Rethinking Risk and the Precautionary Principle

Rethinking Risk and the Precautionary Principle

edited by Julian Morris

OXFORD   AUCKLAND   BOSTON   JOHANNESBURG   MELBOURNE   NEW DELHI

Butterworth-Heinemann
Linacre House, Jordan Hill, Oxford OX2 8DP
225 Wildwood Avenue, Woburn, MA 01801-2041
A division of Reed Educational and Professional Publishing Ltd

℞ A member of the Reed Elsevier plc group

First published 2000

British Library Cataloguing in Publication Data
A catalogue record for this book is available from the British Library

Library of Congress Cataloguing in Publication Data
A catalogue record for this book is available from the Library of Congress

ISBN 0 7506 4683 7

Composition by Genesis Typesetting, Laser Quay, Rochester, Kent
Printed and bound in Great Britain by Biddles Ltd, *www.biddles.co.uk*

Contents

Introduction

Julian Morris

There can be no safety without risk

(Wildavsky, 1988, p. 1)

Risk is often conceptualized as a purely bad thing, and something to be avoided. Some types of risk taking may lead to great rewards, however. Buying Microsoft or AOL shares when they first came to the market would have yielded spectacular returns, although to do so would certainly have been risky. Generally, people who buy stocks accept that the value of their investment can go down or up, but they think the risk of loss is worthwhile because on average the returns are better than safer investments such as bank accounts. Higher returns mean more wealth and more wealth means more safety – which takes us back to Aaron Wildavsky's aphorism. The same is true generally for technology: new technologies entail new risks, but they often enable us to control old risks better. Gas-fired heating entails a risk of explosions from leaks, but it reduces the risk of lung diseases resulting from coal-burning fires. Coal fires themselves reduce the risk of death from hypothermia.

Of course, some risks are probably worth avoiding if possible (nuclear war, for example); but how far should we extend this precautionary approach? A few extremists even wish to apply it to *any* activity that *might* cause catastrophic damage regardless of the probability of the catastrophe occurring. This book is about the ways in which this 'precautionary principle' has been developed and applied. The authors take a critical look at the principle, assess its usefulness as a means of addressing the putative threats against which it is employed; and suggest alternative ways of conceptualizing those threats.

Chapter 1 considers the meaning of the precautionary principle, which, in spite of much discussion remains an ill-defined concept. Environmental and consumer organizations have pushed for a definition that would prevent the emergence of new technologies (including, ironically, the technologies they favour). Governments, reluctant to go so far, have accepted a version that is weaker and may be more readily applied by existing regulatory bodies. Neither definition is philosophically sound and practical implementation often has harmful unintended consequences.

The precautionary principle has become an excuse for imposing arbitrary regulations. Accepted at the national level, it is applied by unaccountable international bodies, such as the UN and its various affiliates, to notional problems promoted by environmental, consumer, and other 'civil society' organizations. These international bodies then promote the drafting of international treaties which, once signed, are used by national regulators to justify the imposition of restrictions that could not have been obtained through purely national legislation.

Aaron Wildavsky points out in Chapter 2 that trial and error is an effective means of discovering both the benefits and the drawbacks of new technologies, and has served humanity well throughout history. Whilst it is clearly inadvisable to try technologies that are known to have serious negative effects and few beneficial effects (the plague and nuclear war are examples), imposing a general prohibition on the use of new technologies until solutions have been found to all their potentially harmful side-effects is a recipe for stasis. This 'trial without error' (which is the environmentalists' favoured version of the precautionary principle) is ultimately likely to be a less good way of regulating the introduction of new technologies than is trial with error. Permitting trials with small errors (a weaker version of the precautionary principle, which is favoured by policymakers) is an improvement on trial without error, but it nevertheless encounters many problems and is ultimately likely to slow down progress, with attendant negative effects both economically and for the health of people and the environment.

In Chapter 3, Wilfred Beckerman argues that the notion of 'intergenerational justice' cannot be used to justify the precautionary principle because we cannot know what people who will be born in the future would wish. Furthermore, uncertainty provides no basis for the precautionary principle; indeed, inasmuch as uncertainty makes it more difficult to know what the effect of any policy will be on future people, it would seem further to undermine the 'intergenerational justice' argument.

The authors of the next few chapters deal with specific applications of the precautionary principle. Tony Gilland (Chapter 4) shows that the precautionary principle was used to justify restrictions on the commercial growing of GM (genetically modified) crops in Britain in spite of the very ambiguous evidence relating to the possible impact of such crops on farmland birds. As a result, British companies are, without good reason, being prevented from developing a technology that may provide enormous benefits.

Henry Miller and Gregory Conko (Chapter 5) argue that the Biosafety Protocol to the Convention on Biological Diversity, agreed in Montreal in January 2000, which has been predicated on the precautionary principle, will most probably have the opposite effect to that intended, namely it will encourage extensive farming at the expense of biodiversity. The authors detail the evolution of the Protocol and its implications, as well as discussing the effects of the recent shift in direction of the Codex Alimentarius Commission.

Charles Rubin (Chapter 6) discusses the problem of how to deal with the (real but small) risk of Earth suffering a catastrophic impact by an asteroid. He notes that the precautionary principle has been used, on the one had, to call for massive spending on defending Earth against impact by asteroids, and on the other to call for a moratorium on the development of such a system, on the grounds that it might increase the risk of a nuclear exchange. To escape from this stalemate it is necessary to apply more conventional risk–risk or cost–benefit approaches. These might lead to the conclusion that it would be worthwhile to develop a monitoring system that can provide several years warning of any impending collision and thereby enable the people of Earth at that time to invest in defensive measures. Meanwhile, some money might be spent on evaluating how to convert inter-continental ballistic missiles (ICBMs) and other nuclear missiles to the purpose of deflecting as yet undetected asteroids.

In Chapter 7 Helene Guldberg shows that in Britain the precautionary principle has infected the way in which child–child and child–adult inter-actions are treated. As a result, children are being afforded excessive protection, which is actually hindering their development. Dr Guldberg contrasts the situation in Norway, where children are more free to experiment.

Bill Durodié describes in Chapter 8 how the European Union's (EU) use of the precautionary principle derives from and interplays with a general fear of new technology, sponsored by environmental and consumer groups, but getting its initial impetus from crisis events such as BSE. A case study of the EU ban on soft toys shows how scientific evidence is manipulated in the context of the precautionary principle in order to achieve a particular end.

Bruce Yandle (Chapter 9) discusses how the Kyoto Protocol, an international agreement justified on precautionary grounds as a means of limiting the possibility of catastrophic global climate change, evolved in a context of lobbying by various interest groups. The Protocol is best seen as a mechanism for creating a more centralized system of energy management for the world, with benefits for certain narrow and well-funded groups (environmental organizations, bureaucrats) and costs for the majority of people.

In Chapter 10 Indur Goklany considers three instances where environmental organizations have argued that the precautionary principle should be applied: the imposition of swingeing restrictions on greenhouse gas emissions, a ban on the use of DDT, and a ban on the cultivation of GM crops. In each case, he shows that the conventional application of the precautionary principle fails to account for the impact on humanity of taking precautionary action. When viewed in a broader context (i.e. considering the desirability of taking precautionary action to prevent the loss of human life and harm to human welfare), the conclusions of applying the precautionary principle differ considerably. He shows that these supposedly precautionary measures would, in fact be imprudent because they would increase overall risks to public health and the environment.

The final two chapters discuss some of the problems posed by subjectivity and the lack of certainty in science. John Adams argues in Chapter 11 that attempting to regulate risk can often have perverse consequences because perception of risk is a subjective matter, depending on a variety of factors many of which are known only to the individual decision-maker. In some cases, attempts to make us aware of very small risks may lead to an over-reaction with worse consequences than the original risk. The negative publicity in the mid-1990s concerning the risk of thrombosis associated with taking the second-generation birth-control pill led to an increase in the number of pregnancies, which carries a higher risk of thrombosis! Where the 'problem' under consideration is merely a threat – a 'virtual risk' – attempts at risk management, through application of the precautionary principle, are even less likely to be successful (and more prone to unforeseen negative consequences) than the attempts to manage real risks.

One of the reasons why the precautionary principle has been able to flourish is that there is, and always will be, uncertainty over the validity of scientific claims. In Chapter 12 Robert Matthews offers insights as to how one might cope better with the inherently subjective interpretation of scientific research. He shows that dogmatic interpretation of research has in many cases slowed down the evolution of scientific understanding, and argues that Bayes' theorem offers a better means of dealing with subjectivity. This theorem might well form the basis of a more rational approach to dealing with threats about which we are uncertain.

Perception of risk and the paradox of precaution

All this is very well, of course, but it is of little relevance unless we understand *why* specious theories are being used as a basis for applying a spurious principle in the name of saving us from supposedly catastrophic risks. At root, I think this must be related to the way in which people perceive risks and the incentives that various parties have to provide information that might affect those perceptions of risk (relevant parties might include: environmental and consumer organizations, the media, government, and corporations).

One of the factors thought to affect perception of risk, or at least attitudes towards particular risks, is the extent to which the individual is able to control his exposure to those risks. The ability to control exposure, which affects whether a risk is seen as voluntary or involuntary, is largely a function of the costs of avoiding the risk. Few people are concerned about the risks of rock climbing, an activity that carries very substantial probabilities of death and injury, because they are not forced to engage in such activities. The costs of avoiding it are zero. Fear of being injured in a car accident is perhaps more prevalent because car travel is one of only a few methods of high-speed transit available. Fear of environmental pollution is widespread because the putative causes of the hazard are ubiquitous. For many, avoiding air pollution would mean moving house or installing expensive air filtration equipment.

However, as people become wealthier, it becomes easier to avoid what would earlier have been seen as involuntary hazards. Richer, more technologically advanced societies tend to be cleaner and healthier societies for several reasons. First, new technologies tend to be more efficient, producing less waste and pollution. Second, richer people are willing to spend more money to protect their legal rights to be free from pollution. Third, richer people have more money to spend on lobbying for more stringent regulations. Fourth, richer people are better able to determine in what circumstances they live and hence to determine their own exposure to environmental pollutants.

In principle, then, wealthier societies should be characterized by a lessening of fear of environmental hazards, as our ability to control them improves. However, there appears to be a peculiar feedback effect resulting from the third factor, namely that by sponsoring organizations to lobby for increased environmental protection, wealthy societies have set in motion a train with great momentum. This train is not easy to stop, even when highly regarded scientists and other commentators erect red lights in very visible areas, because the drivers of the train benefit (psychically and financially) from the journey, even though the destination may have passed. Politicians are happy with this state of affairs because it gives them an excuse to take action and enables them to obtain rewards by claiming that the train has not yet departed or has a long way to go before it reaches its destination. Unsurprisingly, politicians don't want to install ATP on the green train.

A similar thing has occurred in other areas, including protection of children from hazards. Groups set up (perhaps with some justification) to limit the hazards faced by children, discover that their income stream and social status is contingent on perpetuating the notion that children are 'at risk'. So they promulgate action to deal with spurious hazards, which the public at large accept as real because of the credibility the organizations initially gained through the action they took in dealing with more genuine problems.

In general, as significant hazards are dealt with, environmental, consumer and other lobby organizations invent justifications for taking action on less significant and often highly uncertain or 'virtual' threats. As the authors of the chapters in this book show, the primary justification for such action in modern times is the precautionary principle. This is phrased innocuously enough in the terms of Pascal's wager: why take the risk if the cost of avoiding it is so small and the potential benefits so large? Such arguments fail to take into consideration the opportunity costs of not taking the risk, namely the forgone benefits. Until the public can see these benefits (perhaps in terms of the growing wealth of other parts of the world where regulation has been less strict) they will continue to support stricter regulations based on this specious 'principle'.

Reference

Wildavsky, A. (1988). *Searching for Safety*. New Brunswick: Transaction Publishers.

Biographies

John Adams

John Adams is Professor of Geography at University College London. Professor Adams received his BA and MA from the University of Western Ontario and his PhD from the London School of Economics. He is the author of numerous books and papers on the subjects of risk and transport, including a recent report for the OECD on the social implications of hypermobility and, in 1995, *Risk* (UCL Press).

An earlier version of the chapter by Professor Adams was presented to the British Association meeting on environmental risk on 10 September 1997.

Wilfred Beckerman

Wilfred Beckerman is an Emeritus Fellow of Balliol College, Oxford University, having recently retired as a Fellow and Tutor in Economics at the college. Previously, he had been Professor and Head of the Department of Political Economy at University College London. Dr. Beckerman is the author of *Small is Stupid* (Duckworth, 1995), as well as several other books and numerous academic articles on economics, politics and the environment. He has served on the Royal Commission on Environmental Pollution, and chaired the Academic Panel of Economists for the UK Department of the Environment from 1991 to 1996.

Gregory Conko

Gregory Conko is a Policy Analyst and Director of Food Safety Policy with the Competitive Enterprise Institute, a Washington, DC-based public interest group dedicated to the principles of free enterprise and limited government. Mr. Conko specializes in issues of food and pharmaceutical drug safety regulation, the regulation of tobacco use, and in the general treatment of health risks in public policy. He is particularly interested in the debate over the safety of genetically engineered foods and the application of the precautionary principle to domestic and international environmental and safety regulations. He frequently participates in international meetings on food safety and trade as a Non-Governmental Organization representative.

Mr Conko's writings have appeared in such journals as *Nature, Biotechnology Regulation,* and *AgBioForum,* and in such newspapers as *The Financial Times,* the *Journal of Commerce, The Washington Times,* and the *National Post of Canada.* He has also appeared on numerous television and radio programmes as a frequent commentator on public health and consumer safety issues. Prior to joining CEI, Mr. Conko was a Research Associate with the Capital Research Center in Washington, DC.

Bill Durodié

Bill Durodié graduated from the Imperial College of Science and Technology in London, and holds a postgraduate degree in European social policy from the London School of Economics and Political Science, where he now researches the regulation of environmental/health risks.

Mr Durodié has written extensively upon the proposed bans on phthalate softeners in PVC from a perspective that seeks to highlight the wider social cost of, and dynamic behind, such measures. His views have been published in a wide range of newspapers and periodicals, which along with industry-related journals, have included *The Times,* the *Financial Times,* the *Wall Street Journal Europe,* and *LM magazine.* Mr Durodié is a Research Fellow for the European Science and Environment Forum, an Associate of the Royal College of Science and a Member of the Society for Risk Analysis. He also worked for several years as an adviser on European-related matters to both the public and private sectors. He lives in Greenwich in south-east London and may be contacted for comments on: w.j.durodie@lse.ac.uk

Tony Gilland

Tony Gilland is a director of Open Dialogue Limited. He graduated from St. Catherine's College, Oxford University with a degree in Philosophy, Politics and Economics. He has eight years' experience of researching and advising on consumer issues and business regulation, first with the Centre for Regulated Industries and then within the UK energy industry. More recently he has researched and written about the reaction to GM crops and food, and has published various articles on the subject over the last two years, including in *The Times* and *LM magazine.* He has presented on this issue at seminars and public conferences, including those organized by the Department for International Development and the Institute of Grocery Distribution.

Indur M. Goklany

Dr Indur M. Goklany, the author of *Clearing the Air: The Real Story of the War on Air Pollution,* has more than 25 years' experience of addressing environmental and natural resource science and policy issues with state and federal governments and the private sector in the USA. He has published extensively in various peer-reviewed journals on air pollution, climate change, biodiversity and the role of technology in creating, as well as solving, environmental problems. Being Indian-born and bred, he is keenly aware that, despite the best of intentions, First World sensibilities can often aggravate Third World problems – DDT and GM crops being cases in point.

Helene Guldberg

Helene Guldberg studied psychology at University of Edinburgh and gained a PhD in developmental psychology from the University of Manchester. Prior to that, she worked as a primary school teacher. Dr Guldberg is currently working as an associate lecturer with the Open University, teaching an MA module *Child Development in Families, Schools and Society.*

Dr Guldberg was co-publisher of *LM Magazine* and was also co-director of *Interrogating the Precautionary Principle*, a conference which took place at the Royal Institution in July 2000.

Robert A. J. Matthews

Robert Matthews is Visiting Fellow in the Neural Computing Research Group at the Aston University, Birmingham. A graduate in physics from Oxford University, he has published many research papers in fields ranging from astrodynamics and probability theory to the statistical analysis of anomalous phenomena and the mathematical basis of 'urban myths'. A Fellow of the Royal Statistical Society and Royal Astronomical Society, he also acts as science correspondent for *The Sunday Telegraph*, London. His web site is:

http://www.ncrg.aston.ac.uk/People/index.html

Dr Matthews' chapter was originally published as ESEF Working Paper 2/98

http://www.esef.org.

Henry I. Miller

Dr Henry I. Miller graduated from Massachusetts Institute of Technology (MIT) with a BS in Life Sciences and subsequently obtained his MS and MD from the University of California, San Diego. After completing his clinical training at Harvard Medical School, Dr Miller spent almost three years as a Research Associate at the National Institute of Health, helping to refine, and employing, the recombinant DNA ('gene-splicing') techniques that were then emerging.

Dr Miller joined the FDA in 1979 and served in a number of posts involved with the new biotechnology. From 1989–94, he was the founding director of the FDA's Office of Biotechnology. Dr Miller is currently at Stanford University, where he is a Senior Research Fellow at the Hoover Institution. As a consultant, he advises defendants' and plaintiffs' counsel and companies on a wide spectrum of regulatory strategies and problems.

Dr Miller is the author of more than three hundred articles in scholarly and popular publications. He writes frequently for such publications as *The Financial Times, Wall Street Journal, Biotechnology Law Report,* and *Nature Biotechnology.* He is the author of *Policy Controversy in Biotechnology: An Insider's View* (R.G. Landes Co. and Academic Press, 1997).

Julian Morris

Julian Morris read economics at the University of Edinburgh and holds Masters degrees in related disciplines from University College, London and Cambridge University, as well as a graduate diploma in law from the University of Westminster.

Mr Morris is the author and editor of numerous papers and books, including *Fearing Food* (Butterworth-Heinemann, 1999), which he co-edited with Roger Bate. He is a frequent contributor to *The Wall Street Journal Europe* and commentator on radio and television, as well as an occasional contributor to other newspapers and magazines. Mr Morris is a Fellow of the Institute of Economic Affairs in London (www.iea.org.uk), where he commissions, edits and researches papers on technology, trade, environment, and legal issues. He can be contacted by email at: jmorris@iea.org.uk.

Charles T. Rubin

Dr Charles T. Rubin is associate professor of political science at Duquesne University (Pittsburgh), and also graduate faculty for Duquesne's Center for Environmental Research and Education and its Graduate Center for Social and Public Policy. He is author of *The Green Crusade: Rethinking the Roots of Environmentalism* (Rowman and Littlefield), a critical look at the US environmental movement, and editor of a forthcoming volume of essays on the conservation movement, *Conservation Reconsidered: Nature, Virtue and American Liberal Democracy* (Rowman and Littlefield). Much of his work focuses on the interaction between science and public policy in areas of high uncertainty, for example, global warming, and the scientific search for extraterrestrial intelligence.

Aaron Wildavsky

Aaron Wildavsky was one of the greatest political scientists of the twentieth century. His contributions to that discipline ranged from seminal studies of the nature of public finance to an entirely new way of conceptualizing political discourse, known as cultural theory (developed with Mary Douglas, upon whose anthropological grid/group theory it is based, and Michael Thompson). He was the author of numerous books and articles on a wide range of public policy issues. At the time of his death in 1995, Aaron Wildavsky was Professor of Political Science and Public Policy at the University of California, Berkeley.

Professor Wildavsky's contribution first appeared as Chapter 1 of *Searching for Safety* (Transaction Publishers, 1988). The editor thanks the publishers and the estate of Aaron Wildavsky for their kind permission to reprint this chapter.

Bruce Yandle

Bruce Yandle is Alumni Professor of Economics and Legal Studies at Boseman State University and Visiting Fellow at the Political Economy Research Centre, having previously been Executive Director of the Federal Trade Commission. His writings on environmental policy include many journal articles, special reports, and monographs. He is the author of *The Political Limits of Environmental Regulation* (Quorum, 1989), and *Common Sense and Common Law for the Environment* (Rowman and Littlefield, 1997), as well as the editor of numerous books.

Professor Yandle's chapter was first delivered as a presentation at a Hoover Institution programme (12–14 October 1998) on the greening of foreign policy and was subsequently published as an IEA Working paper (http://www.iea.org.uk).

1 Defining the precautionary principle

Julian Morris

Precaution has long been a basis for taking action to prevent harm; and at the level of the individual there are clearly merits in this: it is not advisable, for example, to build a house on the edge of a volcano that is expected imminently to erupt. In a broader context, 'Trying out a nuclear exchange or experimenting with a little plague are inadvisable' (Wildavsky, *infra*, p. 31). The precautionary principle goes beyond this conventional 'look-before-you-leap' prudence, however.

Whilst there are many definitions of the precautionary principle (hereinafter, PP), it is worth distinguishing two broad classes: first, the Strong PP, which says basically, take no action unless you are certain that it will do no harm; and second, the Weak PP, which says that lack of full certainty is not a justification for preventing an action that might be harmful. Both types are problematic, although the latter considerably less so than the former. This chapter presents a discussion of the historical development of the PP, followed by a critique of various definitions of it.

The development of the precautionary principle

The PP has been traced to the German principle of *Vorsorgeprinzip* (literally, 'foresight-planning'), which was a founding principle of German environmental policy in the mid-1970s (Th. Douma, 1996). According to the Vorsorgeprinzip, a distinction is to be made between human actions that cause 'dangers' and those that merely cause 'risks': in the case of danger, the government is to prevent these by all means; in the case of risk, the government is to carry out a risk analysis and may order preventative action if deemed appropriate. As O'Riordan (1994) notes:

> For the Germans ... precaution is an interventionist measure, a justification of state involvement in the day to day lives of its lander and its citizenry in the name of good government. Social planning in the economy, in technology, in morality and in social initiatives all can be justified by a loose and open-ended interpretation of precaution.

> (O'Riordan, 1994)

Although it is often regarded as a German concept, Allan Mazur (1996) shows that PP-like arguments have been used in the USA since the 1950s; at that time, groups of political conservatives opposed fluoridation of water on the grounds that fluoride was used as rat poison and that involuntary fluoridation amounted to mass medication, a step on the road to socialism. In the 1960s, left-wing radicals similarly used PP-like arguments against nuclear power. Fluoride and radiation have in common known negative effects at high doses and thus pose a risk of widespread damage if they are misused. By highlighting this possibility of catastrophe, regardless of the probability of its occurrence, campaigners were able to instil fear of the technology as such.

In the 1970s, these arguments were picked up by social scientists such as Robert Goodin (1980) and David Pearce (1980), who presented them in a more general framework. They argued that where there is a possibility of catastrophic risk from the use of a technology, potential problems created by that technology (such as disposal of nuclear waste) should be solved before proceeding with its use; or else it should not be used at all (Wildavsky, *infra*, p. 23–28).

Consumer groups, hormones, Commissioners and the PP

An early application of this open-ended precautionary approach can be seen in the 1985 decision of the European Commission to ban hormones used for animal growth promotion. The ban was instituted (under EC Directive 81/602) on the basis that 'their safety has not been conclusively proven'.

The history of the ban dates to the late 1970s, when Italian media carried reports that babies had developed breasts and enlarged genitals after eating French veal containing traces of the synthetic hormone diethylstilbestrol (DES) (Cargill, 1999). The Italian government, which had banned the use of DES a decade earlier, promptly restricted imports of veal from other member states. Consumer groups, seeing an issue on which they might garner public support, then began demanding a ban on the use of hormones in all livestock production. In 1981, the EC banned the use of DES and established a body of scientists to look into the effects of five other hormones that are commonly used as growth promoters (ibid.). The body, known as the Lamming Commission after its head, Professor G. E. Lamming, issued an interim report in 1982 which concluded that the three natural hormones (estradiol, progesterone and testosterone) 'would not present any harmful effects to the health of the consumer when used under the appropriate conditions as growth promoters in farm animals' (Cargill, 1999). Indeed, it will not usually be possible to identify meat from cattle treated with these natural hormones as residual levels are typically within the normal variability observed in untreated cattle (WTO, 1998). However, in 1985, before the Lamming Commission had completed its research into the effects of the synthetic hormones, the European Commission – under increasing pressure from consumer groups – banned the use of all growth promotion hormones, with effect from January 1988 (Cargill, 1999; WTO, 1998).

The argument seems to be that only a total ban on all hormones will prevent possibly undesirable use of certain hormones. Three responses to this seem apposite. First, it is almost certainly easier to identify farmers who are using DES than those farmers using hormones in general, since traces of DES can be identified in treated meat whereas traces of additional natural hormones usually cannot. (This might be seen as a good thing by regulators, whose bureaucracy will be expanded, and by consumer groups, who can claim a victory, but it is surely a bad thing in terms of identifying illegal use of potentially harmful chemicals.) Second, if the objective is to prevent farmers using DES, would it not be more just to impose heavy fines and even prison sentences on those who treat their animals with this putatively harmful chemical rather than criminalizing all users of hormones regardless of the harm they impose on society? Third, the ban might be counterproductive because if all growth promotion hormones are illegal, it seems likely that those farmers who are inclined to use (illegal) hormones will tend to use the most cost-effective ones, which might also be the more harmful. Thus, an early application of the PP also exposes some of its flaws.

The precautionary principle as a premise for international agreements

Ten years ago, the PP was described by one leading scholar as 'the most important new policy approach in international environmental co-operation'. The PP had become the cornerstone of an international agreement for the first time three years before. The Ministerial Declaration of the Second International Conference on the Protection of the North Sea, held in London in 1987, stated:

> Accepting that in order to protect the North Sea from possibly damaging effects of the most dangerous substances, a precautionary approach is necessary which may require action to control inputs of such substances even before a causal link has been established by absolutely clear scientific evidence'.

(SICPNS, 1987)

This is clearly a weak PP argument, since the burden of proof remains with those regulating the technology. Developers of new technologies are not required to prove that their technology will have no negative impacts; rather, the onus is on the regulator to imagine harms that might result and to regulate in anticipation of these. It is perhaps not surprising that government officials should prefer such a conceptualization for two reasons. First, it provides them with a reason to act, expanding their authority, whereas the strong PP might lead to a transfer of authority to environmental and other groups (see below). Second, the weak PP is more accommodating, enabling regulators to broker agreements with industries rather than simply shutting them down.

On the basis of this PP, all sewage sludge disposal into the North Sea was subsequently banned under the EC Urban Waste Water Treatment Directive (with effect from 31 December 1998). This increased the cost of sewage sludge dumping in Britain and led to an increase in sewage spreading on land, which may have undesirable effects in terms of exposing farm workers to pathogens and increasing the concentrations of heavy metals in some crops (HSE, n.d.; MAFF, n.d.; Avery, 1999). (Note that this is not an argument against restricting the dumping of sewage sludge at sea. Clearly dumping sewage in shallow coastal waters near popular beaches is a bad idea. It is an argument in favour of implementing systems of sewage disposal that impose fewer costs on society – for example by extending disposal pipes further out to sea.)

Environmental and consumer organizations likewise have used the PP as a justification for their demands for international agreements (viz., the consumer organizations' demands for a precautionary ban on the use of growth promotion hormones). However, not surprisingly, many such organizations favour the strong PP, which accords with their generally anti-industry view of the world; but they may also have other incentives to promote the strong PP. It is conceivable that if the strong PP were to be accepted as a general legal principle, environmental and consumer organizations might be empowered to take legal action against companies which fail to prove that their technologies are safe. This would probably increase both their authority and their income.

In the context of a demand for international regulation of so-called greenhouse gases, Jeremy Leggett of Greenpeace asserted in 1990 that:

> For organizations like Greenpeace, what comes first must be the needs of the environment . . . the modus operandi we would like to see is: 'Do not admit a substance unless you have proof that it will do no harm to the environment' – the precautionary principle . . . the fact that proof of harm might come too late – or that proof is invariably hard to demonstrate with absolute certainty – only augments the license given to the polluters.

(Leggett, 1990)

There is still considerable uncertainty regarding the likely impact of emissions of these gases (which include carbon dioxide, a product of the combustion of carbon-based fuels, such as coal, oil and natural gas, and methane, a product of the digestive breakdown of biological organisms as well as a by-product of rice production). Even at the time of Leggett's statement, it was observed that taking precautionary action to control greenhouse gas emissions might be counterproductive; with our greater knowledge this is more clearly the case (see below as well as Goklany, Chapter 10 *infra*, Morris, 1997b, and Spencer, 2000). Nevertheless, the demands of environmental organizations, certain groups of scientists and national politicians have led to the elaboration of international agreements to constrain greenhouse gas emissions (see below).

In spite of this demand for a strong PP, regulators remained fixated on the weak PP. In the same year, the United Nations Economic Conference for

Europe (ECE) held a meeting on Sustainable Development in the ECE Region in Bergen, Norway. The final Ministerial Declaration of that meeting stated:

> In order to achieve sustainable development, policies must be based on the precautionary principle. Environmental measures must anticipate, prevent and attack the causes of environmental degradation. Where there are threats of serious or irreversible damage, lack of full scientific certainty should not be used as a reason for postponing measures to prevent environmental degradation.

> (ECE, 1990)

This language was adopted more or less verbatim at the Second World Climate Conference later that year, although the ministerial declaration of that conference added that 'the measures adopted should take into account different socio-economic contexts' (cited by Weintraub, 1992, p. 187).

Similar language was again adopted in the Ministerial Declaration of the UN Conference on Environment and Development (the 'Earth Summit') in Rio de Janeiro in 1992 (known as the 'Rio Declaration'), although this time the PP has been watered down further by the additional caveat that measures should be 'cost-effective':

> Where there are threats of serious or irreversible damage, lack of full scientific certainty shall not be used as a reason for postponing cost-effective measures to prevent environmental degradation

> (Principle 15, Rio Declaration, 1992)

This became the international standard definition for the PP amongst policymakers and has been used to justify a number of international agreements including the UN Framework Convention on Climate Change and its subsidiary, the Kyoto Protocol (Yandle, *infra*), as well as the UN Convention on Biological Diversity and its subsidiary, the Cartagena Protocol on Biosafety (Miller and Conko, *infra*.).

However, environmentalists continued to push for the Strong PP and to this end convened their own conference in January 1998 at Wingspread in Racine, Wisconsin, where the following definition was agreed:

> When an activity raises threats of harm to human health or the environment, precautionary measures should be taken even if some cause and effect relationships are not fully established scientifically. In this context the proponent of the activity, rather than the public, should bear the burden of proof.
>
> The process of applying the precautionary principle must be open, informed and democratic and must include potentially affected parties. It must also involve an examination of the range of alternatives, including no action.

> (cited by Montague, 1998)

This has become the environmentalists' own international standard definition, which they promote at every opportunity (an Internet search for 'precautionary principle' brings up literally hundreds of references to the Wingspread definition and tens of references to 'mirrors' (copies) of an article by Montague (1998) from *Rachel's Environmental and Health Weekly*, in which the Wingspread definition is detailed).

A precautionary union

As already noted, the European Union(EU)/European Communities have been grappling with the precautionary principle since the mid-1980s. In response to pressure from environmental and consumer activists, the PP was incorporated into the 1992 Treaty on European Union (the Maastricht Treaty) in Article 130R (2):

> Community policy on the environment shall aim at a high level of protection taking into account the diversity of situations in the various regions of the Community. It shall be based on the precautionary principle and on the principles that preventative action should be taken, that environmental damage should as a priority be rectified at source and that the polluter should pay.

However, no definition of the precautionary principle appears in the Treaty and some confusion has arisen from the fact that it is placed side by side with another apparently similar principle, 'that preventative action should be taken'. The European Court of Justice (ECJ) cited the latter as justification for upholding the ban on export of beef from the UK (Cases C-157/96 and C-180/96, 5 May 1998), but has not employed the former, so there is no clear legal precedent regarding how it might be used.

In response to numerous health scares and subsequent lobbying by consumer and environmental organizations, the European Council of Ministers adopted a resolution on 13 April 1999 urging the Commission 'to be in the future even more determined to be guided by the precautionary principle in preparing proposals for legislation and in its other consumer-related activities and develop as priority clear and effective guidelines for the application of this principle' (EC, 2000, p. 8). The result was the Commission's own *Communication on the Precautionary Principle* (EC, 2000), the summary of which states that the PP should apply:

> ... where preliminary objective scientific evaluation, indicates that there are reasonable grounds for concern that the potentially dangerous effects on the environment, human, animal or plant health may be inconsistent with the high level of protection chosen for the community.

> (EC, 2000, p. 3)

It continues:

> Recourse to the precautionary principle presupposes that potentially dangerous effects deriving from a phenomenon, product or process have been identified, and that scientific evaluation does not allow the risk to be determined with sufficient certainty.

> The implementation of an approach based on the precautionary principle should start with a scientific evaluation, as complete as possible, and where possible, identifying at each stage the degree of scientific uncertainty.
>
> (EC, 2000, p. 4)

On the face of it, this appears to be the weakest version of the PP yet to be developed by any inter-governmental body, implying as it does a requirement that scientific evaluation be a pre-requisite for any application of the PP. Indeed, much of the document reads as though there is eminent sense and logic in the notion that the PP should be the underlying basis for policy towards protection of the environment, human health, etc. Such an interpretation belies some very serious problems, however, as is shown below.

Problems with the precautionary principle

We now turn to a discussion of some of the problems with the PP, starting with a general problem: the fallacy that the merest possibility of catastrophe should justify action. This is followed by a discussion of some more specific problems with the strong and weak versions of the PP.

A Pascal's wager for the environment

Proponents of the PP argue that remoteness of harm is not an excuse for inaction: the *mere possibility* that use of a particular technology *might* kill off the human race is sufficient to prevent that technology being used or at least to limit its use severely. Calling for swingeing restrictions on the use of technologies that burn carbon-based fuels, Jeremy Leggett, for example, asserts that:

> Nobody – repeat, nobody – can deny that there is at the very least a prospect of ecological disaster on the horizon where the greenhouse effect is concerned. Those who choose to ignore the prospect, therefore, wilfully elect to ignore the environmental security of future generations.
>
> (Cited by Manson, n.d.)

This argument, of infinite potential harm, is however susceptible to the counter-argument that preventing the action might also result in the death of all human beings. The philosopher Neil Manson has likened the PP to Pascal's Wager, wherein the potentially infinite benefit one might obtain from believing in God justifies the effort taken to actualize such belief, regardless of how small is the probability of God's existence. Put another way, since the benefit obtained if God does exist is infinite (eternal life), then even if the probability of God's existence is very small, the expected benefit is still infinite, because infinity multiplied by a non-zero number is still infinity. However, as Manson shows, this is susceptible to the 'many gods' argument.

> Consider the ancient semitic sun-god Baal. If we suppose Baal is a jealous god, then on Pascal's reasoning you have equal reason not to believe in God. After all, if Baal exists and you worship a god other than him, you will pay an infinite price, making belief in God a risk not worth taking. Now of course Baal might not strike us as a very plausible candidate for divinity, but we must admit it is *possible* that Baal exists. Given that both Baal and God are possible deities, Pascal's reasoning leads to contradictory demands, and so it cannot be valid.
>
> (Manson, n.d.)

(It should be noted that this is an argument against Pascal's Wager, not against the existence of God.)

In the context of the PP applied to catastrophes (PPC), Manson observes:

> The many-gods objection to Pascal's Wager brings to light the following point: the infinite expected disutility of a particular course of action demands that we do not engage in that course of action only if there is not an infinite expected disutility to *not* engaging in that course of action. Thus even if we grant that an outcome has infinite disutility, it does not follow that we should act to prevent that outcome from occurring (much less that we should disregard the probability of its occurrence). Why? Because it could be that acting to prevent it will bring about a different outcome which *also* has infinite disutility. And the same goes for courses of action which might lead to outcomes that, while not possessing *infinite* disutility, are nonetheless catastrophic. While such courses of action might lead to catastrophe, so might attempting to prevent them. We could be doomed if we do and doomed if we don't. For example, it could be that preventing global warming has some nonzero probability of leading to nuclear winter. Significant reductions in the consumption of fossil fuels might cause global economic collapse, which might cause global war, which might lead to multiple detonations of nuclear weapons, which might lead to a nuclear winter. If the Catastrophe Argument for drastic reductions in the emission of greenhouse gasses is a good one, then, by parity of reasoning, we have an equally good argument *against* drastic reductions in the emission of greenhouse gasses.
>
> Clearly PPC is not a good principle.
>
> (Manson, n.d.)

The precautionary principle is unnecessary

Amongst supporters of the PP, there seems also to be a widespread misconception regarding the normal use of law and regulation as mechanisms for preventing environmental damage. For example, Weintraub (1992) argues that: 'The tort-oriented, non-precautionary approach postpones the regulation of activities until harm occurs and compels states to respond to environmental degradation rather than promote environmental protection.' This is simply incorrect, on the following counts.

First, Anglo-Saxon tort law (and specifically the law of toxic torts, which includes nuisance and the rule in *Rylands v Fletcher*) does permit pre-emptive action where there is imminent danger, through the use of a *quia timet* injunction (*Redland Bricks v Morris* [1970] AC 652; *Hooper v Rogers* [1975] Ch. 43).

Second, the fact that compensation may be payable if a harm can be shown to have resulted from an action creates a strong incentive for individuals and corporations not to cause the harm in the first place. (Of course, in some cases a corporation may decide the fines that are likely to result would be less costly than prevention. But if the objection is that the fines do not reflect the damage done and hence do not discourage inappropriate behaviour, then the answer is presumably to increase the fines, not shut down modern society. In any case, even a supposed prohibition will only be effective if the right balance is struck between the degree of monitoring and the size of the fines imposed.)

Third, the fact that tort law is often not capable of dealing with certain kinds of harm (such a those which affect large numbers of people and those which might affect people in the far future) is the conventional justification for regulation, so it is not clear why a 'precautionary principle' is needed.

Demands for a reversal of the burden of proof are disingenuous

The oft-repeated requirement that the burden of proof be reversed is legally very interesting, especially in the context in which it is supposed to be applied. In certain circumstances a reversal of the burden of proof is considered expedient. In tort law, for example, the principle of *res ipsa loquitur* (literally 'the thing speaks for itself') may be applied when there is only one plausible explanation for a particular harm that has occurred. So, if a person A has been injured by a falling brick and another person B was seen leaning out of a window above the injured man, it may be reasonable to presume that B threw the brick at A and that B should have to prove his innocence. However, this is not the case with potential environmental harms. First, environmental harms often have many different possible causes. Second, the claim here is not that a definite harm has been identified but, rather, that an identifiable technology is to be used and there is some fear that as a result something bad might happen. This, then, is the opposite of the normal justification for applying *res ipsa loquitur* in tort.

The notion that the burden of proof should be shifted to the party developing the technology is in any case an odd one, given the scepticism that the environmental and consumer organizations who promote this view usually exhibit regarding the scientific claims made by corporations. Also, of course, merely reversing the burden of proof says nothing about the standard of proof. In British law, for example, the standard of proof in civil cases is the balance of probabilities. That is to say, if there were a 51 per cent chance that the technology is safe, then under this rule it would be acceptable to adopt it. This is clearly below the standard of proof that is currently required by most regulatory authorities.

One suspects that the real intention of this requirement is an increase in regulatory oversight combined with an expansion of the powers of environmental and consumer organizations to review regulatory decisions – including powers to sue companies directly for any breach of regulations.

General application of the precautionary principle in this way would necessitate the statutory regulation of every new technology, which if taken literally means every new product (including every new product formulation) and every new process. This is in line with another emerging concept known as integrated product policy (IPP), being developed enthusiastically by the Environment Directorate at the European Commission. IPP is an attempt to force product design to take account of all the environmental impacts of a product throughout its life-cycle. This is of course epistemologically impossible; it requires certain knowledge about a wide variety of things that cannot be known by the product designers, including: variability in the production process employed (which is likely to change as new techniques develop); variation in impacts of the same production process employed in different places; variation in the modes of distribution, storage and use of the product; and variation in the impacts of distribution, storage and use of the product contingent on the different environments in which these occur. The end result of both IPP and the PP would amount to more or less direct control of the production process by environmental and consumer organizations, which would foist on us their preferred technologies and ban everything they did not like. It is not clear that this would be desirable environmentally (indeed in the long-term the environmental effects are almost certainly negative) and it would certainly not be desirable economically (Morris, 1997a).

The standard of proof is infinitely high

The demand that a technology should not be admitted until it has been proved to be harmless means an infinitely high standard of proof. Obviously such a standard can never be achieved. It is epistemologically absurd; it demands a level of knowledge that simply cannot be reached. It is not possible to prove something is harmless, any more than it is possible to prove that there are no fairies at the bottom of one's garden. Wildavsky (Chapter 2, *infra*, p. 24) observes: 'One could well ask whether any technology, including the most benign, would ever have been established if it had first been forced to demonstrate that it would do no harm.'

Failure to take account of the fact that 'the dose makes the poison' is counterproductive

The notion that regulations should be based on the presumption that there is no safe dose for any chemical that exhibits carcinogenic properties (be it in animal experiments or as a result of epidemiological studies) has been widely refuted (see, for example, Wilson, 1997; Munby and Weetman, 1997; Ames and Gold, 1999). However, it is repeatedly used as the basis for taking precautionary action (see, for example, Durodie, *infra*.).

Wildavsky (Chapter 2, *infra*, p. 30) observes: '. . . we all know that virtually everything human beings breathe or eat or drink brings them into contact with carcinogens. Poisons are an integral part of nature. So is chemical warfare among plants, animals, and insects. To ban carcinogenic substances, therefore, is to ban life. Remember that the idea is to develop a rationale for regulating the products of industrial technology, not for ending all life.'

A duty to take action to prevent harm would be too broad

Montague (1998) argues that the Wingspread definition of the PP implies that: 'People have a duty to take anticipatory action to prevent harm. (As one participant at the Wingspread meeting summarized the essence of the precautionary principle, "If you have a reasonable suspicion that something bad might be going to happen, you have an obligation to try to stop it.")'

This duty seems too broad. There is no specification of the scale of harm or the extent of action that might be entailed. Does one have a duty to spend one's life savings in order to prevent a Yanomami tribesman from cutting down a tree in Brazil? If so, it seems unlikely that many people would wish to subscribe to this principle. More generally, the lack of apportionment of responsibility would cause chaos: who should be responsible for doing what? There are clearly too many potential harms that might be accorded attention and there is no mechanism within the precautionary principle for deciding which should be addressed and by whom.

Examining the full range of alternatives would be infinitely costly

Montague (1998) also notes that the Wingspread definition entails that 'Before using a new technology, process, or chemical, or starting a new activity, people have an obligation to examine "a full range of alternatives" including the alternative of doing nothing.' This is not only absurd and impossible, it is bad for the environment: examination of the 'full range' of alternatives would take forever and consume an infinite quantity of resources because *all* extant and possible technologies must be considered.

Precautionary decisions are not democratic

Again according to Montague (1998), 'Decisions applying the precautionary principle must be "open, informed, and democratic" and "must include affected parties"'. This assertion belongs in the realms of the mystical. The precautionary principle is typically applied when the effects are reputed to be wide-ranging – often putatively affecting everyone on the planet – and far-reaching, affecting people far into the future. *How* the authors of the Wingspread declaration envisage all the people on the planet to be represented is unclear (one suspects that they envisage themselves as the appropriate parties to do such representing). It is clearly difficult to establish psephocratic systems that represent people who are alive (there is a very large literature on this subject, the general conclusion of which is that voting systems tend to reflect the preferences of the median voter, excluding large minorities – even majorities – whose preferences diverge from this median); it is altogether impossible genuinely to represent the interests of those who have yet to be born, since there is no way for their preferences to be aggregated.

The risks of preventing learning by trial and error

General application of the 'trial without error', strong PP may prevent people from making some mistakes, but it also prevents them learning from those mistakes and from overcoming the mistakes of the past. New technologies generally provide benefits; if they did not, there would be little incentive to produce them. Examples of such benefits include: higher crop yields (pesticides, fertilizer, new crop varieties, better irrigation systems); faster, more efficient transport (the Macadam road, the railroad, Stephenson's Rocket, the internal combustion engine, diesel engines, jet engines, rockets); increased product shelf-life (refrigeration, laminated containers, vacuum-sealed packs); speedier communication (the telephone, packet switching and the internet, fibre-optic cable); better medicine (penicillin, Prozac, the birth control pill); better, less polluting, heating systems (gas central heating, roof insulation, distributed electricity); better, less polluted, water (sewerage systems, reservoirs, PVC tubing).

One result is that humankind is now better fed, less frequently exposed to water-borne pathogens and air pollution, and less likely to die or suffer ill effects as a result of disease. A second result is higher quality of life in other regards, through lower cost and higher quality goods and services of all kinds. The general point is that although new technologies usually bring with them new risks, they often replace technologies that pose greater risks, or reduce the cost of technologies (such as fresh fruit and vegetables) that enable us to reduce our exposure to certain risks. Applying the PP may prevent the adoption of technologies that would make the world a safer place.

To be sure, new technologies bring with them new challenges and often result in the displacement of old jobs. In this process of 'creative destruction' some people lose out and that is unfortunate. However, the benefits of creation generally outweigh the costs of destruction. Who would deny that the replacement of coal fires with gas central heating was a net benefit, though it came at the cost of unemployed miners, coal merchants, and chimney sweeps? (In addition to its benefits in terms of convenience, improved protection from the elements, and lower pollution, central heating of course led to the creation of jobs in the gas, plumbing and boiler-making industries.) And even those who are obsessed with protecting jobs cannot deny that technological stasis reduces humankind's capacity to cope with the many things that are not under its control. Droughts, floods, earthquakes, volcanoes, and other natural events cause disruptions that may require humans to adapt or die. In Ethiopia, two years of drought mean crop failure, malnutrition, disease and death. In technologically more advanced and hence wealthier and more resilient Australia, two years of drought mean little more than an increase in food imports and some whingeing from farmers.

Problems with the weak precautionary principle

If the strong PP were to be applied either generally or 'only' to the environmental and health consequences of new technologies, the unreality of the situation would make PP unworkable as a practical political principle. So it is not surprising that political definitions of the PP have tended to be weaker, always keeping the burden of proof on the side of the regulator and often incorporating notions of cost-effectiveness. However, political definitions, as with other political decisions, are the result of interest-group lobbying and tend to reflect the demands of the interest groups more than they reflect abstract analytical ideas.

In its more political weak form, the PP is about taking a hyper-cautious approach to change. This means imposing very strict controls on the licensing of new technologies and cutting back drastically on emissions of substances into the environment. Although not as devastating as the philosophically dubious strong PP, this more practical approach has serious drawbacks. Consider the 'Earth Summit' definition:

> Where there are threats of serious or irreversible damage, lack of full scientific certainty shall not be used as a reason for postponing cost-effective measures to prevent environmental degradation.

There are several problems with this definition. First, it is not clear what is meant by 'threat'. Is it to be restricted to events with an actuarially ascertainable probability (that is, events whose probability of occurrence can be ascertained by analysing data combined with a theoretical appraisal incorporating relevant variables)? Or is it broader, including all manner of hypothetically possible events the probability of occurrence of which, whilst not zero, *cannot* be ascertained? A problem with this second possibility is that 'threats' thus loosely defined can include everything from the *risk* of the

Thames flooding (which is reckoned to occur twice a century, giving an annual probability of 1 in 50), to the *mere possibility* that there might be an alien invasion.

Second, it is necessary to define damage – and in particular to distinguish 'damage' from mere 'change'.

Third, all change (and hence all damage) is irreversible in the strict sense that the precise structure of the world that pertained before cannot once again come into being. (This is a consequence of the second law of thermodynamics, wherein it is observed that the state of disorder (or entropy) of the universe is constantly increasing. Attempting to reverse some 'damage' will result in other changes occurring to the state of the world. Thus in recycling paper, energy and other resources are consumed and the fibres in the paper foreshortened, with the result that although what results may look very similar to the paper that existed previously, it will not be exactly alike and there will be fewer of whatever resources were consumed in its making.) This ultimately negates the utility of including 'irreversible' as a criterion as distinct from 'serious'.

Fourth, it is then necessary to define 'serious' damage. This is problematic because the notion of seriousness is clearly a subjective one. What one person considers serious another might consider trivial. Thus, a person who has great empathy for elephants might be saddened to see a single elephant being shot by a hunter. By contrast, a person who has only a dispassionate concern for the survival of elephants as a species might be happy to see the same elephant being shot because he knows that the hunter will contribute significantly to the funding of the community that has been husbanding it, thereby encouraging that community to conserve the elephants. (The fact that the elephant might in any case have been culled in order to prevent it consuming other valuable resources, crops and so on, might also enter into the minds of both parties; one suspects, though, that whilst this fact would make someone who was in favour of sustainable use rest easier in their moral acceptance of the hunt, it would make little difference to the person passionately opposed to the killing of elephants.)

Fifth, science has not yet, and is unlikely in the future, to provide a fully-fledged deterministic theory of the universe from which all particular events can be predicted. In other words, there will always be scientific uncertainty, both with regard to environmental effects and with regard to all other matters, especially concerning the future.

The EU definition

As noted earlier, the EU has recently contributed what appears to be a weaker definition of the PP. What is perhaps most interesting about this definition is its requirement that bounds be put on the uncertainty surrounding scientific knowledge. It could be argued, for example, that this will limit the application of the PP to cases when there is very great uncertainty regarding the likely impact of a technology. If that were the case, the PP would be most suitably applied before a technology is even developed, because this is when uncertainty is greatest. In the case of genetically modified (GM) crops, it would provide a justification for preventing field trials, since there is clearly greater uncertainty before the trials take place than afterwards. Indeed, the very purpose of the trials is to reduce uncertainty by expanding scientific knowledge.

Thus the European Commission's brave attempt to define the PP in such a way as to limit its application to cases where it might most usefully serve the purpose of achieving a high level of environmental protection, which is surely admirable, fails in this purpose; this is because if it were applied it would deter the development of technologies (including GM crops) that might very well provide environmental benefits.

The problem of knowledge and the dangers of technological determinism

Although the environmental and consumer organizations promoting the PP might seem at first glance to be anti-technology, on closer inspection it is clear there are certain technologies that they favour and others they oppose. Examples of those they favour include electricity generated from solar and wind energy, organic agriculture, and recycling. Examples of those they oppose include chlorine-based compounds, coal, oil and anything produced by the petrochemical industry. Their preference for what they call 'sustainable' technologies appears to derive from a belief that these technologies are superior to those that are currently dominant; that they are less polluting and will satisfy human wants further into the future. In the long term, they may be correct; but from the perspective of today we cannot possibly know. Robert Bradley (1999) points out that conventional energy technologies are in fact becoming more sustainable, in the sense that they are becoming cheaper and less polluting, whilst in spite of billions of dollars of subsidies the alternatives remain expensive and, in the case of wind and hydro power at least, still have environmental costs. So, a simple extrapolation would seem to favour conventional technologies, at least for the foreseeable future, and the unforeseeable future is precisely that: it is unforeseeable, a place that we have not yet visited and for which we have no maps.

This is perhaps the fundamental philosophical problem with the strong PP: it presumes that we can know the unknowable. Applied consistently, it would prohibit the development of solar technology just as surely as it would prohibit the burning of carbon-based fuel. Jeremy Leggett, a vocal proponent of solar technology, as well as antagonist of carbon-based fuel, might think about how he would prove that there are no harmful environmental effects from using solar technology. He won't be able to do so.

Alternative technologies might not provide the most economically or environmentally viable solutions to our energy demands in the near future, and they may not be admissible according to the criteria for the strong PP; nevertheless they may become the dominant technology as a result of the widely held dogmatic belief that they *should* be the technology of the future. By excluding competing technologies (through regulation and taxes), the state may bring to fruition this environmentalist prophecy. If it does so, it may well be at the expense of precluding the development of better technologies. Imagine what might have happened if in the mid-nineteenth century, environmental activists had managed to convince policymakers around the world that coal would run out (based, perhaps on the popular misconception of William Stanley Jevons' analysis – see Jevons, 1865/1965), and that all monies for development of new energy technologies should be poured into the development of wood-based fuels, whilst simultaneously banning the use of coal, oil and natural gas (for fear that these two would run out). The result would have been wood-powered vehicles, stoves, central heating systems, etc. Generally speaking, all these technologies would be more polluting, because wood has a lower hydrogen to carbon ratio, and more expensive, because the availability of wood would be restricted not only by the absolute availability of woodland but also by the lack of petrochemical-based pesticides. Central heating would be a luxury enjoyed only by the very wealthy (who could afford the automatic wood-feeder or the extremely pricey electricity produced by the few wood-fired power stations). Cars would be far larger (they would have to accommodate a steam engine and sufficient room for the lower-energy wood fuel) and would probably be significantly more expensive. Planes would probably not exist. Agriculture would be significantly less efficient, and much would be wasted in distribution, so food would be scarcer and more expensive. Because of the lower agricultural yields and lower capacity to raise industrial production, people generally would be far poorer. In sum, the lot of the majority of people in the developed world would be more akin to that of those in Bulgaria and Romania, countries that were oppressed for much of the last century by rulers who believed they knew which technologies were best.

For those who protest that such objections miss the point, consider the record that environmentalists have in predicting events. In the 1960s, biologist turned environmental activist Paul Ehrlich predicted that by the 1980s there would be widespread malnutrition in the USA; by 2000 he envisaged that 65 million Americans would starve to death (Ehrlich, 1968). Between 1970 and 1990, per capita consumption in the USA rose from 3192 to 3680 calories – even though the population has been rising by around 1 per cent per year – and continues steadily to increase. (Indeed, there is now more concern about obesity than famine in the USA.) It is important to stress that this was not because the US government heeded Ehrlich's advice: rather, the growth in food production that enabled this increase in consumption was the result primarily of advances in food production technology which Ehrlich had not foreseen. Similarly, the dire predictions of the Club of Rome in 1972, another influential group of environmental doomsayers, did not come to pass. Environmentalists are notoriously poor clairvoyants.

In an attempt to give Ehrlich a stronger incentive than mere academic ridicule to back up his pessimistic claims, in 1980, Julian Simon, then Professor of Economics at the University of Maryland, challenged Ehrlich to choose a basket of five commodities that in Ehrlich's opinion would become more expensive over the coming decade (cost being a measure of scarcity). The two agreed that if the price of the basket (which contained $200 of each commodity) went up, Simon would pay Ehrlich the difference and vice versa. Ten years later, every one of those commodities had fallen in price and the average cost of the basket had fallen by more than half. Ehrlich paid Simon $576.07 (Fumento, 1991).

The precautionary principle would make for a dim future

The last years of the twentieth century saw a technological revolution that may turn out to be as dramatic in its own way as the invention of the railroad in the eighteenth century. High-bandwidth access to the Internet has made home-working, home-schooling and home-shopping more realistic possibilities for a greater number of people. A shift away from the classroom, the office and the supermarket will reduce the number of car journeys taken, which in turn will have benefits for the environment in terms of lower emissions. More broadly, the Internet is increasing the efficiency of markets, bringing down producer costs and consumer prices and thereby stimulating a virtuous circle of growth. Few would have predicted such changes a decade ago. Certainly it formed no part of the proposals of environmentalists. Indeed, the technologies upon which the Internet is based could not have evolved but for the existence of distributed electricity networks, which in turn could not have been created without using highly efficient carbon-based fuels: renewables simply would not (indeed still do not) cut the mustard. The only 'alternative' energy sources that could feasibly have been used to power the growth of telecommunications that we have observed are nuclear and hydroelectricity, both of which have known and potential adverse environmental effects and both of which have been opposed by environmentalists (Mills, 1999; Bradley, 1999).

As Wilfred Beckerman (Chapter 3, *infra*.) observes, similar changes *will* occur in the future and they *will* result in economic growth. Consider merely the possibility of economic growth in so-called developing countries, where output is close to that of the 'developed' countries at the turn of the twentieth century. (Note that the nomenclature of development economics – 'developed' vs 'developing' – is highly misleading, since in most cases the 'developed' economies are those which are developing most rapidly, whilst the 'developing' economies are often doing anything but.) Clearly there is a great deal of room for the economies of many countries in Asia, Africa, Eastern Europe and South America merely catching up with the economies of the US, Japan, Western Europe and Australasia. The transformation has already occurred in South Korea, Singapore, Hong Kong and Taiwan. It is happening in the Czech Republic, Estonia and Chile. As countries such as China and Bolivia liberalize their economies and provide a more secure environment for trade and investment, it is beginning to happen there too (O'Driscoll et al., 2000).

For this change to occur, people must be free to develop and use both new and old technologies, including the technologies that enabled the western world to develop. It is all very well to sit in a comfortable chair high in an air-conditioned office block powered by the latest solar energy technology and imagine that it might be nice for people in Africa and Asia to do likewise. In reality, what most poor rural farmers need in the way of technologies are mechanical farm equipment, cheap carbon-based fuel (to power the machinery), fertilizer and pesticide (to increase yields). Similarly, budding industrialists require access to cheap fuel in order to manufacture and transport their wares. It is thus not only totally unrealistic but also morally offensive to expect such people to rely on non-carbon-based fuels.

As regards the use of new technologies by the people of Africa, Asia and Latin America, it is worth noting that genetic enhancement of crops promises enormous benefits for such people. Virus- and pest-resistant varieties of crops have already been developed, offering farmers in developing countries higher yields (Wilson et al., 1999). Hardier crop varieties, able to withstand drier, hotter, and more saline conditions, are being developed; these would enable farmers in developing countries to grow crops under a wider range of conditions, thereby reducing the risk of crop failure (ibid.).

Many farmers in developing countries are reluctant to use GM varieties, however, because of fears that Europeans will not buy them. The fear of new technology which enabled the precautionary principle to flourish in Europe is being recycled and fed to the people of the developing world, who are now reluctant to utilize technologies that would probably be beneficial both to them and to us.

Eroding the rule of law

The experience of GM crops in developing countries exemplifies the kind of impact that the precautionary principle is likely to have if applied more generally. Civilized people act within a framework of law and meta-legal institutions that encourage trust and foster mutually beneficial forms of association and exchange. It is said that we live according to the 'rule of law', a basic principle of which is the concept of 'legal certainty'. Consider the case of contract law. Let's suppose Andrea makes an agreement today with Benjamin to exchange 100 widgets for £1000 in one month's time. It seems reasonable to expect that Benjamin should make plans contingent on receiving those 100 widgets at the time and place specified. If Andrea decides to withdraw from the agreement at the last minute (perhaps her widget machine has broken down, or she has been offered more for her widgets from someone else), Benjamin may thereby suffer a loss not of his making. It is thus reasonable that Andrea should have to compensate Benjamin for at least some part of his loss. The fact that such a rule exists gives Andrea greater incentive to ensure that her widget machine is in fact working and not to sell her widgets to another buyer. The rule, in sum, creates a more certain environment in which to make transactions.

The precautionary principle undermines legal certainty by providing bureaucrats with an excuse to change the rules of the game in an essentially arbitrary manner. It is a bit like someone breaking into Andrea's factory and throwing a monkey wrench into the widget machine half-way through its production run, crippling it. The result would be that both Andrea and Benjamin would lose out, and there would be no gain other than the psychic pleasure of the vandal). The suggestion that this might be constrained by ensuring that precautionary decisions are founded on science is ridiculous, because the regulator can choose to use whatever 'science' he likes. Moreover, the regulator in these matters is typically influenced less by the quality of the scientific research than by what the most vocal and influential interest groups demand. As Durodié (*infra*) observes, when the precautionary principle is applied, it is the most radical science that is used, not the most reliable. There will always be scientists willing to claim that there is a problem and to support this with 'evidence', just as there will always be vandals who enjoy destroying machines.

Such piecemeal erosion of the rule of law ultimately makes of us less civilized men and women.

Conclusion

Attempts to define the precautionary principle have done little more than restate the views of interest groups and regulators whose antipathy towards the development of new technologies was already well known. Aggrandizing these views into 'principles' risks undermining any faith modern man may have had in the notion that the world should indeed be run according to principles and in particular those true principles, freedom and duty, which are owed betwixt men. Moreover, the slipshod reasoning given by environmentalists, consumer activists and bureaucrats to justify their dubious anti-technology assertions reinforces the view, already widely held by philosophers, economists and others who care for rationality and enlightened thinking, that the modern state has become a corruptible vessel into which the ravings of misanthropes and self-serving lobbyists are poured, stirred and regurgitated on to an unsuspecting public.

Rather than attempting to define the undefinable, policymakers should search for ways of weeding out the more ridiculous claims made by environmentalists, consumer activists and others, the application of which would be a disaster for us, as it would be for our children and our children's children. Robert Matthews' (Chapter 12, *infra*) suggests using Bayes' Theorem to adjudge the quality of scientific claims; that seems seems like a good place to start. Who knows? Maybe it will return policymaking on such issues to the rule of law and the rule of reason.

Acknowledgements

I would like to thank David Henderson, Roger Bate, Tony Gilland and Gregory Conko for their comments on earlier drafts of this chapter. All remaining errors are my own.

References

Ames, B. and Gold, L.(1999). Pollution, pesticides and cancer misconceptions. In *Fearing Food* (J. Morris and R. Bate, eds) pp. 19–37, Oxford: Butterworth-Heinemann.

Avery, D. (1999). The fallacy of the organic utopia. In *Fearing Food* (J. Morris and R. Bate, eds) pp. 3–18. Oxford: Oxford: Butterworth-Heinemann.

Bradley, R (1999). The increasing sustainability of conventional energy. Cato Policy Analysis No. 341, Washington DC: Cato Institute, April.

Cargill (1999). Beef hormones. *The Cargill Bulletin*. http://www.cargill.com/today/bulletin/t101996.htm (accessed 14 April 2000).

European Commission (2000). *Communication from the Commission on the Precautionary Principle* COM (2000) 1. Brussels: Commission of the European Communities.

ECE (1990). *Ministerial Declaration on Sustainable Development in the ECE Region*. Bergen, Norway, May 16, UN Doc A/Conf.151/PC/10. New York: United Nations.

Ehrlich, P. (1968). *The Population Bomb*. New York: Ballantine Books.

Freestone, D. (1992). The precautionary principle. In *International Law and Global Climate Change* (Churchill, R. and Freestone, D., eds) London: Graham and Trotman.

Fumento, M. (1991). The profits of doom. *People Count*. **2** (1), 3–5.

Goodin, R. E. (1980). No moral nukes. *Ethics*, **90**, April, 418–419.

HSE (n.d.). http://www.hse.gov.uk/dst/tt1.htm (accessed 18 April 2000).

Jevons, W. S. (1865/1965). *The Coal Question*. New York: A.M. Kelly.

Leggett, J. (ed.) (1990). *Global Warming: The Greenpeace Report*. Oxford: Oxford University Press.

MAFF (n.d.) http://www.maff.gov.uk/environ/epdnews1/soilprot.htm (accessed 18 April 2000).

Manson, N. (n.d.). The precautionary principle, the catastrophe argument, and Pascal's wager. http://www.abdn.ac.uk/cpts/manson1.shtml (accessed 14 April 2000).

Mazur, A. (1996). Why do we worry about trace poisons. http://fplc.edu/RISK/vol7/winter/mazur.htm (accessed 4 April 2000).

Mills, M. (1999). *The Internet Begins With Coal*. Arlington, VA: The Greening Earth Society.

Montague, P. (1998). The precautionary principle. *Rachel's Environment and Health Weekly*, No. 586, 19 February. http://www.monitor.net/rachel/r586.html (accessed 9 April 2000).

Morris, J. (1997a). *Green Goods? Consumers, Product Labels and the Environment*. London: Institute of Economic Affairs.

Morris, J. (1997b). *Climate Change: Challenging the Conventional Wisdom.* London: Institute of Economic Affairs.

Munby, J. and D.F. Weetman (1997). Benzene and leukemia. In *What Risk?* (R. Bate, ed.) pp. 73–95, Oxford: Butterworth-Heinemann.

O'Driscoll, Gerald, P., Holmes, K.R. and Kirkpatrick, M. (2000). *2000 Index of Economic Freedom,* Washington, DC: Heritage Foundation/The Wall Street Journal.

O'Riordan, T. and Cameron J. (eds) (1994). *Interpreting the Precautionary Principle.* London: Earthscan.

Pearce, D.W. (1980). The preconditions for achieving consensus in the context of technological risk. In *Technological Risk: Its Perception and Handling in the European Community* (M. Dierkes, S. Edwards and R. Coppock, eds.) Cambridge, MA: Oelgeschlager, Gunn and Hain.

SICPNS (1987) Ministerial Declaration of the Second International Conference on the Protection of the North Sea. *ILM,* **835**, 25 November.

Spencer, R. (2000). How do we know the temperature of the earth?. In *Earth Report 2000* (R. Bailey, ed.) New York: McGraw Hill.

Th. Douma, Wybe (1996). The precautionary principle. http://www.eel.nl/virtue/precprin.htm (accessed 14 April 2000).

Weintraub, B. (1992). Science, international environmental regulation, and the precautionary principle: setting standards and defining terms. *New York University Environmental Law Journal,* 173–223.

Wilson, J. (1997). Thresholds for Carcinogens: a review of the relevant science and its implications for regulatory policy. In *What Risk?* (R. Bate, ed.) pp. 1–36, Oxford: Butterworth-Heinemann.

Wilson, M.l, Hillman, J., and Robinson, D. (1999). Genetic modification in context and perspective. In *Fearing Food* (J. Morris, and R. Bate, eds), Oxford: Butterworth-Heinemann.

WTO (1998). *EC Measures Concerning Meat and Meat Products (Hormones).* 16 January 1998, AB-1997–4, WT/DS26/AB/R; WT/DS48/AB/R.

2 Trial and error versus trial without error

Aaron Wildavsky

There are two bedrock approaches to managing risk – trial and error, and trial without error. According to the doctrine of 'trial without error', no change whatsoever will be allowed unless there is solid proof that the proposed substance or action will do no harm. All doubts, uncertainties, and conflicting interpretations will thus be resolved by disallowing trials. Taking 'error' here to mean damage to life, prohibiting new products unless they can be proven in advance to be harmless, is an extraordinarily stringent prohibition. Surely no scientist (or businessperson or politician or citizen) can guarantee in the present that future generations will be better off because of any individual action.

It is true that without trials there can be no new errors; but without these errors, there is also less new learning. Science, its historians say, is more about rejecting than accepting hypotheses. Knowledge grows through critical appraisal of the failure of existing theory to explain or predict events. Learning by criticizing implies that existing theory is in error – not necessarily absolutely, but relative to better knowledge. Rules for democracy say little about what one does in office, but much more about getting officials out of office. 'Throwing the rascals out' is the essence of democracy. Similarly, in social life it is not the ability to avoid error entirely (even Goncharov's Oblomov, who spends his life in bed, cannot do that), but learning how to overcome it that is precious. As Joseph Morone and Edward Woodhouse (1985, p. 230) say: 'This is the classic trial-and-error strategy for dealing with complex problems: (1) establish a policy, (2) observe the effects, (3) correct for undesired effects, (4) observe the effects of the correction, and (5) correct again.'

The current debate on risk, however, which proposes a radical revision of this strategy; results in the opposite doctrine: no trials without prior guarantees against error. I do not mean to imply that proponents of trial without error would never permit error. They see 'no errors' as the goal (albeit one that cannot be fully realized) only for certain classes of situations. In this perspective, trial and error is all right in its circumscribed place. But that place would be limited to conditions in which possible consequences are quite modest (as distinguished from catastrophic) and where feedback is fast. This limitation implies a certain foreseeability of the possible sorts of error and the extent of their consequences. Yet this presumption itself may be erroneous; that is, it ignores the most dangerous source of error, namely, the unexpected. When large adverse consequences probably will occur, and when preventive measures are likely to make things better (without, in other ways, making them worse), of course no one disputes that trials should be regulated. The difficulty, as usual, lies in reaching agreement about whether and when a catastrophe is coming. One side wants special reasons to stop experimentation, and the other wants special conditions to start. Which bias, the question is, is safest?

The outcome of analysis depends in large part on how the criterion of choice is defined. Some prominent environmental economists, such as Allen Kneese, would opt for the standard of efficiency called Pareto optimality, under which actions are justified if they make some people better off without harming others. But this criterion assumes, erroneously, that it is possible to separate harmful from beneficial effects. Thus, a vaccine that saves millions but kills a few would not be justified, even though the health of society as a whole, and of almost all of its members, would be improved. Indeed, the pursuit of Pareto optimality can strangle growth and change, because any developments are likely to hurt someone, somewhere, sometime. Lindblom's criticism is justified:

> Economists often blunder into the conclusion that policy makers should choose Pareto-efficient solutions because they help some persons and hurt no others. Not so. If, as is typically the case – and perhaps always the case – there are still other solutions that bring substantial advantages to large numbers of persons and these advantages are worth seeking even at loss to other persons – for example, protecting civil liberties of minorities even if doing so is greatly irritating and obstructive to others then, there remains a conflict as to what is to be done. The Pareto efficient solution is not necessarily the best choice
>
> (Lindblom, 1984)

In discussing trial without error with participants in the risk debate, I often sense an air of disbelief, as if no reasonable person would support such a practice. But people do; I shall show that trial without error is indeed the prevailing doctrine among the risk-averse and that in important respects it is government policy. For illustrative purposes, I have deliberately chosen the most persuasive exponents of this doctrine.

No trials without prior guarantees against error

Trial without error is proposed as a criterion of choice by David W. Pearce, who wishes to prevent technologies from being introduced 'without first having solved the problems they create. This "reverse solution" phenomenon characterizes the use of nuclear power, where waste disposal problems remain to be solved even though the source of the waste, the power stations themselves, forms part of whole energy programs' (Pearce, 1980, p. 58). There is nothing unusual today about this way of introducing new technologies. In the past, however, it was common practice to solve the problems associated with novelty as they surfaced following adoption of the innovation. One could well ask whether any technology, including the most benign, would ever have been established if it had first been forced to demonstrate that it would do no harm.

In 1865, to take but a single instance, a million cubic feet of gas exploded at the London Gas Works, killing ten people and burning twenty. The newspapers screamed that the metropolis faced disaster.

> If half London would be blown to pieces by the explosion of the comparatively small quantity of gas stored at Blackfriars, it might be feared that if all the gasholders in the metropolis were to 'go off', half the towns in the kingdom would suffer, and to be perfectly secure, the source of danger must be removed to the Land's End.
>
> Anon, 1865, p. 807)

Could anyone who planned to introduce gas heating or lighting have certified in advance that there would be no explosions, no danger of blowing up the city? I think not. Nonetheless, the gas industry, without such guarantees, did flourish.

But Pearce sees otherwise. In order to guard against potential harm from new technology, he suggests amassing information from experts on both sides, with attention being paid to the possibility of refusing to go ahead with a particular technology. By funding the opposition and by bringing in wider publics, Pearce hopes to ensure that 'surveillance of new technology is carried out in such a way that no new venture is embarked upon without the means of control being 'reasonably' assured in advance' (Pearce, 1980, p. 58). This, I say, is not trial and error but a new doctrine: no trials without prior guarantees against error.

The most persuasive and most common argument is that trial and error should not be used unless the consequences of worst-case errors are knowable in advance to be sufficiently benign to permit new trials. For if irreversible damage to large populations resulted, no one might be around to take on the next trial. A strong statement of this view comes from Robert E. Goodin:

> Trial and error and learning by doing are appropriate, either for ... discovering what the risks are or for the adaptive task of overcoming them only under very special conditions. These are conspicuously lacking in the case of nuclear power. First, we must have good reasons for believing that the errors, if they occur, will be small. Otherwise the lessons may be far too costly. Some nuclear mishaps will no doubt be modest. But for the same reasons small accidents are possible, so too are large ones and some of the errors resulting in failure of nuclear reactor safeguards may be very costly indeed. This makes trial and error inappropriate in that setting. Second, errors must be immediately recognizable and correctable. The

impact of radioactive emissions from operating plants or of leaks of radioactive waste products from storage sites upon human populations or the natural environment may well be a 'sleeper' effect that does not appear in time for us to revise our original policy accordingly.

(Goodin, 1980, pp. 418–19)

Past practice had encouraged people to act unless there were good reasons for not doing so. Goodin reverses that criterion, explicitly replacing it with a requirement for 'very special conditions' before trying anything new. His justification, like Pearce's, is the potential danger of nuclear energy, or of any other technology that might lead to irreversible damage.

Yet the argument against taking any irreversible actions is not as broadly applicable as it may appear. On this ground many policies and practices that make up the warp and woof of daily life would actually have to be abandoned. Maurice Richter makes the case well:

Our legal system makes it relatively easy for people to commit themselves to specified courses of action 'irreversibly' through the signing of contracts; a contractual agreement that is too easily reversible may thereby lose much of its value. The movement away from irreversibility in marriage is widely regarded as a social problem. Why, then, should irreversibility, which is sought in so many other contexts, be considered a defect when it appears in material technology? There may be a good reason, but the burden of proof falls on those who insist that reversibility in technology is a valid general principle, and they have hardly proved their case.

(Richter, 1982, p. 97)

Putting it a little differently, we might want reversibility in some areas of life (say, alternation in political office), but not in others (say, diversion of social security funds to other purposes).

With regards to the effects of nuclear radiation, there are extraordinarily sensitive means available for measuring radiation, down to the decay of single atoms. Moreover, human exposure (consider Hiroshima and Nagasaki) has been so intensively studied that it is possible to accurately estimate the health risk of exposure to a given dose, including long-range risk. This comparatively great understanding of radiation notwithstanding, however, no reasonable person could say with complete certainty that any particular dose – for given individuals, or, still more remote, large populations – would never produce irreversible consequences. And there is still doubt about the long-term effects of very small doses. Even when the best estimates of risk (the magnitude of the hazard/error times the probability of occurrence) approach zero, one can always imagine some concatenation of events that make it impossible (viz., Chernobyl) to rule out potential catastrophe. Presumably, then, the only safe action, according to the 'trial-without-error' school, is no trials at all.

Though agreeing that there has been useful learning about nuclear energy, Goodin draws a pessimistic conclusion:

Sometimes, once we have found out what is going wrong and why, we can even arrange to prevent it from recurring. Precisely this sort of learning by doing has been shown to be responsible for dramatic improvements in the operating efficiency of nuclear reactors. That finding, however, is as much a cause for concern as for hope. It is shocking that there is any room at all left for learning in an operational nuclear reactor, given the magnitude of the disaster that might result from ignorance or error in that setting.

(Goodin, 1980, p. 418)

Heads, I win; tails, you lose. Here (as elsewhere) correcting error actually did prove to be an effective route to increased safety. So, since trial and error is exactly what Goodin wishes to prevent, he needs a stronger argument for its inadvisability.

Goodin does argue that nuclear power plants are different because 'we would be living not merely with risk but also with *irresolvable* uncertainties' (Goodin, 1980, p. 418). But I hold that this is not good enough; after all, every technology, viewed in advance, has 'irresolvable' uncertainties. Only experience can tell us which among all imaginable hazards will in fact materialize and hence justify measures to reduce them. 'Irresolvable' uncertainty about the future is a condition of human life. One thing no one can have for sure is a guarantee that things will always turn out all right in the future.

Turning to the only recent and comprehensive study of trial and error as a strategy for securing safety (it covers toxic chemicals, nuclear power, the greenhouse effect, genetic engineering, and threats to the ozone layer), Morone and Woodhouse '. . . were pleasantly surprised to find how much learning from error has occurred. In part because the ecosystem (so far) has been more forgiving than reasonably might have been expected, trial-and-error has been an important component of the system for averting catastrophe' (Morone and Woodhouse, 1985, p. 14). They conclude:

For years, regulation of toxic substances proceeded by trial and error. Chemicals were regulated only after negative consequences became apparent. This type of decision process is a well-known, thoroughly analysed strategy for coping with complex problems. But we had assumed that long delays before obtaining feedback, coupled with severe consequences of error, would make trial and error inappropriate in managing hazardous chemicals. Contrary to our expectations, there proved to be numerous channels for feedback about the effects of chemicals, as demonstrated in detail for pesticides. Regulators were able to take repeated corrective actions in response to the feedback.

(Morone and Woodhouse, 1985, p. 215).

There are many historical examples of feedback from affected citizens that led to corrective measures after the fact. When beekeepers began to complain that inorganic pesticides were harming bees (allegations supported by early entomologists, for instance), agricultural extension agents in the 1890s urged that spraying be delayed until the bees had departed. Again, as it became clear that London Purple (which had supplanted 'Paris Green' as the favourite American insecticide, to choose another of many examples) burned plants, and as substitutes existed that did not have this harmful quality, market and governmental action moved toward a different approach to insect control (Whorton, 1974).

Despite such evidence, the 'no error' criterion has much support. In the Environmental Protection Agency (EPA), Melnick (1983) concludes, this criterion represents the governing principle of the organization. Strong elements in Congress also favour this form of risk aversion. In December 1985, for instance, Senators David Durenberger and Max Bacus introduced a bill to replace voluntary oversight with mandatory regulation of engineered organisms. Any firm that sought to release or use such a product 'must be able to prove that no adverse effect to the environment will occur as a result of its actions' (*Inside the Administration*, 1986a). This is a 'conservative' criterion that is widespread among academics, and it is presented as the epitome of rationality. Peter Nemetz and Aiden Vining concluded that '. . . conservative standard setting procedure is the most desirable course of action. In fact, it can be argued that the maintenance of such an approach is not to err at all, but to adopt the only rational approach to public policy.' (Nemetz and Vining, 1981, p. 137).

It is instructive here to look at the approach that over decades has been in use for determining the allowable level of poisons in food: set up a dose study in animals; determine the dose where 'no effect' is observed; divide this level by 100 (10 times to allow for possible differences in species sensitivity, and another factor of 10 to allow for greater human variability); and declare this level 'acceptable' for anyone to eat during a lifetime. This method has worked well for at least 50 years (as far as anyone knows); yet it lacks all theoretical elegance. It is merely a rule of thumb. Possibly a chemical might turn up to which rats and mice were resistant but that could poison half the human population. Also, the 'no effect' levels are determined in animal tests of limited scope; maybe one really should test many more than just 50 or 100 animals (as usually is done) to exclude 'rare' effects. Were Goodin's criteria (immediate recognizability and correctability) followed in this instance, something as common as salt or pepper or sugar or Vitamin D could never be added to prepared foods. After all, any of these might be carcinogens to which everyone is unavoidably exposed; the last three have in fact been shown to cause cancer in at least one animal test. And, because of the long latency of carcinogens, we could not hope to detect their effects in humans before several decades had passed.

Efforts have been made to distinguish natural from man-made chemicals on the grounds that we could stop or limit use of the latter while nothing much can be done about the former. True, but not, I think, the most important truth. Sometimes it is suggested that human beings have grown up with natural carcinogens and have thus somehow adjusted to them, while this is not true at all or to the same extent of man-made chemicals. Yet no evidence whatsoever exists to show that the body distinguishes differences between the sources of chemicals. Furthermore, were it true, this argument would lead us to expect that rats and mice would not get cancer from natural foods. But, like human beings, rats and mice can get cancer from any number of natural foods. Of course, there could be synergistic effects of two or more chemicals interacting that would increase their potency and hence their danger. So far as is known, however, which is not far, such synergy is as likely to reduce as to increase cancer-causing agents. (Ames, 1983, pp. 1256–1264; Efron, 1984; and Havender and Meister, 1985, pp. 28–30).

Turning to actual policy, the final cancer exposure regulation prepared by the Occupational Safety and Health Administration (some 300 pages long in the Federal Register) contained assumptions, the agency promised, that would err on the side of identifying non-carcinogens as carcinogens rather than the reverse. This is no risk with a vengeance. Even epidemiological studies that failed to show that carcinogens were present or caused harm would be ignored unless:

> (i) The epidemiological study involved at least 20 years' exposure of a group of subjects to the substance and at least 30 years' observation of the subjects after initial exposure; (ii) documented reasons are provided for predicting the site(s) at which the substance would induce cancer if it were carcinogenic in humans; and (iii) the group of exposed subjects was large enough for an increase in cancer incidence of 50 per cent above that in unexposed controls to have been detected at any of the predicted sites.

> (Federal Register, 1980, p. 5287)

Studies showing positive results (i.e., the presence of carcinogens) were exempt from these criteria. As Mendeloff concludes, 'Extremely few epidemiological studies can meet these criteria.' (Mendeloff, 1986, p. 24)

The risk-averse position – no trials without prior guarantees against error – has lately infiltrated the whole arena of public life. What consequences, we may ask, would result from adopting a criterion of choice that would restrict new technologies to those few that might be able to provide such extraordinary advance reassurance?

The 'no-safe-dose' argument

Risk aversion is sometimes justified on grounds that the smallest probability of irreversible disaster overwhelms all other considerations. 'If the extinction of mankind is evaluated at minus infinity,' Jon Elster writes, 'then it swamps all disasters of finite size. We must, of course, have some precise probability attached to this event: mere logical possibility is not sufficient. It does not matter, however, if this probability is extremely small, for an infinite number multiplied by a positive number remains infinite' (Elster, 1979, pp. 371–400). So what do we have? Terribly low probabilities of awfully terrible events. Infinitesimal amounts of strontium 90 may accumulate in enough bodies to kill off entire peoples. Why, just imagine-if everything else is held constant, an increase in goat's milk projected to infinity could drown the earth and everyone on it! 'The weakness of this argument,' Elster continues, 'is that it may turn out that most actions have such total disasters associated with them, at an extremely unlikely but still quantifiable probability. I believe, therefore, that one should be very cautious in arguing along these lines' (Elster, 1979, pp. 371–400). One should indeed be cautious, but many are not, because it is hard to resist the temptation to present a case against which there appears to be no reasonable reply.

Under the designation of the 'no threshold' theory, it is said (and, I add immediately, sufficiently supported to form the basis of governmental policy) that a single mutagenic event can cause cancer. 'The "predisposition", if one can call it that, to cancer builds up over a period of time, perhaps from constant exposures to carcinogens along with individual susceptibility,' Jacqueline Verrett of the Food and Drug Administration wrote, 'and there may come the day when that extra molecule of a carcinogen may overload the system and cancer begins to grow'. Reasoning on that 'last straw' basis, researchers from the National Cancer Institute assured Congressmen that a single molecule of DES (in the 340 trillion or so molecules present) in a quarter of a pound of beef liver might well be enough to trigger human cancer (Verrett and Carper, 1975, pp. 148–9). Should no trials of possibly carcinogenic chemicals be allowed because every error might well kill someone? Let us study this 'one-hit' theory, because it offers insight into what one would have to believe in order to justify a policy of no trials without prior guarantees.

The 'one-molecule' or 'no-threshold' or 'no safe dose' theory of carcino-genesis holds that exposure to the very smallest amount of cancer-producing material may, over time, have some chance of causing a deadly change in the affected cell such that the malignancy multiplies out of control. But, as Marvin Schneiderman of the National Cancer Institute asked, why is it 'prudent . . . to assume no threshold for a carcinogen' (Schneiderman, n.d., p. 10). In the field of toxicology, the traditional method had been to develop empirically a 'dose-response' curve so that exposure below a certain level, called the 'threshold,' to all intents and purposes was safe, while higher doses would be (increasingly) harmful. This method of dealing with hazards is not appropriate for carcinogens, some scientists might say to Schneiderman, because of fundamental differences in mechanism between toxins and carcinogens; also, there are inherent uncertainties in the task of carcinogenic risk assessment. Further, given the difficulty of using large numbers of animals in research, very large doses must be given to small numbers of animals; this makes it hard to say what would happen at the low doses that are more typical of human exposure. Since human variability is so great, moreover, a threshold (or 'safe dose') for one person might be quite different for another. So little is known about mixing carcinogens and non-carcinogens that their interaction might turn out to produce cancer, even at very low levels (Schneiderman, n.d., pp. 88–92 and pp. 335–344). The 'no dose is safe' theory claims either that the last infinitesimal dose will break the camel's back of cancer resistance (increments can kill), or that through evolution 'nature' has learned how to deal with natural but not with industrial carcinogens (technology can kill) (see *inter alia*, Schneiderman, n.d.).

Yet we all know that virtually everything human beings breathe or eat or drink brings them into contact with carcinogens. Poisons are an integral part of nature. So is chemical warfare among plants, animals, and insects. To ban carcinogenic substances, therefore, is to ban life. Remember that the idea is to develop a rationale for regulating the products of industrial technology, not for ending all life.

Viewed as rhetoric, the no-safe-dose argument is superb. If it is accepted, it creates a convincing rationale for forbidding any trials of new chemical substances on the grounds that errors (assuming a large number of people were affected) could be catastrophic. Think of it: a single molecule can kill. Were that not enough, we are to be persuaded that the most sensitive person in a population – running into hundreds of millions of people who have wide variations in susceptibility – should set the standard for regulatory decisions about safety. The ancient tale, 'for want of a nail . . .' ending 'the battle [in this case, for life] was lost' is trotted out as grounds for banning any innovation, however small. And all change one does not like may be prevented merely by claiming that the tiniest part can be catastrophic to some segment of the population. That sounds like a conclusive argument.

Incrementalism as risk aversion

At this point in the discussion, some students of decision making may experience deja vu. They have been there before. The criteria suggested for political and social decisions – errors should be small, recognizable, and reversible – are those usually attributed to the method for making decisions called incrementalism that was popularized in the decades following the Second World War. According to this doctrine, which Karl Popper once called 'piecemeal social engineering' (Popper, 1971), alternatives should (1) be small in size, (2) limited in number, and (3) follow a consistent pattern of relationships. The benefits presumed to follow from incrementalism include an ability to enhance learning because errors, being small, are easier to correct. Political agreement is to be promoted, in addition, by narrowing the range of dispute to a few alternatives, which differ only marginally from existing policy (Wildavsky, 1979; Dempster and Wildavsky, 1979, pp. 371–389; Lindblom, 1959; and Lindblom, 1979).

Although the validity of incrementalism as a description of some (but by no means all) decision processes has been recognized, the normative status of the method has been hotly disputed. In a word, incrementalism has been criticized as an ideology that rationalizes conservatism, and defined as adherence to the status quo (Lustick, 1980). These critics would, in stipulated instances, prefer radical – i.e., fundamental, wholesale, large-scale – policy or political change. In response, defenders of incrementalism have argued that 'it [the conservatism of incrementalism] ain't necessarily so', Runners can get as far by taking many small steps as by a few larger ones (Wildavsky, 1964; and Braybrooke and Lindblom, 1963). Moreover, had they known about the 'one-hit' theory of cancer causation, the defenders of incrementalist doctrine might have been able to point out their more progressive posture.

Incrementalism was also part of the doctrine of the positive, interventionist state. The idea of incrementalist doctrine was not to do nothing; it was emphatically to do something (Popper, 1971). If incrementalism were designed to justify inaction, its supporting doctrine would have stressed the unacceptability, not the desirability, of trying out small moves.

Incrementalism as trial with small errors

Observe that the old incrementalism is conservative, not reactionary. The doctrine does provide a positive justification for change in the form of repeated trials. Errors are welcomed so long as they are small and diverse – i.e. not cumulative. The extent of change may be small and (if knowledge or consent are lacking) slow, but the sign, the direction, is positive. Incrementalism was conceived as a strategy for action, however moderate, not inaction.

This warm, if cautious, welcome to change in areas of public policy has not been extended by everyone to technological development. On the contrary, incrementalism has now been recast as a reactionary doctrine in which the tiniest conceivable increment of error or harm (recall the single molecule test) can halt all change.

Like the strategy of trial and error it resembles, incrementalism (using small doses of experience to discover uncertainties unpredictable in advance) has been attacked as inappropriate for certain risky realms of decisions. Trying out a nuclear exchange or experimenting with a little plague are inadvisable. 'Since incrementalism is a reactive strategy,' Jack Knott sums up the prevailing critique, 'it cannot anticipate sharp discontinuities; because the strategy relies on successive comparisons, it receives no guidance when responses to actions are long term.' (Knott, 1982, pp. 1–2). Decision makers who face such conditions, the argument goes, should not go for the incremental approach. What approach, then, should they use? The major contender as a strategy for decision making was one known as synoptic choice (centralized control of means and ends through prediction of long-term effects). Through comprehensive, large-scale planning, bad things would be prevented and good accomplished. Yet Knott recalls that:

> Earlier efforts to study decision strategies generally concluded that longer feedback loops, . . . complexities, and sharp discontinuities were precisely the kinds of problems for which incremental strategies had a decided advantage over more synoptic (big change] approaches. Martin Landau has argued, for example, that task environments not characterized by sharp discontinuities are most suitable for synoptic decisions, while environments characterized by uncertainty require experimental, open-ended approaches.

> (Knott, 1982, pp. 2–3)

Synoptic decisions based on the assumption of being able to predict and control large-scale change, it was then argued, worked best in situations without discontinuities, i.e., in more readily predictable environments. The greater the uncertainty, therefore, the more reason to adopt the incremental approach of successive, limited comparisons (cf. Landau, 1973, pp. 533–42; Steinbrunner, 1974; Thompson and Tuden, 1959; and many other works). When theory was powerful and discriminating, so was prediction, and hence control of consequences. Problems, therefore, could be prevented by large-scale intervention. When knowledge was weak, however, and better decisions had to be discovered because they could not be figured out analytically in advance, the incremental search procedure called trial and error better fit the circumstances. (Knowledge might grow even more by the invention of new and broader hypotheses that then were subjected to screening through results (Munz, 1985). But it is not easy to develop new and fruitful hypotheses on command or to subject them to test when avoidance of trial and error is part of public policy.)

It would be better to work with powerful and discriminating theories. But when these are unavailable, task environments usually display high degrees of uncertainty. Under such circumstances, vigorous trial and error seemed the best way to proceed – so that there could be mutual adjustment among different sorts of experiences and problems. And, because error was both expected and valued as an aid to learning, decisions (and, hopefully, consequences) were deliberately kept small; this reduced risk and increased the chances of learning from mistakes. Taking fewer risks may ultimately decrease safety, but, as Lewis Dexter advises, 'going slow frequently' may improve our prospects (Dexter, 1986). Large numbers of small moves, frequently adjusted, permitted tests of new phenomena before they became big enough to do massive harm.

Playing it safe

That was another era. Nowadays we find ourselves in a world in which the ancient verities have been turned inside out. Except under improbable conditions – theoretical or laboratory proof that the next move will do no harm on the self-reinforcing grounds that trials permit errors – resort to experience has been ruled out. (Examples abound. For traditional pollution problems where the effluent is obvious, Talbot Page contends, an incremental approach may well be useful in avoiding overly abrupt changes: 'But for environmental risk the process of incremental reaction is not self-correcting. Because of latency, an effect is irreversibly determined before it is clearly observed. ... Rather than relying ... upon the perception of past failures, adequate control of environmental risks requires institutions that anticipate the risks' (Page, 1978, p. 242). Bryan Norton likens incremental choices on the diversity of species to the alcoholic's choice of whether to take a single drink. The one drink here is not a small matter but, rather, a prelude to catastrophe.

'These arguments imply,' he concludes, 'that . . . almost all costs of preserving a species should be considered "reasonable" . . .' (Norton, n.d., p. 22). On this ground, any act, however small, could be prohibited on the grounds that it will hammer the last nail into society's coffin.)

The most seductive form of playing it safe is prudential conservatism. Why be half safe? When in doubt, add margins of safety. Allow nothing new unless pre-guaranteed as harmless. Such fields as toxicology and engineering do present honourable examples of conservatism. A structure or a substance would be estimated to carry a certain load, or to cause a certain degree of difficulty. Concerned that future conditions might lead to change far beyond the parameters of their models, engineers and toxicologists would, as a matter of ordinary procedure, design structures to carry far heavier loads than expected, and decrease allowable exposure to substances far below expected dangerous levels. So far, so good.

But beyond these prudential safety factors, however, there has grown up a tendency to add other levels. Safety margins will be increased on 'worst-case' considerations, and then again increased on the grounds that it doesn't hurt to be even more careful. That is, one first estimates the dangers of a product or practice according to existing knowledge. Then at every step decisions are made as to where uncertainty can be resolved. Prudence, presumably, is the byword. Having arrived at an estimate (or range of estimates), one chooses the upper bound of danger, then multiplies it by a safety factor of, say, ten to a hundred. But observe what has occurred. As uncertainties are resolved by exaggeration, estimates of potential damage also may be increased thousands of times over. So what? Is there anything wrong with being supercautious? What is wrong is that there is no inherent stopping point. If supercaution is the one guiding principle, there is no reason why estimates should not be exaggerated again and again. 'Conservatism' can be pursued to infinity; and since virtually everything contains some harm, the inescapable conclusion is to decide that the activity in question should be disallowed altogether.

In an important paper, H.W. Lewis distinguishes between conservatism that tries to compensate for inherent uncertainties and conservatism for its own sake. 'In the design of bridges and buildings, for example,' he writes, 'a value for the breaking strength of steel is commonly used that is far below its actual breaking strength, but one would obviously not want to use the same value to calculate the real probability that the structure will collapse.' Yet often regulators compensate for uncertainty as though it were as accurate as the best calculation of risk (Lewis, no date, pp. 23–4). Suppose, however, that an actual situation of technological uncertainty exists. How should a regulatory agency behave? Lewis makes the essential distinction:

> One is not dealing here with a situation in which one knows the correct answer for the damage probability, and uses conservatism to set it low enough to be tolerable, but is rather using conservatism to mask ignorance. It is common under such conditions to proceed through the calculation of the risk, dealing with each point at which there is scientific uncertainty by deliberately erring in the direction of overestimating the

risk. There is an essential difference between calculating a risk carefully, and then deliberately choosing a conservative design in such a way as to reduce the risk to a desired level, and deliberately erring in a conservative direction in the calculation of risk. An error in the conservative direction is nonetheless an error.

(Lewis, n.d., p. 30)

It is not, however, an error from which one can learn because, since the error is deliberate and far out of bounds, the magnitude of its excess remains unknown.

The imposition of safety factors is sensible, but only if two considerations are observed: first, the best known probabilities are calculated, and then the adverse effects of increasing the margin of error are taken into account. One could hardly find a better example than Lewis's use of aircraft wings:

The penalty for a conservative design which makes the wing too strong is a heavier airplane, with a negative impact on all the other virtues of flight. The result is that the safety factors on aircraft wings have always been much lower than the factors of five or ten which are common for civil structures, and are in fact substantially lower than a factor of two. This author's experience has been that many engineers are shocked when they learn this fact, since they are accustomed to larger factors of safety. However, in this case, there would be a recognizable penalty for excessive conservatism, and experience with aircraft wings has enabled the designers to reduce the safety margin to the minimum possible. Even in the early days of aviation, when the accumulated experience was not large, the fact that heavy airplanes can not fly was sufficient to reduce the safety factors, and aircraft design has always involved the conflict between weight and structural integrity.

(Lewis, n.d., p. 30)

Making flight impossible or causing crashes is not usually recommended as a conservative measure to increase safety.

Albert Nichols and Richard Zeckhauser claim (correctly, I think) that the practice of 'conservatism' confuses risk assessment (estimating hazards) with risk management (policies to control hazards). They would prefer to estimate hazards as close as existing knowledge will permit and then, as a matter of management, decide how much risk to take. Otherwise, they write, 'Conservatism can lead to less rather than more safety by misdirecting public concern and scarce agency resources' (Nichols and Zeckhauser, 1986, pp. 13–24).

Perhaps this account of risk aversion is a caricature. Quite possibly, advocates of risk aversion wish to be prudent, but not extreme; for that to be so, in a given study, they must establish supportable limits to the number of times conservative estimates ought to be multiplied in subsequent calculation. Also, they must allow estimates of the safety benefits of the product or substance being evaluated to weigh in the balance. The result would be a return to the useful practice of cost-benefit analysis (efforts to compare the gains and losses from proposed projects so as to assess their relative desirability), from which the emphasis on conservative calculation is intended to depart.

This exact issue is at the root of a current conflict between the Environmental Protection Agency (EPA) and the Office of Management and Budget (OMB). The question concerns standards for allowable amounts of carcinogenic substances in ground water. OMB objects to the way EPA makes cascading conservative projections, so that it is impossible to judge the protection provided; instead, OMB feels that EPA should try to calculate the risks and then add a reasonable margin of safety. OMB claims that an individual would face a cancer risk 4000 times higher from drinking a diet soda with saccharin than from the amounts of solvents and dioxins in the ground water (*Inside the Administration*, 1986b, p. 4). Does this comparison, assuming that it is roughly accurate, tell us anything? Or should the faintest prospect of harm dictate regulation to eliminate the offending substance? Are we to reject any new substances that are not risk free? What, then, will be the effects of the attendant decline in innovations for our society?

Safety comes from use

So far as safety is concerned, old dogs *can* learn new tricks, for older products do not necessarily have to remain as unsafe as they are. Relative safety is not static, but is rather a dynamic product of learning from error over time. By 'dynamic', I mean not only that new products may be safer than their forerunners, but also that those older products may be successfully modified in certain aspects.

Pioneers suffer the costs of premature development. But if development is allowed to continue into succeeding generations, the costs of error detection and correction would be shared to some extent with the next generation of future innovators; and the resulting benefits likewise would be passed back down to the now 'old' originators. Needless to say, however, a second generation of products cannot learn from the first if there isn't one.

Technology, as Nathan Rosenberg observes, is not merely the application of theory: 'Technology is itself a body of knowledge, . . . of techniques, methods and designs that work . . . even when one cannot explain exactly why'. But people who do not 'know why' may yet 'know how'. This 'know how' is responsible for much progress. 'Indeed,' Rosenberg concludes, 'if the human race had been confined to technologies that were understood in a scientific sense, it would have passed from the scene long ago.' (Rosenberg, 1982, pp. 121–40).

Existing knowledge may be incomplete. Indeed, in the sense that new and more powerful theories potentially will replace or alter the now-known, knowledge is always incomplete. The presenting problem, moreover, may contain combinations of factors that are new – in this proportion, or that sequence, or the other location. As Fredrich Hayek tells us in his essay 'The use of knowledge in society', the relevant factors may occur only in local combinations (Hayek, 1945, pp. 519–30). The task of decision making in a complex society, therefore, may not be so much to create general theory but more to be in touch with, and apply, knowledge that is attuned to local conditions (Cohen and Lindblom, 1979). An important component of innovation entails applying knowledge to a product even though the consequences cannot be known (i.e., specified in all details) in advance.

How can one make use of this unarticulated 'know-how'? Learning by doing is one way. Kenneth Arrow locates learning as part of the process of production. His argument will set the stage for our consideration of learning how to do better, in terms of health and safety as well as economic productivity. According to Arrow:

> Knowledge has to be acquired . . . The acquisition of knowledge is what is usually termed 'learning' . . . I do not think that the picture of technical change as a vast and prolonged process of learning about the environment in which we operate is in any way a far-fetched analogy; exactly the same phenomenon of improvement in performance over time is involved.
>
> Of course . . . there are sharp differences of opinion about the processes of learning. But one empirical generalization is so clear that all schools of thought must accept it, although they interpret it in different fashions: Learning is the product of experience. Learning can only take place through the attempt to solve a problem and therefore only takes place during activity . . . A second generalization that can be gleaned from many of the classic learning experiments is that learning associated with repetition of essentially the same problem is subject to sharply diminishing returns . . . To have steadily increasing performance, then, implies that the stimulus situations must themselves be steadily evolving rather than merely repeating . . . I advance the hypothesis here that technical change in general can be ascribed to experience, that it is the very activity of production which gives rise to problems for which favorable responses are selected over time.
>
> (Arrow, 1962, pp. 155–73)

No trials, no new errors – but also no new experience and hence no new learning.

We all know the old adage, 'experience is the best teacher'; well, an appropriate, if wordy, interpretation would be to say that error correction through trials increases reliability and efficiency. Think for a moment about the inspection of nuclear power plants by government regulators. Since inspectors differ, and because rules are not always codified or applicable, the thousands of change-orders at each facility may lead power plants – though built from the same or similar designs – to differ considerably. Talking to engineers reveals that the situations of plants can be so different that local experience is essential for controlling their performance. Only a few nuclear power plants, for instance, are on sites containing four or more reactors. Experience reveals that single reactors alone on a site are more likely to break down than reactors on sites with multiple units. 'A reactor seems to "learn" significantly faster,'

Alvin Weinberg notes, 'when it is next to "older brothers" than when it is an "only child" (Weinberg, 1982, pp. 54–8). This family aspect of safety extends also to consumers (users) as well as producers of products (doers).

The distinction between learning by doing (see Arrow, 1962) and learning by using, introduced by Nathan Rosenberg (1982), is essential for understanding innovation and how innovation relates to safety. After a product has been designed, learning by doing (that is, confined to manufacturing) refers to the process of increasing skill and efficiency in production. Now, whereas cumulative gains in production involve 'doing', advantages that occur from utilization have to do with 'using'. Manufacturers 'do' while consumers 'use'. These two types of learning differ, Rosenberg argues, because 'many significant characteristics of . . . products are revealed only after intensive or, more significantly, prolonged use' (Rosenberg, 1982, p. 122).

A vital aspect of the competitive position of a product is its maintenance cost, which is in part a function of reliability. And reliability is often determined by user-sponsored changes (Rosenberg, 1982, p. 135–8). Reliability and safety are closely connected. Where equipment is difficult to reach, as, for instance, in underwater cables or space satellites, extending the time period between maintenance checks and replacements is both cheaper for the user and safer for the fixer. As anyone acquainted with a computer product knows, '. . . the optimal design of software depends upon a flow of information from its customers' (Rosenberg, 1982, p. 139).

Much technological innovation is accomplished by users who modify products, not merely by designers who originate them. A crucial test of this hypothesis is to measure the rate of discovery by research units in large organizations who specialize in new applications by comparison with feedback from the customers who use these products. On an anecdotal level, Thomas J. Peters reports that:

> After 25 years of studying IBM, GE, Polaroid, Xerox, Bell Labs, and the like, he [Brian Quinn] concluded of one of them: 'Not a single major product has come from the formal product planning process.' The offender of rationality: IBM. In two years of using Quinn's line with hundreds of audiences (virtually all with past or present Ambers in attendance), I've only once heard a demurring voice. It came from a Bell operating company vice-president, who said: 'Nonsense. That statement is probably not true for IBM, and I know it's not true for the [Bell] Labs.' He pointed to a very respected Labs vice-president and said, 'You tell him'. The Labs man scratched his chin for ten seconds or so (as my heart skipped beats) and replied: 'Well, I've only been at the Labs for a bit over 30 years, but I can't think of anything that ever came directly from the new product planning process
>
> (Peters, 1983, pp. 12–21).

A substantial majority of major twentieth-century inventions, from the continuous casting of steel to ballpoint pens, as John Jewkes demonstrates in his book *The Sources of Invention*, came from people outside the then-existing industry (Jewkes, Sawers, and Stillerman, 1959). The special role of early users is developed by James Utterback, who concludes that the initial intended use for a new product is rarely the one that catches on (Utterback, 1979, p. 48). After reviewing some 80 studies of the emergence of new products, Peters concludes that 'The great majority of the ideas . . . come from the users' (Peters, 1983, pp. 10–19). This view is supported by Eric Von Hippel's study of 160 innovations in scientific instruments. Users made not only 60 per cent of minor modifications and 25 per cent of the major ones, but also originated all 'first of type' innovations. To qualify for inclusion in the study, users had not only to come up with the idea but also to make a working prototype (Von Hippel, 1984). In the field of pharmaceutical drugs, I should add, there is good reason to believe that the bulk of benefits have come not only from the original discovery, however brilliant, but from innumerable variants produced by a sort of rough-and-ready empiricism, where incremental changes are tried out to see if they would suit a particular class of potential users. Reducing the number and variety of new products, while it may indeed diminish the errors (say, damage to the body) associated with these trials, also can eliminate unsuspected health-giving potential.

Thought of in another way, the user is always right, for the value of a product does not lie in the producer but in the ultimate judges of utility, the users. Users are more numerous and more diverse than producers. Their number and diversity suggest that more tests by users be made under more varied conditions. The larger the number and the greater the variety of hypotheses tested ('Is this product satisfactory under my conditions?'), the greater the probability of learning about good and bad impacts and the conditions under which they apply. The more unsatisfactory, that is, error-like, experiences that come about, the greater the likelihood that efforts to overcome the bad will lead to useful innovation.

Surveying the advantages of a strategy of trial and error makes it difficult to believe that it would be subject to wholesale rejection. Perhaps all that is Uyxeant is the unexceptional view that trial and error is not suitable for every sort of situation. Such a conclusion would indeed appear reasonable, but would it be factually correct?

Not so fast. Do proponents of trial without error ('institutions that anticipate the risks,' as Page put it) actually exist in real life? Maybe it is wrong to claim not only that a viable doctrine of taking no new chances exists, but also that there are serious people who believe it. I think this usage has become quite common. 'I shall consider only the dangers and costs of biomedical advance,' Leon Kass tells us. 'As the benefits are well known, there is no need to dwell on them here.' Perhaps Kass is exceptional in alerting the reader to his premise '*My discussion is, in this regard, deliberately partial*' (Kass, 1985, p. 19). Philosophers are one thing, however, and those who make the law of the land are another. Have I, out of the scribblings of deranged philosophers and madcap activists, created a straw man just for the pleasure of knocking it down? Well, let us look at public policy and see whether this straw man is alive and kicking.

'Trial without error' as public policy

In an article aptly entitled 'Exorcists versus gatekeepers,' Peter Huber demonstrates that the doctrine we have been discussing – no trial without prior guarantees against error – is embodied in current regulatory practice. Producers of old products and substances still operate on a trial-and-error basis, in that the burden of proof (in justifying any regulation) is lodged with the government; but innovations must function under the rule of 'no trials without prior guarantees against error'; here, producers must be able to prove beforehand that their product will do no harm (Huber, 1983b, pp. 23–32).

Regulation, Huber observes, has two, sometimes contradictory, purposes: One is to reduce existing, older risks (such as bad air quality or in digging for coal), and the other is 'to impede technological changes that threaten to introduce new hazards into our lives' – new toxic chemicals, nuclear power, and so on. Attached to old risks is the mode of regulation called standard setting; here, producers are left alone until the federal government forces them to meet a revised standard. New risks, however, are handled by screening procedures under which advance licensing applies. Permission is required both before and after a new thing is done or produced. The Food and Drug Administration (FDA) and the Nuclear Regulatory Commission (NRC) screen or license; the Occupational Health and Safety Administration (OHSA) sets standards.

Sometimes the same agency does both; EPA, for example, screens new pesticides and also sets production standards for old ones (Huber, 1983b, pp. 23–4.). There is a wide gap between 'it can't be allowed to come into existence' and 'let's make it better' As David Foster wrote, responding (as he says, for himself, not for EPA) to Huber's article, the bias against new sources threatens to create

> . . . some negative environmental consequences. As Huber notes, the most effective means of reducing risk may be to encourage the introduction of competitors that impose a lower level of risk. Ironically, our 'gatekeeper' regulations may do just the opposite. Regulations that impose significantly greater costs on new sources than on existing ones may discourage industry from replacing older heavy-polluting facilities with newer and cleaner ones. Rigorous screening of new pesticides and chemicals may unintentionally delay the entry of potentially safer substitutes for existing risky products . . . The new-source bias affects not only consumer goods and services, but also the equipment and technology used in pollution control. Approval for innovative pollution-control equipment takes longer and is more uncertain than for traditional devices. That can make polluters reluctant to take a chance on buying innovative control equipment even if they expect it to be more effective and less costly than more traditional devices.

> (Foster, 1984, p. 2).

These are the practical differences between setting standards for the old, and screening development of the new: 'A screening system admits only the "acceptably safe", while a standard-setting system excludes only the "unacceptably hazardous" . . .' (Huber, 1983b, pp. 25–6). Huber continues:

> Screening systems . . . place the cost of acquiring the information needed for regulation on the regulatee; standard-setting systems place that cost on the agency. This makes all the difference when the product or process targeted for regulation is only marginally profitable. A pesticide manufacturer may have to spend $20 million on tests needed for licensing. Even if a pesticide is completely safe, it will never be submitted for review if the manufacturer stands to make only $19 million from its sale.

> Huber, 1983b, pp. 25–6

Since old dangers are systematically treated more leniently than new hazards, Huber asks, quite rightly, 'What accounts for the double standard?' (ibid.).

The common view that old dangers are treated less strictly because they are well understood, Huber believes, is fallacious. 'Those in the business know that informational problems are pervasive even for hazards as old as asbestos and wood fires' Exactly so. He is also properly sceptical about the psychological view that since people are inured to 'common killers,' the rarer kind should be subject to harsher measures. After all, 'Rare catastrophes are caused by old sources of risk every bit as by new ones' True. In the end, Huber is convinced that 'Congress thinks that it is much more expensive to regulate old risks than new ones.' To wipe out tangible benefits people already enjoy – familiar products, traditional jobs, with their 'identifiable and self-aware constituencies' – is politically more difficult to do than to stop something new that is not yet surrounded with a self-protective belt of interest.(In this regard, Huber's position comes close to Mancur Olson's thesis (Olson, 1982) that nations decline because existing interest groups receive special privileges). 'Legislators care more about political costs than about economic ones,' in Huber's estimation. 'Consumers lose, of course [in being denied the benefits of new products] but-here's the political kicker – they don't know it' (Huber, 1983b, p. 27). Why not?

'Statutes,' Huber observes, 'almost never explicitly address the lost opportunity costs of screening out a product' (Huber, 1983a, p. 1025–1107). The producer of a new product might go to court and succeed in overturning a ban by showing that the agency wrongly estimated the dangers, 'but he will get nowhere by arguing that the decision incorrectly evaluated the potential benefits of the product' (Huber, 1983a, p. 1063). Ignoring the good, even if it might exceed the bad, does not optimize safety for society, though it may be palatable for the polity. The clamouring constituency is worried about safety now. Proponents of safety now, like the planners they resemble, can talk of specific measures on behalf of tangible people. Proponents of trial and error can speak only of safety later, a safety, moreover, not for this or that specific group but because they cannot predict or control what will happen (their very reason for advocating trial and error) for society in general. 'You'll be better off in the 'by-and-by' has never been noted as a politically potent appeal. The benefits lost because of rejected opportunities are seen as inferior political goods.

A question of proportion

In his characteristically inventive, 'The principle of the hiding hand', Albert Hirschman sees negativism rather than over-enthusiasm as the prevailing vice in considering the establishment of development projects in poor countries. Therefore, he wants to bias consideration in favor of action, even (or especially) if that means ignoring possible negative consequences. Hirschman's reasoning is instructive:

> ... each project comes into the world accompanied by two sets of partially or wholly offsetting potential developments: (1) a set of possible and unsuspected threats to its profitability and existence, and (2) a set of unsuspected remedial actions which can be taken whenever any of these threats materializes ... (1) If the project planners had known in advance all the difficulties and troubles that were lying in store for the project, they probably would never have touched it, because a gloomy view would have been taken of the country's ability to overcome these difficulties by calling into play political, administrative, or technical creativity. (2) In some, though not all, of these cases advance knowledge of these difficulties would therefore have been unfortunate, for the difficulties and the ensuing search for solutions set in motion a train of events which not only rescued the project, but often made it particularly valuable. ... Or, put differently: since we necessarily underestimate our creativity, it is desirable that we underestimate to a roughly similar extent the difficulties of the tasks we face, so as to be tricked by these two offsetting underestimates into undertaking tasks which we can, but otherwise would not dare, tackle ... Language itself conspires toward this sort of asymmetry: we fall into error, but do not usually speak of falling into truth.

> (Hirschman, 1967, pp. 10–23)

The disinclination to consider the ability to respond to risks (anticipated or unanticipated) thus creates a bias towards technological inaction.

Trial and error is not a doctrine one would like to see applied to engaging in nuclear war. But at the same time, 'no trial without prior guarantees against error' is unsuitable for everyday life. The question, as always, is one of proportion (how much of each strategy?) and relevance (what kinds of dangers deserve the different strategies?), and ultimately, given uncertainty, of bias (when in doubt, which strategy should receive priority?).

Trial and error is a device for courting small dangers in order to avoid or lessen the damage from big ones. Sequential trials by dispersed decision makers reduce the size of that unknown world to bite-sized, and hence manageable, chunks. An advantage of trial and error, therefore, is that it renders visible hitherto unforeseen errors. Because it is a discovery process that discloses latent errors so we can learn how to deal with them, trial and error also lowers risk by reducing the scope of unforeseen dangers. Trial and error samples the world of as yet unknown risks; by learning to cope with risks that become evident as the result of small-scale trial and error, we develop skills for dealing with whatever may come our way from the world of unknown risks.

Now if these small advances and big disasters are independent of one another, incrementalism works, and search is hardly necessary. But if the two are interdependent, in that you cannot have one (an overall increase in safety by small advances) without the other (occasional disasters) search becomes more complex. For then we have to figure out how to cut down on big losses without simultaneously reducing incremental gains to such a degree that net safety declines.

If the incremental road led to disaster, society already should have suffered substantial losses. Instead, we find that morbidity is way down and life expectancy way up. We would be well advised to ask how these large numbers of small moves have led to our extraordinary improvement in health and safety.

We are faced with an anomaly in studying safety: large-scale disasters (flood, fire, earthquake, explosion, food poisoning) are fairly frequent occurrences (see Chapter 2 of *Searching for Safety*, Wildavsky, 1988); yet decade by decade, people are living longer and experiencing fewer serious accidents, and are healthier at corresponding ages. How is it that safety improves amidst disasters? Incremental advance offers a possible explanation. Large numbers of small improvements in safety may add up sufficiently to overcome a much smaller number of severely damaging episodes.

Just as most accidents occur in or near home (see any of the recent volumes of Accident Facts published by the US National Safety Council) and most foods contain carcinogens (Ames, 1983, pp. 1256–1264), as the axiom of connectedness suggests, so there is some degree of danger getting out of bed or taking a shower or eating a meal or walking across the street; or, need I say, in making love as well as war. Risking and living are inseparable (hospitals make people sick, exercise can hurt you, herb tea is laden with carcinogens); even breathing, according to a prominent theory in which cancer is caused by oxygen radicals created through the burning of fat, can kill.

The direct implication of trial without error is obvious: if you can do nothing without knowing first how it will turn out, you cannot do anything at all. An indirect implication of trial without error is that if trying new things is made more costly, there will be fewer departures from past practice; this very lack of change may itself be dangerous in forgoing chances to reduce existing hazards. Of course, the devil you know may be preferred over the one(s) you don't know. Existing dangers do have an advantage: they are bounded by past experience. If they are not too large, they may be tolerable and indeed preferable to novelty, whose dangers, being uncertain, may be unbounded. Nevertheless, existing hazards will continue to cause harm if we fail to reduce them by taking advantage of the opportunity to benefit from repeated trials.

By reducing dangers that still exist, not merely by avoiding new ones, risk taking becomes socially desirable; old hazards can be eliminated or alleviated in ways that improve human life. These, the 'opportunity benefits' that are lost without a strategy of trial and error, will be discussed in the next chapter.

References

Ames, B. (1983). Dietary carcinogens and anticarcinogens. *Science*, **221** (4617), 23 September, pp. 1256–1264.

Anonymous (1865). *The Journal of Gas Lighting, Water Supply and Sanitary Improvement*, 14 November.

Arrow, K.J. (1962). The economic implications of learning by doing. *Review of Economic Studies*, **29**, June, pp. 155–73.

Braybrooke, D. and Lindblom, C.E. (1963). *A Strategy of Decision: Policy Evolution as a Survival Process*. London: The Free Press.

Cohen, D. and Lindblom, C.E. (1979). *Useable Knowledge*. New Haven, CT: Yale University Press.

Dempster, M.A.H. and Wildavsky, A. (1979). On change . . . or, there is no magic size for an increment. *Political Studies*, **27** (3), September.

Dexter, L. (1986). Letter to the author, 12 July.

Efron, E. (1984). *The Apocalyptics*. New York: Simon & Schuster.

Elster, J. (1979). Risk, uncertainty, and nuclear power. *Social Science Information*, **18** (3).

Federal Register (1980). 29 CFR 1990.144(a), 22 January.

Foster, D. (1984). Letter to the Editor of *Regulation*, March/April.

Goodin, R.E. (1980). No moral nukes. *Ethics*, **90**, April..

Havender, W.R. and Meister, K.A. (1985). *Does nature know best?*. Report by the American Council on Science and Health, October.

Hayek, E.A. (1945). The use of knowledge in society. *The American Economic Review*, **35** (4), September.

Hirschman, A.O. (1967). The principle of the hiding hand. *The Public Interest*, **6**, Winter.

Huber, P. (1983a). The old-new division in risk regulation. *The Virginia Law Review*, **69**, (6).

Huber, P. (1983b). Exorcists vs. gatekeepers in risk regulation. *Regulation*, Nov./Dec.

Inside the Administration (1986a), 2 January .

Inside the Administration (1986b), 24 April.

Jewkes, J. Sawers, D. and Stillerman, R. (1959). *The Sources of Invention*. New York: St. Martin's Press.

Kass, L.R. (1985). *Toward a More Natural Science: Biology and Human Affairs*. New York: Free Press.

Knott, J.H. (1982). Incremental theory and the regulation of risk. Paper presented to the American Political Science Association Annual Meeting, September.

Landau, M. (1973). On the concept of a self-correcting organization. *Public Administration Review*, **33** (6) (referred to in Knott, 1982)

Lewis, H.W. (n.d.): Technological Risk. Typescript.

Lindblom, C.E (1984). Who needs what social research for policy making? Paper for the New York Education Policy Seminar, Albany, New York, May.

Lindblom, C.E. (1959). The science of 'muddling through'. *Public Administration Review*, **19**, pp. 78–88.

Lindblom, C.E. (1979). Still muddling: not yet through. *Public Administration Review,* **6.**

Lustick, I. (1980). Explaining the variable utility of disjointed incrementalism: four propositions. *American Political Science Review,* June.

Melnick, R.S. (1983). *Regulation and the Courts: The Case of the Clean Air Act.* Washington, DC: The Brookings Institution.

Mendeloff, J. (1986). Overregulation and Underregulation: Standard Setting for Toxic Chemicals. Unpublished book manuscript.

Morone, J. and Woodhouse, E. (1985). Averting Catastrophe: Strategies for Regulating Risky Technologies. Typescript, April.

Munz, P. (1985). *Our Knowledge of the Growth of Knowledge: Popper or Wittgenstein?* London: Routledge and Kegan Paul.

Nemetz, P.N. and Vining, A.R. (1981). The biology–policy interface: theories of pathogenesis, benefit valuation and public policy formation. *Policy Sciences,* **13,** (2), April.

Nichols, A.L. and Zeckhauser, R.S. (1986): The dangers of caution: conservatism in assessment and the mismanagement of risk. Discussion Paper Series E-85–11, Energy and Environmental Policy Center, John E Kennedy School of Government, Harvard University, November 1985, published as The Perils of Prudence, *Regulation,* Nov./Dec.

Norton, B. (n.d.). On the inherent dangers of undervaluing species. Working Paper PS-3, Center for Philosophy and Public Policy, University of Maryland.

Olson, M. (1982). *The Rise and Decline of Nations: Economic Growth, Stagflation and Social Rigidities.* New Haven, CT: Yale University Press.

Page, T (1978). A generic view of toxic chemicals and similar risks. *Ecology Law Quarterly,* **7** (2).

Pearce, D.W. (1980). The preconditions for achieving consensus in the context of technological risk. In *Technological Risk: Its Perception and Handling in the European Community* (M. Dierkes, S. Edwards and R. Coppock, eds) Cambridge, MA: Oelgeschlager, Gunn & Hain Publishers; and Konigstein/Ts: Berlag Anton Hain.

Peters, (1983). The mythology of innovation, or A skunkworks tale, Part II. *The Stanford Magazine,* **II,** (3), Fall.

Peters, T.J. (1983). The mythology of innovation, or A skunkworks tale, Part I. *The Stanford Magazine,* **II,** (2), Summer.

Popper, K. (1971). *The Open Society and Its Enemies.* Princeton, NJ: Princeton Univ. Press.

Regulating Risky Technologies, typescript, April.

Richter, Jr . M. (1982). *Technology and Social Complexity.* Albany, NY: State University of New York Press.

Rosenberg, N. (1982). Learning by using. In *Inside the Black Box: Technology and Economics,* Chapter 6, Cambridge: Cambridge Press.

Schneiderman, M. (n.d.). Extrapolating animal and microbiological tests to human. Urban Environment Conference (cited in Efron, 1984, op. cit.).

Steinbrunner, J. (1974). *A Cybernetic Theory of Decision.* Princeton, NJ: Princeton University Press.

The Journal of Gas Lighting, Water Supply, and Sanitary Improvement, 14 November 1865:

Thompson, J. and Tuden, A. (1959). Strategies, structures, and processes of organizational decision. In *Comparative Studies in Administration* (J. Thompson et al, eds), Pittsburgh: University of Pittsburgh Press.

Utterback, J. (1979). The dynamics of product and process innovation in industry. In *Technological Innovation for a Dynamic Economy* (C.T. Hill and J. M. Utterback, eds) New York: Pergamon Press.

Verrett, J. and Carper, J. (1975). *Eating May Be Hazardous to Your Health*. Garden City, NY: Anchor/Doubleday (cited in Efron, 1984, op. cit.).

Von Hippel, E. (1984). *Novel Product Concepts From Lead Users: Segmenting Users by Experience*. Cambridge, MA: Marketing Science Institute.

Weinberg, A.M. (1982). Nuclear safety and public acceptance. *Nuclear News*, October, pp. 54–8.

Whorton, J. (1974). *Before Silent Spring: Pesticides and Public Health in Pre-DDT America*. Princeton, NJ: Princeton University Press.

Wildavsky, A. (1964). *The Politics of the Budgetary Process*. Boston: Little, Brown and Company.

Wildavsky, A. (1979). *The Politics of the Budgetary Process* (3rd edn). Boston: Little, Brown.

Wildavsky, A. (1988) *Searching for Safety*. Transaction Publishers.

3 The precautionary principle and our obligations to future generations

Wilfred Beckerman

Introduction

Whatever the merits of the 'precautionary principle' (PP) one thing is clear: it does not apply where it is most supposed to apply, namely over long periods encompassing distant generations. In environmental areas, such as pollution of our rivers or coastlines, or of the air in our cities, or the lack of clean drinking water and decent sanitation or shelter in the Third World, and so on, the facts and the range of environmental risks are relatively well known, so that the policies required do not have to rely on fragile projections into the distant future. Hence, appeal is rarely made to the PP in such environmental contexts.

It is where there are great uncertainties about the future course of events, such as those surrounding climate change, loss of biodiversity, or exhaustion of supplies of non-renewable resources, that the PP is believed to come into its own. For these are the areas where (1) we are concerned with the distant future and (2) the prospects are so full of uncertainties. Consequently it is in areas such as these that there is room for divergent future scenarios, and the greatest need for some new principle to guide us in our choice of policies.

Paradoxically, it is precisely when we are considering policies affecting distant generations that environmental thought in general and the PP in particular are based on an ethical assumption that is totally unfounded. This ethical assumption is that our policies affecting future generations should be constrained by respect for the 'rights' of future generations, including, in particular, a 'right' to inherit an unchanged environment. On this view, almost any price has to be paid by the present generation in order to avoid our violating the rights of future generations to inherit the same environment as we have now or to transgress the claims in 'justice' that define our obligations to future generations. (This chapter is not concerned with the problem of overlapping generations, since natural benevolent motivations of concern for one's children or grandchildren usually predominate. This means that one's actions are not constrained by any claims arising out of 'rights' or 'justice'.)

Now, of course, taken literally such a policy prescription would be absurd. The human race has exploited the environment since the beginning of its existence, but has also greatly improved and enhanced it in many respects. Consequently, most sensible environmentalists advocate a version of 'sustainable development' which allows the environment to be used up to some extent as long as there is a compensating increase in man-made capital. In this case, all that is claimed is that the rights of future generation consist of a right to enjoy the same standard of living. However, the question I wish to discuss is not so much which particular rights future generations can be said to have but whether they can have any at all. It will be argued below that they cannot, but that this does not absolve us from the obligation to take account of the *interests* that they will have in deciding which of our policies will make the most important contribution to their future welfare. It is then argued that the most important bequest we could make to the welfare of future generations is not in the environmental field but in the field of the extension and protection of basic human rights.

The 'rights' of future generations

The implications of not existing

The crux of my argument that future generations cannot have rights is that 'properties', such as being green or wealthy or having rights, can only be predicated of some subject that exists. Outside the realm of mythical creatures or hypothetical discourse, if there is no subject then there is nothing to which the property can be ascribed. (When rights are attributed to mythical creatures, they are not believed to be rights that they have in the real world outside the myths in question, and hence they are not believed to impose any obligations on real world people, such as us.) Propositions such as 'X is Y' only make sense if there is an X. If there is no X then the proposition is meaningless. If I were to say 'X has a fantastic collection of CDs' and you were to ask me who is X and I were to reply 'Well, actually there isn't any X', you would think I was mad. And you would be right. Thus the fact that future generations cannot *have* rights follows from the meaning of the present tense of the verb 'to have'. (This fundamental and decisive point was made by De George (1981) and a similar point was made in the same publication by Macklin. But with some exceptions, notably de-Shalit (1995) and Merrills (1996), it does not seem to have been given due weight in the literature on this subject, perhaps because it was not regarded as sufficiently subtle or obscure.) Unborn people simply cannot *have* anything. They cannot have two legs or long hair or a taste for Mozart.

The consequences of ignoring the significance of this point is clearly seen in many of the arguments used to justify attributing rights to unborn people. For example, one widely quoted authority on intergenerational equity, Edith Brown-Weiss, refers to the Preamble to the Universal Declaration of Human

Rights, which states that 'Whereas recognition of the inherent dignity and of the equal and inalienable rights of all members of the human family is the foundation of freedom, justice and peace in the world', and she then goes on to argue that the 'reference to all members of the human family has a temporal dimension, which brings all generations within its scope' (Brown-Weiss, 1989, p. 25). The problem here is that future generations (of unborn people) are not 'members of the human family'. They are not members of any family, or of any tennis club or national legislature or of anything at all. They do not exist. In the absence of some global catastrophe there will be members of the human family in the future; but whether or not they can be said to have rights here and now is the whole problem and cannot be simply side-stepped in the way that Professor Brown-Weiss tries to do.

The wide acceptance in some sections of the population of the notion that unborn people can have rights may owe something to the error of thinking about unborn people as some special class of people waiting out in the wings for the cue for them to enter on to the stage and play their many parts. But there is no such class of people as unborn people. In his devastating critique of the notion of attributing rights to future generations, Hillel Steiner put it admirably in saying that 'In short, it seems mistaken to think of future persons as being already out there, anxiously awaiting either victimization by our self-indulgent prodigality or salvation through present self-denial' (Steiner, 1983, p. 159).

It is true that there are difficult border-line cases in the allocation of rights; for example, to children, animals, severely handicapped people, and so on. However, unborn people do not seem to be a borderline case, as they fall into a different logical category. It may be *physically* impossible for a small child or a handicapped person to claim a right or to delegate it to somebody else, but it is *logically* impossible for a member of a distant future generation to do so. (For the sake of clarity, it is important to stress that this analysis is not intended to apply to overlapping generations, where younger members of any generation may have rights in relation to older people alive at the same time, such as their parents.) For example, even if it is accepted that those of us alive today have certain 'rights' to enjoy the existing environment, it does not make sense to complain that the inhabitants of Mauritius three centuries ago violated our rights by hunting the Dodo or failing to take action to preserve it. Nor could we, if we so wished, waive our right to see a live Dodo by saying 'O.K. Go ahead. Hunt it if you like. We think it is a rather silly bird anyway'.

In other words, the fact that future generations may have rights in the future does not imply that they have rights to anything that exists today. At best, as far as rights to resources are concerned, they would only have rights to what is available at that time. If it were logical to say that future generations have rights to what exists today, then it would be logical for us to complain that the inhabitants (or visiting seamen) who were responsible for the extinction of the Dodo three centuries ago have deprived us of our right to see a live Dodo. Where does one stop? An infinite number of acts of commission and omission in the past may have resulted in welfare today being less than it would otherwise have been. One may be justified in deploring the failure of past generations to take adequate account of the effect of their activities on our welfare; but that is not the same as saying that all such past acts of commission or omission represented ancient violations of our rights. We may deplore somebody refusing to allow a neighbour to use his telephone to make an urgent call but this does not mean that we believe the neighbour had a right to do so. Whatever rights future generations may have to any asset or resources, therefore, must be restricted to rights over what is available when they are alive.

According to one traditionally accepted interpretation of the term 'rights', all rights imply obligations , though not vice versa, e.g. Hohfeld, 1923; Hart, 1982, footnote 7, p. 80; Rawls, 1972., p. 113; O'Neill, 1996, chapter 5). Most rights – and certainly those that are relevant in the present context – are what are known (following Hohfeld) as 'claim rights'. They are the counterpart of valid claims, on legal or moral grounds, to have or obtain something, or to act in a certain way. (In contrast, reference is sometimes made to the concept of 'manifesto rights', introduced by Feinberg in 1970, which need not be correlated with counterpart duties – see Baier, *loc. cit.*, p. 182, n3, and Feinberg, 1970/98 p. 612.) A claim right implies that somebody or some institution is under obligation to provide or permit whatever is claimed. If X has a universal right, such as a right to free speech, everybody has an obligation to allow him to say what he likes. If X has a specific claim right, for example, to own something or have access to some service, some person or institution has an obligation to ensure that X can exert his right. This means that no generation can have a right to something that no longer exists, since there is no person or institution who has a counterpart obligation to provide it.

The defence of the rights of future generations

Despite the argument of the above section, some eminent philosophers or authorities on intergenerational 'equity' explicitly or implicitly believe that future generations can be said to have rights. A representative and important selection of articles on the subject of the rights of future generations published in 1981 brought together many advocates (as well as critics) of the proposition that future generations have rights (Partridge, 1981). Most of the defenders of the rights of future generations based their argument partly on the fact that future generations *will* have 'interests' (interpreted very widely to mean anything that might be believed, rightly or wrongly, to add to one's sense of well-being). For example, the distinguished philosopher, Joel Feinberg, who is also the author of authoritative articles on the concept of 'rights', writes of the interests of future generations: 'The identity of the owners of these interests is now necessarily obscure, but the fact of their interest-ownership is crystal clear, and that is all that is necessary to certify the coherence of present talk about their rights'. He concludes by saying that 'Philosophers have not helped matters by arguing that animals and future generations are not the kinds of beings who can have rights now, that they don't presently qualify for membership, even "auxiliary membership", in our moral community' (Feinberg, 1981, pp. 148–9; see also Sterba, 1980, 1999).

However, there seem to be two objections to the argument that because future generations *will* have interests, they must *have* rights now (see, in particular, Feinberg, 1981, and Elliot, 1989). First, having interests is, at best, merely a necessary condition for having rights contemporaneously, not a sufficient condition. Many people have an interest in seeing the horse they have backed to win a race winning it; but they have no right to such an outcome and, indeed, it would be internally inconsistent to maintain that they all did. It is not necessary to scrutinize the border-lines between 'interests', 'needs', 'desires' and so on in order to see that 'If we had rights to all that is necessary for the good life, rights would be too extensive' (Griffin, 1986, p. 227).

Secondly, the fact that future generations will have interests in the future (and may well have rights in the future) does not mean that they can have interests today, i.e. before they are born. It may well be that having certain interests implies having certain rights. But future generations do not 'at this point in time' (as politicians like to say) *have* any interests.

The weakness in the argument that future generations have 'rights' because they have interests cannot be dispelled by the assertion that their rights or interests are being represented today by environmentalist pressure groups and the like. It is *logically* impossible, as well as physically impossible, for future generations to delegate the protection of their rights to somebody alive today. Unborn people cannot delegate anything, in the same way that they cannot *do (in the present tense)* anything. Even if we thought that our moral right to see a live Dodo had been violated by people living in Mauritius three centuries ago, it is unlikely that we could find a lawyer, even in the USA, to lodge a complaint about this violation of our right. Of course, anybody can *claim* to represent the interests of future generations, but that is another matter. As it happens, I claim to do so.

Assessing our moral obligations to future generations

The fact that future generations cannot be said to have any 'rights', including rights to any environmental asset, does not mean that we have no moral obligation to take account of the way that our policies will affect their interests. 'Rights', like 'justice', do not exhaust the whole of morality. If my neighbour asks me if he can use my telephone or toilet because his has broken down, I would let him do so out of my characteristic benevolence, not because he had any 'right' to do so. Hence, without accepting that future generations have some special right to inherit the same environment as exists today we can still accept that we have a moral obligation to take account of the *interests* that they will have. How then should we weigh our various obligations to future generations in order to assess their relative importance?

Of course, one cannot draw up a lexicographical ranking of our various obligations to future generations. In addition to environmental obligations, we should also give great weight to the reduction in widespread poverty and to the extension of basic human rights, as well as dealing with numerous other of the ills that plague modern society, such as crime, violence, family breakdown, and so on. It would be illogical to refuse to do anything under any one of these and many other worthy objectives until everything possible had been done to promote some particularly favoured objective to which one might be tempted to give priority. Economists are trained to recognize conflicting objectives and to reject all or nothing solutions, and to seek, instead, to make trade-offs at the margin in the light of the relative costs and benefits of specific possibilities in specific areas. However, this does not rule out our judging that, at any point in time, some problems are more important than others.

If we are dealing with the very long run, i.e. the long run in which we are talking about unborn future generations and in which uncertainties rule the day, there are good reasons to believe that some of the major ills of modern society will be largely overcome. For example, although it will be impossible to totally eliminate pockets of poverty since bad luck, unfortunate family background, evil and despotic regimes, and a host of other random circumstances will always ensure that, in some parts of the world, some people will be very poor, it is argued below that there is reason to believe that mass poverty will be a far less important problem is the case today. It is also argued that, in the light of the prospective growth of incomes, what are perceived today as major environmental threats, notably climate change, will actually have relatively minor impacts on overall world prosperity.

How much richer will future generations be?

In principle, one of our major objectives as far as future generations are concerned would be to avoid policies that would condemn them to dire poverty. Apart from that, what would be fair to bequeath to them must depend chiefly on how much richer we can expect them to be. The average growth rate of real national income per head in the world over the last forty years or more has been 2.1 per cent per annum (Maddison, 1995). It is true that the first decade of this period includes possibly exceptional growth when Europe might still have been catching up on the large productivity gap compared with the USA, and the first half of the period was when Japan was reaping the benefits of an even more striking catch-up phase.

On the other hand, much of the slowdown of the period 1975–2000 or so represents an adjustment to the 1973 oil shock followed by a major deflationary shift in economic policy in most of the advanced countries of the world; this took the form of far more reluctance to ensure full employment on account of a far greater fear of re-igniting inflationary pressures. While the productivity growth rate of that 25 years period has been below that of the preceding 20 years, this may have been just as much a below-potential growth rate as the previous period had been an above-potential growth rate; so the underlying potential growth rate could still be not far off the 2.1 per cent recorded over the last 40 years or so.

The future growth rate is likely to be at least as high as this, if not higher. For in the long run, the main source of growth in incomes per head is technological and scientific progress. This is a function of the number of highly educated people in the world, particularly those having technological and scientific qualifications, and the speed of transmission and dissemination of technological progress. As regards the former, the number of people with technological and scientific training in the world is increasing so rapidly that it far surpasses the corresponding number of people having similar qualifications only two or three decades ago, and is likely to go on expanding rapidly. And as regards the latter, the speed of transmission of technical and scientific knowledge has been accelerating as a result of globalisation and the information revolution. These two underlying forces for *long-run* growth suggest that the long-run growth rate over the next century should be above that of the last forty years. In the light of this a projection of a growth rate over the next century of between 1 and 2 per cent per annum would seem to be on the cautious side.

To simplify the argument, therefore, let us assume a single figure of 1.5 per cent as the annual average compound growth rate of real incomes per head over the next 100 years. The power of compound interest being what it is this means that world average real incomes per head after 100 years, say in the year 2100, would be 4.43 times as high as they are now! And it should not be thought that the above guess at the annual average growth rate of Gross World Product (GWP) per head over the next 100 years is a fanciful figure. The various scenarios of possible growth rates used by the IPCC (the UN Intergovernmental Panel on Climate Change) to estimate the likely range of carbon emissions put per capita GWP at between 4.3 times as high as it is today and 20 times as high! (Anderson, 1998) In other words, our guesstimate is at the bottom of the range adopted by the IPCC. It is thus a conservative and modest estimate.

In the light of this growth in per capita (real) incomes, it is reasonable to assume that mass 'absolute' poverty on the scale that currently exists in many parts of the world can and will be eradicated. It is also in this perspective that one should appraise predictions of global environmental disaster, such as those associated with predictions of climate change. A recent report by the IPCC has suggested that a doubling of the atmospheric carbon concentration could reduce GWP per head by between 1 and 2 per cent*. In other words, the world's population in the year 2100 will have to wait until the year 2101 or 2102 to enjoy the level of income that they would otherwise have enjoyed in the absence of climate change. It is to be hoped that they will not be too impatient. Instead of average incomes per capita being 4.4 times as high as today, they would be only about 4.3 times as high.

---

* IPCC, 1996, Table 6.6, p. 205. The studies to which reference is made above and quoted in the IPCC report are by Fankhauser (1995) and Tol (1995).

It is true that this figure is close to (slightly above, in fact) most of the estimates of the damage that climate change would inflict on the USA; and estimates of the effect on developing countries, while much more fragmentary and flimsy, suggest that the damage would be greater, since they are much more dependent on agriculture (Mabey et al., 1997, especially. p. 237ff). But it is these countries whose growth rates are, rightly, expected to be the fastest as they catch up on the rest of the world and shift their patterns of output over the course of the century towards those prevailing today in the developed countries. Consequently, if the world as a whole can be expected to be about four times as rich as today (per capita) the per capita incomes in the developing countries will no doubt increase even faster.

Furthermore, the precautionary principle as a guide to decision-making under conditions of uncertainty suffers from one major drawback. This is that if the future is really all that uncertain, how can one be confident that action taken today will not make things worse, rather than better. For example, if effective action had been taken in the late 1960s and early 1970s to combat the fear, widespread among certain climatologists, that the world was entering a new Ice Age, the consequences now would have been most unfortunate. As regards concern today for the impact of global warming on the developing countries, the IPCC makes the very pertinent point:

> If we take aggressive action to limit climate change they may regret that we did not use the funds instead to push ahead development in Africa, to better protect the species against the next retrovirus, or to dispose of nuclear materials safely ... Alternatively, if the developed countries choose to embark on an aggressive control regime now, and if this cuts into their growth rates, the result will shrink export markets for developing countries and thus reduce growth there. In addition, if developed countries view their greenhouse efforts as, in effect, aid to developing countries, they may cut back on other programmes (sanitation, education for women, etc.) that have a more immediate impact on life expectancy, health and well-being.

(IPCC, 1996, p. 33)

The estimates of the impact of global warming referred to above may be far too modest; but presumably, whatever the PP is supposed to mean, it should take such account as it can of the orders of magnitude involved. So let us suppose that there is some very unpleasant surprise – e.g. some unfavourable positive feedback effect of climate change or loss of biodiversity – resulting in a cut in gross world product (GWP) that was ten times as great as that predicted to be caused by climate change if nothing is done to prevent it. In other words, suppose that world output would fall by about 10 per cent, which is about the top of the range of various estimates in a survey of such possibilities quoted by the IPCC (IPCC, 1996, Tables 6.7 and 6.8). This would mean that, in the year 2100, instead of world per capita income levels being about 4 times as high as they are now, they would be only about 3.6 times as high. Of course, the reduction in output would not just affect the terminal year 2100. It would presumably be spread over earlier years, so that output per head in earlier years would also be lower than could otherwise be expected, but this does not significantly affect the *proportionate* reduction in GWP over the whole period.

Nevertheless, it is still not an unmitigated disaster. It might be a disaster for individual countries or regions, especially those that might still be heavily dependent on agriculture; and it is to be hoped that the rest of the world will find more effective ways of helping poorer countries than it has done in the past. Whether or not it is feasible to do much is, of course, a contentious issue. But that is beside the point. In a world which accepts with some equanimity the existence of widespread poverty it is humbug to urge the present generation to make major sacrifices in order to shield distant generations, who will be far richer, from the remote possibility of some environmental disaster that would still be a relatively modest proportion of the very much higher income levels that can be predicted for the next century.

In any case, much of the hype about disaster scenarios is not based on serious science. For example, every time there is a serious storm anywhere it is widely advertised as one of the consequences of global warming. As the eminent scientist Bert Bolin, who was until recently the Chairman of the IPCC, put it: 'Environmental activists, for example, seize eagerly on the occurrence of extreme events (hurricanes, floods, droughts, etc.) as signs of an ongoing change of climate. Even though extreme events may be harbingers of change, there is still as yet little scientific evidence to prove this, nor can we as yet ascribe such changes to human interference' (Bolin, 1997, p. 107). The Prime Minister, Tony Blair, is not an environmentalist activist but he seems to have been misled by some of them to attach great importance to the idea that global warming will increase storms (*The Times*, 4 December 1997). This is the only piece of evidence he gives in the article on climate change in which he wrote that '. . . it is clear that, unchecked, climate change . . . will impose enormous human and business costs . . . Global warming could lead to an increase in stormy weather . . . To give some idea of that threat, the great storm of 1987 cost our economy about £3 billion at today's prices. That is nothing compared with what could happen if we allow global warming to go unchecked'. In similar vein, the Minister for the Environment, Michael Meacher, wrote that 'The north (i.e. the developed countries) is right to be concerned about worsening degradation that seriously threatens the viability of the planet . . . global warming, which will generate hurricanes, droughts, floods and severe crop losses across the world' (*The Financial Times*, 4 June 1997).

In fact far from storms increasing there has been some evidence of a downward trend in the frequency of storms (Henderson-Sellers et al, 1997; Landsea, et. al., 1996; Schiesser et al., 1997). Even the IPCC is neutral on the danger of increasing storms as a result of climate change: '. . . climate models give no consistent indication whether tropical storms will increase or decrease in frequency or intensity as climate changes; neither is there any evidence that this has occurred over the past few decades' (IPCC, 1990, p. xxv; the same conclusion is re-iterated in IPCC, 1996, p. 11). Of course, the damage done by a storm of any given intensity is likely to be greater today than 50, or even 10, years earlier; but this is simply because there are more buildings around to be damaged and their prices are much higher. Naturally, the steadily rising value of storm damage these days is used by insurance companies as an excuse to jack up their premiums on the grounds that it is a legitimate response forced on them by climate change. In fact, it has nothing to do with climate change and is simply the result of increased urbanization and buildings and continuous inflation.

There is equally little substance to the claim that climate change will greatly add to the incidence of insect-spread diseases, such as dengue fever and malaria, which are widespread in many poor tropical countries. Any likely increase in this type of disease on account of warmer climates would be negligible by comparison with the high incidence of these diseases in countries where it is clearly the result of poverty and all its accompanying features: lack of drainage, clean water and sanitation and public health systems. In an article in *The Lancet*, Paul Reiter, the Chief Scientist of the Dengue Fever branch of the US Center for Disease Control writes: 'The distortion of science to make predictions of unlikely public health disasters diverts attention from the true reasons for the recrudescence of vector-borne diseases. These include large-scale resettlement of people, rampant urbanization without adequate infrastructure ... and the deterioration of vector-control operations and other public-health practices' (Reiter, 1998). For example, malaria and cholera were major health problems in the USA in the nineteenth century; and malaria was widespread in southern Europe until the mid-twentieth century when good health practices and the use of insecticides and drainage programmes wiped out large mosquito-breeding areas.

A recent report by the UN World Health Organization (WHO) also emphasizes that poverty is by far the major cause of infectious and parasitic diseases, not climate. The WHO states: 'As the new millenium approaches, the global population has never had a healthier outlook', and it goes on to say that the only significant growth threat to human health is HIV/AIDS, which also has no relationship to climate (WHO, 1998).

Bequeathing a just society

Common predictions of environmental disaster have been made over the course of the centuries which have been falsified; they include those predictions of imminent mass starvation on account of world food output failing to keep pace with world population that have been made and repeatedly falsified during the last thirty years or more by 'prophets' such as Paul Ehrlich (1968) and Lester Brown (1974). By contrast, there is one prediction about the future that one can make with even more confidence than my prediction that future generations will be very much richer. This is that there will always be some source of possible conflict between people. Except in some Utopian scenarios, human wants will always expand more or less in line with what is available, so that whatever we do now about the future availability of resources and however much technical progress expands our potential for producing goods and services, there will always be conflicting interests in the way that output is shared out. Some people will want a larger share and others will be unwilling to provide it. Future generations may not have the institutions that ensure that, whatever level of output is available in the future, it is shared out peacefully, if not equitably.

In any case, conflicts over resources are by no means the only possible source of conflict between human beings. Ideological, ethnic, and religious conflicts have also been a source of immense human suffering throughout history. Human compassion has not kept pace with technical progress. Given then that future generations will always experience conflicts, a major obligation to future generations is to bequeath to them a 'decent society' (see the brilliant analysis of what constitutes a 'decent society' in Margalit, 1996). The chief characteristics of a 'decent society' would be respect for basic human rights and liberties, tolerance for differences in conceptions of the good life, and just and democratic institutions that enable people to sort out their inevitable conflicts peacefully. We should give high priority to protection of basic human rights, particularly when their widespread violation today is indisputable, whereas the predictions of inevitable catastrophe on account of environmental developments are no more likely to be fulfilled than similar predictions over the last two thousand years.

It is true that there are immense obstacles to the extension of greater respect for human rights in most countries in the world where these rights are largely ignored. Given the conventional limits on the extent to which international bodies feel they can interfere in the internal situation of sovereign states, it is not easy for the world community to do much to improve human rights in those countries where they are flagrantly violated. However, there have been instances of international action to override national sovereignty to prevent gross and widespread abuses of basic human rights. So although pessimism regarding the prospects for rapid progress may be justified, despair is not. For this can only lead to inaction; and without a continuous struggle on behalf of human rights the forces of tyranny and oppression would continually gain ground. The struggle is necessary in order to help stop the world slipping backwards – as it has been doing in many parts of the world throughout much of this century (see the moving and devastating account of violations of human rights in the course of the twentieth century in Jonathan Glover, 1999).

Thus instead of having to invoke some dubious and vague precautionary principle to avoid, possibly at great cost, some totally uncertain event that would deprive future generations of their 'rights' to inherit the environment as we find it today, we can give priority to a policy that is based on a virtual certainty. This is that the need for society to find ways of resolving its conflicts in a just and tolerant manner will indisputably be a permanent feature of the human condition. And it is one that exists today, so that making a contribution to future welfare also makes a contribution to welfare today, instead of imposing any sacrifice on people living today. By contrast, while no precise quantities can be attached to the alternative outcomes, simple recognition of the likely rise in incomes per head by comparison with even serious environmental 'disaster' scenarios, suggests that there can be no case for imposing heavy burdens on the current generation in order to reduce the risk of even a large fall in incomes of people who, by the end of this century, will be incomparably richer than we are today.

Conclusions

Much of the pressure to adopt the precautionary principle to ensure against any damage to the environment is based on the notion that future generations have some over-riding 'rights' to inherit more or less the same environment as we experience today, or, as in most conceptions of 'sustainable development', the right to enjoy the same level of welfare that is experienced today. In fact, future generations have no rights; but since rights and justice do not exhaust the whole of morality, this does not mean that we have no moral obligations to take account of the impact of our actions on the *interests* that future generations will have. However, this implies that we have to weigh up what, in fact, will be the most important interests that future generations will have in the sense of the conditions that will make the most important contribution to their future welfare.

It has been argued above that there is good reason to assume that continued world economic growth will, over the very long run, i.e. during the course of this century, be nearly as fast (if not much faster) than the rate of 2.1 per cent per annum per head achieved during the last forty years or so. A rate of only about 1.5 per cent would mean that average real incomes in the world in the year 2100 would be over four times as high as they are now. This means that the magnitude of loss of incomes that are predicted to be caused by a failure to tackle global warming, for example, would be negligible by comparison with future income levels; and even if the actual damage done by global warming were to be, say, ten times as great, it would still leave future generations far richer than we are today. Furthermore, whereas the predictions of environmental catastrophe that dominate much environmentalist thought and that give rise to the emphasis on the precautionary principle are invariably shaky and similar past predictions have always been falsified, there is one prediction about the future that one can make with complete confidence. This is that there will always be conflicts between people, whether over resources, ideologies, race or religion, or conflicting conceptions of 'the good life'.

The most important bequest we can make to future generations, therefore, is to cultivate institutions and traditions that enable them to resolve their inevitable conflicts in as peaceful, just and harmonious manner as possible. This means bequeathing 'decent' societies that are more just, free and democratic than those prevailing in many parts of the world today.

References

Anderson, D. (1998). On the effects of social and economic policies on future carbon emissions. *Mitigation and Adaptation Strategies for Global Change*, **3**, 419–53.

Baier, A. (1981). The rights of past and future persons. In Partridge (1981) op.cit.

Bolin, B. (1997). 'Scientific assessment of climate change'. In *International Politics of Climate Change* (G. Fermann, ed.) Oslo: Scandinavian University Press.

Boyle, A. and Anderson, M. (1996). *Human Rights Approaches to Environmental Protection*. Oxford: Clarendon Press.

Brown, L. (1974). *In the Human Interest: A Strategy to Stabilize World Population*, New York: Norton.

Brown-Weiss, E. (1989). *In Fairness to Future Generations: International Law, Common Patrimony, and Intergenerational Equity*. New York: Transnational Publishers.

De George. R.T. (1981). The environment, rights, and future generations. In Partridge (1981) op.cit.

de-Shalit, A. (1995). *Why Posterity Matters*. London: Routledge.

Ehrlich, P. (1968): *The Population Bomb*. New York: Ballantine.

Elliot, R. (1989): The rights of future people. *Journal of Applied Philosophy*, **6**, pp. 159–71.

Fankhauser, S. (1995). *Valuing climate change: the economics of the greenhouse*. London: Earthscan.

Feinberg, J. (1970/98). The nature and value of rights. *Journal of Value Inquiry*, **4**, 1970. Reprinted in *Ethics: History, Theory and Contemporary Issues* (S.M. Cahn, and P. Markie, eds) Oxford: Oxford University Press, 1998.

Feinberg, J. (1974/81): The rights of animals and unborn generations. In *Philosophy and Environmental Crisis* (W. Blackstone, ed.) University of Georgia Press (Reprinted in Partridge, 1981, op.cit.).

Glover, Jonathan (1999). *Humanity, A Moral History of the Twentieth Century*. London: Cape.

Griffin, J. (1986). *Well-Being*. Oxford: Clarendon Press.

Hart, H.L.A. (1982). Are There Any Natural Rights? In *Theories of Rights* (Waldren, J. ed). Oxford: OUP.

Henderson-Sellers, A., et al. (DATE). Tropical cyclones and global climate change: a post-IPCC assessment. *Bulletin of the American Meteorological Society*, **79**, 19–38.

Hohfeld, W.N. (1923). *Fundamental Legal Conceptions*. Newhaven, CT: Yale University Press.

IPCC (1990). *Climate Change: The IPCC Scientific Assessment*.(Houghton, Jenkins and Ephraums eds.), Report of the Intergovernmental Panel on Climate Change, Cambridge University Press.

IPCC (1996). *Climate Change 1995: Economic and Social Dimensions of Climate Change*, Contribution of Working Group III to the Second Assessment Report of the Intergovernmental Panel on Climate Change, Cambridge University Press.

Landsea, C., et al. (1996). Downward trend in the frequency of intense Atlantic hurricanes during the past five decades, *Geophysical Research Letters*, **23**, 527–30.

Mabey, et. al. (1997). *Argument in the Greenhouse*, London: Routledge.

Macklin, Ruth (1981). Can future generations correctly be said to have rights? In Partridge (1981) op.cit.

Maclean, D. and Brown, P.G. (eds) (1983). *Energy and the Future*. New Jersey: Rowman and Littlefield.

Maddison, A. (1995). *Monitoring the World Economy*. Paris: OECD.

Margalit, A. (1996) *The Decent Society*. Cambridge, MA: Harvard University Press.

Merrills, J.G. (1996). Environmental protection and human rights: conceptual aspects'. In Boyle and Anderson (eds) op.cit.

O'Neill, O. (1996). *Towards Justice and Virtue*. Cambridge: Cambridge University Press.

Partridge, E. (ed.) (1981). *Responsibilities to Future Generations*, New York: Prometheus Books.

Rawls, J. (1972). *A Theory of Justice*. Oxford: Clarendon Press.

Reiter, P. (1998). 'Global warming and vector-borne disease in temperate regions and at high altitude', *The Lancet*, **351**.

Schiesser, H., et al. (1997): Winter storms in Switzerland north of the Alps, *Theoretical and Applied Climatology*, **58**, 1–19.

Steiner, H. (1983). The rights of future generations. In *The Rights of Future Generations* (Maclean and Brown, eds.) New Jersey: Rowman and Littlechild

Sterba, J.P. (1980) Abortion and the rights of distant peoples and future generations. *Journal of Philosophy*, **77**, 424–40.

Sterba, J.P. (1998). *Justice for Here and Now*. Cambridge: Cambridge University Press.

Tol, R.S.J. (1995). The damage costs of climate change; Towards a more comprehensive calculation. *Environmental and Resource Economics*,. **5**, 353–74

WHO (1998). *Life in theTwenty First Century – A Vision for All*. Geneva: World Health Organisation.

4 Precaution, GM crops and farmland birds

Tony Gilland

Introduction

Abiding by the precautionary principle, in November 1999 the UK government reached a voluntary agreement with industry to withhold from the commercial growth of genetically modified (GM) crops until the results of a three-year programme of farm-scale trials had been evaluated. This followed an earlier voluntary agreement whereby industry would not grow GM crops commercially during 1999 whilst a methodology for the trials was being established. With the last harvest of the evaluation programme taking place in 2002, the first commercial harvest of GM crops grown in the UK will now be 2003 at the earliest – a full seven years after the first US harvest in 1996. According to the Department of the Environment, Transport and the Regions (DETR), the purpose of the trials is to 'investigate the null hypothesis that there are no differences in the diversity and abundance of wildlife associated with the management of GM herbicide tolerant crops compared with the management of equivalent non-GM crops' (DETR, 1999b). This precautionary position was championed by the UK's Prime Minister in a high profile statement published in *The Independent on Sunday* 27 February 2000. Tony Blair was clear: 'no GM crops will be grown commercially in this country until we are satisfied there will be no unacceptable impact on the environment' and went on to contrast this position with the more "cavalier" approach of the US 'where an area the size of Wales is already under cultivation' (Blair, 2000).

Never before has an agricultural development been put on hold to examine its effects on wildlife. However, the theoretical threat posed by GM crops to wildlife builds upon mounting concerns amongst conservationists about the detrimental impact of modern farming methods more generally on the populations of birds found on farmland. The significant decline in some 'farmland birds' recorded by the British Trust for Ornithology (BTO) have become a regular feature of newspaper coverage accompanied by alarming headlines such as 'Silent Spring 2020' (Nuttall, 1998) or 'Farm subsidies have brought death to millions of songbirds' (Watson-Smyth, 1999), and copy which accepts that intensified farming practices must be to blame. Indeed, the recorded figures, at first sight, are very striking. According to the BTO's data, tree sparrow have declined by 87 per cent, grey partridge by 78 per cent, corn bunting by 74 per cent and reed bunting, turtle dove, skylark, and yellowhammer all by 60 per cent or more between 1972 and 1996 (Crick et al., 1998).

Concerns about the relationship between agriculture and wildlife are not new, and have been an increasingly topical issue amongst conservationists since the 1960s, following the publication of Rachel Carson's book *Silent Spring* (1962) which brought to attention fears about the poisonous impact of DDT on wildlife. What is new is the influential impact these concerns now have.

Since signing up to the United Nations Convention on Biological Diversity, agreed at Rio in 1992, the UK government has sanctioned 436 habitat and species biodiversity action plans (BAPs) which commit it to reversing these declines in wildlife and habitats (DETR, 1999a). 26 of the species BAPs are for birds, many of which are common species for which significant declines have been recorded. Improving the fortunes of wild bird populations is also a component of the government's sustainable development strategy and their population indexes are being used as one of 15 key 'headline indicators' of quality of life (DETR, 1999b). Whilst the overall index of 139 'more common' species of wild birds has never fallen below its original index value in 1970, and an index of rarer species rose by over 150 per cent between 1970 and 1997 (DETR, 1998), attention has focused primarily on the index for 20 farmland species. This has fallen by around 35 per cent since 1970; a trend which the government aims to reverse (DETR, 1999). Building on the existing range of 'agri-environment' schemes introduced since the late 1980s, in December 1999 Agriculture Minister Nick Brown announced a £1.6 billion package for the rural economy over seven years, of which £1 billion was for agri-environment schemes. The move was welcomed by the Royal Society for the Protection of Birds (RSPB) as a 'firm step in the right direction' and by English Nature as 'the most important decision on the countryside for 20 years' (Meikle, 1999).

It is not just government that has become sensitive to the concerns of conservationists about modern farming. Image conscious supermarkets have also made a commitment. Tesco Stores Ltd is the official champion of the UK skylark biodiversity action plan and has funded research into the decline of the skylark, to demonstrate the company's commitment to 'encouraging responsible farming methods which benefit wildlife and local communities' (RSPB, 2000a). As part of its commitment to reduce its impact on agricultural land and to 'protect endangered species' J Sainsbury plc now requires its produce suppliers to implement Integrated Crop Management protocols to reduce pesticide usage and has developed a Farm Biodiversity Action Plan to which it encourages suppliers to sign up (Sainsbury, 1998).

In this context, and given the more general and severe hostility to genetic modification expressed by sections of the media and many consumer and environmental groups, it may appear unsurprising that the government responded to English Nature's precautionary demand for a moratorium on GM crops, by brokering the voluntary agreement with industry to meet this demand. Indeed, the government's Chief Scientific Advisor, Sir Robert May, has frequently expressed his concerns about the possibility that GM crops may have a negative impact on wildlife. In a paper addressing public concerns about GM, May found little cause for concern except in the case of its potential impact on wildlife. According to Sir Robert May:

> Setting aside emotional preferences, one thing stands out: these agricultural changes are all in the direction of realizing the ages-old dream of growing crops that no one eats but us. This has obvious consequences for the invertebrates, mammals and birds that also depend on the fields we use. The Royal Society for the Protection of Birds and others have documented dramatic declines in many bird populations, and although the evidence for corresponding effects on invertebrate and plant diversity is less well documented, I nevertheless find it convincing. The thrust of GM crops is, entirely understandably, to accelerate this trend.

> (May, 1999)

Clearly, then, concerns about 'farmland birds' and modern farming extend well beyond conservation organizations. These concerns, which emphasize the unintended and destructive impact of human activity on the countryside, increasingly exert a precautionary influence over society: best illustrated by the GM farm-scale crop trials and a seven-year lag in the introduction of a technology currently being usefully employed in the USA. What is surprising, though, is how few hard questions have been asked about whether our impact on wildlife is really so bad. Before jumping to the conclusion that this precautionary measure places UK GM policy in a progressive light, it is worth stopping to consider the evidence upon which this unprecedented decision is based.

Who counts the birds?

In the debate following English Nature's call for a moratorium on the commercial growth of GM crops, a great deal of emphasis was placed upon the fact that approximately 75 per cent of the UK land surface is farmed. This fact not only underscores the significance of the relationship between UK farming and wildlife, but deters comparisons between the UK's position and that of the USA, where the impact of farming on wildlife is apparently mitigated by the large areas of land which are set aside for nature conservation. Consequently, the recorded declines of birds found on farmland are all the more important to the abundance of wildlife in the UK's countryside, and therefore provide an apparently good reason for the UK's more precautionary approach towards GM crops.

However, given that the land use category 'farmland' covers a number of distinct land uses (for example, 25 per cent of farmland is used as rough grazing and 25 per cent for intensively managed crops; see Figure 1) it is worth being clear about what is known about the population trends of birds in different habitats. Despite precise figures for the declines in the UK populations of some birds regularly featuring in newspaper print, at present, long term data representative of UK habitats and different types of farmland does not exist. So what does exist?

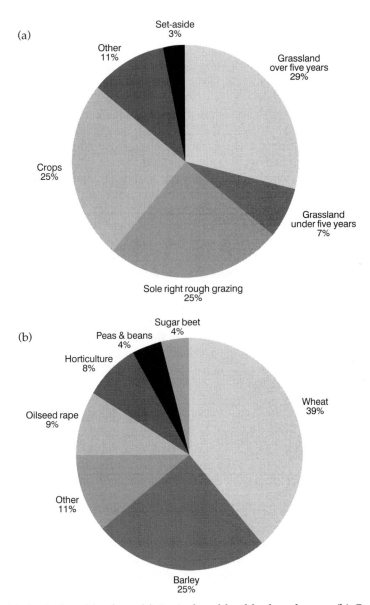

Figure 4.1 Agricultural land use (a) Agricultural land by broad usage (b) Cropped area by type of crop

Currently, the primary source of data for the population trends of common breeding birds is the BTO's Common Bird Census (CBC). The CBC has been running from 1962 and, as the BTO points out, was the 'first national breeding bird monitoring scheme of its kind anywhere in the world' (Crick et al., 1998). The census involves a team of volunteers of around 250 people surveying between 200 and 300 plots of land annually. The surveys take place between late March and early July and require the volunteers to visit their plots ten times. However, due to the time-consuming nature of the fieldwork and subsequent analysis, the BTO readily admit the 'constraints imposed by the relatively small sample size' of their data such as the census' primary focus on farmland and woodland habitats. One result of this is that 'bird population trends in built-up areas and the uplands are little known' (Crick et al., 1998). Another consequence of the CBC's relatively small sample size is its geographical bias towards where the greater number of BTO volunteers live – the south and east of the country. Consequently, most of the specialist literature investigating the relationship between farming and bird populations rightly acknowledges that CBC farmland plots are only representative of rural land use in southern and eastern Britain. (Note: Table 4.1 provides figures for the percentage declines of a number bird species recorded by the CBC and published in three recent reports).

The significance of these data limitations, in terms of the restricted geographical and habitat coverage of the CBC, led the BTO, Joint Nature Conservation Council (JNCC) and the RSPB jointly to introduce the Breeding Bird Survey (BBS) in 1994. The intention was to survey a larger number of plots by simplifying the process, requiring volunteer observers to visit their plots three times a year, instead of ten. The survey method used is also simpler, and according to the BTO is 'relatively quick and convenient to undertake, thereby encouraging a larger number of volunteers to take part' (Noble et al., 1999). As anticipated, the number of volunteers participating has increased and according to the latest BBS report 2297 plots were surveyed in 1998 and much of the country reached 'optimal coverage'. However, despite this increased level of coverage, the necessarily initial short time-span of the data means that currently the more limited Common Bird Census remains the main reference point for measuring trends in the UK's bird populations.

Recent research by Gregory and Baille (experts working for the RSPB and BTO respectively) underlines the importance of representative data. Referring to the concentration of most surveys in southern Britain they point out that 'we have limited data on population trends over a wider area and in other habitats. There is therefore a need to place such population changes in the context of the British population as a whole' (Gregory and Baille, 1998). Using data from the more nationally representative BBS survey the authors have estimated the relative proportions of various bird species found in different habitats (the results of their work are summarized in 4.2). For many of the birds, cropped areas and managed grasslands (which the authors jointly term 'farmland') hold large proportions of their populations; though for only two (corn bunting and linnet) do they estimate that cropped areas alone hold

Table 4.1 The ups and downs of bird populations recorded by the CBC

Species	BAP (1)	Specialist/ Generalist (2)	1970–98 (3) % Index	1972–96 (4) % CBC A	CBC F	CBC W	1968–95 (5) % Index	LCL	UCL
Redpoll			−92	−89					
Tree sparrow	Y	F	−87	−87	−76		−83	−97	
Corn Bunting	Y	F	−85	−74			−61		
Grey partridge	Y	F	−82	−78			−74	−86	−52
Turtle dove	Y	F	−77	−62	−85	−53	−65		
Snipe			−74	−90					
Grasshopper warbler			−73	−59					
Woodcock			−70	−55					
Marsh tit	Y		−69	−37		−42			
Spotted flycatcher				−68	−78	−78	−78		
Willow tit			−63	−50					
Redshank			−60	−72					
Tree pipit			−62	−56					
House sparrow			−58	−64					
Starling		F	−58	−45	−32	−77	−40	−61	−11
Song thrush	Y	G	−55	−52	−66	−39	−63	−72	−53
Lapwing		F	−52	−42	−46		−38	−80	240
Skylark	Y	F	−52	−60	−75		−49	−58	−37
Reed bunting	Y	G	−52	−64	−40		−27	−60	27
Sedge warbler		G	−45	−12	9		−62		
Yellow hammer		F	−43	−60	−37	−71	−26	−42	−6
Lesser spotted woodpecker			−42	−76					
Bullfinch	Y	G	−40	−62	−62	−36	−45	−75	−10
Linnet	Y	F	−38	−41	−40	−30	−41	−59	−13

Table 4.1 *continued*

Species	BAP (1)	Specialist/Generalist (2)	1970–98 (3) % Index	1972–96 (4) % CBC A	CBC F	CBC W	1968–95 (5) % Index	LCL	UCL
Tawny owl			-30	-33					
Blackbird		G	-29	-33	-31	-4	-41	-50	-33
Curlew			-28	-26					
Moorhen		G	-26	-10	-18	4	-33	42	
Willow warbler		G	-23	-23	-10	-39	-22	-40	3
Dunnock		G	-21	-31	-40	-41	-33	-48	-19
Mistle thrush		G	-21	-34	-48	-25	-47	-61	-28
Meadow pipit			-20	-28					
Kestrel			-17	-24					
Swallow		G	-16	20	26		-3	-34	41
Yellow wagtail			-13	-25					
Cuckoo		G	-12	3	9	-31	17	-21	62
Red-legged partridge		F	-6	-30	-32		-13		
Jay			-4	-1	-33	1			
Tree creeper		G	-2	13	-8	23	-9		
Greenfinch		G	-2	3	19	-11	3	-23	48
House martin			-1	-1					
Goldcrest			0	-60	-54	-61			
Goldfinch		F	10	2	18		59	8	130
Coot			17	-22					
Little owl			17	8					
Lesser whitethroat		G	17	-3	-24		9	-56	187
Chiffchaff		G	26	7	1	3	-2	-34	57
Redstart			30	109					
Chaffinch		G	30	25	27	23	28	11	48

Species								
Whitethroat	F	34	83	105	-14	-38	-58	-15
Garden warbler	G	35	27	-7	20	-48	-88	95
Blue tit	G	35	28	23	27	33	8	49
Pied wagtail	G	39	5	0	7	64	15	141
Robin	G	42	21	17	63	35	13	53
Coal tit		55	28	41				
Great tit	G	57	22	32	16	78	45	112
Long-tailed tit	G	61	19	8	9	132	50	309
Pheasant	G	65	83	102	125	87	6	179
Wren	G	69	4	4	0	99	68	128
Mallard	G	82	29	65		131	52	205
Green woodpecker		92	15	-7	-1			
Magpie	G	113	94	63	130	83	48	125
Nuthatch		118	82		68			
Carrion crow	G	120	101	75	106	115	62	181
Stock dove	F	140	124	185		162	42	491
Jackdaw	G	148	117	118	123	60		
Blackcap	G	155	54	83	27	120	58	220
Great spotted woodpecker		161	185	179	89			
Sparrowhawk		162	294					
Reed warbler		194	228					
Woodpigeon		201	55					
Buzzard		224	29					
Collared dove		782	514	474				
Barn owl	not monitored by CBC							
Rook	not monitored by CBC							

(1) Y = Biodiversity Action Plan exists for the species.

(2) F = 'farmland specialist', G = 'farmland generalist', Siriwardena et al (1998).

(3) Gregory et al. (2000). The State of the UK's Birds 1999, RSPB and BTO.

(4) CBC A = 'all plots index', CBC F = 'farmland plots' index, CBC W = 'woodland plots' index. Crick et al. (1998). Breeding Birds in the Wider Countryside: their conservation status (1972–1996), BTO.

(5) Index value followed by 95% lower and upper confidence limits, Siriwardena et al (1998).

Species in bold are the twenty species which make up the DETR's 'farmland bird' quality of life index.

50 per cent or more of their national populations. For two other birds featuring in the 'farmland birds debate' (house sparrow and starling) around 50 per cent of their populations are estimated to occur in 'human' habitat types. For skylark, they estimate that 35 per cent of the population occurs in tilled habitats but estimate that an approximately equal proportion, 33 per cent, occurs, on semi-natural grass and heath habitats. Many of the farmland birds, then, are not found exclusively on farmland.

As a result of their research, the authors counsel against conservation focusing solely on farming:

> Our analysis also shows that substantial proportions of particular species occur outside farmland, but that different species occur in different habitats. A considerable proportion of skylarks occur on upland moor, bullfinches in wooded habitats, and reed buntings in riparian habitats. Conservation of this group of species thus requires appropriate management of the wider countryside as a whole. We should also not lose sight of the value of human-made environments for birds; sites associated with human settlement (i.e. urban, suburban, and rural human sites) hold > 20 per cent of the British populations of blackbird, song thrush and starling and considerable numbers of other species

> (Gregory and Baille, 1998).

Gregory and Baille argue for the importance of 'appropriately designed monitoring schemes that provide representative coverage of species and habitats' (ibid.).

These data limitations are particularly significant because the various hypotheses put forward about the impact of farming relate to specific farming practices which vary across the country. For example, when the practice under discussion relates to arable farming (as is often the case) CBC data is relevant because so much of lowland farming in the south and east of Britain is arable. Thus a study into the indirect effects of pesticides on farmland birds notes the limitations of the CBC data, but reasonably argues that 'the CBC does provide data that give a reliable measure of broad trends in numbers within the area most likely to be affected by pesticides' (Campbell et al., 1997). However, when discussing the relevance to changes in livestock farming, such as stocking densities or the shift from hay to silage production, the CBC data provides a far less reliable guide to what is happening to bird populations in the parts of the country where various forms of livestock farming are more dominant (western and northern regions).

Consider the example of the skylark, one of the most widely distributed breeding birds in Britain (Gibbons et al., 1993), and regularly featured in newspaper coverage and headlines concerning declining farmland bird populations. A RSPB press release in January 2000 announced the results of new research it had carried out (but which was still 'in press') into 'drastic declines in the UK's skylark numbers' (RSPB, 2000a). According to the press release, the research shows that the move from spring-sown to autumn-sown cereal crops by UK farmers 'has contributed significantly to a drop in the UK

Table 4.2 Habitat use of some 'farmland birds'

Species	Till	Grass/ Till	Intens. Grass	Unintens. Grass	Farm Total	Grass & Heath	Wood & Scrub	Urban	Suburban	Rural	Human Total	Water	Misc.	Total
Skylark	34.8	5.5	11.2	6.7	58.1	32.9	2.9	0.1	0.9	–	1.0	0.6	4.5	100.1
Dunnock	22.0	6.0	25.0	6.4	59.4	2.7	13.3	1.8	6.9	7.5	16.2	2.2	6.4	100.2
Blackbird	15.0	4.3	18.9	6.8	45.0	2.4	15.0	4.1	13.7	9.4	27.2	2.7	7.6	99.9
Song thrush	11.4	2.1	16.7	5.6	35.8	4.7	24.2	3.1	9.5	11.1	23.7	3.5	8.0	99.9
Starling	8.7	2.8	16.2	7.2	34.9	1.7	4.4	11.0	28.7	9.1	48.8	1.5	8.7	100.0
House Sparrow	10.1	2.3	13.9	4.6	30.9	0.6	2.0	9.9	30.7	15.6	56.2	2.5	8.1	100.3
Tree Sparrow	25.5	7.5	27.0	5.3	65.3	11.8	6.9	–	0.3	5.1	5.4	5.3	5.1	98.8
Chaffinch	19.1	5.2	24.4	6.3	55.0	3.9	24.7	0.7	2.2	5.1	8.0	2.8	5.8	100.2
Greenfinch	16.4	5.0	21.5	6.3	49.2	1.1	8.0	3.0	12.5	17.2	32.7	2.4	6.6	100.0
Goldfinch	15.6	5.9	29.4	5.9	56.8	4.2	9.1	2.3	5.7	11.6	19.6	4.0	6.1	99.8
Linnet	30.4	6.4	22.5	6.5	65.8	10.4	9.7	0.8	2.4	4.9	8.1	1.0	4.8	99.8
Bullfinch	11.1	4.6	15.3	7.0	38.0	5.0	36.4	0.4	3.0	8.0	11.4	3.0	7.1	100.9
Yellow Hammer	50.9	9.7	16.8	5.8	83.2	3.0	6.3	0.1	0.2	1.6	1.9	1.6	4.1	100.1
Reed Bunting	27.2	6.1	9.2	7.9	50.4	24.6	5.6	–	0.6	0.6	1.2	11.5	6.5	99.8
Corn Bunting	65.0	5.4	16.4	6.5	93.3	–	2.7	–	0.4	0.5	0.9	–	3.2	100.1

Estimated percentages of the British population within major habitat categories in 1995 and 1996.

Sources: Gregory and Baille. (1998) and Gregory, Richard (1999).

Note:

Intens. Grass = intensified grassland

Unintens. Grass = unintensified grassland

Grass & Heath = Semi-natural grassland and heaths combined

Wood & Scrub = deciduous woodland, coniferous woodland, mixed woodland and scrub land combined.

Caveat: 'In interpreting the results it is important to recognise that the associations between birds and habitats are at a broad, landscape scale and that they depend on the specific definitions of habitat type.' Gregory, Richard (1999).

skylark numbers of 75 per cent on UK farmland'. However, more accurately, the research is only relevant to skylarks breeding in farmland where cereal crops are grown. The reference to 'UK skylark numbers' is actually a reference to the CBC 'farmland plots' survey statistic, which is not representative of parts of the country and habitats where large proportions of the skylark population are found.

Given the widespread acknowledgement of the importance of these data limitations, it is notable how rarely these data caveats are referenced in the public debate. Indeed the latest report, *The State of the UK Birds 1999* (Gregory et al., 2000), produced jointly by the RSPB and the BTO, begins with a discussion of the importance of the inclusion of the wild bird indicator in the DETR's 'quality of life' headline indicators and notes the 'notable' contribution made to this by the CBC. According to the report 'Birds have been chosen partly because the data are so good, but also because their widespread distribution across the UK allows them to be used as barometers of change in the wider environment'. Yet nowhere in the report, or in the government's own reporting of the indicators, are the data limitations discussed above explained.

On occasion, the discussion based on these figures can be highly misleading. For example, in the accompanying press release to *The State of the UK Birds 1999*, Dr Jeremy Greenwood, Director of the BTO, states:

> Our volunteers, who provide the bulk of the observations on which our results are based, survey all the main habitats in Britain. . . . Even some familiar urban birds, such as starlings and house sparrows, have undergone dramatic declines. All are candidates for addition to the nation's set of Biodiversity Action Plans.

> (Gregory et al., 2000)

As a result of the BBS volunteers may now survey all the main habitats in Britain, and the CBC records 45 per cent and 64 per cent declines for starling and house sparrow respectively. However, as the BTO acknowledges, due to the historic limitations of the CBC, 'bird population trends in built-up areas' are 'little known'.

It is also worth noting that whilst, for the areas and habitats for which they are representative, most of the CBC indexes are regarded as a reliable indication of trends, the degree of reliability can be variable. For example, a recent BTO report, which provides conservation alerts for declining species, points out that though past alerts were issued for three species (swallow, goldfinch, and little owl) because they had declined by more than 25 per cent in the last 25 years, 'reanalysis using the more advanced techniques employed in the current report suggests that these species no longer fall into this category (c.f. Siriwardena et al., 1998)' (Crick et al., 1998). It is also the case that, for a few 'farmland' species whose large percentage declines have placed them at the forefront of the debate (tree sparrow, corn bunting and turtle dove), the statistical confidence limits on their population changes are very wide. The reanalysis of the CBC indexes by Siriwardena et al. (1998) omitted confidence limits for corn bunting and turtle dove 'because they were too wide to be informative, owing to sparseness in data'. They point out that the sparseness in data was the result of a recent reduction in the number of CBC plots on which they occur, and that therefore they 'can almost certainly be added to the list of declines' though their indices 'must be considered to be less reliable.' For the tree sparrow, confidence limits are included but are still very wide at the 95 per cent level, indicating a decline of between –5 per cent and –97 per cent (see Table 4.2).

GM crops: the final blow for farmland birds?

> The environmentally untested introduction of GMOs could be the final blow for such species as the skylark, corn bunting and the linnet, as the seeds and insects on which they feed disappear. We must adopt the precautionary principle if we are to maintain England's biodiversity – its wealth of wildlife – and honour Government's commitments under the Rio Convention.
>
> (English Nature 1998b)

When, in July 1998, English Nature published its influential position statement on Genetically Modified Organisms, calling for a moratorium on the commercial release of GM crops, apart from reminding the government of its commitment to biodiversity and to reversing the declines of a number of 'farmland birds', its primary concern about GM crops related to the indirect effects of pesticides on bird populations. One of the many hypotheses put forward to explain the decline of birds on farmland is that intensive pesticide usage has an unforeseen and indirect effect on bird populations, by reducing the abundance of weeds and invertebrates which form important components of their diets. Whilst English Nature accepts that the use of GM crops 'may have potential benefits for farmland wildlife, particularly if their use results in better targeted or lower usage of agrochemicals', it argues that there is 'little evidence that such benefits are being realized' (English Nature, 1998a). The purpose of the farm-scale trials is therefore to compare the diversity and abundance of plants and invertebrates associated with the management of GM crops and equivalent non-GM crops. Birds and mammals are not being directly studied due to the difficulty of making such direct comparisons, because they are not confined to single fields. However, according to the DETR 'by sampling organisms at the lower end of the food chain, knock-on effects to the larger organisms can be well predicted' (DETR, 1999b).

What is surprising in the response to the farm-scale trial proposals is the relative lack of comment about how little is known about the indirect effect of pesticides on bird populations. Indeed, the DETR statement that 'the knock-on effects to the larger organisms can be well predicted' appears a little over-confident. A major study of the indirect effects of pesticides, commissioned by the DETR and English Nature (on behalf of the JNCC), provided inconclusive results on these questions. The report concluded: 'Lack of data has hampered the extent to which it has been possible to assess which features of agricultural activity or change are most important in determining the abundance of bird foods and birds.' (Campbell et al., 1997).

Though the report recommends, 'in the absence of clear evidence', a precautionary approach 'when trying to determine appropriate policy and conservation strategies' it clearly acknowledges the importance of these data problems. It notes:

> The most important gap, which has severely reduced the extent to which it has been worthwhile or even possible to look for detailed relationships between bird food and pesticide usage, is the lack of detailed data on the diet of the majority of farmland bird species' and that there has been 'rather little work on the effects of pesticide usage on broad-scale abundance of invertebrates, plants and seeds at the scale likely to have an impact on bird populations.

(Campbell et al. 1997)

Given a general lack of data and knowledge to demonstrate cause-and-effect relationships (with the exception of only one species), the report places a great deal of emphasis on the correlation between declines in population trends recorded by the CBC for different farmland bird species and increases in the proportion of cropped areas sprayed with pesticides each year. The report finds that 'the starts of the current declines of at least ten of the declining species broadly coincides with the period between 1974 and 1982 when crop spray levels for fungicides, insecticides, and molluscicides started to approach or exceed 50 per cent', and argues that, whilst equivalent herbicide levels are estimated to have been reached by as early as around 1959 (and therefore preceded the starts of the declines of most species), 'a time-lag of several years, depending on the plant species involved, would not be unexpected'.

Based on a number of factors – whether a bird population species is declining; items included in its diet are declining; whether the bird decline coincides with increases in pesticide use; and any evidence of pesticides having caused the decline of the bird – the authors of the report assess the likelihood that pesticides have had an indirect effect on 40 species of birds found on farmland. Sixteen of the species have not declined and so it is assumed for these that there is no indirect effect of pesticides. For a further nineteen species, which have declined in population, the authors conclude 'that it is possible that pesticides could be having an indirect effect' (see Table 4.3). For eight of these species this is deemed to be less likely because of the lack of coincidence between the starts of their declines and the period of increased pesticide usage identified by the authors. For the remaining eleven, in the absence of any evidence either way as to whether pesticides have caused a decline, the report can only find that such a relationship is possible, or, in other words, that we do not currently know. Indeed, as the report points out, recent detailed research for the cirl bunting suggests that its decline is 'unlikely to be indirectly affected' by pesticides, despite the start of its decline

Table 4.3 Summary of evidence of a possible indirect effect of pesticides on 'farmland birds'. Compiled from Campbell et al. (1997)

Species	UK population trends (%) 1969–1994 Farmland	Woodland	Are diet items declining?	Does the bird decline coincide with pesticide use?	Is there any evidence that pesticides have caused the bird declines?	Conclusion: is there an indirect effect of pesticides?
Grey partridge*	–82	nd	Y	?	Y	Y
Tree sparrow	–89	nd	Y	Y	?	P
Turtle dove	–77	–74	Y	Y	?	P
Bullfinch	–76	–54	Y	Y	?	P
Song thrush	–73	–50	Y	Y	?	P
Lapwing	–62	nd	Y	Y	?	P
Reed bunting	–61	nd	Y	Y	?	P
Skylark	–58	nd	Y	Y	?	P
Linnet	–52	–61	Y	Y	?	P
Swallow (1)	–43	nd	Y	Y	?	P
Blackbird	–42	–25	Y	Y	?	P
Starling	–23	–65	Y	Y	?	P
Corn bunting*	–80	nd	Y	?	?	(P)
Spotted flycatcher	–73	–82	Y	?	?	(P)
Sand martin	nd	nd	Y	?	?	(P)
Mistle thrush	–39	14	Y	?	?	(P)
Yellow wagtail*	–31	nd	Y	?	?	(P)
Dunnock	–29	–48	Y	?	?	(P)
Yellowhammer	–17	–48	Y	?	?	(P)
Red-backed shrike	nd	nd	Y	?	?	(P)

Key: nd = no data; Y = Yes; ? = No evidence either way; P = possible effect; (P) = qualified possible effect
* for these species the population trend is for all CBC plots
Source: Campbell et al. (1997).
(1) Note: The BTO now record a 26% increase for swallow for the period 1972–96 – based on reanalysis using more advanced techniques. Crick et al. (1998).

coinciding with increased pesticide use. Only for one species, the grey partridge, is there well-established evidence that its decline is linked to the indirect effects of pesticides. Another species, the swallow, following the BTO's recent adjustment to its CBC index showing a 26 per cent increase in its population on farmland rather than a 43 per cent decline, should presumably now be ruled out as a candidate example of the indirect effects of pesticides.

This reliance on statistical correlation, rather than evidence of cause and effect relationships, is characteristic of the many arguments linking declines in farmland birds to changes in agricultural practices.

Statistical correlation or cause and effect?

A paper by three BTO experts examining the question of why more species of birds on farmland are decreasing than increasing argued that a number of agricultural factors are 'implicated', including: 'the intensification of cereal growing, the loss of winter stubbles, reductions in mixed farming, the drainage and improvement of pasture and direct mortality from agricultural operations'. However, their review found that for only four of the more widespread species (those under discussion in this debate) is information 'available on the environmental causes of the declines'. Consequently they conclude: 'We remain ignorant of the precise causes of the majority of farmland bird declines and identifying these is an urgent priority.' (Baille et al., 1997).

Two related factors explain this lack of hard evidence. First, conducting the necessary field experiments is a difficult and expensive business. As discussed above, the only species for which there is reliable evidence of pesticides having an indirect and significant negative impact on a bird population is the grey partridge. The Game Conservancy Trust, who have conducted much of the research into the decline of grey partridge, have spent over 33 years studying the bird. In 1990 the BTO estimated that some '200 man-years' had been 'invested in partridge studies' (Marchant et al., 1990). Such work is clearly expensive.

Second, there is a large number of hypotheses to be tested. Each bird species has particular ecological needs in terms of nesting habitat, chick rearing and adult diet. Some species nest in fields whilst others nest in hedgerows; some are seed-eaters and others insectivores. For each species a complexity of factors need to be untangled to explain its population dynamics. In particular, a key question is whether changes are being driven by changes in breeding productivity (which itself may be either as a result the result of a reduction or increase in the number of nesting attempts made by a species or a change in the productivity of each nest) or a change in the survival rates of chicks or adults. As the BTO points out, 'without access to good long-term datasets of productivity and survival, remedial conservation action has to be taken without a sound basis or has to wait until some detailed investigative research has been undertaken' (Crick et al., 1998). Analysis can be further complicated by short-term effects of bird populations, such as adverse weather. These can have temporarily dramatic impacts on bird populations and can require several years for species to recover from (Newton, 1998).

When you multiply the number of bird species of interest to conservationists by the number of ecological factors which impact upon their population levels, and finally by the number of changes in farming practices over the last thirty years, the number of hypotheses to be tested becomes very large. As one paper points out, to conduct intensive studies for each of the species which have declined on farmland 'would clearly require a large, perhaps prohibitive investment of time and resources' (Siriwardena et al., 1998). As a result of such barriers to our knowledge, in a similar fashion to the arguments put forward about the indirect effects of pesticides, much attention has been focused on a correlation between changes in certain agricultural practices and the decline of a number of species which appears to have begun around the same time – the mid 1970s to early 1980s. An increasing amount of research has gone into interrogating the BTO's data using sophisticated statistical techniques to identify clusters of turning points in the population trends of various birds found on farmland. The idea is to identify similarities in ecology between species sharing similar turning points, in the hope that this will help to identify the role played by specific changes in agricultural practices which occurred at around the same time, thus helping to guide conservation efforts.

Using these statistical techniques, Siriwardena et al. (1998) conducted ten tests against the species characteristics of 42 birds found on farmland and reached the conclusion that farmland specialization 'was the only significant determinant of changes in abundance'. Using this result, four leading ornithologists recently answered the question 'Can we be sure that the bird declines in the United Kingdom are caused by agricultural intensification?' in the following way:

> Most of the evidence is by association, but in sum total it is damming. For example, annual BTO censuses of 42 species of breeding birds show that 13 species living exclusively in farmland, such as the skylark and corn bunting, declined by an average of 30 per cent between 1968 and 1995, while 29 species of habitat generalists, such as the carrion crow and the wren, have increased by an average of 23 per cent.
>
> (Krebs et al.,1999).

The argument is that generalists are more able to adapt to change, to nest and feed elsewhere, whilst those whose ecological requirements are more specific to farmland are more vulnerable to changing agricultural practices.

To an extent the argument is highly plausible. Birds found on and around farmland are living in a habitat heavily shaped by man's activities and therefore one would expect to find that changes in those activities have had an impact on some of the birds living there. However, this more imprecise approach can hide a lot of important contextual information. For example, aside from the 'farmland specialist' category, the statistical analysis by Siriwardena et al. (1998) found that 'clear groups were absent from both the declining and (especially) the increasing species data sets' and that 'most long-term relationships between the environment and abundance have been species-specific . . . the groupings of species we have identified are notable for their ecological and phylogenetic diversity: the groups are not simply the product of the environment acting similarly on several ecologically similar or closely related species'. They conclude that 'the range of long-term trends we have found argues against a single, simple explanation for the recent declines in the abundance of farmland birds'. Nevertheless, they go on to argue that it is 'likely that the intensification of agriculture, in general, is responsible', and cite the detailed studies of the corncrake (linking its decline with the earlier cutting of grassland) and the grey partridge (indirect effects of herbicides) to substantiate this point.

However, when one considers what is known and not known about the 13 farmland specialists the study refers to, the danger of simplistic, though striking, aggregate statistics becomes clearer; as do the reasons why it is wrong to jump to the conclusion that all these changes are the result of changing agricultural practices.

Take the 13 farmland specialists identified by Siriwardena et al. (1998) as having declined on average by 30 per cent between 1968 and 1995, according to CBC farmland plot data. For two of these seed-eating specialists, stock dove and goldfinch, their populations increased over the period (162 per cent and 59 per cent respectively). For another, whitethroat, its recorded decline of 38 per cent over the period has been attributed to a population crash of 75 per cent between 1968 and 1969 'due to drought in West Africa (cited in Crick et al., 1998 referring to an earlier report) where it migrates to for the winter. According to the BTO (Crick et al., 1998), its population remained low until the late 1980s and then increased on farmland plots (the CBC recorded an increase of 105 per cent over the period 1972–96) but not on woodland ones (on CBC woodland plots a decline of 14 per cent is recorded over the same period). And for the migratory turtle dove, there remains doubt over the relative impacts of 'over-wintering' problems in Africa, hunting during migration, and changed agricultural practices.

For others of the 13 farmland specialists of concern here, such as the starling, yellowhammer and tree sparrow, there is little direct evidence that the changes in their population levels recorded by the CBC have been caused by agricultural changes. For the starling, its CBC woodland index fell by more than twice the recorded fall in its farmland index (a fall of 77 per cent compared with 32 per cent) over the period 1972–96 (Crick et al., 1998). The woodland index for the yellowhammer has also declined more steeply than its CBC farmland index (a 71 per cent fall compared with a 37 per cent from 1972–96) and its decline, beginning at the very end of the 1980s, does not coincide with the period of the mid 1970s to early 1980s – the period identified as significant with regard to the start of agriculture-induced declines in farmland birds.

As for the tree sparrow, which often heads the list of declining farmland birds with its startling 87 per cent decline, today's low numbers are not a unique feature of modern times. As the Biodiversity Action Plan for the tree sparrow notes:

> The tree sparrow appears to undergo irregular fluctuations in numbers. In Britain there was a high population from the 1880s to the 1930s, but numbers then decreased to a low point around 1950 . . . Numbers then increased again from 1960 to 1978, possibly due to an influx of birds from mainland Europe. . . . Little is known about the factors affecting numbers of tree sparrows.
>
> (English Nature, 1998c)

Research by Summers-Smith (1998) suggests that today's remaining 10 per cent of the tree sparrow may well be equivalent to 100 per cent of its population in 1950. Further perspective on the significance of tree sparrow numbers is offered *by The Historical Atlas of Breeding Birds in Britain and Ireland, 1875–1900* (Holloway, 1996) which refers to a nineteenth century account of the tree sparrow by Yarrell (1837–43) suggesting that the tree sparrow 'was not a well-known species anywhere in its English range in the early 1800s'.

For skylark and linnet, where greater evidence exists for agricultural changes having an adverse impact on their population levels, the stark statistics for their declines on CBC farmland plots (–75 per cent and –40 per cent respectively) can easily give the impression, in the context of the current debate, that their populations are in 'free fall'. But these headline statistics obscure the fact that their recorded populations have not declined significantly since the mid 1980s (approximately 15 years ago). According to the BTO, skylark populations have 'remained relatively stable' since the mid 1980s, whilst linnet 'have since shown signs of recovery' (Crick et al., 1998). It has been suggested that the recovery of the linnet is linked to the introduction and expansion of oil seed rape crops since the 1970s, rape seeds being taken 'avidly by Linnets and other finches' (Marchant et al., 1990).

And even in the case of the grey partridge, one of the few common breeding birds for which there is substantial direct experimental evidence to support the argument that changes in modern agriculture have had a major impact on its population, it is worth noting that its general decline predates modern agricultural practices. As an earlier BTO report points out (Marchant et al., 1990), 'The modern decline of the grey partridge can be traced back to the closing decades of the nineteenth century, as is apparent from old records in game books. Only in regions such as East Anglia where game-bird management, with game-keeping, was paramount were maximum population levels maintained into the 1940s'. The report notes the decline in game-keepers during the First World War and the even greater declines in game-keepers during the Second World War and argues 'The decline in the number of gamekeepers was crucial, because the level of nest predation is an important factor in the population regulation of the grey partridge (Aebischer and Potts, 1989)'.

As a result of all these uncertainties, usually bypassed in the current debate, not all bird experts and enthusiasts are equally happy with the level of attention being paid to the 'farmland birds'. Dr Dick Potts is the Director General of the Game Conservancy Trust, where he and others have conducted much of the research on the decline of the Grey Partridge. Potts is convinced that changing agricultural practices are the primary cause of the decline of six to eight species. For others he believes 'the jury is still out' due to other possible factors such as 'problems in Africa' for the migratory turtle dove. According to Potts, 'There is no study of a bird which comes anywhere near what we have done with the grey partridge, so a lot of it is speculation'. He believes that 'people have been too hasty altogether to blame farming which in recent years has improved in many ways' (personal communication, 1999).

So even for the 'farmland specialists' in decline, there may be other factors which need to be taken into account. One such factor which causes immense controversy is predation. According to Dick Potts, others 'tend to dismiss claims that magpies or sparrowhawks are an important factor. Nobody has looked at the predation side as critically as they have the farming side'. One of the problems of assessing the weight to attach to the various hypotheses, when the cause and effect experimental evidence is weak, is that people's views can be coloured by other preoccupations. Predation might be a more appealing hypothesis to some farmers and those interested in game birds compared to others more convinced about the destructive nature of modern farming. And in the conservation world, many will admit in private that the organizational agendas of concerned parties can, at least in part, drive the issues being pushed.

It is also important to keep in mind that there are many more bird species to be found breeding on farmland than the 'farmland specialists' (which themselves are generally found in other habitats also). As Siriwardena et al. (1998) found, 29 generalists breeding on farmland 'have increased by an average of 23 per cent'. They also found that, of the 42 species studied in total, 'the abundance of 12 species declined significantly' but that of 14 had 'increased'. So although 75 per cent of UK land is used for farming and the specialists are thought to have declined by around 30 per cent on CBC plots, our countryside is not becoming devoid of bird life. Indeed, more generally, there seems much that is positive about the state of the UK's birds. According to the BTO's report on breeding birds in the wider countryside, based on CBC data over twenty five years, 'the number of species showing long-term trends of declining population size approximately equalled the number showing increases' (Crick et al., 1998). The latest results of the more representative BBS, covering the period 1994 and 1998, found that for the 101 species that could be indexed, 32 had increased significantly and 21 had decreased significantly. According to the joint RSPB and BTO report, *The State of the UK's Birds 1999* the number of bird species breeding in the UK has increased by nearly 40 since the beginning of the nineteenth century (one third as a result of human introduction and the remainder due to natural colonization) and 'in the last 30 years there has been a net increase of four species per decade' (Gregory et al., 2000).

Declining farmland birds: 'So what?'

Given the complexity of factors impacting upon bird populations, partial data and incomplete knowledge of individual species' ecology, the most important question of all is how we should interpret the more uncertain picture which lies behind the public chastisement of modern farming methods and the invoking of the precautionary principle to suspend the introduction of commercially grown GM crops in the UK. One thing that is clear from the CBC data is the immense amount of change, both up and down, that there has been in bird populations since the survey began. Due to the absence of survey data prior to the 1960s, we can only really speculate as to whether such a degree of change is a peculiar feature of modern times. However, what is clear from the ornithological publications of the nineteenth century is that changing bird populations, up and down, associated with agricultural changes, are nothing new.

An interesting review of some of this literature, and other historical accounts, is provided by Simon Holloway (1996). His account suggests, for example, that following an increase in the area of arable land from the late eighteenth century onwards, 'it seems likely that the population and range of the corn bunting was its height during the last half of the nineteenth century'. However, the agricultural depression from the 1870s to the 1930s, which led to a substantial decline in the area of cereals in Britain, is thought then to have caused a major decline in the corn bunting population. According to Marchant et al. (1990): 'the turtle dove is known to have increased in numbers and range around the middle of the nineteenth century, for reasons we do not understand' and 'another upsurge in the early decades of the present century coincided with agricultural recession' – the same time that the corn bunting was in decline. Then there is the reed bunting, whose population is thought to have remained broadly stable during the nineteenth century due to the counteracting effects of lost habitat due to land drainage and expanded habitat due to the expanding network of canals, flooded clay and gravel pits, and large new reservoirs (Holloway, 1996). A useful overview is provided by O'Connor and Shrubb (1986), who explain how much of Britain's avifauna is of a forest or woodland origin (dating back to the domination of the land by woodland and marsh prior to its cultivation) and how species of open country – such as lapwing, skylark, and partridges – would have expanded as increasing amounts of land was cleared for farming. They also point out how the Enclosure Acts of the eighteenth and nineteenth centuries, and con-sequent expansion of hedgerows, resulted in an increase in songbirds in the countryside (much commented upon by writers of the time). However, according to O'Connor and Shrubb, the problem today is that wildlife 'cannot keep pace with the speed of modern technological development'.

Not all experts take the same view. Dr Tim Sharrock, Managing Editor of *British Birds* ('the longest established monthly ornithological journal in the world') and co-ordinator of the BTO's first *Bird Breeding Atlas* in the early 1970s, is more sanguine. Prompted by mass media coverage of 'the latest doom-and-gloom story', Dr Sharrock wrote an editorial for the September issue of the journal, entitled 'Panic ye not', which counselled against looking for 'the one simple answer' and for the need to keep the population statistics in perspective: 'just as it takes time for a speeding juggernaut to be stopped or for a steamroller to build up speed, there is also a momentum to change. Thus it takes time for a population decline to be reversed, even if conditions are propitious'. It would appear that Sharrock's concern is not only with the media: 'even those who really should know better seem to ignore the fact that a decline may merely be a contraction from a previous expansion phase which led to the species extending beyond its "natural" range and also perhaps into unsuitable habitats'. Sharrock's philosophy seems to be that, whether due to 'natural' effects or human impact, change is to be expected and should be no cause for alarm: because there 'will always be winners and losers' (Sharrock, 1999). Consequently, for Sharrock 'It is ridiculous to blame the decline of these birds on farmers becoming more efficient; what would you expect them to do? And as some species decline others increase and take their place' (personal communication).

Such views are in stark contrast to the views expressed by the RSPB in press releases and promotional literature:

> drastic declines in farmland bird species such as skylark, tree sparrow and corn bunting mean that the natural environment is in grave danger'
>
> (RSPB, 1998)

and

> The wildlife is being cut out of our countryside. . . . The staggering losses of farmland birds coincide with the major changes which have taken place in UK farming over the last 30 years. The broad conclusion must be obvious. Intensive farming practices are devastating the populations of wild birds, and other wildlife too.
>
> (Wynne, 2000)

are just two recent examples. Such statements have generated strong criticism from some quarters. One of the more high profile critics is Lord Derek Barber, who was the Chair of the RSPB from 1976–81 and Chair of the Countryside Commission from 1980–90. According to Lord Barber:

> in terms of a balance sheet type approach, conservation is gaining something every day. What people ignore is the fact that we are getting better rather than worse. Everything as far as the RSPB are concerned is

always in grave danger. Bodies like the RSPB and WWF are now in the hands of sophisticated marketers and so they cry wolf at every opportunity. They tend to go for exaggerating all the time and they tend in due course to believe their own exaggeration.

(Personal communication)

Conclusion

However, while there may be some truth to this, such arguments miss the more important points about what is really going on. Clearly changes in agricultural practices can and do have an impact on different bird species. This is nothing new and these changes are not the only contributing factors. Whether the pace of agricultural change since the 1970s is having an unusually significant impact on the balance of bird populations is far from clear. However, what is clear is that the increasing level of attention being paid to wildlife issues by government and industry is not simply the result of the marketing success of the RSPB.

The debate about the impact of modern farming on bird populations and the potential impact of GM crops reflects a growing preoccupation with the fortunes (ups and downs) of common bird species. It has little, if anything, to do with more traditional conservation concerns about endangered species. Over 1100 of the worlds 10 000 identified bird species have been listed as 'globally threatened'. Yet only 24 of these 1100 species breed in Europe, and only a handful in the UK (Heredia et al., 1996) – none of them are the species making the newspaper headlines. The government's endorsement and encouragement of this preoccupation – with its commitment to biodiversity action plans for birds such as tree sparrow, corn bunting and skylark, which breed in their millions around the world; the publishing of a 'wild bird' headline indicator of quality of life alongside GDP; and the brokering of the precautionary moratorium on GM crops despite a complete lack of evidence of harm – demonstrates a tendency for society to interpret modern technological achievements in the most destructive and negative way possible.

It is this sentiment, rather than any concrete evidence about the dangers GM crops pose to wildlife, that inform the precautionary principle in relation to this discussion. Only when this is recognized, and challenged, will a useful and informed analysis of the future of Britain's countryside be possible.

References

Baille et al. (1997). Farmland Bird Declines: Patterns, Processes and Prospects. 1997 BCPC Symposium Proceeding No. 69, 65–87.

Blair, Tony (2000). The key to GM is its potential both for harm and good. *The Independent on Sunday*, 27 February.

Campbell et al. (1997). A review of the indirect effects of pesticides on birds. JNCC Report No. 227. Peterborough: Joint Nature Conservation Committee.

Crick et al. (1998). *Breeding Birds in the Wider Countryside: Their Conservation Status* (1972–96), Thetford: BTO.

DETR. (1998). Sustainability counts. Consultation paper on a set of 'headline' indicators of sustainable development. London: Department of the Environment, Transport and the Regions.

DETR (1999a): Quality of life counts. Indicators for a strategy for sustainable development for the United Kingdom: a baseline assessment. London: Department of the Environment, Transport and the Regions.

DETR. (1999b). Farm-scale evaluations of the impact of the management of GM herbicide tolerant oil-seed rape and maize on farmland wildlife. Fact Sheet. London: Department of the Environment, Transport and the Regions, 26 May.

DETR. (1999c). Voluntary agreement on GM crops extended. Press release. London: Department of the Environment, Transport and the Regions, 5 November.

English Nature (1998a). *Genetically Modified Organisms.* Position Statement. Peterborough: English Nature.

English Nature (1998b). Government wildlife adviser urges caution on genetically modified organisms – the new agricultural revolution. Press Release, 8 July. Peterborough: English Nature,

English Nature (1998c). UK Biodiversity Group Tranche 2 Action Plans, Volume 1 – vertebrates and vascular plants. Peterborough: English Nature.

Gibbons et al. (1993). *The New Atlas of Breeding Birds in Britain and Ireland: 1988–1991.* London: T & A.D. Poyser.

Gregory, Richard (1999). Broad-scale habitat use of sparrows, finches and buntings in Britain. *Vogelwelt*, **120**, 47–57.

Gregory, R. et al. (2000). *The State of the UK's Birds 1999.* Sandy: RSPB and BTO.

Gregory, R. and Baille, (1998). Large-scale habitat use of some declining British birds. *Journal of Applied Ecology*, **35**, 785–799.

Heredia et al. (1996). *Globally Threatened Birds in Europe – Action Plans.* Brussels: Council of Europe.

Holloway, S.. (1996). *The Historical Atlas of Breeding Birds in Britain and Ireland 1875–1900.* London: T & A.D. Poyser.

Krebs et al. (1999). 'The second Silent Spring?' *Nature*, **400**, 611–612.

MAFF (2000). *Agriculture in the United Kingdom 1999.* London: HMSO.

Marchant et al. (1990). *Population Trends in British Breeding Birds.* Thetford: BTO.

May, R. (1999): Genetically modified foods: facts, worries, policies and public confidence. A note by the UK Chief Scientific Adviser, Sir Robert May. February 1999. London: Parliamentary Office of Science and Technology.

Meikle, J. (1999). Brown diverts cash to green farming. *The Guardian*, 8 December.

Newton, I. (1998). *Population Limitations in Birds.* London: Academic Press.

Noble et al. (1999). *The Breeding Bird Survey 1998.* Thetford: BTO.

Nuttall, N. (1998). Silent Spring, 2020. *The Times*, 13 July.

O'Connor and Shrubb (1986). *Farming and Birds.* Cambridge: Cambridge University Press.

RSPB (1998). Birds are key indicators of healthy environment. Press Release, 23 November. Royal Society for the Protection of Birds.

RSPB (2000a). Autumn crops blamed for skylark declines. Press Release, 19 January. Royal Society for the Protection Of Birds.

RSPB (2000b). Lowest ebb on record for many UK birds. Press Release, 6 February. Royal Society for the Protection of Birds.

Sainsbury (1998). *1998 Environment Report.* London: J Sainsbury plc.

Sharrock, T. (1999). Panic ye not. *British Birds*, **92**, 442–444.

Siriwardena et al. (1998). Trends in the abundance of farmland birds: a quantitative comparison of smoothed Common Birds Census indices. *Journal of Applied Ecology*, 1998, **35**, 24–43.

Summers-Smith, D. (1998). *British Birds*, **91**, pp. 124–138.

Watson-Smyth, K. (1999). Farm subsidies have brought death to millions of songbirds. *The Independent*, 12 August.

Wynne, G. (2000). Become a Founder of the RSPB's Hope Farm. Promotional letter. Sandy: Royal Society for the Protection of Birds.

5 Genetically modified fear and the international regulation of biotechnology

Henry I. Miller and Gregory Conko

Introduction

International biotechnology regulation planned, promulgated and implemented by various agencies and instruments of the United Nations (UN) illustrates some of the perverse effects of applying the precautionary principle (PP). The PP states that often action ought to be taken to avoid a risk even when there is incomplete scientific evidence as to its magnitude or potential impacts. In practice, it has been interpreted to mean that a technology should not be used unless and until it has been shown to be absolutely safe. This means that the usual burden of proof is reversed: new technologies are assumed to be guilty until their innocence can be proven to a standard demanded by their critics which is impossible. Using the PP as justification, half a dozen UN programs or agencies have targeted biotechnology with a sweeping array of burdensome new regulations.

The UN's major regulatory and policing initiatives relating to biotechnology include a code of conduct and a Biosafety Protocol. These regulations have already severely compromised the potential of the new technology. Agricultural biotechnology has been particularly vulnerable, because while innovation is high, market incentives are small and fragile. Putting this another way, the regulations remove an important tool of crop breeders: the ability readily and rapidly to test large numbers of new varieties in field trials. In traditional plant breeding, each year an individual breeder of corn, soybean, wheat, or potato commonly tests in the field as many as 50,000 distinct new genetic variants (NRC, 1989). But stultifying regulation prevents this level of research activity for genetic variants developed with the newest and most precise techniques, variously known as genetic modification (GM), recombinant DNA technology, gene-splicing, or the new biotechnology. The new regulations have vastly increased the paperwork and costs of field-testing plant varieties created with the new biotechnology and offered cover to overly risk-averse, incompetent, or corrupt regulators, and have thus become potent disincentives to research and development (R&D) in many countries.

Ironically, many of the products of this R&D would offer environmental benefits, such as crop plants with greater yields and requiring less agricultural chemicals, biological alternatives to chemical pesticides, and various biological methods of cleaning up toxic wastes. As a result of unscientific and excessive regulation of biotechnology, however, companies around the world have seen their regulatory expenses skyrocket and their potential markets shrink. Many agricultural biotechnology companies have failed. In contrast to the biopharmaceutical sector, there are actually fewer 'agbiotech' companies in the United States now than a decade ago. Ultimately, consumers will pay inflated prices for over-regulated products and higher taxes to support bloated bureaucracies, and they will have fewer options in the marketplace. Agricultural biotechnology, touted in the 1970s as promising to increase food productivity in the developing world, has increasingly become a boutique technology applied to commodity crops for making high value-added products targeted at affluent consumers in industrialized countries, and relatively few plant species are in the commercial pipeline.

The precautionary principle

The underlying justification for these regressive, burdensome regulations is the precautionary principle, whose essence is that in the face of incomplete data, worst-case scenarios should dictate government policy. Dr Elizabeth M. Whelan, the president of the American Council on Science and Health, notes objections to the PP:

> First, it always assumes worst-case scenarios. Second, it distracts consumers and policy makers alike from the known and proven threats to human health. Third, it assumes no health detriment from the proposed regulations and restrictions. By that I mean that the PP overlooks the possibility that real public health risks can be associated with [expending resources on] eliminating minuscule, hypothetical risks.

> (Whelan, 1996)

Christopher Douglass at the Center for the Study of American Business has described the stepwise process by which the PP is incorporated into international public policy for, say, 'an environmental problem':

> The ultimate goal (of bureaucrats) is to attain the twin goals of bolstering 'scientific support' for the most risk-averse public policy outcome and for reaching a binding international agreement. UN agencies, national governments and NGOs work in concert, often in a carefully orchestrated way, to develop consensus on an international agreement via five steps: 1. scientific or interest group concern; 2. agenda-setting at unofficial conferences; 3. intergovernmental (usually ministerial level) meetings; 4. creation of a voluntary, or 'soft', multilateral agreement; and 5. development of a binding, or 'hard', agreement.

> (Douglass, 1998)

The PP has infiltrated many multilateral treaties, including the 1987 Montreal Protocol on Substances that Deplete the Ozone Layer, the 1992 Convention on Biological Diversity, the 1992 Climate Change Convention, the 1992 Treaty on European Union, the 1992 Convention for the Protection of the Marine Environment of the North-East Atlantic, and the 1992 Helsinki Convention, dealing with protection of the marine environment of the Baltic. International declarations containing the PP include the 1990 Bergen Declaration, issued by ministerial representatives from European countries (as well as Canada and the US), and the 1992 Rio Declaration on Environment and Development.

Biotechnology and the United Nations

Biotechnology is the immediate target of an increasing number – now exceeding a half dozen – of UN programs or agencies, which have proposed a sweeping array of new and unnecessary regulations. These regulatory and policing proposals have compromised the new technology's potential. In the face of over-regulation that has inflated the costs of R&D and consumer products, and created uncertainty about both the course of development and ultimate product acceptance, whence will come the impetus to work on plants that are the staples of subsistence agriculture, such as millet, yams, sorghum and cassava? There won't be any such impetus, of course, and the UN regulatory policies will contribute to famine, disease, and death. Especially disadvantaged with be those Asian countries that have made substantial investments in agricultural biotechnology – including the Philippines, Thailand, India, Singapore and China, whose programme is among the largest and most vigorous in the world – and African countries where hunger and nutritional deficiencies are endemic.

One of the new biotechnology's great advantages is that it became available almost immediately to those outside the industrialized countries. Since it builds on traditional agriculture and microbiology to help improve regionally important crops, the new biotechnology could be an important element in increasing food production in developing countries; but a burdensome international bureaucracy enforcing ill-conceived and excessive regulation will stall many of these benefits. Agricultural biotechnology is particularly vulnerable, because while innovation is high, market incentives are often small and fragile. Vastly increased paperwork and costs for field testing will be potent disincentives to R&D in many countries. For these nations whose economies have been ravaged by the economic 'Asian flu' of the late 1990s, in particular, it is difficult to imagine a worse time to cripple an important new enabling technology that could raise economic productivity and the efficiency of food production. Ironically, many proposed UN biotechnology regulations will also actually harm the environment. They will stifle the development of innovations that could help clean up toxic wastes, purify water, replace agricultural chemicals, and avoid cultivating additional land for farming. Classical plant genetics has already supplanted some chemical pesticides with pest- and disease-resistant varieties of wheat, rice, soybeans, corn and other staple crops, but further advances of this kind resulting from the use of gene-splicing will be slowed by UN policies.

Two regulatory documents are of particular concern to the future of agricultural biotechnology: the UN Industrial Development Organization's (UNIDO) 1992 'code of conduct' for field trials and the Biosafety Protocol (BSP) of the 1992 Convention on Biological Diversity (CBD, or informally, the 'Biodiversity Treaty'). The CBD's goals seem positive, but the BSP, finalized in Montreal in January 2000, has become the UN's Trojan horse, surreptitiously delivering ruinous biotechnology-averse regulatory policies to the developing world. The UNIDO code of conduct shares many of the disadvantages of the CBD but offers none of the latter's ostensible benefits. In addition, a task force of the Codex Alimentarius Commission, the joint food standards program of the UN's World Health Organization and Food and Agriculture Organization, met in Chiba, Japan, in March 2000 to begin discussions of issues related to biotechnology and food that will likely culminate in still more international standards.

The UNIDO Code of Conduct

UNIDO's unscientific and ill-conceived proposal was published on behalf of three other UN agencies: the United Nations Environment Program (UNEP), the World Health Organization (WHO), and the Food and Agriculture Organization (FAO). The preamble states that the purpose of this (currently) voluntary code of conduct is to 'provide help to governments in developing their own regulatory infrastructure and in establishing standards' for research and use of GMOs ('genetically manipulated organisms', defined as those crafted with the most advanced recombinant DNA techniques). Then it proceeds to dictate regulatory requirements in the most stringent, unscientific and self-serving terms. The document asserts that '[t]he UN is an obvious system through which to co-ordinate a world-wide effort to ensure that all [research and commercial applications of GMOs are] preceded by an appropriate assessment of risks' (*Anon.*, 1992), but it demonstrates a lack of even a rudimentary understanding of risk analysis. The document also defines as a principal goal to 'encourage and assist the establishment of appropriate national regulatory frameworks, particularly where no adequate infrastructure presently exists' (ibid.), but provides no economic strategies by which such frameworks could be created and sustained in developing countries.

The code requires the establishment of new environmental bureaucracies and demands that impoverished developing countries divert resources to the regulation of researchers who wish to perform even small-scale field trials of crops of local agronomic value, such as cassava, potatoes, rice, wheat and ornamental flowers. (By contrast, no oversight, no paperwork, no bureaucracy is required for the testing of new variants of indigenous plants or micro-organisms crafted with traditional genetic engineering techniques.) 'Every member country should designate a national authority or authorities to be responsible for handling enquiries and proposals, i.e., all contacts concerning the use and introductions of GMOs. More than one authority may be necessary ... Case-by-case evaluation should be the rule ...' (ibid.).

Finally, we get to the pay-off for the international regulators-in-waiting themselves. The code proposes that the UN 'establish an international biosafety information network and advisory service'. These entities would have a number of functions, among them information-gathering, advising and technical assistance on monitoring the environmental impacts of GMOs, and 'on request provide advice to assist in working toward the setting up of a designated national authority(ies) in each country'(ibid.).

Because UNIDO has produced this code of conduct, it should come as no surprise that 'UNIDO should take the lead ...' in offering these new consultancy services. The resources required would include 'a scientific steering committee ... [and] a small technical/administrative secretariat.' In addition, 'as a starting point, the service should conduct an international survey to identify existing expertise in the various scientific disciplines required for the safety assessment of biotechnology use.'(ibid.).

Nothing at all redeems these regulations or the 'make-work' program they require. Having got wrong the scope of what requires government review, the drafters hopefully and naively invoke the language but not the intent of the scientific consensus about biotech regulation: 'Regulatory oversight and risk assessment should focus on the characteristics of the product rather than the molecular or cellular techniques used to produce it'(ibid.). The world-wide scientific consensus on this point calls for the scope of oversight, and the degree of scrutiny, to be based on the risk-related characteristics of products – whether inert or living organisms. It categorically rejects the approach of the UN, in which regulatory triggers and discriminatory treatment are based on the use of genetic manipulation. The UN drafters reduce that pivotal point of scientific consensus to mere rhetoric as they forge ahead with a contradictory, expensive, and regressive regulatory system. In the process, they erect steep barriers to R&D, particularly for developing countries that aspire to meet some of their economic development and food security goals through the new biotechnology.

The obsession with regulating the new biotechnology is clearly contrary to the remit of the UN, and especially UNIDO, diverting resources away from health promotion and protection, where they could be of some genuine use. Better surely to spend money on research into the prevention of schistosomiasis, malaria, and AIDS; immunizing children against cholera, polio, and hepatitis; and developing genetically improved cultivars of staple crops such as millet, yams, rice, potatoes, and cassava.

The Biosafety Protocol (BSP) of the Convention on Biological Diversity (CBD)

A product of the 1992 UN Conference on Environment and Development (UNCED) – the so-called 'Earth Summit' held in Rio de Janeiro, Brazil – the CBD addresses a broad spectrum of issues related to the protection of biological diversity. Its stated intention, 'the conservation of habitats in developing nations', is commendable; and the agreement's specific goals are crafted to sound universally unobjectionable:

1 identifying and monitoring components of biological diversity, such as specific ecosystems and communities (Article 7);
2 establishing a system of protected areas (Article 8);
3 adopting measures for ex situ conservation (that is, preserving seeds or sperm in repositories under appropriate conditions);
4 integrating genetic resource conservation considerations into national decision-making and adopting incentives for the conservation of biological resources (Articles 10 and 11); and
5 developing assessment procedures for ensuring that impacts on biological diversity are considered in project design (Article 14).

Whilst on the surface these goals may appear unobjectionable, further inspection reveals that they are heavy on centralized planning and implementation, making them cumbersome and inflexible – not perhaps desirable characteristics to include in a piece of legislation intended to protect the most dynamic system on the planet. However, whatever one may think of the overall goals, they pale into insignificance in comparison to the proposed international Biosafety Protocol, which was to be developed as part of the CBD.

It is difficult to determine from the vague and sometimes contradictory language of the treaty whether the CBD actually required that a Biosafety Protocol be adopted by ratifying countries. For example, Article 8 calls for measures to 'regulate, manage or control the risks associated with the use and release of living modified organisms resulting from biotechnology which are likely to have adverse environmental impacts that could affect the conservation and sustainable use of biological diversity . . .'. Living Modified Organisms (LMOs) is yet another neologism for plants, animals, and microorganisms developed with new biotechnologies – an unscientific distinction based solely upon the techniques used in their development. Article 19 specifies that 'the Parties shall consider the need for and modalities of a protocol setting out appropriate procedures, including, in particular, advance informed agreement, in the field of safe transfer, handling and use of any living modified organism resulting from biotechnology that may have adverse effect on the conservation and sustainable use of biological diversity.'

At the heart of controversy over the protocol is the meaning of the CBD's phrase, 'any living modified organism resulting from biotechnology.' Among field trials of living organisms including micro-organisms, insects, fish, farm animals, crop plants and ornamental flowers, what, exactly, would be subject to regulation? All field trials? Certain organisms or field trials judged to be high-risk? Organisms crafted with certain specific genetic techniques? The CBD's scope is potentially broad: 'Biotechnology means any technological application that uses biological systems, living organisms or derivatives thereof, to make or modify products or processes for specific use' (CBD, 1992). And the advantage of such a broad definition is that, in theory, it provides latitude for circumscribing categories of organisms to be field-tested that deserve a government safety review, that is, a risk based approach focused on the product. In other words, case by case review could be limited to those categories judged to be of possible significant risk. Such a risk-based approach (Miller et al, 1990, Miller et al., 1995) would be more defensible scientifically than the process- or technique-focused approaches of the European Union (EC, 1994), the UNIDO code of conduct (Anon., 1992), or the biotechnology regulations of the US Environmental Protection Agency and Department of Agriculture (Miller, 1997). However, as discussed below, the scope of what is to be subject to case by case review has been narrowed in a way that focuses only on organisms modified with the newer, more precise molecular techniques, an approach that is wholly unrelated to the likelihood of risk that might be posed by their testing or use. This violates the fundamental principle of regulation that the degree of oversight should be commensurate with risk.

The slow development of an irrational protocol

The rational possibilities afforded by the wording of the CBD have however been overlooked. From the beginning, the international bureaucrats charged with crafting the details of the regulations have consistently and purposefully ignored the scientific consensus which repudiates their regulatory approach. An official document that describes the April 1993 proceedings of the expert panel established to implement these aspects of the CBD clarified the scope of the proposed regulations. According to paragraphs 57 and 58:

> . . . a majority of the Panel members believed the organisms covered by a possible protocol should be restricted to genetically modified organisms, along the lines of the EEC-Directive 90/220 on the Deliberate Release into the Environment of Genetically Modified Organisms which defines GMOs as organisms in which the genetic material has been altered in a way that does not occur naturally by mating and/or natural recombination. Annex 1 A of the Directive further specifies which techniques are covered and which are not.
>
> (Anon., 1993)

Annex 1 of that document states explicitly that the scope of regulation 'does not include organisms modified by traditional breeding methods', regardless of pathogenicity, likelihood of constituting an environmental nuisance, or other potential risks. Thus, the panel unabashedly endorsed an unscientific, technique-based definition of what requires regulation, which is unrelated to the risks posed. It is noteworthy that they did so in spite of a minority viewpoint cited in the panel's report that argued against limiting the scope to GMOs. The dissenting (and correct) view held that such a scope would be irrational and counterproductive because it 'would ignore organisms actually known to present a threat to biodiversity, while focusing on others for which only hypothetical analyses can be offered'(ibid.).

Why did the scientific view not carry the day? Representatives of the EU and, separately, those of Holland and the United Kingdom successfully convinced developing countries that their regulatory and development needs could be met by the same technique-based regulatory approach that currently impedes biotechnology research and commercialization in Europe. In characteristically paternalistic, if not imperialist, fashion, they offered themselves as consultants, to perform the required environmental assessments for their less-prepared counterparts in developing countries.

The miasma surrounding the crafting of the CBD's Biosafety Protocol was aptly summarized by (then) senior US Department of Agriculture scientist Val Giddings:

> It reveals how factions, driven more by hostility to biotechnology and other goals than concern for biodiversity, brought about the hijacking of a major portion of the energy and resources of the Convention. The impetus has thus been directed away from real and present threats to biodiversity toward an area (biotechnology) that is not a significant threat; furthermore, one that promises to enable major strides toward improved agricultural sustainability in both the industrial and developing worlds. A sadder litany of missed opportunities and misdirected efforts would be hard to find.

Giddings,1996

Paragraphs 74 and 75 of the April 1993 CBD panel proceedings report contain an ominous observation:

> a majority of the Panel members interpreted the language of Article 19.3, 'safe transfer, handling and use,' as if both international transfer of organisms and domestic handling and use of organisms were covered. The majority of the Panel members thought that domestic regulation should be covered by a possible protocol.'(emphasis added).

(Anon, 1993)

The implication is that CBD should be used to justify the elaboration of unscientific regulations, under the auspices of a Biosafety Protocol, that would exert negative impacts not only on R&D in the developing world and on international transfers and transactions, but also on domestic R&D.

After several meetings and the production of prodigious amounts of paper by participants on discussant panels, the nations that have ratified the CBD appeared to reach agreement on this issue at a conference in Jakarta in November 1995. At first, it appeared that the regulations would encompass both international (that is, trans-national) and domestic research and development. Then, according to a report in the Bureau of National Affairs (BNA) *Environment Daily* (20 November 1995), one of the key decisions made by the 1000-plus delegates at the Conference of the Parties was 'an agreement to draw up a protocol governing the transboundary movement of living modified organisms' (BNA, 1995) (emphasis added). Thus, signatory nations agreed to formulate an international protocol regulating the transfer of GMOs between states, and the agreement appeared not to extend to regulation of purely domestic testing or uses of organisms. As the journal *Nature* reported at the time, 'The agreement represents a compromise between the Group of 77 (G77) countries, which favored early enactment of a comprehensive protocol on biosafety, and the industrialized nations, which have been seeking the adoption of looser guidelines' (Masood, 1995). An open-ended Biosafety Working Group (BSWG), whose function was actually to craft definitions, procedures, and the other details of regulations, was created at that meeting. (The issue of exactly which activities will be regulated remains unresolved.)

At a meeting held in Cairo, 11–14 December 1995, by the United Nations Environment Program (UNEP), the group adopted the 'final text' of the UNEP Guidelines for Safety in Biotechnology and requested the UN to distribute them widely. Despite appearances to the contrary, this was not the actual Biosafety Protocol. That was to be produced by yet another panel, an 'open-ended Ad Hoc Working Group to develop in the field of the safe transfer, handling and use of living modified organisms, a protocol on biosafety'. But since it was expected to (and indeed did) take several years to conclude the protocol, it was deemed that 'a number of countries and intergovernmental, private sector and other organizations will need technical guidance of the kind contained in these Guidelines to fulfil their commitments under such an international agreement'(ibid.). That technical guidance was offered in a forty-two page treatise, entitled, 'Report of the Global Consultation of Government-Designated Experts on International Technical Guidelines for Safety in Biotechnology' (UNEP, 1995). Whilst appropriating the concept of 'familiarity' from earlier work such as the 1989 report of the US National Research Council (NRC, 1989) and various OECD publications (e.g. OECD, 1995), the UNEP group in Cairo tortured and misrepresented the concept, asserting that:

> there is generally less familiarity with the behaviour of organisms whose genetic make-up is unlikely to develop naturally, such as organisms produced by modern genetic modification techniques, than with the behaviour of organisms developed traditionally. This has been the reason why many countries have focused on such organisms and products containing them . . .'
>
> The guidelines provide assistance for identifying organisms whose characteristics may differ from those of the parent organisms from which they are derived in ways that would suggest additional scrutiny might be appropriate. This may be because they produce substances which are not found in the species concerned . . .'

(UNEP, 1995)

These are precisely the rationales that the scientific community has repudiated consistently and categorically during the past fifteen years. Intentionally or otherwise, the UNEP document misapprehends and misrepresents various concepts, including novelty, familiarity and risk. The conferees seem not to understand that the introduction into an organisms of a new gene 'even one in a location unlikely to occur in nature' does not necessarily affect an organism's relative risk. For example, a micro-organism or plant may have been modified to carry a biochemical or visual marker (such as firefly lucifierase, the protein that makes the insects glow in the dark) introduced by recombinant DNA techniques. If the host organism is known to pose negligible risk and the introduced gene does not make the new construct 'unfamiliar' in some way related to risk, then the modified organism should be treated no differently than the host organism or organisms with similar traits modified by traditional techniques. (Field tests of living organisms are traditionally unregulated, except in those rare instances where they are known or suspected plant or animal pathogens, or otherwise known to be a hazard.).

At the first meeting of the Biosafety Working Group, held in Aarhus, Denmark, in July 1996, the group tried to begin the drafting of a protocol but accomplished little. Rather, it was little more than a forum for defining issues and staking out positions. Governments listed issues for future discussion and negotiation and outlined the information required to guide their future work (Bai et al., 1998).

At the second BSWG meeting, held in May 1997 in Montreal, the participants addressed Advance Informed Agreement' (AIA), that is, notification procedures for transfers of LMOs; competent authorities/focal points; information-sharing and a clearing house mechanism; capacity-building; public participation and awareness; risk assessment and management; unintentional transboundary movement; handling, transportation, packaging and transit requirements; and monitoring and compliance (Bai *et al.*, 1998).

At the third BSWG meeting, held in Montreal in October 1997, delegates produced a draft text to serve as the basis for negotiation. Two 'Sub-Working Groups' were established to address the basic issues to be addressed in the protocol, as well as a 'contact group' on 'institutional matters' and 'final clauses.' In plenary, the issues addressed included: objectives, socio-economic considerations; liability and compensation; illegal traffic; non-discrimination; trade with non-Parties (countries that have not ratified the CBD); and other housekeeping issues (Bai *et al.*, 1998).

The Montreal Agreement and its consequences

A meeting of the parent group, the Conference of the Parties (COP) to the CBD, took place in May 1998 in Bratislava, Slovakia, provided for two more meetings to finalize the Biosafety Protocol, the first in August 1998 and the second in early 1999, to be followed by an 'extraordinary' meeting of the COP to adopt the protocol (Bai *et al.*, 1998).

The BSP was finalized and adopted at a meeting in Montreal in January 2000. Not surprising in view of the sordid history of negotiation described above, the parties agreed on a scheme that violates the principle that the degree of scrutiny should be commensurate with risk. The agreement singles out recombinant DNA-manipulated products for extraordinary regulatory scrutiny in spite of a total lack of evidence that such products deserve such special attention. The trigger for the regulatory regime is merely the fact of manipulation with recombinant DNA techniques, independent of risk, while other (non-recombinant) organisms known to be pathogenic or environmental nuisances may be subject to no oversight at all.

The goal of the UN's biosafety protocol is ostensibly to ensure that the development, handling, transport, field testing and use of recombinant DNA-manipulated organisms into the environment are 'undertaken in a manner that prevents or reduces the risks to biological diversity, taking also into account risks to human health' (BNA, 2000). It was also hoped that a multilateral agreement would promote regulatory uniformity and predictability, in order that the global development of beneficial recombinant DNA-manipulated organisms could proceed. But even a cursory examination of the protocol shows that the agreement has less to do with legitimate concerns about public health and the environment and more to do with trade protectionism and pandering to anti-technology sentiments.

The protocol is certain to slow the pace of technological progress. Although the unnecessary restrictions to the international trade in goods produced with the new biotechnology will no doubt be debilitating, its greatest effect will be to hobble the work of academic researchers and small, innovative companies, ultimately delaying or denying the benefits of the 'gene revolution' to much of the world.

The primary regulatory mechanism of the protocol is the Advanced Informed Agreement (AIA) provisions mentioned above, which require the importing nation's government to approve or reject the first shipment of each new variety of Living Modified Organism intended to be released into the environment – that is, genetically modified seeds, or live plants, animals, or micro-organisms (Article 7). Under the protocol, the importing nation is given 270 days in which to make its decision, but there is no provision for the enforcement of this time limit, and the government's failure to respond does not imply consent (Article 9). 'Co-operative procedures and institutional mechanisms to promote compliance' were left to be negotiated at a later date (Article 34).

The essence of agricultural research is getting large numbers of experiments into field trials as rapidly and easily as possible, so one can imagine how a regulatory delay of at least nine months will adversely impede the transboundary flow of improved seeds and other agricultural products. Yet, though the entire Advanced Informed Agreement process could have been opposed on principle, political manoeuvring by the major agricultural exporting nations attempted only to secure a carve-out exemption from the AIA provisions for their large agribusiness constituents. This ploy succeeded, but at the expense of researchers interested in creating crop plants, animals, and beneficial micro-organisms for planting and propagation in other countries.

A coalition of six major agricultural exporting countries, known as the Miami Group, were able to get an exemption from the burdensome Advanced Informed Agreement procedures for shipments of grains, fresh fruits and vegetables, and other harvested agricultural goods, which are intended for use as food, animal feeds, or for processing (Article 11). This alternative approval mechanism provides at least temporary protection for large shipments of commodity grains, the largest current source of LMO export. With this provision secured, both the Miami Group governments and the biotechnology industry now believe that the Biosafety Protocol establishes a uniform international framework under which they can operate, and gives importing nations no more right to exclude biotech products than they had before the Montreal agreement (Hodgson, 2000). In the end, however, they may get much less than they bargained for.

Following the consensus reached in Montreal, the final protocol will enter into force once it is ratified by 50 member nations, which is likely to occur by the end of 2000. The question for policymakers will then become one of implementation. The agreement requires participating nations to construct regulatory systems that promote the goals of the protocol, but it leaves them wide discretion as to how this was to be done. That discretion gives government officials political cover for all manner of dubious objections to the testing and use of GMOs. One can only hope that the concerted influence of the scientific community and those committed to free trade might encourage governments to establish risk-based regulatory schemes focused on legitimate risks. Such speculation, it is admitted, exemplifies the triumph of hope over experience.

The protocol is based on a 'precautionary approach' to regulation, as described in the 1992 Rio Declaration on Environment and Development: 'Where there are threats of serious or irreversible damage, lack of full scientific certainty shall not be used as a reason for postponing cost-effective measures to prevent environmental degradation.'(UN, 1992). The completed Protocol refers to or paraphrases the Rio Declaration's precautionary language some five times (Preamble, Article 1, Article 10, Article 11, and Annex III) (BSP, 2000). This precautionary approach is simply a euphemism for the 'precautionary principle' itself, as discussed above, a neologism coined by opponents of technology who wish to rationalize banning or over-regulating things they don't like, such as gene-splicing, cellular phones, oil exploration and carbon dioxide emissions.

Precaution, in this sense, shifts the burden of proof from the regulator, who once had to demonstrate that a new technology was likely to cause some harm before intervening in its use, to the innovator, who now must demonstrate that the technology will not cause any harm. Thus, rather than creating a uniform, predictable, and scientifically sound framework for effectively managing legitimate risks, the BSP establishes an ill-defined global regulatory process that permits overly risk-averse, incompetent, and corrupt regulators to hide behind the precautionary principle in delaying or deferring approvals. Witness the regulatory feeding frenzy spawned by unscientific approaches to biotech regulation in Europe and at the US Environment Protection Agency (EPA) and Department of Agriculture. The result has been the virtual disappearance of gene-spliced foods from the shelves of European markets, inhibition of agbiotech research at US universities, and the near-elimination of US biotech companies' once highly-touted research on microbial pesticides and bioremediation.

Furthermore, while its proponents advise that the Precautionary Principle should not be used 'as a disguised form of protectionism' (see, for example, EC, 2000), there is no clearly defined evidentiary standard that could be used scientifically to satisfy demands for an assurance of "safety." Under this new standard of evidence, regulatory bodies are free arbitrarily to require any amount and kind of testing they wish. Consequently, claims of disguised protectionism are inherently difficult, if not impossible, to prove. Nor is their any procedural safeguard in the Biosafety Protocol – or any other document that incorporates the precautionary principle – that would serve to make such (barely) disguised protectionism less likely.

In Europe, the PP is becoming an ever more popular excuse to limit the introduction of new technologies. In February 2000, the German government decided arbitrarily and capriciously – and at the eleventh hour – to block the commercial-scale cultivation of gene-spliced Bt-corn by the biotechnology company Novartis. This action came one day before the new variety was expected to be approved for commercial use by the Ministry of Agriculture, which specifically cited the need to respect the precautionary principle and called for more research into the crop plant's potential hazards.

Yet, while the planting of biotech seeds may be prohibited within a given nation's borders, the Miami Group governments believe that language included in the Biosafety protocol's preamble, will protect shipments of harvested agricultural goods from their jurisdictions. This 'savings clause' holds that 'this Protocol shall not be interpreted as implying a change in the rights and obligations of a Party under any existing international agreements' (Preamble, BSP, 2000).

In particular, the Miami Group nations wanted to ensure that the protocol did not take precedence over certain trade agreements, including the General Agreement on Tariffs and Trade (GATT) and its World Trade Organization (WTO). Miami Group representatives believe that this savings clause will prevent overly risk-averse or protectionism-minded governments from shutting off trade in biotech commodities. One spokesman for the US Biotechnology Industry Organization has argued that, regardless of what the Biosafety Protocol allows nations to do, under the WTO, international shipments of biotech goods may not be refused without a valid scientific demonstration of a true risk (Hodgson, 2000).

In general, this is a reasonably valid understanding of nations' rights and obligations under the WTO. The GATT/WTO Agreement on the Application of Sanitary and Phytosanitary Measures (SPS) has provided generally strong protection for trade. When challenged, the SPS ostensibly requires nations to introduce compelling scientific evidence in defence of their environmental and public health measures; but the WTO has, at times, been somewhat permissive when evaluating nations' environmental laws. With a finalized agreement for the international regulation of the new biotechnology, it is at best unclear whether or not the WTO will act to overrule unscientific regulatory decisions made under the aegis of the Biosafety Protocol.

As is noted in a recent communication from the Commission of the European Communities on the precautionary principle, the WTO specifically gives countries leeway in enacting regulatory measures intended to protect the environment (CEC, 2000). Although WTO member nations may not take regulatory actions that clearly discriminate against imported goods *vis-à-vis* domestic goods, Article XX of the GATT specifically allows WTO members to place environmental goals above their general obligation to promote trade, provided that the actions do not improperly discriminate against imports (GATT, 1994). Conceivably, the Biosafety Protocol could become a regulatory 'safe harbour' – that is, so long as nations prohibit agbiotech products domestically, they may then also be free to prohibit agbiotech imports, finding justification for this unscientific posture under Article XX of the GATT.

An interesting object lesson is provided by the now infamous WTO Shrimp-Turtle case, often cited (improperly) by environmental activists as an example of trade superseding environmental protection. In that case, the WTO's dispute settlement panel and its Appellate Body both overruled a US ban on shrimp imported from countries that did not require fishermen to use Turtle-Excluder Devices in their nets. The Appellate Body specifically held that the environmental goal of protecting endangered sea turtles was a valid one under the WTO, because it 'relates to the protection of exhaustible natural resources' permitted under Article XX of the General Agreement on Tariffs and Trade (GATT) 1994. The Appellate Body ruled the US restriction invalid only because it would have forced fishermen in the exporting countries to use a specific technology to achieve that goal and would have precluded all imports from those countries even if only some fishermen were found not to be using the devices (WTO, 1998). Given its more recent history, it is not unreasonable to speculate that the WTO will find precautionary regulatory actions to be valid, even when they do not meet the standards of scientific evidence otherwise demanded by the SPS, solely because they have been taken under the Biosafety Protocol.

A source of additional confusion is Article 22 of the Convention on Biological Diversity, of which the Biosafety protocol is a part; it stipulates that rights and obligations under existing international agreements are not to be affected 'except where the exercise of those rights and obligations would cause serious damage or threat to biological diversity' (CBD, 1992). Although what kinds of activities might constitute 'serious damage or threat to biological diversity' is likely to be a matter of some dispute, it is conceivable that this clause too could be interpreted by the WTO Trade Policy Review Mechanism as permitting unscientific restrictions on GMOs enacted by nations under the aegis of the Convention and its subsidiary Protocol. Ultimately, it is not clear, ex ante, that the WTO will overrule all but the most blatant abuses of precautionary regulation.

The Codex Alimentarius considers food biotechnology

Because there still is some uncertainty in how the WTO is likely to handle its relationship to the Biosafety Protocol, the European Union and environmental activists are trying to undermine the WTO more directly by writing the precautionary principle into the SPS itself and the agreements of the Codex Alimentarius Commission, the joint food standards program of the United Nations' World Health Organization and Food and Agriculture Organization. Parties to the Codex Alimentarius Commission are not directly bound by its regulatory principles, but the WTO tends to defer to Codex principles for guidance on acceptable regulatory decisions. Naturally, Codex measures have a great influence on international trade.

In March 2000, a task force of the 165-member Codex Alimentarius Commission, met in Chiba, Japan, to begin discussions of issues related to biotechnology and food. It began auspiciously, with Thomas J. Billy, the temporary chairman of the Codex (and senior US Department of Agriculture official), noting that biotechnology is merely 'a new name or label for a process people have used as long as we have been baking bread, fermenting wine or making cheese, or cultivating crops and breeding animals.' He alluded to the scientific consensus that biotech is a continuum of new and old technologies, and that modern gene-splicing techniques are 'essentially a refinement of the kinds of genetic modification long used to enhance micro-organisms, plants and animals for food.' Then he posed the central question about biotech regulation: 'Is the method by which a product was created the important issue, or is it the [product's] characteristics' that should be a trigger to regulatory oversight? He concluded rightly that scientific consensus and the lengthy history of food regulation argue that the risk-based characteristics of a new product – for example, changes in allergenicity or levels of endogenous toxins – are most important, regardless of the production techniques used.

Neither Billy's scientific approach nor his pivotal conclusions were heard from again. Instead, the group moved deliberately toward circumscribing only food products made with gene-splicing for various draconian and even bizarre regulatory procedures and requirements that will impair the competitiveness of these products in the marketplace. The creation of obstacles was, of course, exactly the agenda of many of those assembled. Their motivations vary: The

Europeans, especially the European Commission and France, want to stop gene-spliced products because they're mostly made by American companies, and the radical environmental NGOs (who are permitted to participate in Codex meetings) are ideologically opposed to new technology.

Faced with initial antagonism to the USA's positions from other countries and NGOs, which is not unusual at international negotiations on regulatory issues, the US delegation commonly sets the tone by insisting on adherence to scientific principles and explains the scientific basis for its own regulatory policy. For example, the Food and Drug Administration's (FDA) exemplary 1992 policy on 'new plant varieties' applies irrespective of whether the plant arose from gene-splicing or 'conventional' genetic engineering methods. The FDA does not routinely subject foods from new plant varieties to pre-market review or to extensive scientific safety testing. Instead, it considers that the usual safety and quality control practices used by plant breeders – mostly chemical and visual analyses and taste testing – are generally adequate for ensuring food safety. The FDA's policy does, however, define certain safety-related characteristics of new foods that would require consultation and review by the agency. Foods lacking such characteristics are not required to undergo pre-market review, although the FDA maintains a 'voluntary consultation procedure' under which food manufacturers consult with the agency before marketing a biotech-derived food. This policy has worked admirably for eight years.

What was anomalous at the Codex task force meeting was that the US delegation, headed by FDA food regulator Robert Lake, never cited the important principle that the degree of regulatory scrutiny should be commensurate with risk. They never invoked the scientific consensus about the essential equivalence between old and new biotech. They never mentioned the FDA's risk-based approach. Instead, they went with the flow, which seems destined to carry food biotech down the drain.

This first session of the task force, which is scheduled to complete its work in 2003, was dominated by the relentlessly anti-biotech European Commission, which advocates both the creation of overt obstacles to gene-splicing applied to food and agriculture, and also vagueness in regulatory definitions and concepts. This ensures that regulators can be as arbitrary and capricious as they wish. Their opposition to biotechnology was nothing new. What was new was the USA singing the Europeans' anti-biotech tune. The reasons for this change are purely political. Under pressure from anti-technology extremists and the Clinton administration, according to senior FDA officials, the FDA plans to repudiate both its well-tested, much-praised policy on new plant varieties and its 20-year-old commitment not to discriminate against gene-spliced products generally: the agency expects to announce a new requirement that all gene-spliced foods come to the agency for pre-market evaluation. FDA officials orchestrated the phoney 'pressure' for such a change by holding public meetings at the end of last year that offered activists an opportunity to stuff the ballot box, and at which radical opponents of biotechnology were given vastly disproportionate representation.

This impending deterioration in domestic regulatory policy tied the US delegation's hands at the Codex task force – and will continue to do so in other international forums. Knowing that their own policy will soon contravene the scientific consensus about biotech regulation constrains FDA officials from pushing the scientific line. As a result, the Codex task force is en route to codifying various procedures and requirements more appropriate to potentially dangerous prescription drugs or pesticides than to gene-spliced tomatoes, potatoes and strawberries. They include long-term monitoring for adverse health effects and batteries of tests for genetic stability, toxins, allergenicity, and so on. Among the most egregious is something called 'traceability,' an array of technical, labelling and record-keeping mechanisms to keep track of a plant 'from dirt to dinner plate', so that consumers will know whom to sue if they get diarrhoea from gene-spliced prunes, and providing, in the words of the European Commission delegate, 'a tool governments can use to remove products from the market.'

The prospect of unscientific, overly burdensome Codex standards for gene-spliced foods is ominous, because members of the World Trade Organization will, in principle, be required to follow them, and they will provide cover for unfair trade practices. Jean Halloran, of the anti-biotech group Consumers International, characterized Codex standards as a legal defence against WTO challenges to countries that arbitrarily stop trade in biotech foods. 'The Codex is important because of the WTO. If there is a Codex standard, one country cannot file a challenge [for unfair trade practices] against another country which is following the Codex standard. But when there is no Codex standard, countries can challenge each other on anything.' (Anon, 2000).

The unprincipled precautionary principle

Focusing mainly on the possibility that new products may pose theoretical risks, the precautionary principle applied to agricultural and food bio-technology ignores very real, existing risks that could be mitigated or eliminated by those products. If the precautionary principle had been applied decades ago to innovations like polio vaccines and antibiotics, regulators might have prevented occasionally serious, and sometimes fatal, side effects by delaying or denying approval of those products, but that precaution would have come at the expense of millions of lives lost to infectious diseases. Instead of demanding assurance of safety that approaches absolute certainty, the goal should be to balance the risk of accepting new products too quickly (Type I error in the parlance of risk-assessment) against the risks of delaying or forgoing new technologies (Type II error). Because individuals' tolerance for risk is so heterogeneous, regulators should be open to greater informed choice by the end-users of technology.

More than one billion people in the world now live on less than a dollar a day, and hundreds of millions are severely malnourished (World Bank, 1997). By increasing the efficiency of agriculture and food production in myriad ways, recombinant DNA-derived products can significantly increase the availability and nutritional value of foods and reduce their cost. However, the application of the precautionary principle will stall progress and exact a substantial human toll. The huge stakes – both in human and commercial terms – demand that within the flawed regulatory paradigm agreed upon in Montreal, regulators create scientifically sound, risk-based frameworks for the regulation of GMOs.

In view of these extraordinary efforts to craft wrong-headed regulation, one might wonder at what motivates UN and national officials to implement anti-social public policy. It may be that they feel there is reason to believe that the products of the new biotechnology do genuinely pose incremental hazards, that public concerns argue for excessive regulation, or perhaps that the PP is valid. However, careful examination of the positions and interventions of various nations suggests that the underlying agenda is self-interest.

Consider, first, the regulators. More specifically, consider the conduct of regulators in the context of economist Milton Friedman's observation that individuals and institutions most often act in their own self-interest, even if those actions are inimical to the public interest. Most regulators participating in the drafting of the Biosafety Protocol were environmental regulators, whose mandates, domains and budgets traditionally have not been large. It is hardly surprising, then, that these regulators welcomed a new international agreement that dictates new regulatory responsibilities 'namely, the requirement for case by case reviews of proposals and approvals before field testing can proceed (or expand to larger scale, additional sites or the use of other distinct but similar genetic variants). A more rational, risk-based approach (as exists for non-gene-spliced organisms, where in general, only organisms known to be plant pests or hazardous in other ways trigger case by case evaluation) would leave the vast majority of field trials exempt from case by case government review, denying regulators any enhancement of their professional responsibilities, budgets and influence. (The PP may be seen to be a useful tool to the ambitious bureaucrat in this strategy: 'erring on the side of caution' is a convenient rationale for excessive, anti-innovative regulation.)

Second, and less obvious, many developing countries' interventions at the BSP and Codex meetings reveal their hunger for 'capacity-building and financial resources' along with compensatory guarantees through liability and socio-economic considerations'. These are the code words for more largesse, more welfare flowing from north to south. Specifically, officials from the developing countries appear to believe that the industrialized countries are going to bankroll the establishment and maintenance of their new regulatory apparatus; and to pay large compensatory damages if, say, Japanese microbiologists develop a yeast that produces extractable vanilla and disenfranchises exporters of vanilla beans in Madagascar and Mauritius.

Third, it seems obvious that the extravagant and gratuitous regulation required by the Biosafety Protocol (and in the future, perhaps, Codex standards) will not be implemented in developing countries if industrialized countries do not provide the resources for the 'capacity-building and financial resources', both in-country and internationally. Even if regulatory infra-structures were established, in many countries they would likely be inefficient and corrupt, a particular concern where every field trial would be subject to the vagaries of case by case pre-testing and pre-marketing review. One cannot ignore the likelihood that in order to perform testing in certain countries, bribes – either overt or camouflaged – will change hands between government regulators and those wishing to perform the field trials. One has to ask whether this arrangement will create positive incentives for R&D using a new technology?

Biotech-regulator 'wannabes' in developing countries may think mis-takenly that they are in a no-lose situation; that is, that the worst-case scenario is that the excessive regulatory regimes will leave them with virtually no biotech R&D activity, which is where they expect to end up with anyway. These officials reason, therefore, that any outside support for such 'capacity-building', even if it is part of an anti-innovative regulatory regime, is advantageous: they can, after all, cannibalize the resources for other things, and R&D be damned. (For most countries, biotech field trials will be rather a rare occurrence in the best of circumstances). However, the myopic or cynical decisions of their regulators have real costs for citizens of the UN's member nations, for it is these citizens who continue to pay for both the direct expense of the recurring international seances, as well as the indirect expense of ultimate compliance with the new regulations. In the longer-term, the added expense of unnecessary case by case review of essentially negligible-risk activities will, as discussed above, serve as a potent disincentive to R&D, especially on low value-added products such as those involved in agriculture in general and subsistence farming in particular. The result will be that many countries will become no more than spectators to the revolution in agricultural biotechnology.

Conclusion

New regimes for the international regulation of biotechnology have been discussed. These regimes, spearheaded by various UN agencies, are planning or have promulgated programmes that are unscientific and over-regulatory. They favour bureaucrats' self-interest but stifle the innovation and use of products that might help to increase food production, clean up toxic wastes, purify water, supplant agricultural chemicals, and reduce the need for putting additional land under cultivation.

Regulators and environmentalists from industrialized countries regard the third-world as an opportunity to impose regulations based upon their own minority view of unique biotechnology risks, and to promote their own importance as policy players on a larger stage. They invoke the precautionary principle to justify policies that will systematically undermine research on precisely the kinds of products that are most needed in developing countries: more plentiful and nutritious foods and biological alternatives to chemical pesticides and fertilizers.

One wonders what the positive impacts would have been if, instead of imperiously anointing itself the world's biotechnology-regulator, the UN had undertaken to explain to the world's opinion leaders and citizens the continuum between old and new biotechnology, the greater precision and predictability of the newer techniques, and the benefits that would accrue from overseeing the new biotechnology in a scientific and common sense way. Perhaps there would truly have been a brave new world.

References

Anon. (1992). *Biotech Forum Eur* **9**, 218–21.

Anon. (1993). Expert panels established to follow-up on the convention on biological diversity. Report of Panel IV, UNEP/Bio.Div/Panels/Inf. 1, 28 April.

Anon. (2000). GMO foe sees standards as WTO lever. *Japan Times*, 18 march, p. 3.

Bai, C., Burgiel, Rajmani, L., Prather, T., and Wagner, L. (1998). *Earth Negotiations Bulletin* **9**, 31 August www.isisd.ca/linkages/download/asc/enb09108e.txt.)

BNA (1995). *Bureau of National Affairs Environment Daily,* November 20.

BNA (2000). Draft Protocol on Biosafety Issues to UN Convention on Biological Diversity, Daily Environment Report. Washington DC, Bureau of National Affairs, January 31, E1–10.

BSP (2000). Cartagena Protocol on Biosafety to the Convention on Biological Diversity.

CBD (1992). United Nations Convention on Biological Diversity. New York: United Nations.

CEQ (1982). Council on Environmental Quality Annual Report. Washington, DC: Council on Environmental Quality.

Cohrssen, J. (2000). The world through emerald-colored glasses. In *The Greening of US Foreign Policy* (T. Anderson and H. Miller, eds). In press.

Douglass, Christopher (1998). Environmental crossing guards: international environmental treaties and US foreign policy. Center for the Study of American Business, Working Paper 168, May.

European Commission (EC) (1994). *Biotechnology Risk Control.* Luxembourg: Office for Official Publications of the European Communities.

European Commission (EC) (2000). Communication from the Commission on the Precautionary Principle. Brussels, 2 February, COM (2000) 1.

GATT (1994). General Agreement on Tariffs and Trade as Amended.

Giddings, L.V. (1996). A convention unmasked. *Nature Biotechnology,* **14**, 1304–5.

Hodgson, J. (2000). Biosafety rules get thumbs up. *Nature Biotechnology,* **18**, 253.

Masood, E. (1995). Biosafety rules will regulate international GMO transfers. *Nature,* **378**, 326.

Miller H.I., Burris R.H., Vidaver A.K et al.(1990). Risk-based oversight of experiments in the environment. *Science,* **250**, 490.

Miller, H.I., Altman, D.W., Barton, J.H. et al. (1995). Biotechnology oversight in developing countries: a risk-based algorithm. *Bio/Technology,* **13**, 955.

Miller, H.I. (1997). *Policy Controversy In Biotechnology: An Insider's View*. Austin, TX: R.G. Landes Co. and Academic Press.

National Research Council (NRC) (1989). *Field Testing Genetically Modified Organisms: Framework for Decisions*. Washington, DC: National Academy Press.

OECD (1995). *Safety Considerations for Biotechnology: Scale-up of Microorganisms as Biofertilizers*. Paris: OECD.

United Nations (UN) (1992). Rio Declaration on Environment and Development. New York: United Nations, UN Doc. A/CONF.151/26 (I); 31 ILM. 874.

United Nations Environment Program (UNEP) (1995). UNEP/Global Consultation/ Biosafety/4. Nairobi: United Nations Environment Programme, 19 December

Whelan, E.M./ (1996). Our 'stolen future' and the precautionary principle. *Priorities*, **8**, 32–33.

World Bank (1997). *Rural Development: From Vision to Action*. Washington DC, The World Bank.

World Trade Organization (1998). United States – import prohibition of certain shrimp and shrimp products. Appellate Body Report. WTO Doc. WT/DS58/AB/R (October 12).

6 Asteroid collisions and precautionary thinking

Charles T. Rubin

Introduction

Not all threats to the integrity of natural ecosystems are man made. One such threat receiving increasing attention is the possibility of collision between Earth and asteroids or comets that cross Earth's orbit, called 'near Earth objects' or NEOs (Lewis, 1996b; Morrison, 1992). A recent spate of movies, popular books and articles follows a steadily increasing interest among scientists and engineers. While to my knowledge the precautionary principle has not been explicitly introduced into considerations about what might be done with respect to this hazard, it has implicitly played an important role in framing discussions of the nature of this threat and what to do about it. The discussion below highlights the paradoxical result produced by precautionary thinking in this case. On the one hand, such thinking emphasizes the importance of taking urgent action to forestall the potentially devastating harm of a collision. On the other hand, it emphasizes the grave danger of taking such action. In order to resolve this paradox alternative ways of conceptualizing the problem are considered.

Bits and pieces of space debris slam into Earth all the time; on almost any night we see pea-sized chunks burning up in the form of shooting stars. About 40 000 tons of material of this size and smaller enter the atmosphere every year (Steel, 1995, p. 113). Larger chunks, from 1–15 metres in size, collide on a monthly to yearly basis. They usually explode high in the atmosphere; we see some of them as fireballs; sometimes they are even bright enough to be visible during the day. The explosive power involved can be substantial; it is estimated that once a year an explosion occurs high in the atmosphere that has the force of the Hiroshima nuclear bomb (10–20 kilotons) (Morrison et al., 1994, p. 63). Sometimes conditions (primarily the object's physical composition) allow chunks of the NEO to reach the ground to become what we call meteorites. Recovered meteorites weigh from ounces to tens of tons (Verschuur, 1996, p. 33). There are no recent, well documented cases of meteorites killing anyone, although it seems not unknown to history (Lewis, 1996b, p. 162). They do knock into cars and houses, and not long ago a golfer had a small one dig up a divot right at his feet.

As compared with these daily to yearly harmless and nearly harmless events, on a time-scale of centuries to thousands to millions of years, much larger objects produce far more serious consequences, ranging from the locally to the globally catastrophic. For example, in 1908 an object exploded over the Tunguska river valley in Russia, flattening trees for about 18 miles in all directions (Lewis, 1996, p. 54). It is estimated that the explosion took place at about 24 000 feet and was in the range of 10–20 megatons (ibid., p. 62). The body causing it was probably about 60 metres in diameter (Morrison, 1992, p. 8). An event of this sort probably happens once every 100 to 1000 years; it might strike a populated area every 3000 years. Were such an object to explode over a large city, hundreds of thousands of people would be killed (ibid., pp. 8, 11). Objects from 100 m to one km in diameter probably strike the Earth about every 5000 years; if they impact on land they would produce a crater about 2 km in diameter, and have a zone of destruction of over 10 km in diameter (ibid., p. 9). Landing in the ocean, a 200 m object might produce a tsunami (tidal wave) that would be 200 m high when the wave broke on shore – enough to inundate Holland, Denmark, Long Island and Manhattan. Hundreds of millions of people might die (Verschuur, 1996, p. 153).

Objects from 1 to 5 km in diameter probably strike land once every 300 000 years, producing craters 10 to 15 times their size. Even at the lowest end of the scale, these objects (of which there are an estimated 2000) are big enough, it is argued, to produce global scale catastrophe, due both to their immediate impact effects and the climate changes it is argued they would produce (Morrison, 1992, p. 9). Finally, every 10 to 30 million or so years, we can expect a strike from an object larger than 5 km. It was an object on this scale that is theorized by many to have brought about the extinction of dinosaurs. It is thought to have been in the range of 10–15 km, with an explosive force of over 100 million megatons (ibid., p. 10).

Precautionary thinking about NEOs

The picture emerging, then, is that we can be certain that at some point in the future – however far away – seriously dangerous NEO impacts will take place. The situation with regard to Earth-crossing NEOs is clearly one that involves a grave, if not at any given moment likely, threat at least to the well being of vast numbers of human beings, and also to natural ecosystems. There are various approaches to risk management under these circumstances.

The first might be called the strong precautionary principle, a fair summary of which has been provided by Daniel Bodansky (1991, p. 4): 'In essence, this principle says that, rather than await certainty, regulators should act in anticipation of environmental harm to ensure that this harm does not occur . . .'. Thus, in 'its strictest interpretation it suggests that no action should be taken if there is any likelihood at all, however small, that significant environmental damage could occur. This likelihood may be independent of the scientific evidence. That is, unless there is certainty that there are *no* detrimental effects, actions should not be taken which, for example, release harmful pollutants into the environment' (Pearce, 1994, p. 132) So understood, one rationale for the principle is that 'conventional scientific methods . . . may not be enough to instil confidence', particularly with regard to 'possible catastrophic convulsions in human use of the Earth. . . .'(O'Riordan and Cameron, 1994b, pp. 14, 15).

The 1992 Rio Declaration enshrines a weaker version of the principle, given that there are added, limiting characterizations of the 'harm' in question and of the nature of appropriate responses: 'Where there are threats of serious or irreversible damage, lack of full scientific certainty should not be used as a reason for postponing cost-effective measures to prevent environmental degradation' (cited by Th. Douma, 2000). Not any and every damage justifies precautionary measures, then, and in cases where 'serious or irreversible damage' is in question, the response must still be cost-effective.

In both cases, the net result of precaution, it has been noted, is 'a high degree of risk aversion on the part of the decision maker' (Pearce, 1994, p. 132). The difference between strong and weak precaution is further obscured to the extent that this risk aversion is intended to apply particularly to supporting the 'intrinsic natural right' of those systems (O'Riordan and Cameron, 1994b, p. 18). Serious harm within this context is not the same as serious harm to nature understood as a legitimate tool for human use. Furthermore, given the potential decoupling between present empirical knowledge and the problem foreseen (Costanza and Cornwell, 1992), precautionary thinking amounts to a form of worst-case analysis, or more precisely the worst *imaginable* case. This tendency, along with the deliberate 'bias' in favour of natural ecosystems (Bodansky, 1991, p. 5), undercuts the element of 'proportionality of response to risk' that the weaker formulations of the principle attempt to introduce, since it will always be difficult to argue that we should not expend resources to forestall the worst we can imagine.

The precautionary principle, however, is not the only way of formulating a response to NEO risks. Comparative risk assessment, placing the NEO danger in context with other risks we face and respond to, may help decide whether the NEO threat is of such a magnitude that we need to respond to it, what level of response is appropriate, given the policies developed in comparable cases – if there are any. Alternatively, different responses to NEO collision could be analysed in terms of the risk trade-offs they would produce. Such trade-offs result from the possibility that in doing away with one adverse outcome, another is generated. More worryingly perhaps (especially in terms of evaluating the trade-off), it may be that in reducing the risk to one group of people, another group of people are exposed to a new risk. Knowing the extent to which these trade-offs exist is a necessary prelude to efforts to reduce the risk faced by society (Graham and Wiener, 1995b).

It is argued below that although elements of comparative risk assessment and risk trade-off approaches are seen in discussions of what to do about NEO impacts, they are typically framed by precautionary thinking. This is most probably a result of the fact that the threat of a large NEO collision is *sui generis* – no other natural hazards are known which pose such dramatic possibilities of global havoc as those at the upper ranges of NEO collisions (Morrison et al. 1994, p. 78). At the same time, a case for action against NEOs made on comparative risk grounds might be biased by the fact that within the comparison pool will be hazards against which action is taken already on precautionary grounds (in other words, action against these other hazards is not justified by a rigorous comparative risk-benefit assessment).

Before considering the implications of applying the precautionary principle to the NEO threat, it is first necessary to ask whether the precautionary principle should be applied to this class of threat at all. From an 'ecocentric' perspective, it might be argued that interfering in the course of nature is wrong. NEOs are no less part of the natural order than are volcanoes and earthquakes, so following ecocentric reasoning nothing should be done about them. However, this objection is convincing only if we are willing from the start to read human beings out of nature entirely, that is, if the precautionary principle is not just anti-anthropocentric but overtly misanthropic. Other species are, within their capacities, expected to act in ways that preserve themselves and foster the conditions necessary for their existence. Furthermore, if it were possible to forestall an NEO collision, it would not only be humankind that would benefit, but the order of nature on Earth as we presently know it as a whole. Inasmuch as the precautionary principle favours the status quo above anything else, it would seem to be incompatible with the ecocentric argument against actions to avert NEO collisions (O'Riordan and Cameron, 1994b, p. 16).

The worst case scenario

Two key elements of precautionary reasoning are inherent in the case for action as developed by proponents: worst case thinking and the elision of unknowns that it produces. For example, in a popular book, radio-astronomer Gerrit Verschuur spends a chapter trying to imagine what it would have been like 60 million years ago when the asteroid strike some believe brought about dinosaur extinction (known as the K/T impact) took place:

> As regards the likelihood of survival at the time of the K/T impact, any creature above the surface within about 5 000 kilometres would not live. If you weren't roasted, killed by the pressure of the blast, blown away, cooked in the hot winds, or dashed to death by the earthquake ripples, drowned in enormous tsunamis or the floods produced by torrential acid rain, you'd soon perish of starvation or freezing

> Verschuur, 1996, p. 124)

Starvation or freezing are due to climate changes said to be wrought by the injection of soot, dust, heavy metals, water, etc from the blast into the atmosphere. As noted above, a K/T size event is among the largest and least likely strikes. Indeed, it is probable that if an asteroid this size were in a threatening Earth crossing orbit we would know of it by now (Morrison et al, 1994, p. 61), although the same could not be said of the long-period comets that might produce such a catastrophe.

In an article in *Sky and Telescope*, the largest amateur astronomy magazine in the United States, Verschuur quotes astronomer Michael Baillie pointing out that even a much smaller object – on the scale of 500 metres – could lead to the collapse of modern civilization:

> The trouble is . . . that a significantly smaller impact could still do the trick, especially if over an ocean . . . Civilization is a thin veneer. Take away all air travel, restrict global food supplies, demonstrate that the military and governments are ineffective, demonstrate that coastal zones should be avoided, and where would we all be? That is not to mention the problems when all the dead sea life washes up.

> (Verschuur, 1998, p. 29)

Here the precautionary thinking becomes extremely clear. Each of Baillie's concerns really should be preceded by an 'if' and even then one could hardly say for certain that the result would be the collapse of modern civilization. Yet neither can one say that such things could not happen, with the claimed result.

Not all efforts at developing scenarios are quite this blatantly worst case. John S. Lewis provides ten accounts of a variety of collisions of various sized bodies in various places that might have taken place in the course of this century, producing a range of results from no fatal events per hundred years to 250 000 people dead in four distinct disasters (Lewis, 1996, pp. 188–205). On the other hand, the chapter begins with a mock newspaper report of an asteroid strike off the Chinese coast. Millions are already feared dead, and scientists give times for when the impact tidal wave will reach various locations around the Pacific rim. To prevent the reader from thinking such stories are pure imagination, ancient tales and myths of catastrophe are given literal interpretations designed to suggest that our forebears at least might have had actual experiences with terrors coming from the sky (Verschuur, 1996, pp. 95–107; Baillie, 1997).

Such efforts to state the case are supplemented by a rhetoric rich in threatening images. 'We live in a cosmic shooting gallery' begins Chapter 1 of *Doomsday Asteroid: Can We Survive?* by Cox and Chestek (1996, p. 29). Verschuur (1996, p. 220) is similarly apocalyptic: 'We have incontrovertible proof that we live in a violent universe . . . We are perpetually poised on the edge of extinction.' It tells us something when a book titled *Rogue Asteroids and Doomsday Comets: The Search for the Million Megaton Menace that Threatens Life on Earth* is actually one of the most thoughtful popular volumes written on this subject.

While it is true that some of the most feverish rhetoric is reserved for lay audiences, similar tendencies can be found even within the more technical literature on this subject. A subtle effort is found in a graphic at the very beginning of the National Aeronautics and Space Administration (NASA) *Spaceguard Survey* report that in 1992 first proposed a system of telescopes to locate potentially Earth-crossing NEOs (Morrison, 1992). (The picture, in updated form, is frequently republished.) The orbits of the already known Earth-crossers, a small fraction of the number that it is expected will eventually be found, are plotted against the orbits of Mercury, Venus, Earth and Mars, producing a graphic of about 2 × 2 inches that is a dense, and hence dangerous looking, birds' nest of intersecting orbital paths (Morrison, 1992, p. 1). Of course, at this scale even the thinnest of visible lines would vastly over-represent the volume of space occupied by a given asteroid's orbit.

In its worst-case premise, a 1995 position paper of the American Institute of Aeronautics and Astronautics comes very close to an explicit statement of the precautionary principle:

> If some day an asteroid does strike the Earth killing not only the human race but millions of other species as well, and we could have prevented it but did not because of indecision, unbalanced priorities, imprecise risk definition, and incomplete planning, then it will be the greatest abdication in all of human history not to use our gift of rational intellect and conscience to shepherd our own survival, and that of all life on Earth

> (Marcus, 1998)

David Morrison and Edward Teller, two of the most prominent scientists concerned with the NEO threat, have argued that in three ways the 'impact hazard is qualitatively different from other natural hazards' (Morrison and Teller, 1994, p. 1135). The first point is the difficulty that exists in getting rare events taken seriously; the third is that, unlike many natural hazards, this one can be avoided. But their second point builds on the worst case:

> Cosmic impacts are capable of producing destruction and casualties on a scale that far exceeds any other natural disasters; the results of impact by an object the size of a small mountain exceed the imagined holocaust of a full-scale nuclear war ... Even the worst storms or floods or earthquakes inflict only local damage, while a large enough impact could have global consequences and place all of society at risk. ... Impacts are, at once, the least likely but the most dreadful known natural catastrophes.

> (Morrison and Teller, 1994, p. 1136)

Imagining and describing worst-case scenarios of course has its place but focussing on those worst-case scenarios as a predicate to action sets up a rather unhealthy dynamic with regard to the development of policies towards NEO threats. On the one hand, it creates a situation where debate centres on how bad a catastrophe has to be before it merits attention. On the other, it sets up expectations the policies advocated might not satisfy.

Building the worst case requires submerging unknowns concerning the extent and nature of the threat, thus implicitly increasing their imaginative content. For starters, there is still a good deal of estimation going on with respect to the frequency and effects of the larger and rarer impacts. For example, while models of immediate impact effects are based in part on a body of geological evidence and well-established norms based on the effects of nuclear weapons, the longer range consequences of the larger strikes with respect to climate effects are built on the far less solid foundations of computer climate modelling of phenomena such as nuclear winter and global warming. A K/T size event can only tell us so much about global climate change from smaller scale impacts. Indeed, given that vertebrate palaeontologists do not widely accept this explanation for dinosaur extinction, it might not tell us much about its impact on life on Earth generally.

This point is important because attempts are made to define the size of impact that would produce a 'globally catastrophic event', which definition is taken by some to suggest a cut-off point for what needs to be done about the NEO problem. Such an event is categorically distinct from smaller events, such as the Tunguska impact. As Morrison and Teller (1994, p. 71) put it: 'The risks associated with Tunguska-class impacts, while not insignificant, represent mortality rates that are substantially less than those associated with many smaller and more frequent natural hazards such as earthquakes, hurricanes, volcanic eruptions, floods, or mudslides. Thus the hazard from Tunguska-like impacts does not inspire special concern or justify heroic efforts either to predict such events or to attempt to avert them.' Of course, this carefully phrased suggestion does not deny the legitimacy of *some* level of concern, or even of *some* non-heroic efforts. Nevertheless, its intention seems to be to define a threshold.

Sometimes these definitions are fairly straightforward, for example, David Morrison and Clark Chapman's suggestion that global catastrophe be defined in terms of disruption of 'global agricultural production' and the death of more than 25 per cent of humanity (Chapman and Morrison, 1994, p. 35). However, the NASA *Spaceguard Survey's* attempted definition is at once more sophisticated and more problematic. It sought to specify (for example) the kinds of events that would 'destroy most of the world's food crops for one year' and/or create threats to 'the stability and future of modern civilization' (Morrison, 1992, p. 10). The former would be characterized by a large number of unknowns (particularly given the link to climate modelling), but that number would pale in comparison with efforts to estimate the latter, involving as it would an attempt to specify the current level of stability of modern civilization as well as to predict its future. Perhaps what is really at work here is yet another element of precautionary thinking, the bias towards the status quo, with the 'future of modern civilization' simply a surrogate for threats to whatever we hold dear at the moment.

Still, on the basis of the case made so far, one might think that strong precautionary thinking would recommend some rather aggressive measures for protecting the Earth from the threat of collision with an NEO. We know it will happen; we just don't know when. We know it could be terrible; we just don't know how bad. Some ability to deflect or destroy incoming NEOs seems appropriate, and since we don't know what out there has our name on it, having such a system in place sooner rather than later would seem to be prudent. Strong precaution may require measures over a wider range of impact sizes and scenarios than weak precaution, particularly if we were to factor in the fate of the species that might be forever lost even with a relatively small strike in the Amazon rainforest. Then again, cost-effectiveness is notoriously difficult to assess if the fate of the coastal North Atlantic is at stake.

The prima facie case for action seems to be supported by a comparative risk assessment. It has been suggested that for a given individual the chance of dying by an asteroid strike is between 1 in 3000 and 1 in 250 000. At the lower limit, these odds suggest that a person living in a developed country is more likely to be killed by an asteroid than electrocuted. At the upper limit, he is more likely to be killed by an asteroid than to die of botulism poisoning, or by exposure to solvents such as trichloroethene (TCE) (Chapman and Morrison, 1994, p. 39). For a given individual, then, the chance of dying by asteroid impact is greater than by other causes that already garner regulatory and meliorative attention – although in the case of some of the less likely threats that we take action to forestall, the justification of so doing is probably itself precautionary in character.

Cost/benefit analysis likewise seems to favour action. Gregory H. Canavan (1994) performed cost/benefit analysis of various NEO detection and deflection systems. Such estimates are highly sensitive not only to the cost of the system, but to the magnitude of the expected impact, and to assumptions made about exactly what one expects to be destroyed. Yet Canavan finds that in a variety of circumstances, there are both detection and deflection systems that have favourable cost/benefit ratios.

NEO detection

What, then, are the scientists, engineers and researchers who are calling our attention to the problem saying should be done? Despite the frightening scenarios that have been described, and in contrast to the demands made by environmentalists in response to much lesser threats, they are reluctant to recommend even the development of such protective measures as seem plausible given current technology. Nobody is advocating that we start building today a fleet of missiles or spaceships that could be used to destroy or deflect threatening NEOs (the closest anyone comes to this is Oberg, 1998). Instead, there is general agreement that what is necessary, first is a reasonably complete sky survey with an eye to identifying, more precisely than we now can, just what is the population of such Earth-crossing NEOs and, to the extent possible by calculating their orbits, when an actual collision threat is likely. Nevertheless, differences remain as to precisely how this should be done. To understand why this is the case, it helps to know a bit more about the politics behind efforts to deal with incoming asteroids.

In 1990 the United States Congress authorized NASA to perform two studies concerning the NEO threat. Its justification for so doing was that whilst 'the chances of the Earth being struck by a large asteroid are extremely small . . . the consequences of such a collision are extremely large . . . [so] it is only prudent to assess the nature of the threat and prepare to deal with it' (Morrison, 1992, p. 2). One study was to develop a program for the detection of Earth-crossing asteroids; this became the 1992 *Spaceguard Survey* report. Another study was about deflection or destruction of threatening NEOs; this was published as *Proceedings of the Near-Earth-Object Interception Workshop*. According to one participant, the reasonable distinction between the two efforts proved to be fateful, for the two committees ended up being staffed by different kinds of scientists with different views of what the NEO problem really looked like (Steel, 1995, p. 232).

The detection committee consisted for the most part of astronomers, a number of whom were already engaged in successful but small-scale efforts at NEO detection. They began with two related assumptions. First, the most serious collision threat was to be found in 1 km and larger asteroids whose orbits needed to be determined for as long in advance as possible. Second, the search program should cost about $US300 million, roughly the price of a NASA space mission. To some extent, then, the problem – 1 km and larger asteroids, i.e. those capable of producing global catastrophe as they defined it – was framed in such a way as to produce a certain solution: a $US300 million price tag (see Steel, 1995, p. 213, who suggests that this definition of the problem was too narrow). As a result *Spaceguard Survey* suggested a system of six telescopes that, in a search extending over a period of some 25 years would be expected to find the great majority of the 1 km or larger NEOs (Morrison, 1992, pp. 30, 31). It was expected that such a system would also find many smaller bodies in the normal course of its operations, and that indeed if kept running long enough, or if sufficiently subject to technical improvement, it could even identify the next Tunguska-class collider (ibid. p. 34). However, to design a system to detect smaller asteroids from the start would have increased the size of the telescopes necessary, and hence the price, as well as the data-processing requirements. To attempt to detect long-period comets that would otherwise appear with very little warning time would have required at least more telescopes.

The interception committee, on the other hand, had for obvious reasons a large representation of people who had been active in the Star Wars strategic missile defence program. While they eventually came to be constrained by the program of the detection committee in their planning, they came to the table with a very different idea of the threat. They assumed that their systems should be built to destroy smaller asteroids which would be detected much closer to the actual time of impact – in other words, a threat that would look much more like the one for which they had been designing systems to date (Steel, 1995, p. 233).

There was a clash of scientific cultures here, and it produced a certain amount of acrimony on the interception committee. The astronomers, having laboured to produce what they considered to be an effective but modest proposal, were taken aback by the free spending and fanciful-seeming assumptions of those who had worked in the defence establishment. The Star

Warriors felt unduly constrained by the narrow problem definition of the detection committee, which they felt would not produce the range of options Congress would want (ibid., pp. 232–4).

It is not as if either side was building on premises that were impregnable. For the kind of survey undertaken depends on assumptions that are in part empirical, with respect to the questions of timing and size of potential colliders, and in part moral, with respect to the size of threat that is deemed worthy of response. As noted above, the *Spaceguard Survey* defines the problem as one of tracking asteroids of a certain size; it does this because of assumptions that were made regarding what makes for a global catastrophe and because of certain self-imposed cost restraints. Yet it is clear that far smaller bodies, of which there are many more and with which collisions are more likely, have the potential for doing some very serious harm as well, particularly if they impact in the ocean (which is not at all unlikely, given that two-thirds of the surface area of the earth is water) or burst over populated areas (which is less likely, given the very small surface area covered by dense human habitation). The question is, what are we willing to pay to avoid the negative impacts that the inundation of coastal areas that a less than 1 km asteroid might produce? In a classic instance of precautionary hyperbole, Edward Teller makes it clear that no price is too great:

> And I think that whenever it should occur . . . whether it is ten people in the middle of Siberia or a hundred thousand people in a city or a hundred million people on a continent or the whole human race, we should do what we can to prevent it

> (Teller, in White, 1997)

Teller might be accused, as a key figure in Star Wars efforts, of making such a statement to maximize the prospects for funding programs close to his heart, but the issue these remarks raise is real enough. The logic of precaution suggests that once we could be reasonably confident that we could secure ourselves from global catastrophe, it would be terrible to risk hundreds of millions of lives. And once those hundreds of millions were safer, would it not become obvious that cities needed to be secured? Given all that we do not know about impact effects, how does one justify a particular stopping point? It is this characteristic of precautionary arguments which opens the door to the kind of large scale spending on distant and uncertain risks that could divert resources from being spent in ways that would make us safer with respect to more common risks (Wildavsky, 1988; Rubin, 1998).

The Spaceguard style survey has been said to be vulnerable on other points. It would not be good at giving much advance warning of hitherto undiscovered long-period comets, which come as it were out of nowhere. Alan Harris has claimed that as a result the Spaceguard search is 'only about half of the solution to the problem' given the threats it is *not* designed to detect (Harris, 1996; Chapman, 1999). This dispute is connected with a deeper one concerning the nature of the threat itself. While the Spaceguard-style survey assumes it comes from the lone rogue asteroid, Australian astronomer

Duncan Steel and other critics suggest that collisions between Earth and smaller bodies may 'cluster' even on a time-scale of days, producing some periods when collisions are more likely than others (Steel, 1995, p. 125). If this were the case, it might be well for a survey to direct its attentions more systematically to smaller potential impactors, rather than finding them as by-products of the search for larger sizes. Indeed, it has been suggested that in light of the difficulty of observing such smaller bodies significantly in advance of their impact it might also be desirable to develop a 'stand-by' defence system (Steel, 1995, p. 243).

A 1995 revision of the detection plan, taking advantage of advances in astronomical equipment, thought that the survey could be completed in 10 years at about $US50 million (NASA, 2000). Neither the original nor this revised system has to date been built as planned, and indeed even the *Spaceguard Survey* found it 'inconceivable that a fully fledged network of completely equipped observing stations will start operating simultaneously and at full efficiency' (Morrison, 1992, p. 34). Instead, in the USA NASA has funded asteroid and comet searches at about $US1 million per year; in April of 1998 it announced it would establish a new program office in the area and boost funding to about $US3 million per year (David, 1998). A small community of researchers around the world, including at least one amateur astronomer, have created a de facto network of searching telescopes (Aguirre, 1999). It is having growing success at the discovery of new asteroids, none of which to date seems to pose a threat, despite a notorious scare in March 1998 when asteroid 1997XF11 was reported in the newspapers as a potential collider. In a January 1999 update on the status of Spaceguard efforts, Alan Harris and David Morrison (1999) note the accelerating pace of discovery. They conclude that if the trend continues, by the end of 1999, 'we should be within a factor of a few of the Spaceguard capability' as outlined in the as yet unfunded program – certainly a tribute to the dedication and skill of those involved at making much out of modest resources.

Beyond the survey, there have been and are in the works space probes designed to study asteroids and comets more closely, as to some extent the best way for destroying or deflecting them would depend on what they are made of and how they are put together (Asphaug et al., 1998, pp. 437–40; Weissman, 1994, pp. 1197–99). A little is already known about asteroids and, by combining innovative radar images (Ostro, 1997) with the relatively few available photographs, we have important suggestive information about the latter. For all that, it has to be emphasized that *little* is known about asteroids and *even less* about comets.

The deflection dilemma

Far from there being many who believe it is appropriate to start building a deflective or destructive system now, the proposal even to *test* a defensive system now has been described as 'one of the most divisive issues raised in this debate' (Morrison and Teller, 1994, p. 1139). A 1993 workshop in Erice, Sicily, produced a final document that while approving searching and exploring concluded that: 'Many of us believe that unless a specific and imminent threat becomes obvious, actual construction and testing of systems that might have the potential to deflect or mitigate a threat may be deferred because technology systems will improve.' (ibid.)

So building an NEO defence system can wait until the results of the sky survey. It has been argued, though, that it can also wait until a potential collider is discovered, because the likely warning time will be of the order of decades.

Where does this reluctance to take aggressive defensive measures come from? The first published objections to building defences looks to be an example of risk/risk analysis. Part of the case against anti-NEO technology seems to be based on an acknowledgement that such measures would amount to risk shifting, rather than risk reduction, because any deflective or destructive technology is itself potentially quite dangerous. Not only would it be likely in the near future to involve nuclear weapons, but it is claimed that the same techniques that can deflect an asteroid that might hit Earth can aim an asteroid towards Earth that might otherwise have passed by in a near miss.

The reliance of the interception committee on nuclear or nuclear-derived weapons in much of their planning seems to have been the proximate cause of concern. It does not seem coincidental that within a few months of the interception committee's meeting in January of 1992, Carl Sagan, himself an antinuclear advocate of note, published an essay in *Bulletin of the Atomic Scientists*, an anti-nuclear journal of note, that called into question the whole notion of building a defence system against asteroids in the first place. Yet Sagan went beyond the nuclear issue to pose what has come to be called the deflection dilemma.

Sagan begins by casting doubt on the whole enterprise of asteroid deflection by associating it with cold warriors who need some new enemy to justify their budgets and build ever bigger bombs in the wake of the end of the cold war. It also 'poisons the waters for space exploration' by military involvement (Sagan, 1992, p. 25). But these ad hominem arguments are not the essence of his point, which is simply this: any technology that could deflect an asteroid away from Earth could be used to deflect asteroids towards Earth. 'Both cases – disintegration and deflection – require developing technologies of mass destruction many orders of magnitude more dangerous than those that now exist' (ibid.).

What would happen, Sagan wondered, if such technologies should 'get into the hands of a Hitler or Stalin, some misanthropic sociopath, someone in the grip of unusually severe testosterone poisoning, or technically incompetent or insufficiently vigilant in handling the controls and safeguards?'. Such threats seem to be far more common and immediate than those posed by NEOs. Hence the 'risks seem far greater than the potential benefits' (ibid.).

In was only later at a conference in January 1993 that Sagan, in a more technical publication. of which he was one of four authors, could provide a quantitative, comparative risk assessment that purports to nail down his conclusion. The seemingly blanket condemnation of any effort to build a defensive system is also moderated. By this time, it had already been well established that the purpose of any Spaceguard system should be to detect potential colliders as early as possible. However, the authors' quantitative risk analysis assumes a system that would deflect with only a few days warning – the kind of system the Star Warriors initially assumed would be appropriate but had already abandoned. This straw man was clearly chosen because it would, in the authors' minds, be readily open to abuse. A somewhat less capable system (i.e. less energy, more warning time) is less susceptible to abuse, but the chance of misuse they judge to be 'about 100 times greater than the probability' of its being needed. Only the build-on-demand system produces a 'minimal threat' (Harris et al., pp. 1154–55).

Understanding the logic here requires knowing that the trick for NEO deflection is to change its orbit as far in advance of the collision as possible, for the more distant the time to collision, the less energy is needed to change the NEO orbit so as to avoid it. An imperfect analogy would be to imagine two cars on a collision course, one whose movement is fixed and another that can be steered. If you are driving the steerable car and observe the oncoming car half a mile away, a gentle and slight movement of your wheel will put your car on a track to avoid the other vehicle. If you don't see it until it is 20 yards away, a much sharper and larger correction is necessary.

Similarly, a defence system that is predicated on long warning times will have more modest requirements for deflecting energy (probably explosive energy, but other possibilities exist) than one that requires action in the face of a more imminent threat. So not only does there seem to be general agreement that a properly conducted search program would give us sufficient warning of a threatened collision to allow the deployment of necessary protective measures on a build as necessary basis, but that the system so constructed would be less dangerous than one we would have to build if warning times were shorter, requiring the system to 'stand by'.

Oberg (1999) argues that Sagan and his co-authors are wrong about the ability to deflect being the same as the ability to aim, at least with respect to present capacities: 'Such systems would be fully effective in diverting dangerous asteroids, but would be physically unable to do the opposite, bring them into contact with Earth. As a threat for misuse, they would panic only those who don't understand real space operations.'

While Sagan's point may appear at first to be directing our attention to risk-shifting, precautionary thinking is still playing a crucial role. This role is evident not only from the fact that Sagan had reached much the same conclusion before the quantitative analysis had been done, when basing himself on explicitly worst-case assumptions about Stalins and sociopaths. One can see it also from a close look at the risk assessment itself. The analysis ends with an estimate of the frequency with which a given deflective system could be abused, in light of the projected knowledge at a given point in time of potentially usable NEOs. No effort is made to operationalize the last element necessary for disaster to occur: the frequency of sufficiently powerful and successful madmen and/or sufficiently negligent operations and the chance of both opportunity and misuser coming together. The implicit worst-case assumption is that a system that can be misused will be misused. Perhaps it is assumed that over the long time-scales that a system might have to stand by, misuse would be inevitable. Against this, however, it might similarly be argued that over the long haul we might become more adept at dealing with such dangers, even if they can never be eliminated, so that the increase in likelihood of abuse is countered (perhaps even overcompensated for) by the increase in capacity to prevent abuse.

Indeed, one wonders whether the earlier, less nuanced form of his argument, with its general mistrust of defensive systems, was not the more consistent. Even a build-on-demand system begs a number of questions if we apply the underlying logic of precaution. Granting the force of Sagan's concern about the Stalins, sociopaths and incompetents of the world, why assume that a build-on-demand system will not, for however long it exists, be subject to deliberate misuse, or to fatal error – the more so if it is operated under pressure (even pressure on a decadal scale) of an event of sufficiently compelling probability to call for the building of the system in the first place? Of course, to secure a 'one-shot' system from being hijacked and to secure a 'stand-by' asteroid defence infrastructure are different tasks, but no security is perfect.

More importantly, once we know how to build an NEO defence system (stand-by or otherwise), our archetypal madman could in principle build one for himself. Both space and nuclear technology are undergoing a process of proliferation, so the basic tools needed to build the system – while technically 'rocket science', of course – are ever more readily available.

What is not now widely known, but will be in the future, is the population of practically deflectable NEOs. The deflection dilemma is based not only on deflection technology, but on the knowledge of the specific orbits of the potentially deflectable Earth-crossing NEOs. There would be no deflection dilemma if such orbital elements were a closely guarded secret – but secrets will out. So there would be much less of a deflection dilemma if we stopped looking for NEOs tomorrow; Sagan himself is said to have 'mused' about this possibility (Chapman, 1999).

Various other arguments against building a defensive system now are presented that apparently reflect different ways of defining the NEO risk and dealing with risk generally. Yet in so of these also we see at work implicit worst-case assumptions. For example, the Erice statement speaks of waiting for improved technology, and it has also been noted that any defensive system we build today will be quickly antiquated. This argument is probably based on a concern for cost-effectiveness. As anyone who has purchased a computer knows, even a system that is not the best we can imagine or as good as what will shortly be possible can be useful. Additionally, the argument also presumes that we know something we do not yet know regarding the timing of the next impact, and about our ability to build a workable system on demand.

Another argument, by Robert Park, Lori Garver and Terry Dawson, is that our experience with nuclear weapons suggests how hard it would be to maintain spending for a stand-by system over the long haul; governments do best at dealing with immediate and obvious threats (Park, et al., 1994, p. 1226). This outlook is at first glance overtly anti-precautionary, with its emphasis on acting on the basis of relative certainties. The same conclusion could be drawn from their warning against worst case thinking: 'While it is important to inform the public, it is dangerous to encourage fear mongering.' (p. 1229). That is not the way to overcome what the aptly initialled P.R. Weissman (1994, p. 1202) speaks of as the 'giggle factor'.

How then should the issue be presented? Clearly, waiting to build a deflection system until there is a known incoming NEO solves part of the problem; calling attention to it is not fear mongering. Until that time comes, 'The asteroid-comet community needs only to insure that everything is fully and accurately explained; the message will take care of itself: (1) the energy deposited by cosmic impacts is enormous; (2) this is a process that is still going on' (Park et al. 1994, p. 1230). But what message is this exactly? 'Enormous' and 'still going on' cover a good deal of ground, while Park and company need to get across a rather finely tuned message that justifies government actions to 'evaluate the threat' *without* making it seem the kind of hazard that would prompt building systems that would create a yet more 'immediate hazard'. Accepting the deflection dilemma means accepting one kind of worst case thinking even as they reject another. It is likewise not clear that their initial premise is consistent with the deflection dilemma, since governments are assumed to be *more* competent with respect to just the kind of *immediate* hazard the deflection system is assumed to create. Starting from Park, Garver and Dawson's premise, a sufficiently Machiavellian actor might conclude that the best way to ensure continued attention to the distant and uncertain NEO problem would be to build a deflection system that required constant monitoring.

Another argument relies on our present uncertainty with respect to the structure and physical composition of NEOs; we do not know what kind of deflection or destructive system to build until we know what we are dealing with (Weissman, 1994, pp. 1197–99). To that extent this argument, with its emphasis on greater certainty, seems to look to a non-precautionary risk management strategy, or to a weak precaution that is concerned with cost effectiveness. But in either case, it seems to be made within a framework where the deflection dilemma is assumed; nowhere have I seen it suggested that more complete structural knowledge should be the signal for constructing a defensive system.

The problems with precautionary thinking about NEOs

It has been noted that the prospect of asteroid impacts stands at the crux of two factors that are important to people's risk perceptions. On the one hand, it is very rare, and rare risks tend to be ignored. On the other hand, it is quite dreadful and in some sense unknown. Despite the fact that the threat is better understood scientifically than many other threats to nature (Chapman and Morrison, 1994, p. 39), we have no experience of the most serious catastrophic results. That can lead to overestimation of risk (ibid., p. 38). Through their desire to grab the public's attention, many NEO authors have highlighted the dreadfulness, through construction and promotion of worst-case scenarios, in order to overcome the problem of rarity. But that may prove too much, and promote a perceived need for more aggressive preventive measures than are deemed necessary. So worst-case thinking is applied again via the deflection dilemma. When there are plausible but diametrically opposed worst cases, how is one to decide between them? Within such a framework, quantitative risk assessment and risk/risk analysis lose their discriminatory power, which is just another way of saying that precautionary thinking undermines their very legitimacy. (For an example of the muddleheadedness that results from this juxtaposition of rational risk assessment procedures with precautionary presumptions, see Chapman's Congressional testimony.)

The point of highlighting this particular antinomy of precaution is not to say that the precautionary principle is an imperfect decision principle, since there are no perfect decision principles in any case. Nor is it to suggest that there are not legitimate concerns that would flow both from not building a deflection system and from building one. The real difficulty is that precautionary thinking frames the NEO collision issue – one might even say skews it – in a way which compounds the difficulty of addressing it, rather than pointing in the direction of reasonable policies.

As we saw earlier, the precautionary principle puts a premium on the hopes and fears of the present moment in its risk averse efforts to protect a given status quo. At the same time, its propensity to act on the basis of incomplete knowledge discounts greatly the usefulness of acquired knowledge. In essence, then, it presents us with a relatively static view of human possibilities. While it purports to be making protective decisions with an eye to the long term, it really privileges our current hopes, fears, abilities and knowledge. A striking example of this point is when Steel (1995, p. 127) notes how 'within a million years' the very large asteroid Chiron may experience a change in orbit that 'would spell disaster for mankind even if the Earth did not receive an impact by Chiron itself. . .'. What exactly is being assumed here about where (or even what) 'mankind' will be that far into the future?

The problem of the precautionary principle's static and time-limited view can be suggested by a historical thought experiment. Imagine our distant ancestors had brought the precautionary principle to bear on the problem of fire. Here was this thing that could save lives and make life more comfortable. But it was terribly dangerous. They might even have thought that let out of control, it could destroy human civilization. If they had decided that, in order to ensure no harm was done, they should not use fire until it could be made safe from misuse, we *might* thank them today – but chances are we would be doing so as we were huddled around whatever sort of burning pile they might, out of their ingenious efforts to relieve the future of a dangerous menace, have contrived. Instead, dangerous as it was, fire was used. Over time it became ever more constrained within an imperfect framework of practices, customs, rules, laws, businesses and institutions. To this day it has not been tamed entirely – it still causes terrible events – but gradually we become more adept with it.

When we remember the persistence of change, the situation with regard to NEOs begins to look different. Duncan Steel (1995, p. 94) is both brave and insightful enough to speculate that at least up to a certain point it is possible to imagine good coming from an asteroid strike. Even if we do not wish to see the possibility put to the test it is a useful reminder of a different way of thinking about risk. Our ability to 'do something' about NEOs might be seen as part of a larger framework of all kinds of knowledge and abilities that might contribute to the effort and to which the effort might contribute, rather than as pre-planned and unified 'program' of detection and deflection. In this respect, the actual history of present search efforts to date – as opposed to what some astronomers seem to continue to put forth as more ideal search circumstances – is quite telling.

Suppose that a consortium of governments had immediately funded the 1992 *Spaceguard Survey*. Within a very few years it might have been up and running. However, given the drop in price and increase in efficiency that occurred between 1992 and 1995 when the proposal was revised, one is entitled to suspect that the thus institutionalized survey would have been behind the curve the moment it came on line. It might even have slowed the development of the opto-electronics that have in fact become available, since resources would have gone into building to the earlier specification, not developing new techniques. Looking at the change from 1995 to the present, when a system has evolved that approaches the hoped-for Spaceguard capacities without the formal infrastructure initially conceived to be necessary, simply reinforces the same point. Even the original *Spaceguard Survey* acknowledged that some sort of incremental development would be more likely than the co-ordinated implementation of its own recommendations – but that did not cause any modification of those recommendations. To the credit of those involved, there is, it seems, something to be said for tight budgets, creativity in dealing with them, and co-operative rather than centrally co-ordinated efforts.

The Spaceguard survey as it is actually developing gives us reason to step back and re-examine the way in which NEO collisions have been framed as a threat. When the stress is on a risk to 'global civilization' is threatened, then a 'civilizational' response seems appropriate. It is almost taken for granted that NEO search efforts should be multinational in character, that ideally they would be in some fashion centrally co-ordinated – despite the reality of current efforts. Given that reality and that global threats are not the only or even the most likely NEO problems, what accounts for these blinders? The centrally planned and co-ordinated search ideal echoes a sense that the NEO threat presents us with a chance to develop a more mature civilizational plan. Planning, as an effort to take the risk out of the future, is perfectly consistent with the risk-averse and status-quo oriented thinking that is encouraged by the precautionary principle.

As Verschuur (1996, p. 199) puts it, 'no one can begin to make coherent long-term plans for the future of civilization without knowing what's out there posing a threat'. Who is it exactly that is responsible for making long-term plans for civilization? It is not a coincidence that the very name for the effort – Spaceguard – was drawn from the science fiction of Arthur C. Clarke, who wrote of mankind's [sic] response to the destruction of a goodly chunk of Italy by 'the hammer blow from space' in 2077:

> After the initial shock, mankind reacted with a determination and a unity that no earlier age could have shown. Such a disaster, it was realized, might not occur for a thousand years – but it might occur tomorrow. And the next time, the consequences could even be worse.
>
> Very well; *there would be no next time.*
>
> A hundred years earlier, a much poorer world, with far feebler resources, had squandered its wealth attempting to destroy weapons launched, suicidally, by mankind against itself. The effort had never been successful, but the skills acquired had not been forgotten. Now they could be used for a far nobler purpose, and on an infinitely vaster stage. No meteorite large enough to cause catastrophe would ever again be allowed to breach the defense of Earth.
>
> So began Project SPACEGUARD . . .'
>
> Clarke, 1973, p. 2

Verschuur presents explicitly a sub-text of such arguments about global purposes:

> In order to assure long-term survival, every action we take on a collective, and perhaps even personal, level may have to be taken consciously and in full awareness of how it will impact our future. For this task we may, as yet, be lamentably ill-prepared, largely due to the psychological immaturity of our species.
>
> (Verschuur, 1996, p. 218)

Benny Peiser has portrayed us as at a crucial juncture:

> By turning away . . . NEOs and the threat they pose to civilisation, man has acquired the capability of changing the course of nature and halting the vicious cycle of cosmic cataclysms. Scientists have the responsibility to meet this challenge head-on and to ensure that mankind takes its fate into its own hands. This would certainly mark the start of a new turning point in the development of cosmic-consciousness and auto-evolution.
>
> (Peiser, 1997)

Verschuur (1996, p. 215) likewise suggests that we have to 'take charge of evolution in a conscious manner'. There is a lurking sense that failure to grasp the magnitude of the problem and opportunity is an indicator of a certain lack of seriousness – even that if we don't take the necessary measures we will get what we deserve when the big one comes.

If, as it turns out, one can rather successfully search for asteroids through efforts more flexible, adaptable, and individualized than initially expected, perhaps this quest for the unified civilization purpose and plan is similarly overblown, and there is some usefulness of muddling through, if only by the skin of our teeth. (For an example of this attitude, consider Chapman's congressional testimony, in which he criticizes non-government forms of funding as implicitly not 'real' money and derides volunteer support. That would change if the outlook recommended here were to be widely adopted.)

Deflection or destruction efforts might be thought about in the same way. It is true that they may well depend on scary things like development of yet more powerful atomic weapons. That may be all the more reason to note that they also depend on what engineers and scientists might come up with in the way of 'mass drivers' (space propulsion systems) of all sorts – systems whose usefulness would far transcend this one area, as they would open further the door to space exploration and exploitation. Indeed, leading popular authors in this field have argued that NEOs (like fire) represent not just a threat but a resource-rich opportunity, both in themselves and in the space-faring capacities that exploiting them would necessarily develop – a point that (as the case of nuclear energy suggests) may be lost if NEOs are in all other respects being demonized (Lewis, 1996; Hartman, 1994).

There would of course be risks related to these benefits. Inevitable human error and the world-destroying Goldfingers to which the deflection dilemma calls our attention will always be with us, if indeed it is correct that the power to deflect an NEO is also the power to aim it at earth. Within the framework of the usual precautionary conceptualization of the NEO problem, the murderous lunatic of the deflection dilemma stands out starkly as perhaps the most dramatic constraint on the hopes for a risk-minimizing rationalization of human affairs. From this point of view, and from the point of view of the technical capacities of today, it looks necessary, forever jealously and zealously, to guard deflection capabilities against this fly-in-the-ointment – all the while perhaps searching for the supposed means consciously to evolve ourselves out of such dangers as error and testosterone poisoning can cause.

That NEO detection and deflection technologies have risks will always be the case more or less, of course, but to have less grand and comprehensive hopes for a new phase of human development might serve to reduce fears as well. If space research and development continue along relatively serious lines, several centuries from now – and, after all, the infrequency of the collision problem prompts thinking in the long term – the development of space-faring abilities might make dealing with these evils something more on the order of a military rescue operation. Once upon a time, house fires meant watching houses, even neighbourhoods, burn or heroic efforts on the part of an entire community. Now, it means telephoning an emergency number and letting the professionals take over.

We can speculate that to try to eliminate all the risk of intermediate stages by waiting until a 'safe' system can be put into place may have the paradoxical consequence of delaying the day such a system might exist. There is after all some point in building systems that become obsolete; the experience teaches you how to build the systems that will *make* them obsolete. If we should wait to build a system until the human race is sufficiently 'mature' to handle it without risk, we could wait for a very long time indeed. It is certain at least that so long as we have both a nuclear and a space travel capacity, somebody could build a misusable system. The danger of the precautionary arguments is that they would prove far too much with respect to the sort of research that might be done in related areas. It not only discounts the usefulness of knowledge with respect to decision making, but it creates a bias against knowledge by highlighting its dangers. This problem is a real one. It is evidenced by the discomfort expressed by Sagan about asteroid investigation missions that are involved with military and Star Wars technology, or when the dangers of thinking of asteroids as resources are highlighted (Lewis, 1996a and Sagan, 1992, p. 26).

I am not arguing that progress will magically solve all of our problems with respect to NEOs or anything else. As I have already suggested, such extreme optimism would in fact tend to result from precautionary thinking, with its belief that progress should mean a risk-free world, where we can have all the things we want. My point instead is that precautionary thinking promotes efforts to find some finite solution to the NEO collision problem, when in fact there is no more a finite solution to that problem than to the fire problem. There will always be an NEO problem so long as human beings, whom Teller has rightly called problem creating animals, are around (Canavan et al., 1993, p. 279). It will look different as time goes by, and the knowledge and capacities we have relative to it will change. In contrast, precautionary thinking privileges our particular vision (or nightmare) of what it looks like. Because it is relatively new to us – very new, in terms of any serious thinking about what might be done – the deflection dilemma looks particularly intractable; but the problem is compounded by the risk aversion and static-mindedness of precautionary thinking.

A terrible catastrophe could be on its way towards us at this very moment; but the same worst case thinking that grabs some headlines in the short term will raise expectations that will make longer-term efforts more difficult. The worst may not even be that helpful in the short term, encouraging as it does the kind of 'Let's do something as soon as possible' thinking that is most likely to cast today's inadequate understandings into stone. When we turn from Spaceguard rhetoric to the reality of the efforts that dedicated scientists are currently undertaking, we see what can be done by incremental and innovative research efforts (and the web of associations and institutional structures they produce) across the broad variety of science, technology and aerospace fronts. This is the work that may some day be of great benefit to the human race. It is the best model for action concerning the NEO threat, and a strong hint that there are better ways of thinking about it than the precautionary principle.

References

Aguirre, E.L. (1999). Sentinel of the sky. *Sky and Telescope*, March, 76–80.

Asphaug, E., Ostro, S.J., Hudson, R.S., Scheeres, D.J. and Benz, W. (1998). Disruption of kilometre-sized asteroids by energetic collisions. *Nature*, June.

Baillie, M.E. (1997). Natural catastrophes during Bronze Age civilizations. http://impact.arc.nasa.gov/news/1997/dec/15.html, accessed 16 March 2000.

Bodansky, D. (1991). Scientific uncertainty and the precautionary principle. *Environment*, September.

Canavan, G.H. (1994). Cost and benefit of near-earth object detection and interception. In Gehrels (1994), pp. 1157–89.

Canavan, G.H., Johndale C.S., Rather, J.D.G. (eds) (1993). *Proceedings of the Near-Earth-Object Interception Workshop*. Los Alamos: Los Alamos National Laboratory.

Chapman, C.R. (1999). The asteroid/comet impact hazard. http://k2.space.swri.edu/clark/hr.html, accessed 26 March 2000.

Chapman, C.R. and Morrison, D.(1994). Impacts on the Earth by asteroids and comets: assessing the hazard. *Nature*, 6 January.

Chapman, C.R. Statement on the threat of impact by near-Earth asteroids before the Subcommmittee on Space and Aeronautics of the Committee on Science of the US House of Representatives.

Clarke, A.C. (1973). *Rendezvous With Rama*. New York: Bantam Books.

Costanza, R. and Cornwell, L. (1992) The 4P approach to dealing with scientific uncertainty. *Environment*, November. http://http://www.aloha.net/~jhanson/page33.htm, accessed 26 March 2000.

Cox, D.W. and Chestek, J.H. (1996). *Doomsday Asteroid: Can We Survive?* Amherst: Prometheus Books.

David, Leonard (1998). New NASA Office to Focus on Asteroid Detection, *Space News*, April 6–12 http://impact.arc.nasa.gov/news/1998/apr/13.html, accessed 26 March 2000.

Gehrels, T. (ed.) (1994). *Hazards Due to Comets and Asteroids.*, Tucson: University of Arizona Press.

Graham, J.D. and Wiener, J.B. (1995) Confronting risk tradeoffs. In *Risk vs. Risk: Tradeoffs in Protecting Health and the Environment* (J.D.Graham and J.B.Wiener, eds), Cambridge, MA: Harvard University, pp. 17–25.

Harris, A. and Morrison, D. (1999). Spaceguard asteroid survey: how are we doing? 15 January http://impact.arc.nasa.gov/news/1999/jan/17.html, accessed 26 March 2000.

Harris, A.W. (1996). Can we defend Earth against impacts by comets and small asteroids. *Mercury*, November/December.

Harris, A.W., Canavan, G.H., Sagan, C. and Ostro, S.J. (1994). The deflection dilemma: use versus misuse of technologies for avoiding interplanetary collision hazards. In Gehrels (1994) op.cit.

Hartmann, William K. and Andrei Sokolov (1994). Evaluating space resources in the context of Earth impact hazards: asteroid threat or asteroid opportunity. In Gehrels (1994) op.cit.

Lewis, J.S. (1996a). *Mining the Sky: Untold Riches from the Asteroids, Comets and Planets*. Reading, MA: Addison Wesley.

Lewis, J.S. (1996b): *Rain of Iron and Ice: The Very Real Threat of Comet and Asteroid Bombardment*. Reading, MA: Addison-Wesley.

Marcus, S.J. (1998).What to do about bolts from the blue. *IEEE Spectrum*, archived at http://impact.arc.nasa.gov/news/1998/dec/23.html, accessed 26 March 2000.

Morrison, D. and Telle, E. (1994). The impact hazard: issues for the future. In Gehrels (1994) op.cit.

Morrison, D. (ed.) (1992). *The Spaceguard Survey: Report of the NASA International Near-Earth-Object Detection Workshop.* Pasadena: Jet Propulsion Laboratory.

Morrison, D., Chapman, C.R. and Slovic, P. (1994). The impact hazard. In Gehrels (1994) op.cit.

NASA (2000). FAQ on asteroid and comet impacts.
http://impact.arc.nasa.gov/related/FAQ.html, accessed 26 March 2000.

O'Riordan, T. and Cameron, J. (eds) (1994a). *Interpreting the Precautionary Principle.* London: Cameron.

O'Riordan, T. and Cameron, J. (1994b). The history and contemporary significance of the precautionary principle. In O'Riordan and Cameron (1994a) op.cit.

Oberg, J. (1998). Planetary defence, asteroid deflection and the future of human intervention in the earth's biosphere.
http://abob.libs.uga.edu/bobk/oberg.html, accessed 26 March 2000.

Ostro, S.J. (1997). Radar observations of Earth-approaching asteroids. *Engineering and Science*, **LX**, p. 2.

Park, R., Garver, L. and Dawson, T. (1994). The lesson of Grand Forks: can a defence against asteroids be sustained? In Gehrels (1994) op.cit.

Pearce, D. (1994).The precautionary principle and economic analysis. In O'Riordan and Cameron (1994) op.cit.

Peiser, B.J. (1997). Essay on cosmic consciousness: the threat to civilization due to comets and asteroids and why we need to change the course of nature (and that of some NEOs).
http://impact.arc.nasa.gov/news/1997/nov/20.html, accessed 26 March 2000.

Rubin, C.T. (1998). The hazard of avoiding hazards. *Sky and Telescope*, August.

Sagan, C. (1992). Between enemies. *The Bulletin of the Atomic Scientists*, May.

Steel, D. (1995). *Rogue Asteroids and Doomsday Comets: The Search for the Million Megaton Menace that Threatens Life on Earth.* New York: John Wiley and Sons.

Th. Douma, Wybe (2000). The precautionary principle.
http://www.eel.nl/virtue/precprin.htm, accessed 26 March 2000.

Verschuur, G.L. (1996). *Impact! The Threat of Comets and Asteroids.* New York: Oxford University Press.

Verschuur, G.L. (1998). Impact hazards: truth and consequences. *Sky and Telescope*, June.

Weissman, P.R. (1994). The comet and asteroid impact hazard in perspective. In Gehrels (1994) op.cit.

White, S. (1997). The day the Earth got hit. TV documentary, Channel 4 (UK), broadcast at 9.00 p.m. Monday 17 November. Synopsis at:
http://impact.arc.nasa.gov/news/1997/nov/17.html, accessed 26 March 2000.

Wildavsky, A. (1988). *Searching for Safety.* New Brunswick: Transaction Publishers.

7 Child protection and the precautionary principle

Helene Guldberg

Introduction

This chapter discusses how the precautionary principle has been adopted in the realm of child protection. It is clear that a 'better safe than sorry' attitude informs the outlook of regulators, charities and schools. There is a paradox here because adults are increasingly encouraged to guide and mediate between children, while at the same time their relationships with children are treated with heightened suspicion. Teachers are encouraged to question the behaviour of parents; parents are encouraged to keep a watchful eye on teachers; sports coaches are distrusted, and so on. The objectives of this chapter are thus:

- To chart the changing attitudes towards children's safety.
- To describe the changes in children's lives that have resulted from the preoccupation with children's safety.
- To appraise the real risks that children face through investigating statistical measures of such things as: mortality and morbidity rates, the number of abductions, road accidents, playground injuries, and home injuries.
- To assess the likely impact of the change in attitude towards child safety on child development.
- To elucidate the impact of the obsession with supervision of adult-child interactions on adult-child relationships.

A The rhetoric and reality of children in danger

The popular imagination is informed by fears for children's safety – from stranger danger and abduction to child abuse and bullying. Government authorities, charities and schools have responded to the increase in perceived risk by encouraging further guidelines and regulations – the result of which is that the sense of children's vulnerability is felt more intensely. The precautionary principle – phrased in terms of Pascal's wager: why take risks if the cost of avoidance is so small and the benefit so large – is informing today's attitude to children and child rearing.

Stranger danger

One instance of this is the fear of 'stranger danger', which was highlighted again in the UK in August 1999 by the Full Stop campaign of the National Society for the Prevention of Cruelty to Children (NSPCC). Almost every household in the UK was sent a pledge form 'to further protect our children' as part of the largest mail-shot ever carried out by a UK charity. Television and billboard advertising campaigns – expressly aimed to shock viewers – complemented the mail-shot. Shortly afterwards an National Opinion Poll (NOP) survey found that almost 80 of parents gave 'a fear of strangers' as the main reason to stop their children from playing outside. The survey was conducted for the Children's Society and the Children's Play Council, charities that aim to promote play. Ian Sparks, the Children's Society chief executive, was concerned about the results of the survey – indicating that children's freedom to play outside is increasingly limited. 'There is a danger of our bringing up a generation of children who will have missed out on the independence and freedom that play brings', he warned (quoted in *The Daily Telegraph*, 3 August 1999).

Jim Harding, chief executive of the NSPCC, recognizes that the danger of child abduction is often exaggerated: yet he justifies the campaign. 'The greatest fear of parents is that their child will be abducted and murdered by a stranger. Although most children are killed by someone they know, it is important for us to alert children to the possible dangers they may face outdoors this summer, without causing fear or panic.' Yet the NSPCC was, quite rightly, accused of scare mongering. The chance of a child aged between one and four being killed by a stranger is less than one in a million, and has fallen by a third since 1988 (*The Guardian*, 2 August 1999). The NSPCC is perfectly aware of these figures – but justifies its campaign on the basis of the 'better safe than sorry' outlook. Even if the danger is minuscule, it is still there – so why take the risk, we are warned. This may seem like common sense. Nobody wants to put children lives at risk, do they?

But is it not possible that the encouragement of such a heightened sense of risk could be detrimental to both children and parents? June McKerrow, director of the Mental Health Foundation, a charity that has commissioned research on children's well-being thinks so: 'We don't need any more of these messages. If anything, the whole thing has already been taken too far.' (quoted in *The Guardian*, 3 August 1999). The foundation recently published findings of an inquiry linking children's mental health problems to their no longer being allowed to take risks through unsupervized play. McKerrow points out that there 'are risks to children in insulating them and not letting them develop their own coping mechanisms, or do things their own way'. Michele Elliott, director of Kidscape, was similarly dismayed by the NSPCC's campaign, arguing: 'It feeds our already inflated fears about their safety and drives kids indoors, when all you can do is give them the strategies and confidence to go out into the world, then hope and pray that any mistakes they make will not be fatal', she said (*Independent on Sunday*, 8 August 1999).

However, the same Michelle Elliot last year co-authored a government-sponsored safety pack *Protecting our Children*, which aims to protect children from paedophiles. The pamphlet encourages parents not to let their children play alone in quiet places, suggests ages at which they might be allowed to run errands alone, and advises parents on how to vet people who work with children. Most of these safety campaigns – highlighting everything from stranger danger and child abuse to sunbathing and dangerous toys – are based on the precautionary principle. This 'better safe than sorry' attitude can only reinforce the exaggerated sense of children's vulnerability.

Fearful parents and teachers have become reluctant to give children the space and the freedom that we, in our childhood, took for granted – feeling the need to keep a watchful eye on children at all times. A MORI poll in the summer of 1999 found that 80 per cent of parents surveyed said they would not allow their children to play unsupervised in the park during the school holiday due to fears of their children falling prey to abduction, assault or bullying. The NSPCC's response was to launch a campaign for more park rangers and play supervisors to make parks safe for children. 'We are not trying to exaggerate the risk. In general, parks are relatively safe but there is a perceived danger by parents. They are worried and we want measures to reassure parents they are safe places,' said Hilary Cross from the charity (*Independent* 27 August 1999). The NSPCC is working with the Local Government Association, the Institute of Leisure and Amenity Management and 40 local authorities to increase security in parks. At Thomas Coram Fields in Camden adults are not allowed into the play area unless accompanied by a child. The Mile End Project in Tower Hamlets plans to introduce close circuit television (CCTV).

Across the UK, the government has spent an extra £22 million to improve security in schools. Many nurseries have installed more sophisticated security and surveillance equipment, such as CCTV cameras. The nursery chain Child Base conducted a survey of parents' concerns and found that security was highlighted as a major issue. Mike Thompson, managing director of Child Base, stated that 'we did CCTV trials on one site and it was well received, so we rolled them out in all of the nurseries. It is clear from the feedback we get that parents are concerned their children should not be exposed to any outside risk' (quoted in *Nursery World*, 8 April 1999). Happy Times nursery in Hammersmith, London, has also made security a priority. They even have a videophone, where parents with the necessary equipment at work or home can supervise their children playing in the nursery.

Such security measures are likely to exacerbate fears in parents, who will wonder why they are necessary. In addition, if local authorities, schools and nurseries are fuelling parents' fears about safety by encouraging constant surveillance, not only will children's freedom to play unsupervised be limited but also the fears and insecurities of parents and teachers will ultimately be transferred to children. The highly suspicious attitude to adults encouraged by all these security measures will also be transferred to children. Do we really want the next generation of children growing up always suspecting the basest of motives in the behaviour of adults towards them?

Parent danger

The behaviours of parents, teachers and all those working with children are continually questioned. We are encouraged not to trust adults to know what is best for children. Grown men and women are supposed to need constant guidance on how to behave with children. For instance, the government recently put forward proposals – in the consultation document *Protecting Children, Supporting Parents* – to ban parents from 'smacking children on the head or face or to use implements that may injure them when inflicting punishment'. Obviously we are not expected to trust parents to administer reasonable force when disciplining their children.

The documentary maker, Philippa Walker, draws a tenuous link, based on a Canadian survey, between being spanked and slapped as children, and drug and alcohol abuse in later life (*Guardian*, 19 January 2000). 'The point is this,' she states 'even if it were only the teeniest, hardly measurable bit harmful, why should we want to take the risk with those we love most?' So the 'better-safe-than-sorry' attitude is applied to the regulation of adults' relationships with children. It is presumed that the benefit of regulation is 'so great' (the prevention of the descent into drug addiction in later life) and the cost 'so small' (preventing parents from using force to discipline their children). However, that the cost may *not* be 'so small'. These kinds of guidelines and forms of regulation may undermine the confidence of parents and breed distrust for those who care most for the very children that these measures are purported to protect.

Not only are we encouraged not to trust parents but we are led to believe that dangers lurk in just about every adult–child relationship. Current attempts to enforce the law against child pornography has encouraged an atmosphere where adults are worried about intimacy with children – even with their own. Stepfathers, boyfriends and grandfathers, and even fathers, are suspected of having base motives when trying to get close to children in their family. Teachers, in particular male, and family members are encouraged by 'experts' to rethink their attitude to physical contact and a flood of new guidelines and rules have emerged. Claims of abuse in sports have led to demands for further guidelines and codes of behaviour for institutions from the England and Wales Cricket Board to the Scout Association. Even the Salvation Army advises its members to 'arrange that, as far as possible, an adult is not left alone with a child or a young person where there is little or no opportunity for the activity to be observed by others'.

In our suspicious times we can all be caught in the web of suspicion, being viewed as potential paedophiles. In 1995 Julia Somerville and her boyfriend were arrested for taking snapshots of her young daughter in the bath – naked, of course. The Protection of Children Act (1978) states it is a criminal offence to take 'indecent' photographs of children. It seems that to some people 'indecent' means naked. A Boots photo-lab assistant reported Somerville's film to his superiors, in line with the company's guidelines, because it contained 28 images of Somerville's daughter during bath-time. It quickly became clear that the photographs were perfectly innocent but it is worrying when photos of children in the nude, that would in the past be a typical part of any family photo-album, are treated with such suspicion.

As a result, those who have regular contact with children – parents, grandparents, aunts or uncles, teachers, scoutmasters or sporting coaches – have come to fear that their behaviour may be misconstrued. Frank Furedi, a British sociologist, warns that:

> the regulation of adult–child encounters fosters insecurity and confusion. Paradoxically it also weakens people's ability to negotiate some of the real problems faced by parents. Experience has shown that human relations are best worked out informally. People learn from their families and friends how to react to ambiguous situations and to distinguish between a difficult relationship and a dangerous one. Rules and guidelines pre-empt this process. The resolution of problems is left to professionals who are endowed with authority to determine what is and what is not acceptable behaviour. Their formal procedures are intolerant of ambiguity and exploration.
>
> (*Independent on Sunday*, 24 August 1999)

Neither is it any good for children. As Meg Henderson points out, 'Children need spontaneous physical contact with both parents, with aunts and uncles, without implanting in their minds that there is something wrong about it. Unless, that is, we want future generations unable to form relationships with the opposite sex.' (*Guardian*, 22 August 1996)

Children danger

It is not only adults' relationships with children that are under the spotlight. Children's peer relations are also often assumed to be damaging. Their opportunities to play freely without adult supervision are therefore increasingly restricted.

It is undoubtedly true that unsupervised outdoor play results in some accidents and injuries – sometimes more serious than grazed knees. In Norway, where I was brought up, outdoor activities were encouraged from a very early age. Therefore, a childhood with no broken bones was said to be 'no good childhood'. The commitment to unsupervised outdoor play was put to the test a few years ago, after the tragic death of Silje, a five-year old girl, in my hometown Trondheim. Silje's death sent shock waves through the entire nation. She had been beaten up by three boys of her own age, knocked unconscious and left to freeze to death in the snow. However, the popular and media consensus quickly emerged that the risk of serious accidents, which are exceptionally rare, were worth taking in order to allow the vast majority of children a healthy and rich childhood.

In the UK we seem to be more ready to place restrictions on children's spontaneous outdoor play. Children's freedom and creativity is being restricted. They get less space to roam freely and rarely even make their own way to and from school. In 1971 80 per cent of seven to eight-year olds were allowed to travel to school on their own or with other children. By 1990 only 9 per cent did. The first national Travel Survey reported a fall of around 20 per cent in the annual distance walked and 27 per cent in the distance cycled between 1985 and 1993. School break-time, one of the few arenas where children's play has tended to be free from adult domination, is being shortened (Blatchford, 1998). Also, partly as a result of anti-bullying policies, a more conscious management and supervision of children's play is taking place.

The dangers of bullying are highlighted by charities, the government, the media and academics. Bully Online, the web site of the UK National Workplace Bullying Advice Line, opens with the statement, 'Half the population is bullied ... most only recognize it when they read this' (successunlimited.co.uk). ChildLine describes bullying as: 'being called names; being teased; being pushed or pulled about; being hit or attacked; having your bag or other possessions taken and thrown around; having rumours spread about you; being ignored and left out; being forced to hand over money or possessions; being attacked because of your religion or colour'. For the Metropolitan Police it is more simple and straightforward: 'Having fun at someone else's expense is bullying.'

It seems that the concept of 'bullying' is increasingly broadly defined. The behaviours and experiences described above surely do not feature too infrequently in all children's everyday lives? Going by the ChildLine definition of bullying, it would be rather surprising if only half the population were being 'bullied'. In January this year the National Association of Head Teachers (NAHT) issued guidance on bullying claiming that anything from pushing, kicking, hitting, pinching, threatening behaviour, as well as sarcasm, name-calling, spreading rumours, ridiculing and excluding from groups or activities can be defined as bullying. In order to ensure against being sued for not taking action, teachers were encouraged to always take the word of the child claiming to be bullied. We are therefore witnessing an increasing supervision of children's break times. At the same time there has been a reduction in the opportunities for peer-interactions outside of school (Hillman, 1993).

Danger danger

The heightened sense of risk and the 'better safe than sorry' attitude may therefore be detrimental to children's well-being. By increasingly focusing on potential risks we are in danger of limiting known benefits. An obvious example is the scare-mongering about the measles, mumps and rubella (MMR) vaccine at the end of the 1990s. The panic was ignited by studies published in the *Lancet* in 1995 and 1998 which seemed to demonstrate a link between the triple vaccine and autism and Crohn's disease. However, subsequent studies failed to replicate the findings – and found no evidence of a link with autism and serious bowel disease. However, the damage was already done. Many parents decided not to take the one-in-a-million chance of a serious reaction to the vaccine. They did not want to expose their children to even the slightest of risks. Vaccination rates therefore fell. According to the Public Health Laboratory Service 95 per cent of babies need to be given the triple MMR jab by the age of 16 months in order to keep the immunity level high enough to prevent an epidemic. By the end of the summer of 1999, however, the vaccination rate had fallen to 87 per cent leading to warnings from public health experts that if vaccination rates continue to fall, the MMR scare could lead to a measles epidemic next year.

This may be a rather obvious example of the detrimental effect of what the Social Issues Research Council (SIRC) have termed 'riskfactorphobia'. But what about today's generally protective climate and the broader fears for children's safety – are they detrimental to children's well-being? What are the implications of this climate for children's development? Are we restricting children's development by restricting their freedom? What are the effects of anti-bullying policies on children's social development? Do they limit their ability to form independent meaningful relationships? What will be the outcome of minimising unsupervised play? Will preoccupations with safety limit children's physical prowess and mobility? And how will children learn road sense if prevented from coping with traffic independently?

The realities of risks faced by children

The reality is that children are healthier, wealthier, safer and better educated than ever before. At the turn of the last century, infant mortality in England was very high – approximately 150 babies in every 1000 died before they reached their first birthday. Their nutrition was poor and lack of vaccinations led to deaths from smallpox, diphtheria, measles, typhoid and cholera, amongst many others. Children are now being immunized against all major inoculable diseases, including mumps and measles. Also, significant medical advances over the last decades have led to improved rates of survival for children diagnosed with cancer, such as leukaemia. Due to medical advances and improved nutrition and hygiene infant mortality has dropped to 5 per 1000 babies born. Over the last hundred years five to seven-year-old children have increased in average size by 1–2 cm per decade.

The major cause of death in children under 15 years of age is no longer malnutrition or disease, but accidental injury, particularly road accidents. However, despite injuries now being the leading cause of death in children over one-year-old, child mortality from accidental injury declined by 34 per cent between 1985 and 1992. (DiGuiseppi, 1997). In 1997 133 pedestrians under 15 years of age were killed by cars. In addition, 57 car occupants and 30 cyclists under 15 years of age were killed in car accidents. Every accident is an individual tragedy; but it should be noted that there are today significantly fewer deaths and serious injuries as a result of road accidents than in previous decades. For instance, the number of cyclist and pedestrian fatalities among children under 19 halved between 1985 and 1997. Of course, this figure partly reflects the decline in distances children walked and cycled. However, there has also been a decline in deaths per mile walked. The Child Health Monitoring Unit found that child pedestrian deaths declined by 24 per cent per mile walked between 1985 and 1992 (DiGuiseppi, 1997). The average distance travelled by car increased by 40 per cent in the same period. Yet there was still a fall in the number of children killed as passengers.

Accidents in the home are also declining, mainly due to higher standards of living, with open fires and unreliable gas heaters being replaced by central heating, candle light by electric lighting, and frayed wires by safer wiring. In 1994, 158 children under 15 died in home accidents by 1998 the figure had fallen to 118 (Home Accident Death Database).

B   Danger and development

In Part A, it was suggested that play is an essential part of development. In Part B, the developmental significance of giving children the freedom to play freely without adult supervision is explored in greater detail.

Peer relations and play

A wealth of developmental research has demonstrated the importance of peer relations in giving children the opportunity to acquire skills that will only be learned through interactions with equals – such as co-operation and competition. Symmetrical relations encourage children to learn skills such as turn-taking, sharing, leadership qualities and how to cope with hostility and conflict. They help children develop the ability to empathize and control their emotions without adult intervention, and to express, and learn the limits of, their own aggression. In this sense play could be described as providing an 'apprenticeship for independent living'. Through play, children develop the ability to negotiate social rules and create rules, as well as help appreciate and challenge the boundaries of their abilities. Playing, fighting and stumbling into difficult situations – the very things adults rush out and stop – help shape children into competent, independently minded individuals.

Some theorists see peer relations as all-important for children's healthy development. Judith Harris (1999) draws on developmental psychology and genetics to argue that parents don't matter and that the key influence comes from peers. Children tend to pick up their attitudes from peers rather than from teachers and parents, she claims. Her writings have caused a storm across the Atlantic. However, although peers are important, research in developmental psychology has established the unquestionable importance of asymmetrical relationships and adult created environments – whether in formal school settings or informal home environments – for children's learning. Adult direction, guidance and supervision are essential for children's cognitive, linguistic, social, moral and emotional development. However, children also need the space to test their limits independently of an adult framework. Children must be allowed to make their own mistakes and to learn from them and their emerging appetite for adventure should not be stifled.

According to one of the most influential theorists in developmental psychology, Lev Vygotsky, the basis for development is overcoming the contradiction between the demands of a particular situation, forcing the individual to undertake new forms of behaviour, and the inadequacy of the individual's existing forms of thought to cope with the tasks at hand (Vygotsky, 1978). He showed how play challenges the ability of the child to deal with the task at hand. 'In play the child is always higher than his average age, higher than his usual everyday behaviour; he is in play as if a head above himself.' (ibid, p. 102). The Swiss psychologist Jean Piaget similarly explored the developmental significance of play. He pioneered comprehensive observational studies of children's interactions. He concluded that children grow out of egocentric modes of thinking by being confronted with other's points of view through peer interactions. Piaget and Vygotsky provided insights into the significance of play, not just in terms of physical and intellectual development, but also in terms of emotional and social development. Piaget was one of the few psychologists to map out in detail the ontogenetic development of play.

In the course of development, children's contact with peers gradually increases. Their contact with adults, on the other hand, decreases. A study by Ellis, Rogoff and Cromer (1981) observing children's interactions between one and 12 years of age found that by three years of age they had started to interact more with other children than with adults.

Children do go through a number of age-related stages in the development of their peer group interactions.

Toddlers: Children under two-and-a-half years of age, before being aware of principles such as sharing and turn-taking, tend mainly to engage in solo play. But already in the toddler period, peer interactions are becoming increasingly frequent. By the end of their second year of life they spend more time in social than in solitary play. Reciprocal play takes place, where children are able to exchange roles – such as in hide and seek – and turns – such as in the use of toys.

The function of play is not only to develop these kinds of social skills but also to develop cognitive skills. Young children are dominated by their situational constraints. Their minds are very much tied to the here and now. They find it difficult to deal with ideas separate from their immediate environment. Play, however, forces them to do just that – to move beyond the constraints of their immediate environment into the imaginary sphere. They start engaging in pretend play – inventing increasingly complex and fascinating make-believe situations. However, as Piaget showed, their make-believe situations at this stage are limited to events experienced by the child and are expressed with a focus on the self. Although this type of pretend play is self-directed, it does rely on children's ability to receive and express ideas, and in turn refines their social communications.

Pre-school children: Before three to four years of age, children tend to play in smaller groups – mainly dyadic – in close contact with one or more familiar adults. However, as they approach their fourth year, having developed an understanding and acceptance of the importance of sharing, turn-taking and fair play, children make rapid strides in their socialization skills, widening their circle of playmates, and demand less adult attention. Their developing capacity for symbolic play and the development of verbal skills transform the nature of their interactions. Vygotsky described their play as both liberating and constraining. Pre-school children are 'free' to explore new roles in play, but as role-playing with their peers is a co-operative activity, they also have to exhibit an unprecedented level of self-control. They need to be able to act against their impulses, subordinating themselves to the rules of the game. Although a vivid make-believe world is created with improvised rules, these rules have to be meticulously observed. There is also a tacit acknowledgement of leadership. The dominant child decides who should play which major roles and children who do not conform are soon tacitly excluded.

School-age children: Corsaro (1999) draws attention to the important feature of peer-group play in the school playground – in that it is largely separated from the adult-dominated aspect of children's lives. Activities and games, such as marbles, hopscotch and skipping – relatively durable features of the playground culture – involve minimal adult intervention. These activities provide an important context for children to assert their relative autonomy, especially from adults on whom they are dependent, to construct a more reflective perspective on their asymmetrical relationships and acquire skills associated with more symmetrical relationships.

Influential descriptions of children's outside play are provided by Opie and Opie (1969). Through detailed observations of play they conclude that control of the games has to be with the children themselves. Their observations centred on play outside school. Sluckin (1981), on the other hand, investigated children's play in school break-times, again concluding that play provides children with skills relevant to adult life. Children become more proficient in 'reading' not only others' perspectives and points of view, but also their emotional states, motives and intentions. They therefore become more adept at participating in joint tasks with a common goal. Friendships become more 'durable, meaningful, intimate and sustained'. Rather than their friendships being based on ad hoc encounters, children start to choose their friends based on a similarity of interests.

Behaviours that adults tend to try to intervene to stop are in fact found to play an important developmental function. Even teasing is recognized as sometimes serving a positive function. An Institute of Education longitudinal study found that teasing was widespread in interactions between peers throughout school. Pupils often emphasized that teasing was not seen as harmful, but more a part of everyday banter, often between friends. According to Blatchford (1999): 'Some teasing no doubt serves a social purpose, helping to denote limits, helping to define and consolidate friendships, showing off sharpness in social discourse, and jostling for status. Pupils showed that considerable skill could be required in determining what form of teasing was appropriate with particular people.'

A local head-teacher in Skudeneshavn in Norway, Asbjørn Flemmen, recognizes the role of play in challenging children's existing levels of competence and, through taking risks, developing new skills. He has therefore pioneered the building of a school playground that positively encourages potentially dangerous 'thrill seeking'. The children whirl around in the 'jungle', an area where balancing, swinging and climbing dominate, dangling from ropes at great heights. The aim of the playground – with its many activity areas, such as the jungle, 'hut-building' and 'hide and seek' – is to maximize spontaneous, unsupervised play. Adults are encouraged to back off at all times. Accidents may be inevitable in such a risk-taking environment, but the worst that has happened in three years is two broken arms and one broken leg. Most injuries were incurred when the playground first opened. It seems the children quickly appreciated their own limitations and adapted their speed and movements to their abilities.

Adults are also discouraged from intervening in conflicts that arise between the children. This has raised some concern among anti-bullying professionals in Norway, but the children seem to have learned how to resolve conflicts of their own accord. The children's improved levels of not only fitness and physical mobility but also social skills have stunned the parents and teachers.

Adults need to appreciate that conflicts of interest are as inevitable in childhood as they are in adulthood. Children are, of course, not as sophisticated in resolving conflicts as adults, and therefore do need the experiences that will help them develop their social skills. It seems children's play – where 'teasing' and 'physical aggression' occurs – serves an important function in developing children's social understanding and social abilities. Conflicts and disputes are not necessarily negative experiences in children's development. Recognizing the existence of conflicts of interest, and learning how to negotiate those conflicts and how to respond to and respect others' points of view, are inevitable and desirable childhood experiences.

But by focusing on and problematizing bullying, are we not denying children these experiences? Because of fears about bullying there is an increasing hostility to school break-times. However, break-time is an important context for children to develop, consolidate and break off friendships. Children learn to share activities and interests, and experience the rewards and joy of loyal relationships and the anger, frustration and sadness of betrayal and loss.

The detrimental effect of parental fears on children's development has been suggested in the Mental Health Foundation report, *The Big Picture*. It notes that, 'Concern about safety and the risk of abuse or violence have limited the amount of time children play outside unsupervised, travel alone or are allowed to attend clubs and youth groups' (Mental Health Foundation, 1999). McKerrow, director of the foundation, said: 'There are risks to children in insulating them and not letting them develop their own coping mechanisms, or do things their own way.'

Similarly, a few years earlier, a Barnardo's report, *Playing it Safe* (1995), warned against the anxieties over children's safety – seen to have reached unprecedented levels. 'Children today are living in an increasingly restrictive environment. Dangers from traffic and fear of strangers are reducing the freedom of children to play and develop independent lives. Large numbers of children spend most of their lives under adult supervision. Children have less opportunity to develop coping skills, independence and the capacity to take responsibility for themselves.' (McNeish and Roberts, 1995).

There is of course the danger that the detrimental effects of today's changes in children's lives are exaggerated. The NSPCC warns: 'The increasing tendency to keep children at home and the rise in computer entertainment at home has led to a rise in "battery children"' (*Independent*, 2 September 1999). Similarly, Barry Hugill says: 'Hundreds of thousands of children are being "reared" by over-protective parents in conditions comparable to those of battery hens ... At the age of five they are emotionally and socially repressed.' (*The Observer*, 19 March 1998). Research commissioned by the Swiss government investigating the lifestyles of young children in Zurich found that frightened parents denying children the opportunity to play outside put them at risk of obesity and restricted their emotional, social and motor development. However, Sonia Livingstone, a social psychology lecturer at the London School of Economics has investigated the effect of the 'bedroom culture' on children's development, trying to put the impact of new media, for instance, into perspective. In *Young People, New Media* Moira Bovill and Sonia Livingstone show that only one in a hundred children can be classed as 'screen addicts':

> The average child is hardly glued to the screen. On the contrary, most children engage in a wide variety of activities. They do watch a lot of TV – on average for two and a half hours a day – but really they prefer playing with their friends.
>
> (Interactions, November/December 1999)

The term 'battery children' may therefore be a bit of an exaggeration. However, parental concerns for children's safety have led to profound changes to the very meaning of childhood.

Conclusion

Children are increasingly deprived of opportunities to engage in rough-and-tumble play, roam freely and to socialize freely with their peers. By placing children under constant supervision they are denied the opportunity to develop in particular ways. Children must be able to plan and take control; they must be free to experiment so that they develop their own abilities to solve problems. It takes a brave parent in our fearful times to grant children this kind of freedom. But unless we chill out a little, we may suffocate our children with a constant consciousness of safety, stifle their potential and prevent them from growing into mature, competent and independently minded individuals.

References

Blatchford, P. (1999). The state of play in school. In *Making Sense of Social Development* (M.Woodhead, D. Faulkner, and K.Littleton, eds). London: Routledge

Blatchford, P. (1998). *Social life in schools: pupils experiences of breaktimes and recess from 7 to 16 years.* London: Falmer.

Corsaro, W. (1999). Preadolescent peer cultures. In *Making Sense of Social Development* (M.Woodhead, D. Faulkner, and K. Littleton, eds). London: Routledge.

DiGuiseppi, C. (1997). Influence of changing travel patterns on child death rates from injury: trend analysis. *British Medical Journal,* **314** (710).

Ellis, S., Rogoff, B. and Cromer, C. (1981). Age segregation in children's social interaction. *Developmental Psychology,* **17**, 399–407.

Harris, J. (1999). *The Nurture Assumption: why children turn out the way they do.* London: Bloomsbury.

Hillman, M. (1993). One false move . . . In *Children, Transport and the quality of life* (M. Hillman, ed.). London: Policy Studies Institute.

Mental Health Foundation (1999). *The Big Picture.* London: Mental Health Foundation.

McNeish, D. and Roberts, H. (1995). *Playing it Safe, Today's Children at Play.* London: Barnardo's.

Opie, I. and Opie, P. (1969). *Children's games in street and playground.* Oxford, England: Clarendon Press

Sluckin, A. (1981). *Growing up in the playground.* London: Routledge and Kegan Paul.

Vygotsky, L. (1978). *Mind in Society.* Cambridge, MN: Harvard University Press.

8 Plastic panics: European risk regulation in the aftermath of BSE

Bill Durodié

Introduction

On 3 March 2000 the European Commission decided to prolong temporary measures which had been adopted in December 1999 to prohibit the use of phthalate softeners in PVC toys and childcare articles intended to be placed in the mouth by children under three years of age. The move, criticized by the chair of the Commission's own Scientific Committee on Toxicity, Ecotoxicity and the Environment (CSTEE), marked the culmination of a two-year campaign by environmental and consumer protection groups. It was a significant victory for the politics of emotionalism over reasoned debate and shows that many, including some scientists and industrialists, are guilty of seeking to legitimate their authority by pandering to consumer fears under the guise of protecting health.

Taking phthalates as a paradigmatic case, this chapter explores the changing attitudes towards risk regulation in the European Union. The chapter begins with a brief discussion of the BSE crisis. The response to two scares over choking on non-food items found in food products, one before, the other after the BSE scare, is evidence as to the impact of this episode. The phthalate case is then considered in detail, exploring in particular the way in which the precautionary principle has been used to act as a kind of lowest common denominator. The chapter ends with a discussion as to the potential social impact of the exaggerated risk consciousness and the attack on objective reason, which are both being promoted by the newly empowered, yet unaccountable, consumer groups.

Mad cows

The impact upon the contemporary European imagination of the scare surrounding the suggestion that bovine spongiform encephalopathy (BSE), commonly known as 'mad cow disease', might cause Creutzfeldt-Jakob disease (CJD) in humans, should not be underestimated. On 20 March 1996,

Stephen Dorrell, then the UK Health Secretary, quoting from an official report by the Spongiform Encephalopathy Advisory Committee, stated to Parliament that there was evidence of a causal link between BSE and CJD. Since then, attitudes to consumer protection and public health services across Europe have undergone a momentous and total transformation.

A month after Dorrell's statement, John Major, then Prime Minister, described the ensuing panic as 'the worst crisis a British government has faced since the Falklands'. For the European Community's agriculture and rural development commissioner Franz Fischler, speaking in September 1996, it was 'the biggest crisis the EU had ever had'.

Ironically, evidence as to a causal link between BSE and CJD remains to be proven (Axelrad, 2000), and in any case the actions taken by ministers and officials in 1988, well before the panic, were wholly sufficient to prevent future harm. The 1988 ban on ruminant protein in cattle feed led to the number of BSE cases by year of birth falling from a peak of 36,861 in 1987 to 1 in 1996, the year of the panic (Ministry of Agriculture, Fisheries and Food (MAFF), 2000). Thus those who helped engender a new low in levels of public confidence by claiming that the death rate might be as high as 500 000 per annum, are not without criticism (Fitzpatrick, 1996). To date the actual number in the UK has been 50.

Irrespective, the crisis acted as a catalyst for a more profound reorganization of the industry and beyond. Subsequent developments, referred to by the European Commission variously as 'farm to fork', 'plough to plate', or 'stable to table', to indicate how all-encompassing they are to be, will allow for faster and tougher responses to perceived problems, food-related or otherwise. These will have far-reaching implications long after the destruction of the last suspect beef herd has been completed.

The European Commission, the executive body of the European Community, was shocked into action by BSE. Over a two-year period, the crisis was referred to in almost every speech by Jacques Santer, then Commission President, as well as other Commissioners and officials. These all pointed towards the need for substantial organizational and legislative reform. Launching this reorganization in 1997, Santer made 'a plea for the gradual establishment of a proper food policy which gives pride of place to consumer protection and consumer health'.

The potential for more Commission intervention within the fields of human health protection, consumer protection and the environment, had been established in Articles 129, 129a and 130r respectively of the 1992 Treaty on European Union (Maastricht Treaty). The BSE crisis triggered these into action as well as providing justification for a new Article 153 in the 1997 Amsterdam Treaty, which further expanded the Commission's remit, placing consumer policy and health protection more centrally as 'rights'.

The Consumer Policy Service at the Commission, which itself only became established as a new directorate-general, DG XXIV, in 1995 (now known as DG SANCO, an abbreviation of the French for health and consumer affairs), was expanded to take on health protection matters and witnessed a truly astonishing pace of transformation. The number of staff trebled and it became responsible for providing scientific advice, risk analysis and control.

Over the course of 1997 a wave of landmark documents was produced, including a communication on 'Consumer health and food safety', and a Green Paper on 'The general principles of food law in the European Union'. An 'Inter-services operations manual' soon followed, establishing co-operation procedures between the directorate-generals responsible for industrial policy; employment, industrial relations and social affairs; agriculture and rural development; and consumer policy and consumer health protection.

A Multidisciplinary Scientific Committee, set up in 1996 to deal specifically with BSE, was replaced by a Scientific Steering Committee with a far broader mandate. Some 131 leading European scientists (selected from a pool of 1126 who had applied), were then co-opted to sit on its eight new scientific sub-committees, thereby replacing the six former scientific committees. (The 1999 White Paper on Food Safety looks set to further reorganize and enlarge the scope of these arrangements.)

Most notably, the Commission established a Rapid Alert System and a Risk Assessment Unit within DG XXIV, and overtly adopted the precautionary principle as the basis of its approach to all future investigations. The latter is popularly understood to imply that in all matters involving uncertainty, one is to err upon the side of caution. Critics would claim that, since there is always uncertainty, the principle is a recipe for paralysis.

Similar adaptations and transformations have occurred within the UK, where a well-publicised fatal outbreak of the *E.coli* 0157:H7 bacterium also occurred over the same period. In 1997, a Joint Food Safety and Standards Group (JFSSG) was formed between the Ministry of Agriculture, Fisheries and Food (MAFF) and the Department of Health. A Risk Communication Unit established within the JFSSG was already making decisions on a 'safety first' principle prior to the formal establishment of the Food Standards Agency in April 2000.

Choking fears

In February 1997, the Belgian authorities notified the European Commission of two (non-fatal) incidents involving children choking on parts of toys contained in food products. In May 1997, Belgium banned all such non-edible items from inclusion in food products. The introduction of what was in effect a new national technical standard required the Commission to be notified as it created a non-tariff barrier to the free movement of goods within the internal market.

This notification was referred to the Commission's Committee on Product Safety Emergencies (CPSE), which had by then relocated to DG XXIV. At its June 1997 meeting, the CPSE decided to issue a 'serious and immediate risk to health' warning. It requested all 15 member states to: examine the risks associated with the inclusion of unwrapped non-food articles mixed with food products (essentially toys in chocolate eggs, crisps and cereal packets); review national policy on such matters; and report back to the Commission by September 1997 so that it could consider 'further steps' at its October meeting.

The effect of the BSE crisis can be seen by comparing the response to a similar incident a year earlier, when a 68-year-old Belgian pensioner choked to death on a 'flippo' (or 'pog') contained in a packet of crisps. The Belgian minister for public health, Marcel Colla, then tried to ban similar items but the media response was satirical, contrasting the regulatory haste to ban 'flippos' in crisps with the minister's lethargic and bureaucratic approach to more pressing health issues.

By 1997, the public mood had become more attuned to safety issues, and the relevant Commission staff, now more numerous, were prepared and expected to react. However, there was little evidence relating to incidence and incidents of choking that could justify the measures being sought.

Research presented to the Commission detailing the numbers of such choking events indicated that 'accidents now represent the most important cause of childhood morbidity and mortality' (Petridou, 1997). Few of these accidents are caused by choking, however.. The figures given in the report suggest that fewer than two people a year die by choking on such 'food products containing inedibles'. This tallied with research commissioned in 1996 by the UK Department of Trade and Industry (DTI, 1996).

Whilst choking fatalities are undoubtedly tragic, they are fortuitously rare. Of over 550 000 deaths per annum in England and Wales for example, only 6000 involve children under the age of 10. Three quarters of these are under the age of one. Of the total deaths, 16,000 can be attributed to external factors; and after excluding road accidents and suicides there remain approximately 6000 accidental deaths among people of all ages, of which about 5 per cent involve choking. Approximately 200 of the accidental deaths involve children under 10 and 15–20 per cent of these (some 30 to 40 cases a year) are the result of choking.

Unsurprisingly perhaps, the vast majority (84 per cent) of deaths by choking involve food items. Sweets, peas, sausages, bananas, apples and nuts are all cited as potentially hazardous. Of the non-food items leading to choking incidents, coins form by far the largest single category. The remaining accidents are caused by a wide variety of items, not many of which involve toys. Cotton wool, conkers, stones, silver foil, tissue paper, even a child's dummy and half a penicillin tablet have proved fatal. Very few incidents ever involve toys, let alone toys associated with food products. In the UK there have only been three recorded child fatalities relating to toys enclosed with food items over the last 15 years and the association between the toy and the food item was not even central to each of these. The first of these, in 1985, involved the wheel and axle of a toy lorry that had been assembled by the child's father and subsequently broken during play. As was argued by the responsible Minister in response to Parliamentary questions on the matter at the time, 'all fatalities are regrettable, but the world is full of small objects which can cause death by choking'. While the death of the little boy was very regrettable, it would be of no consequence to prohibit the sale of such products.

During Court proceedings surrounding the second incident, which occurred in 1989 and involved the foot of a 'Pink Panther' model, Ferrero, manufacturers of Kinder Surprise eggs, pointed to world-wide sales in excess of 4600 million since 1974, 218 million of which had been in the UK, and 58 million of those in the preceding 12-month period. It was suggested that Birmingham City Council had reacted emotionally rather than rationally in issuing a suspension notice against the eggs. Legislating on such matters would prove futile as well as being irrational.

It is just such reasoned objective evidence that should have led the CPSE to conclude that there was little risk and no need to issue a warning to all member states in the first instance.

Of course, due caution is taken in preventing choking incidents where possible. Children between one and three years of age are particularly vulnerable. At this age, children learn to use their thumb and first finger as a pincer and experiment by placing objects into their mouths but they do not have a coughing reflex or a fully developed cricoid (the narrowest part of the larynx and trachea). Reasonable actions have in the past been taken by companies, including the labelling of toys containing small parts as unsuitable for those under 36 months of age, and the creation of ventilation holes in the tops of pen caps. The 'small parts cylinder test' provides a reliable guide as to the potential hazard proffered by such items.

As the DTI report pointedly indicates, 'putting objects in the mouth is an important part of learning and should not be restricted', and further that it is 'unrealistic to segregate toys at all times, and in all circumstances.' With respect to those children who are outside the main danger zone, the report asks the question, 'is it realistic or practical to stop three and four year olds from playing with marbles, small building bricks or tiddlywinks?' (DTI, 1996).

By contrast, the research presented to the Commission suggested that 'a minute probability is never negligible', and, presumably concerned by the small numbers recorded due to 'reporting limitations', proposed that in future there should be 'epidemiological investigation of events, that are more frequent than those that represent major health risks but sharing the same risk profile (in the way near misses are studied to identify risk factors for the very rare air-crashes)'.

However, scientifically, it is vital clearly to differentiate choking incidents, caused by the ingestion of a food or non-food item, from other similar yet substantively different problems. In particular these are: (a) choking on a regurgitated food item; (b) external blockage of the nose and mouth; (c) external compression of the chest; and (d) blockage of the oesophagus leading to a restriction on the passage of air. The first of these is usually not disaggregated from other causes of choking in morbidity statistics, whilst the others are commonly confused with choking in non-fatal accidents that do not necessitate a post-mortem. Choking itself involves the prevention of the passage of air to the lungs. When fatal, the victim is usually unconscious within one minute and by two minutes will have suffered irreparable brain damage; death follows swiftly.

Such differentiation is extremely important if the suggestion to record 'near misses' is to be considered, especially as the swallowing of foreign bodies or their complete inhalation into the lungs, which are rarely fatal, are also commonly confused with choking amongst accident reports. According to the DTI report these latter are 'less serious, even trivial, and, though alarming to a parent, are probably not life threatening', and further, 'it appears that accidents are often classified as choking when a foreign body or piece of food in the mouth causes concern or discomfort even if it has no more than very temporarily obstructed the airway'.

The recording of 'near misses' then, far from providing a wealth of new scientific evidence, would only serve to confuse the issue and raise anxieties. Choking is extremely rare and sometimes fatal; most other incidents involving ingestion of foreign bodies are neither choking nor potentially fatal. These sets of circumstances should never be allowed to become confused, yet it is easily done, even by medically trained professionals, when there is no need for a post-mortem.

When the CPSE met to discuss the outcome of their investigations, they concluded that sufficient protections were already in place. In most EU states, non-edible items contained in food products had been separately wrapped for a number of years and those countries where this was not the case were soon to harmonize their procedures.

Despite the evidence, consumer groups vowed to continue their campaign to see all such products, including those under wraps, removed from the market place. More recently, the parents of the three such UK child fatalities over the last 15 years have been encouraged to petition the European Parliament to introduce mandatory safeguards.

Similar pressures have elsewhere already led to self-restriction. Following emotional campaigns by, amongst others, the Consumers Federation of America and the US Public Interest Research Group, Nestlé withdrew its 'Nestlé Magic', a chocolate ball containing Disney characters, from the US market two years ago. This was before any ruling had been reached as to whether it satisfied the food regulations in place there (which are considered by many to be more stringent than those in Europe). The product, whose parts are substantially larger than those found in 'Kinder Surprise' eggs, subsequently satisfied the Food and Drug Administration requirements and those of the Consumer Products Safety Commission who undertook 'small parts' and 'use and abuse' tests on it, but it was not put back on the market. Moreover, 'Nestlé Magic' continues to be widely available outside the USA and has not apparently caused any of the problems claimed by the protesters.

In spite of the lack of evidence of harm, Nestlé appears to have agreed to pay out some \$US1.5 million in compensation after being approached by

13 attorneys representing the families of children supposedly distressed through choking incidents related to the product. If this is true, the likely explanation is that Nestlé sought to avoid adverse publicity. Companies often settle such suits for this reason even when they feel confident in their product (Füredi, 1999a).

Such developments should serve as a salutary warning to companies such as Kellogg, Smiths, Ferrero and Westimex, who may also find themselves on the receiving end of an irresistible wave of demands for self-restraint marshalled by the increasingly vociferous self-appointed 'representatives' of consumer interests. One can only be left wondering how it was possible for previous generations of young children to have survived being brought up by the apparently thoughtless parents who encouraged them to hunt for the threepenny coins once concealed in traditional British Christmas puddings, or the fève in the French Galette des Rois!

Plastic panics

Polyvinyl chloride (PVC) is a rigid material that can be made soft by the addition of plasticizers. The most commonly used PVC plasticizers are esters of o-phthalic acid, or phthalates, including DEHP, DINP, DIDP, DNOP, DBP and BBP (di-ethyl-hexyl phthalate, di-iso-nonyl phthalate, di-iso-decyl phthalate, di-n-octyl phthalate, di-butyl phthalate and di-pentyl phthalate respectively). Phthalates have been in widespread use for almost 50 years and are found in products as common and diverse as: medical devices: in particular, fluid containers, tubing and gloves; children's toys – including teethers, rattles and bathtime rubber ducks – and household and industrial items–such as wire and cable coating, flooring and clothing. They are also used to a more limited extent in printing inks and perfumes.

As a result of their diverse and widespread use and relative resistance to degradation, phthalates are frequently found in the environment (JFSSG, 1995). Yet, compared to many other commonly used products, such as solvents, they can readily be removed by photochemical, oxidative and biological processes. They also break down in low oxygen environments such as sediment, but at a lower rate (Shanker et al., 1985), and levels in natural waters are reported to be decreasing (RIVM, 1991).

The quantity of phthalate plasticizer added to a PVC product can be determined by measuring weight loss after diethyl ether extraction. For example, at the Laboratory of the UK Government Chemist, over 100 plastic teethers and toys have been assessed for plasticizer content. In these and other laboratory investigations using a low molecular weight solvent, as well as others using chromatographic methods (including those by Greenpeace), losses of up to 50 per cent are fairly common. However, whilst it is not difficult to extract phthalates from PVC using a suitable solvent, it is problematic to determine the level of migration of phthalates from PVC into saliva.

In April 1997, the European Commission services were approached by the Danish authorities regarding three emergency notifications taken out five days earlier on the recommendation of the Danish Environmental Protection Agency (Vikelsoe et al., 1997), and concerning various teething rings manufactured in China for the Italian company Chicco – Artsana. According to these notifications, the analyses carried out showed that the articles released certain phthalates in quantities considered to be unacceptable for babies. The Danish importer had thus withdrawn these products from the market.

The manufacturers, who considered that the teethers were in conformity with Community legislation, and did not present any danger, nevertheless on a preventative basis, and awaiting the results of their own analyses, also decided voluntarily to withdraw them from the market. The results of their analyses, which took into account the latest working draft proposing a test method to determine the migration of phthalates in articles destined for child-use and care, conflicted with those of the Danish authorities.

Reactions by other member states to these notifications indicated important differences regarding test methods used to measure phthalate migration, focusing specifically on such assumptions as period of exposure, contact area, and type of stimulus. An experiment in the Netherlands that led to reported doses marginally above the tolerable daily intake (TDI), itself set at a very cautious level, has been criticized by others for its methodology of mimicking chewing through the use of an ultrasonic bath which produces a 55 000 Hz vibration. Not exactly what one would expect from a child's mouth!

Some took account of the TDIs fixed by the Scientific Committee for Food, in its 1996 Opinion on phthalates in infant formulae. However, Belgium and the UK in particular required the Commission's services to ask for the opinion of experts and/or relevant scientific committees at the European level, prior to proceeding with the matter. The CPSE was thus unable to issue a 'serious and immediate risk to health' warning, as it had done over choking scare, and had to refer the matter on to the new Scientific Committee on Toxicity, Ecotoxicity and the Environment (CSTEE). Due to reorganization, this did not meet for its first plenary session until November 1997.

The Greenpeace campaign

No doubt encouraged by the Danish notification to the Commission and its impact upon the Italian-owned distributors, as well as the results of the disputed Dutch 'in vitro' experiment and longer standing Swedish concerns regarding PVC use, Greenpeace began approaching the Commission on the matter. Since August 1996 the organization had been contacting major toy manufacturers around the world requesting meetings to discuss concerns about PVC toys. This formed part of what appears to be a wider Greenpeace agenda against PVC in particular and the chlorine industry in general.

Perhaps frustrated by the prevarication caused by the need to substantiate and corroborate scientific data, Greenpeace continued independently to approach politicians and officials in member states at a local, regional and national level, as well as manufacturers and retailers and their professional associations. It sought to use the various notifications, voluntary withdrawals and early investigations as proof of a wider concern.

On 17 September 1997 – 100 days before Christmas – Greenpeace launched the 'Play Safe' campaign in New York and London. This included a list for parents of PVC and non-PVC infant toys, as well as a message outlining the supposed adverse health effects – purported to be liver and kidney damage leading to cancer, the mimicking of sex hormones and reproductive abnormalities. The campaign was set to target major toy manufacturers such as Mattel, and retailers such as Toys 'R' Us, who were refusing to conform to the scare, which had by now affected a number of retailers in Denmark, the Netherlands and Sweden, as well as clients of the Italian suppliers in Spain, Portugal, Greece and Italy itself.

Greenpeace claim that they 'first drew attention to the problem by releasing a scientific study'. This actually amounted to no more than a Technical Note identifying the types and amounts of phthalates contained in PVC (Greenpeace, 1997). However, the level of phthalate contained by a compound is not an indication of the amount that actually leaches from it, and even if this latter quantity can be determined, it remains to be proven whether this poses a risk to human health.

In October a number of prominent politicians entered the fray. Austrian Consumer Affairs minister, Barbara Prammer, stated that 'based on precautionary consumer protection, PVC toys are not desirable', whilst Belgian minister for Public Health, Marcel Colla (who had previously tried to ban 'flippos' from crisp packets), urged retailers to 'voluntarily discontinue marketing these products'. Reinvigorated by this political intervention, Greenpeace obtained an agreement from the senior management of Toys 'R' Us in Austria to withdraw ten specific PVC toys from the shelves, although these were subsequently reinstated at the behest of the US head office. In Belgium, FEDIS, the retail federation, agreed immediately to withdraw all soft PVC products designed to be chewed by young children.

No doubt FEDIS and the Austrian management of Toys 'R' Us thought they could placate the anti-PVC activists with their agreements. What happened was quite the opposite: each agreement was seen as a battle won in the war against chlorine, fuelling further activity and leading to more alarmist press releases by the campaigners. In Italy activists entered the Ministry of Health in Father Christmas costumes carrying boxes full of PVC toys. Three weeks later Italian Health Minister, Rosi Bindi, was also encouraging manufacturers to look into alternative materials.

In Germany it was the Association of Toy Retailers, Vedes, which in December took the lead and called upon its members to withdraw such products, whilst the Federal Institute for the Protection of Consumer Health and Veterinary Medicine, BgVV, urged manufacturers and industry to act responsibly by doing likewise. This was then, predictably, followed by statements from the Ministry of Health and the Ministry of Family Affairs suggesting that it would be highly desirable for industry to voluntarily refrain from selling such products.

Everyone now seemed to be getting in on the act. The Spanish municipality of Bilbao introduced its own ban, a measure to be widely repeated by other local and regional assemblies, including many in Italy. These, no doubt, were keen to be seen to be taking a greater interest in their electorates' well-being than that taken by central government, in order to confirm their own legitimacy and purpose.

Revealing its own loss of nerve, in February 1998 the European Commission removed all soft PVC teething toys from its own childcare facilities. This further fuelled the anti-phthalates campaign, with protesters now understandably complaining that if the products were not good enough for the Commission, then they should not be inflicted upon the rest of the population. Relentless pressure by Greenpeace, including the placing of adverts in newspapers seeking to 'name and shame' firms who would not comply led many retailers, including Dutch chain Bart Smit, to order their shops to remove all listed soft PVC toys.

Effectively, retailers and governments across Europe had removed soft PVC products from their shelves and markets on a voluntary basis. This was carried out on the grounds that although the activists' claims against such products had 'not been scientifically substantiated', nevertheless 'we choose to give our customers the benefit of this doubt'.

The CSTEE investigation

It is within this evolving climate that the European Commission invited its new Scientific Committee on Toxicity, Ecotoxicity, and the Environment (CSTEE), at its first plenary meeting in Brussels on 17 November 1997, to give its opinion as to:

- the impact on children's health of the use of soft PVC containing phthalates from child-care articles and toys that children of a young age could put in their mouth;
- the limits which ought to be respected in relation to the migration of phthalates from these products;
- the test method to be followed and the standards or parameters that should be taken into consideration to measure the phthalate migration level.

The CSTEE established a working group which first met in December 1997 and formulated a preliminary position expressed at the Second CSTEE plenary meeting in February 1998. This related to the six phthalates (DEHP, DNOP, DINP, DIDP, DBP and BBP) found in infant teething rings, and was based on the documents and literature available to it at that time. It confirmed the existence of different methodologies and highly variable results for the estimation of emission of phthalates from toys. Nevertheless, true to the precautionary approach, it used the highest reported emission levels as a baseline and sought to homogenize all available research evidence to an equivalent exposure dose.

The exposure dose was initially based upon the maximal amounts extracted over 12 hours, from a phthalate containing PVC-toy surrogate of 10 square cm, by a saliva solution under dynamic conditions, and assuming an infant body weight of 5 kg for the risk assessment. This was changed at the time of the expression of its formal opinion on the matter by the CSTEE at its third plenary meeting in April 1998, to a more realistic extraction for 6 hours using an infant body weight of 8 kg.

A margin of safety was estimated for each phthalate by dividing the No-Observed-Adverse-Effect-Level (NOAEL) values obtained through animal experimentation, by the worst predicted exposure dose. A level of little concern was assumed for exposure situations with margins of safety in excess of 100. This arbitrary figure is derived by allowing an extra factor of 10 for variation between species, and a further factor of 10 for variation between individuals.

A further opinion expressed as answers to four new questions put to the committee on the occasion of the CSTEE fourth plenary meeting in June 1998, emphasized the need to wait for the outcome of an 'in vivo' Dutch study using adult human volunteers, expected later that year. This was expected to provide more realistic estimates for the quantities of phthalate leached, as well as the duration of exposure.

Predictably however, Greenpeace used the launch of investigations by the Commission and the publication of preliminary opinions as a further stick to beat recalcitrant governments, manufacturers and retailers. Under increasing pressure to be seen to be taking action, which included inflammatory comments by Greenpeace about 'corpses' and playing 'Russian roulette', the Commission agreed the need for a directive specifically to address soft PVC toys intended for young children and babies. The then Consumer Policy and Consumer Health Protection commissioner, Emma Bonino, drew up proposals for an emergency ban, reducing its scope to objects designed to be put in the mouth. However, fearing that an outright ban might be successfully challenged in court, the Commission voted against it adopting instead a non-binding recommendation.

The recommendation covered child-care articles and toys made of soft PVC containing phthalates and intended to be put into the mouth by children under the age of three. It invited member states to take appropriate safety measures whilst Community legislation for permanent protection was under way. Indicating that such products 'are considered to be liable to provoke negative health effects at high level of exposure', it also requested member states to check levels of phthalate migration, comparing these to limits now proposed by the CSTEE. It also effectively conceded the importance of non-scientific factors by indicating that 'Other Member States had announced that they would act on their own if the Commission does not find a Community solution' (CSTEE, 1998a).

One of the major problems throughout this process has been the adoption of continuously shifting baselines and data. The margin of safety, arbitrarily considered as needing to exceed 100, is determined by dividing the NOAEL value by the exposure dose. Yet each of these quantities has varied according to particular experiments or has been the subject of systematic revision or reinterpretation. Even samples from parallel batches of PVC and using identical techniques, yield low correlative precision due to the uneven release of phthalates from within them.

In all instances the worst data or the worst-case approach was adopted in order to err on the side of caution, even if this meant variations as great as four orders of magnitude (10 000) between experimental data! Such an approach was considered reasonable, as no account was being made for exposure to more than one phthalate in a toy, and for additional exposures through food, air, or skin contact.

The various opinions did recognize however, that where calculable, intake from toys was not the only, or indeed the major, source of exposure. A European Committee for Standardization draft report in 1997 estimated exposure from toys to be 10 per cent of total exposure for a given phthalate. For at least one such compound (BBP), 'Food is by far the major source contributing over 90 per cent of intake'. A UK MAFF information sheet indicates that far from being caused by plastic containers or wrapping, the presence of phthalates in food is due to general environmental conditions, as core content levels of phthalates in food items often exceed surface content levels (JFSSG, 1996). Indoor air provides most of our remaining exposure to phthalates.

In all, well over one hundred documents have now been presented to the CSTEE in evidence over the issue of phthalate toxicity. Whilst some are merely member state notifications of intended action, others are of a more scientific nature. One of the key, and shifting, areas for debate and experimentation has been over what is assumed to be the critical end point of phthalate toxicity. This means an indication as to the type of adverse effect to be expected from each compound.

Are phthalates carcinogenic?

NOAEL values are determined by administering phthalates in varying concentrations to the diet of test animals, usually rats. Typically concentrations go up in factors of ten, and after a specified period the animals are anaesthetized, terminated, and analysed for abnormalities with respect to a control group. The NOAEL value is then taken to be the highest dose producing no statistically significant variation, whilst the critical end-point is the type of variation first noticed. In certain instances, when appropriate data did not exist, Lowest-Observed-Adverse-Effect-Level (LOAEL) values were taken, and in consequence a further factor of 5 was incorporated in determining their safety margins.

From early on in the proceedings, the two phthalates to come under most scrutiny were to be DEHP and DINP. This is because they had been the most commonly found phthalates in toys and various child-care articles, but also because they each had a margin of safety determined right from the start as being below 100. These particular margins were based on the least reliable available data, provided by Greenpeace and the Danish authorities that had initiated the matter, and varied by factors of 2500 and 10 000 respectively from other experimental sources.

Initially, DNOP also produced a margin of safety below 100 and in its preliminary position of February 1998 the CSTEE declared all three phthalates as giving cause for concern. Later revisions to NOAEL values and exposure doses removed DNOP from the list. By the time of the formal opinion expressed in April 1998, the CSTEE had concluded that only the very low margin of safety for DINP (8.8) caused concern, 'since humans appear to be less sensitive towards the critical effect of DEHP (hepatic peroxisome proliferation; an increase in those parts of cells which generate or break down hydrogen peroxide in the liver) identified in rats'.

DEHP has been found to be hepatocarcinogenic (liver cancer-inducing) in rats and mice (Ashby et al., 1994), as it is accepted that after long-term exposure, peroxisome proliferation which is the most sensitive change found (RIVM, 1992), acts as an early indicator of this. However, there is a marked species variation in response to peroxisome proliferation. Rats and mice are very sensitive, whereas guinea pigs and monkeys appear to be relatively insensitive or non-responsive at dose levels that produce a marked response in rats. There is no indication of human sensitivity.

Yet now, based upon figures 2500 times greater than from other sources; scaled up by a further safety margin of 100; using the most sensitive critical end-point of dubious relevance; and despite the fact that a 1996 risk assessment of DEHP, which reviewed more than 500 studies, concluded that the threat of human liver cancer is extremely unlikely under any anticipated exposure dose (Huber et al., 1996), DEHP was considered as giving cause for concern.

Campaigners against phthalates have attached great importance to the fact that the US Environmental Protection Agency (EPA) classified DEHP as a 'probable human carcinogen'. This decision was taken over 10 years ago, however, and had, until very recently, not formally been re-evaluated. Not only has the relevance to humans of liver tumours in rodents induced by peroxisome proliferation become more questionable, but our understanding of carcinogenic processes themselves have evolved. Nevertheless, in the mid-1980s the US toy industry had removed DEHP from children's products to maintain consumer confidence until further scientific research could be conducted.

Regulation of carcinogens in the United States is still based on the 'no-threshold' assumptions adopted over thirty years ago, the famous 'Delaney Clause' enacted as part of the 1958 amendments to the Food, Drug and Cosmetic Act. Since then however, not only have we become more conscious of the various non-zero doses which the body can tolerate, but our understanding of the biological processes involved, particularly in relation to mitogenic (cell division rate) and mutagenic (cell replication error) carcinogens, which have allowed for a far more sophisticated view than the 'one hit, one cancer' approach which used to determine EPA policy (Wilson, 1997). In addition, according to the biochemist who developed the primary test for carcinogenic substances, Dr Bruce Ames, about one-half of all chemicals tested, both natural and man-made, are toxic when tested at high doses in either rats or mice (Ames and Gold, 1997).

Recently the head of the EPA's Science and Policy Staff stated: 'No evidence exists to suggest that these agents [peroxisome proliferators] are carcinogenic in the human liver', (Cattley et al., 1998). Health Canada has classified DEHP as 'Unlikely to be Carcinogenic to Humans', the European Commission's own official decision states that DEHP, 'shall not be classified or labelled as a carcinogenic or an irritant substance', whilst the World Health Organization (WHO) Environmental Health Criteria document for DEHP concludes: 'Currently there is not sufficient evidence to suggest that DEHP is a potential human carcinogen'.

In February 2000, the International Agency for Research on Cancer (IARC), part of WHO, decided 'on careful consideration of the vast scientific evidence that was generated after DEHP's initial classification in the 1980s', to reclassify DEHP as a Group 3 agent – meaning the substance cannot be classified as causing cancer in humans. In purely scientific terms this is a severe blow to the anti-phthalates campaign.

For DINP there is a recognition that 'different commercial products may vary in composition', which might explain the factor of variation in excess of 10 000 between experiments to measure the exposure dose. It has also been found to cause hepatic peroxisome proliferation in rats, but an even more sensitive critical end-point has been established. This is an increase in liver and kidney weight after feeding significant dietary levels of DINP for up to two years (Lington et al., 1997). Scaled up to human levels this is equivalent to a child consuming a sizeable chunk (50 gm) of plastic each day. As Michael Fumento, senior fellow at the Hudson Institute, has said, 'If your child *eats* toys, phthalates are the least of your worries'!

Are phthalates gender benders?

If the potential carcinogenicity of phthalates, in high doses and over long periods of time on rodents, would not be sufficient to obtain the desired restrictions upon their use, campaigners had already prepared themselves to move on to a more emotive critical end point. This shifting of the argument had begun through focusing media attention onto the most extreme possible outcome, presenting phthalates as so-called 'endocrine disrupting chemicals' (EDCs), calling them 'gender benders', and claiming that they mimic oestrogen. This approach successfully generated shock headlines such as

'Human sperm count could be zero in 70 years' and 'Sex change chemicals in baby milk', in the two UK national newspapers; *The Mirror* and *The Independent on Sunday* respectively.

The endocrine system is held to be that complex of processes whereby a number of fundamental bodily functions are kept in check through the action of an appropriate balance of hormones. An endocrine disrupter is then considered to be any chemical which interferes with the synthesis, secretion, transport, binding, action or elimination of the natural hormones which are responsible for homeostasis, reproduction, development and/or behaviour.

The popularity of this hypothesis, and the belief that artificial hormones released into the environment through human activity are responsible for unexplained phenomena upon the endocrine systems of various organisms, in particular aquatic-related life forms, stems from the publication in March 1996 of *Our Stolen Future* by Theo Colborn, Dianne Dumanoski, and John Peterson Myers. A review of 'Our Stolen Future' by Professor of Environmental Toxicology, Michael Kamrin, at Michigan State University, appeared under the title 'The mismeasure of risk', in the September 1996 issue of *Scientific American*. This described the book as 'not scientific in the most fundamental sense', arguing that 'the authors present a very selective segment of the data that has been gathered about chemicals that might affect hormonal functions', and further that 'it obscures the line between science and policy to the detriment of both.' (Kamrin, 1996).

Nevertheless, Greenpeace released their own version a month later under the title *Taking Back Our Stolen Future: Hormone disruption and PVC plastic* (Greenpeace, 1996) which also repeated a widely criticized study published in the *British Medical Journal* earlier that year that claimed to provide evidence of a serious decline in the quality of human semen in the UK (Irvine et al., 1996). Yet even if this widely disputed claim were to be proven true, it would remain to be demonstrated whether this had any causal connection with the release of artificially produced endocrine disrupting chemicals.

The authors of a 1992 study considered to provide the most conclusive evidence of declining sperm counts, Niels Skakkabaek and Richard Sharpe, have since indicated that the implications of their work have been overstated. In *The Independent* (7 July 1995), the two accused Greenpeace of 'taking something which is a clearly stated hypothetical link and calling it fact'.

Others meanwhile have indicated that 'the major human intake of endocrine disrupters are naturally occurring oestrogens found in foods' (Safe, 1995). This exposure is several orders of magnitude higher than the exposure to pesticide EDCs. Such naturally occurring phyto-oestrogens, commonly found in plants and vegetables such as soya, hops, peas, beans, sprouts and celery, appear to be overlooked by environmental campaigners.

Safe calculated daily human intakes of such oestrogens, based on potencies relative to 17 β-oestradiol. Oral contraceptives are found to represent 16 675 μg equivalent per day, and postmenopausal oestrogen therapy would provide 3350 μg per day. By contrast oestrogen flavonoids in food represent 102 µg per day, whilst daily ingestion of environmental organochlorine oestrogens a mere 0.0000025 µg!

Rather obviously then, substances designed to be endocrine disrupters, such as the contraceptive pill, are, whilst those which are not, such as phthalates, are not. However, presumably recognizing the sensitivities of potentially alienating over half the constituency they seek to influence, Greenpeace and other environmentalists chose tactically not to highlight the extent to which the presence of such substances in the environment, in addition to naturally occurring substances, actually stems from the widespread use of oral contraceptives.

Evidence in support of the putative oestrogenic effect of phthalates is extremely weak even at relatively high doses (Jobling et al., 1995; Zacharewski et al., 1998). At the doses to which humans are likely to be exposed, even young children sucking teethers, there is no known effect. The same is true for putative effects on offspring. The most recent two-generation studies demonstrate that exposure of rats to DINP and DIDP in utero, during lactation, puberty, and adulthood does not affect testicular size, sperm count, morphology or motility, or produce any reproductive fertility effects.

Nevertheless the CSTEE set up a Working Group to investigate such matters. In March 1999 they published their own 'Opinion on Human and Wildlife Health Effects of Endocrine Disrupting Chemicals, with Emphasis on Wildlife and on Ecotoxicology Test Methods' (CSTEE, 1999b). Shortly afterwards, in July 1999, a similar study entitled 'Hormonally Active Agents in the Environment', commissioned by the US National Research Council (NRC, 1999) was also released. Both documents indicate 'growing concern' as their rationales and cite Colborn's widely refuted book as their opening reference. No doubt Greenpeace and their allies, who have been responsible for a substantial element of the 'growing concern', will draw upon these documents themselves as further evidence as to the objectivity of their claims.

Whilst the original intention of the EDC Working Group, as revealed through the various CSTEE plenary meeting minutes, was 'to finally produce a report that covers human health and environmental effects of EDCs' (CSTEE, 1998b), the final product placed a far greater emphasis upon wildlife, 'due to the fact that it is where the greatest impact is felt. The human health effects part was therefore correspondingly reduced' (CSTEE, 1999a). In other words unable to come up with sufficient evidence for effects upon humans, the committee simply decided to play this down rather than highlight the fact. The document accepts that for humans 'a *causative* role . . . has not been verified', and that 'for most reported effects in wildlife (however) the evidence for a *causal* link with endocrine disruption is weak or non-existing', adding further that 'the mechanisms of pollutant-induced reproductive toxicity observed in wild mammalian species generally remain unclear but could also involve endocrine disruption'.

Needless to say, many of the purported effects upon wildlife are themselves speculative. Two studies in the journal *Science* for example, concluded that defects found in frogs throughout the western United States, cited in the CSTEE document as possibly due to EDCs, may be caused by a trematode, a simple parasitic flatworm, which infects tadpoles and leads to multiple or malformed hind legs (Sessions et al., 1999; Johnson et al., 1999). No doubt some will now argue that chemical pollution was responsible for the increase in water snails which act as a key host of the parasite. However, this is to reveal such views as based upon simple association, rather than the scientific analysis necessary to provide insights into causal mechanisms and metabolic pathways.

Applying the precautionary principle

The only logical outcome of adopting the precautionary principle is to accommodate to the lowest common denominator. This effect was perfectly exposed by reactions to the outcome of the Dutch 'Consensus Group' study into the oral leaching of phthalates by adult human volunteers (RIVM, 1998). This coincided with a review of other data made available to the CSTEE subsequent to April 1998, such as an Austrian investigation which appeared to corroborate the results of the Dutch study, and a US Consumer Product Safety Commission report on DINP which showed that the high levels of release that had previously been used could not be reproduced (CSTEE, 1998d).

Notably, the final report by the Dutch 'Consensus Group' study, indicated that the possibility of a baby exceeding the recommended limits was 'so rare that the statistical likelihood cannot be estimated'. It also revealed that previous estimates as to the amounts of time spent chewing on soft PVC products by children had been grossly exaggerated reducing this from six hours to a maximum of three hours exposure. A joint press release issued by Toy Industries of Europe, the European Council of Plasticizers and Inter-mediates, and the European Council of Vinyl Manufacturers, assumed that their position had now been vindicated.

The Greenpeace view on the Dutch study at this stage was predictably antagonistic, arguing not only that it had failed in its task to develop a standardized procedure for measuring the quantities of phthalates leached from PVC, but also, and more pointedly, questioning the integrity of the study group for having representatives from both the toy industry (Mattel), and the chemical industry (Exxon), upon its technical committee. Activists had systematically targeted Exxon production facilities during their cam-paign because it is the world's single largest producer of phthalates. A little over two months later, however, when the CSTEE announced its own views on the new research, Greenpeace was endorsing the change in emphasis. A new and less extreme determination of the NOAEL value for DINP had been made available; however as this yielded a value four times greater than that derived from the earlier research (Lington et al., 1997), the CSTEE decided 'from a precautionary standpoint', to maintain its use of the pre-existing value in its revised assessment. In other words the new evidence was quite simply sidelined.

In addition, a study which had examined the effects of exposing female rats to DEHP in drinking water from the first day of pregnancy to the twenty-first day after delivery, indicated damage to the testes of the offspring (Arcadi et al., 1998). In spite of the poor test methodology, including inaccurate measurement of water intake, the LOAEL derived from this study was taken to substantiate an earlier low NOAEL value which had, at the time of the April 1998 opinion, been ignored in favour of that derived from 'a well-performed study'. Now, however, the critical effect was taken to be the testicular effects rather than hepatocarcinogenicity, despite that study's flawed methodology ruling it out at the time of the earlier opinion (Poon et al., 1997).

The recalculated margin of safety for DINP, whilst providing improvement due to the reduction in exposure time, remained below 100, thereby suggesting continued cause for concern. That for DEHP was now both lower than the previous value and also had a critical end-point assumed to be of greater relevance than hepatic peroxisome proliferation, thus actually raising the level of concern. These views were submitted to the DG XXIV Risk Evaluation Unit who in January 1999 suggested 'that the Commission should be looking for a phase out of phthalates as soon as possible'.

The official view from the Commission was, by now, hardly contentious as a number of member states had, since the issuing of the last formal opinion on the matter in November 1998, finally been convinced by the various voluntary restrictions in operation, as well as pressed through the actions of environmentalists and consumer groups, to take matters into their own hands. They had started notifying the Commission of their intentions to introduce formal restrictions on such products, particularly those aimed at children under three years of age and intended to be placed in the mouth.

When the Commission finally introduced its ban in December 1999 based upon the decision of the Committee on Product Safety Emergencies, eight EU member states had already introduced their own restrictions on the production and sale of such products. Far from being a 'decision' it was no more than a cowardly and rearguard gesture to legitimate its authority by appealing to consumers under the guise of protecting health.

Under the ban, PVC articles intended to be put in the mouths of children aged under three cannot contain more than 0.1 per cent by weight of the six phthalates investigated by the Commission services, despite the fact that only two of these actually gave 'cause for concern'. In addition, soft PVC toys for children under three which could be placed in their mouths, even when this is not intended by the manufacturer, will need to carry a warning label indicating the presence of phthalates. The chair of the CSTEE, Professor Jim Bridges of the University of Surrey, has questioned the ban indicating that 'I don't think the science is saying at all that there's an immediate risk'. Other members of the Committee have complained that the restrictions are being applied too widely as the evidence was only derived from teethers which are designed to be chewed. One member even voiced consternation as to the purpose of their continued deliberations as it had become obvious that 'no matter what the scientific input' it would 'not be the decisive input anyway'.

Ever decreasing circles

It is interesting to note how the gradual collapse by member states across the EU increased the pressure for the USA to follow suit. Despite one commentator's view that 'Multinational companies are under attack every-where – but nowhere more than in Europe', it may yet prove to be the case that Europe is just a stepping stone to actions further afield. In the USA, the Greenpeace campaign took a longer time to become effective, in part due to the fact that DEHP had already formally been withdrawn as a precautionary measure in 1986. Also most pacifiers on the American market are made of latex rather than PVC.

Nevertheless concerned by the direction of events in Europe, the US Ambassador to the European Community, Vernon Weaver, had sent a blunt letter to the EU Directorate General for External Affairs in February 1998, stating that 'a sudden ban on products which have been sold for years and which is based on incomplete and perhaps erroneous information could cause trade misunderstandings between the US and the EU'. With widespread restrictions in place across most of Europe by the autumn however, Greenpeace accelerated its American campaign, releasing a new report on phthalates in November 1998. This amounted to little more than a press release with footnotes, but led to a flurry of toy manufacturers, including Toys 'R' Us, issuing assurances, as to their intentions to phase out the products. At the opening of the International Toy Fair in New York activists abseiled down the side of a building to unfurl a banner that read 'Play Safe, Buy PVC Free'. The stunt was repeated the following year at the Tokyo Toy Fair leading to the arrest of three campaigners and yet more publicity.

Three days after the release of the Greenpeace report, Health Canada, a government consumer protection body, issued an advisory calling for soft PVC teethers and rattles to be removed from shelves and calling on parents and childcare facilities to immediately dispose of these toys. Then, in December 1998, the US Consumer Product Safety Commission (CPSC) released its latest results of a study on DINP which showed that 'the amount ingested does not even come close to a harmful level'. Nevertheless, due to the overall mood, it requested industry, 'as a precaution while more scientific work is done', to remove phthalates from soft rattles and teethers.

In those countries where there had been regulatory successes against toys, the campaign now moved on to medical devices. PVC softened with phthalates provides amongst other products flexible tubing, intravenous bags, catheters and protective gloves. It allows hospitals access to quality disposable items which are durable, flexible, inexpensive and safe.

Yet building upon earlier gains, the Greenpeace-backed Health Care Without Harm in the USA are seeking to limit or prohibit the use of PVC in healthcare facilities; this is despite there being no evidence as to adverse effects, even amongst patients receiving dialysis for kidney disease, the group most exposed, and hence supposedly at risk, from such products.

PVC plasticized with DEHP is the only flexible material approved by the European Pharmacopoeia for life-saving medical devices such as blood and plasma transfusion equipment. The safety of these materials has been confirmed by more than 40 years of use, with five to seven billion patient days of acute exposure and one to two billion patient days of chronic exposure without any indication of adverse effects. But again companies with a vital interest at stake, both private and public, have proven to be remarkably defensive in their stance. Baxter Healthcare's own environmental manager in Sweden, Birgitta Lindblom admits for example that 'It's unfortunate that [the Stockholm County Council] have taken a decision that may have tragic consequences for many people. We probably have to shoulder part of the blame ourselves as we have not succeeded in informing the politicians in the County Council about the necessity for PVC in medical products'. Baxter, a world leader in healthcare products, has come under increasing pressure to develop alternative materials to PVC by its own shareholders, despite seeking to indicate that 'in many applications, PVC remains the material of choice'. Unfortunately one of those new materials is currently recognized as having odour problems and causing skin irritation.

Not surprisingly, therefore, the European Commission's CSTEE has already initiated investigations into the potential problems associated with their possible replacements (CSTEE, 1998c). Both adipates and citrates which have started to be used as substitutes in countries where phthalates are no longer available, have been criticized, not least for appearing to offer little toxicological documentation in the literature (CSTEE, 1999a). In this, the inevitable logic of the precautionary principle has come to the fore. The fear of phthalates has simply been transferred onto the supposed solution.

Finally, it should be noted that the campaign against phthalates forms part of a wider Greenpeace agenda against PVC specifically and the chlorine industry in general. Greenpeace has made it clear that it has no intention of calling a halt to its campaign subsequent to the demise of phthalates, having argued explicitly that 'PVC is a poisonous plastic – replacing phthalates won't solve the problem'.

Retreat from reason

In her speech to the Joint European Parliament and Commission Conference on Food Law and Food Policy in November 1997, the then Consumer Policy and Consumer Health Protection Commissioner, Emma Bonino, placed great emphasis on the increasingly important agenda-setting role of consumers. Stating that 'pressure from public opinion and interested bodies has often appeared to be the strongest driving force to guarantee that all necessary measures to protect public health are effectively taken', she endorsed the enormous boost which such organizations had received over the course of the BSE debacle.

Earlier that year Agriculture and Rural Development Commissioner, Franz Fischler, had actively encouraged this approach in direct relation to BSE, indicating that 'It is time we heard from the consumers. These are the most important people of all in this equation'. Environment Commissioner, Ritt Bjerregaard, also echoed this line, commenting that, 'Retailers can play a crucial role. They are ecological gatekeepers.' Clearly then, the consumer voice, in all its guises, is actively being sought and promoted across the board.

This is because the activism of the lobbyist allows politicians to retain a semblance of accountability in an age when political participation is at an all-time low. Deliberation with advocacy groups creates the impression that genuine consultation is taking place. Lobbyists have thus moved from the margins to the mainstream and are courted and even financed at the highest levels within the European Union. They exert considerable influence over, and enjoy a mutually beneficial relationship with, both politicians and the media, who present them as neutral experts representing the interests of the general public (Füredi, 1999b).

But whilst the advent of a better informed and more questioning attitude by consumers could be welcomed as long overdue, there appears to be a lack of serious debate as to who 'the consumers' actually are (Heartfield, 1998). Such views appear to express an inherent assumption that there is a singular, or at least majoritarian, consumer voice or interest, which finds expression through existing consumer groups. Further, consumerism at its heart is built upon the promotion of mistrust. This can only exaggerate fears and breed passive cynicism.

At the same time the broader climate within which such new roles, structures and procedures are arising should be recognized as one which prioritizes caution over production, and risk over opportunity (Füredi, 1997). This is not to suggest a wilful desire to engender panics or impose restrictions, but rather that society as a whole has become increasingly risk-conscious, and even risk-averse (Beck, 1992).

It has been argued that 'We no longer choose to take risks, we have them thrust upon us', and further, that 'Society becomes a laboratory, but there is no one responsible for its outcomes' (Beck, 1998). As a consequence, the drive to regulate, or re-regulate, to restore a form of moral responsibility, has become a strong one in the 1990s. But there is also a growing aversion to official regulation, which suggests that to be effective regulation may need to occur more informally, at the level of the firm or the individual, through self-imposed restrictions, which may be externally-monitored (Ayres and Braithwaite, 1992).

Echoing this mood, Emma Bonino herself suggested that 'There are times when legislation does not happen, and we need to ask ourselves whether it is better to have nothing at all or self-regulation in some form or other'. In a similar vein, *Financial Times* columnist Lionel Barber astutely observed in relation to the Commission, that 'the flood of EU legislation accompanying the single market has slowed to a trickle. Today, Brussels is using peer pressure and voluntary codes of conduct to encourage minimum standards of compliance'.

As a consequence a climate has been created whereby social control is increasingly exercised, or moderated through self-restraint, and marshalled by the explosion of highly vociferous, and inevitably self-appointed representatives of consumer interests. If left unchecked this can only lead to instances of overreaction and unnecessary interference, justified through an appeal to a supposed consumer mandate.

In addition it has been suggested that 'consumers are not easily convinced by scientific evidence and advice' (European Parliament, 1997). Indeed the Commission's own Consumer Committee, responded to the Green Paper on The General Principles of Food Law by proposing the application of the precautionary principle 'even where there is no known scientific uncertainty'. It argued that when the scientific evidence, which it recognized to be necessary, was available, that 'too great an emphasis on this may be undesirable from the consumer's point of view'.

This presents science as just one of many 'readings' of the world, suggesting that no amount of experimentation or evidence would ever suffice to determine the outcome of an issue, and effectively recognizing that the assessment of risk is a social, rather than a scientific, exercise. Such an approach continues that proposed by the official Commission documentation itself, which had called for the precautionary principle to be highlighted, and had even gone so far as to suggest that 'there may be demands ... to go further in the area of the health protection measures than the scientific evidence suggests is necessary'.

The 'First biannual BSE follow-up report', communicated to the European Parliament in May 1998, took this approach to its logical conclusion, suggesting the need for 'the possibility of taking into account minority scientific views', in other words, of accepting worst-case scenarios regardless of what the majority of scientists say. When hard facts and analysis are replaced by individual views, however, emotion can take over from reasoned debate, and in a climate of heightened sensitivity to risk, the only possible outcome is to adapt to the lowest common denominator.

The hard-done-by consumer has become the alternative voice, which now has to be taken into account within all decision making. Such views, supported by the supposed authority of the precautionary principle, and endorsed by environmentalist and feminist critiques of science, have increasingly become accepted by many social actors. They look set to have a profound impact upon the scientific community, as well as the business and social worlds dependent upon it.

If scientific reason, based upon quantifiable and repeatable evidence, is just one amongst a number of competing views, then it need no longer be the arbiter for decision making, particularly when the concerns of consumer groups or environmentalists have been raised. As Environment Commissioner, Ritt Bjerregaard rhetorically asked in a speech given at a brainstorming workshop on chemicals in the EU, 'Should a lack of sound scientific evidence stand in the way of action?'

The precautionary principle departs from the usual scientific rationale in that it effectively reverses the burden of proof. Science proceeds on the basis of evidence, which is a positive finding that is reproducible. The precautionary principle on the other hand, postulates that all assumptions can be considered valid unless the contrary has been demonstrated. This negative proof is impossible to ascertain. The precautionary principle thus contributes to the deconstruction of the process leading to scientific opinion, since it distances conclusions from evidence-based rationale. It further considers that valid decisions can be made on beliefs without requiring solid evidence.

An international agreement on the precautionary principle was reached during the United Nations Conference on the Environment and Development in Rio de Janeiro in 1992, becoming part of Agenda 21. This is laid down for environmental matters within the European Community, in the Maastricht Treaty under Article 130r. Recently the Commission's Consumer Committee has argued for the principle to be extended into the realm of food law and the Commission has now published its own 'Communication on the Precautionary Principle'. This appears to justify use of the principle on the circuitous application of legal precedent.

The principle is subject to much debate, particularly in relation to the tension between demonstrated actual risk and anticipated plausible risk, as well as the problems associated with enforcing what are inevitably variable standards. A further problem of using the precautionary principle is that all results inevitably become provisional. Targets are relative, and no conclusive outcomes can ever be reached, as situations continuously await clarification through further analysis. In this respect the investigations into phthalate toxicity have been perfect exemplars.

Such an approach has also inevitably encouraged the release and use of results prior to peer-reviewed publication. In addition, frank and open discussions held by interested parties are increasingly entering into the public domain through a desire for greater 'transparency'. The views expressed through both of these means are not the same as reasoned reflection or verified evidence, though, and should therefore not be used in the establishment of policy, as was for instance the case in the then UK Agriculture Minister's decision to ban beef on the bone.

Of more direct concern to the main subject of this chapter has been the fact that some supposed research into the endocrine disrupting properties of phthalates was released through the media, rather than the academic literature. Indeed in one such high-profile instance, a full peer-reviewed version of the work had still failed to appear over two years after raising significant concerns through articles in the popular press, despite assurances that the work 'is still in the phase of being written up'.

Dr. André Prost, Director of Non-Communicable Diseases at the WHO Headquarters in Geneva, has also expressed reservations as to the use of the precautionary principle arguing that, 'precaution becomes a political instrument used on a selective basis by certain sectors of society in support of their own beliefs' (Prost, 1998). He goes on to suggest that situations can only be made worse through the advent of a 'victimization culture', concluding that, 'If the dilemma facing the policy-makers results in a systematic application of the precautionary principle, it will lead to abstention and paralysis in innovation and technology development'.

Conclusions

Implicit within the Commission's approach has been the assumption that the precautionary principle is a zero-cost, or something-for-nothing option. In reality, apart from the narrow economic costs to those businesses directly concerned, there is a far greater social cost which has yet to be taken into account. At an immediate level, replacing plastic medical devices or toys opens the door to the dangers of injury and infection from replacement materials, which are either less flexible or have been subject to less scrutiny. Phthalates are amongst the most understood of organic compounds. There is simply not a single shred of evidence that they have ever harmed any human being. Similarly, banning toys from chocolate eggs or crisp and cereal packets would quite simply make bad law. The statistical evidence and logic show that it is the food items themselves which should be banned, or alternatively all small objects.

More important has been the amount of time and effort, let alone cost, expended by all sides of these disputes. Whilst the attention of large numbers in the scientific community and others have been turned onto these products, countless numbers of people, right across the globe, continue to die of diseases for which cures might be found if only the resources expended elsewhere were to be made available.

Both cases reveal the growing credence afforded to emotional arguments put forward by environmentalist and consumer protection groups. These have learnt how to manipulate the media to good effect and generate their own research to support their views. By appealing to the lowest common denominator amongst manufacturers, retailers and trade associations, they have encouraged a tendency towards self-regulatory behaviour through fear. If needed, official bans can be a rearguard action, formalizing a state of affairs already largely in existence. This allows the authorities to respond to the public concerns generated and yet not to appear over-zealous in their interventions.

While it is now widely recognized that the public no longer trusts state institutions and industry, what has been less debated is how these latter have allowed or encouraged the very rationality of science to be drawn into question. Pointing to the fact that science can never provide definitive answers is hardly a major new discovery, let alone one that deserves to be dressed up with the title precautionary principle. Yet the resulting concerns have allowed the irrational ideas of unaccountable environmentalist and consumer advocacy groups to resonate more widely.

By discovering risky products and activities everywhere, these groups have shifted their focus to one which increasingly seeks to regulate all forms of human activity. Their campaigns may take the form of radical critiques of business and governments, but at their heart, by encouraging mistrust and prioritizing feeling and emotion over thinking and reason, they are a threat to all of us.

Clearly, those orchestrating the scare campaigns are mere messengers within a far broader process of social transformation. This continually lends itself to elevating fears and denigrating our achievements. Although much of the research and reasoned opinion examined in these examples indicated little cause for concern, the actions taken and policies implemented assumed the worst. This suggests that what has changed is not so much the evidence upon which decisions are to be made, but rather the confidence of those responsible for making them.

The panic and hysteria created around these issues reflects a far wider loss of nerve within society rather than any inherent problem with the products themselves. The real cost will be that of a generation of young people brought up to live in fear from the dangers posed by harmless products, and questioning the ability of science to cast light on such issues. A broader climate of fear is being created which in turn will lead many to an even more misguided assessment of risk and greater inflexibility towards innovation and change.

References

Ames, B., and Gold, L.S. (1997).Pollution, pesticide and cancer misconceptions. In *What Risk? Science, Politics and Public Health*. (R. Bate, ed.). Oxford: Butterworth-Heinemann.

Arcadi F.A., Costa, C., Imperatore, C., Marchese, A., Rapisarada, A., Salei, M., Trimarchi, G.R. and Costa G., (1998). Oral toxicity of bis(2-ethylhexyl)phthalate during pregnancy and suckling in the Long-Evans rat. *Food and Chemical Toxicology,* 963–970.

Ashby, J., Brady, A., Elcombe, C.R., Elliott, B.M., Ishmae, J., Odum, J., Tugwood, J.D., Kettle, S., and Purchase, I.F.H. (1994). Mechanistically based human hazard assessment of peroxisome proliferator-induced hepatocarcinogenesis. *Human Toxicology* **13**, Supplement 2.

Axelrad, J. (2000). BSE – A disaster of biblical proportions or a disaster of British science?, ww.iea.org.uk/env/bse.htm.

Ayres, I. and Braithwaite, J. (1992). Enforced self-regulation. *In Responsive Regulation: Transcending the Deregulation Debate*, Oxford

Beck, U. (1992). *Risk Society*. London: Sage,

Beck, U, (1998).Politics of risk society. In *The Politics of Risk Society* (Franklin J., ed.), Cambridge: Polity Press.

Cattley, R.C., DeLuca, J., Elcombe, C., et al. (1998). Do peroxisome proliferating compounds pose a hepatocarcinogenic hazard to humans? *Journal of Regulatory Toxicology and Pharmacology*, **27**, 47–60.

Colborn, T., Dumanoski, D. and Myers J.P (1996). *Our Stolen Future: are we threatening our Fertility, Intelligence and Survival? A Scientific Detective Story*. London: Penguin.

CSTEE (1998a). Phthalate migration from soft PVC toys and child-care articles. Opinion expressed at the CSTEE Third Plenary Meeting, Brussels, 24 April.

CSTEE (1998b). Minutes of the fifth plenary meeting of the Scientific Committee on Toxicity, Ecotoxicity and the Environment (CSTEE), Brussels, 14–15 September.

CSTEE (1998c). Minutes of the sixth plenary meeting of the Scientific Committee on Toxicity, Ecotoxicity and the Environment (CSTEE), Brussels, 26–27 November.

CSTEE (1998d). Opinion on phthalate migration from soft pvc toys and child-care articles – Data made available since the 16th June 1998', expressed at the Sixth CSTEE Plenary Meeting, Brussels, 26/27 November.

CSTEE (1999a), Minutes of the 7th plenary meeting of the Scientific Committee on Toxicity, Ecotoxicity and the Environment (CSTEE), Brussels, 18 January.

CSTEE (1999b). CSTEE Opinion on Human and Wildlife Health Effects of Endocrine Disrupting Chemicals, with Emphasis on Wildlife and on Ecotoxicology Test Methods. Report of the Working Group on Endocrine Disrupters of the CSTEE of DG XXIV, March.

DTI (1999). Consumer Safety Research – Choking Hazards for Children in the European Community'. Department of Trade and Industry, London, 13 June 1996.

Durodié, W.J.L.V (1996). Poisonous dummies–European Risk Regulation after BSE. European Science and Environment Forum, Cambridge..

EP (1996). Final Consolidated Report to the Temporary Committee of the European Parliament on the Follow-up of Recommendations on BSE. Brussels.

Fitzpatrick, M. (1997) CJD and BSE. Scientists who inflame public anxieties must share responsibility of resulting panic. *British Medical Journal*, **312**, 1037, 20 April

Füredi, F. (1997). Culture of fear: risk-taking and the morality of low expectation. Cassell.

Füredi F. (1999). *Courting Mistrust – The hidden growth of a culture of litigation in Britain*. London: Centre for Policy Studies.

Füredi F. (1999). Consuming democracy: activism, elitism and political apathy. *European Science and Environment Forum*.

Greenpeace (1996). Taking back our stolen future. www.greenpeace.org/toxics/reports/tpostf/tbosf.html

Greenpeace (1997). Determination of the composition and quantity of phthalate ester additives in PVC children's toys. Technical Note 06/97. Greenpeace Research Laboratories, September 1997.

Heartfield, J. (1998). *Need and Desire in the Post-Material Economy*, Sheffield Hallam University Press.

Huber, W.W, Grasi-Krauup, B, and Schulte-Herman, R. (1996). Hepatocarcinogenic potential of di(2-ethylhexyl)phthalate in rodents and its implications on human risk. *Critical Reviews in Toxicology*, **26**(4), 365–481.

Irvine, S., Cawood, E., Richardson, D., MacDonald, E. and Aitken, J. (1996). Evidence of deteriorating semen quality in the United Kingdom: birth cohort study in 577 men in Scotland over 11 years. *British Medical Journal*, 24 February

JFSSG (1995). Phthalates in Paper and Board Packaging. Joint Food Safety and Standards Group food surveillance information sheet number 60, London: Ministry of Agriculture Fisheries and Food, May.

JFSSG (1996). Phthalates in Food. Joint Food Safety and Standards Group food surveillance information sheet number 82, London: Ministry of Agriculture Fisheries and Food, March.

Jobling, S., Reynolds, T., White, R., Parker, M.G. and Sumpter, J.P. (1995). A variety of environmentally persistent chemicals, including some plasticizers are weakly estrogenic. *Environmental Health Perspectives* **103**, 582–7.

Johnson, P.T.J., Larde, K.B., Ritchie, E.G. and Launer, A.E. (1999) .The effect of trematode infection on amphibian limb development and survivorship', *Science* 284, 29 April.

Kamrin, M. (1996). The mismeasure of risk. *Scientific American*, September.

Lington, A.W., Bird, M.G, Plutnick, RT.(1997). Stubblefield WA, and Scala RA, Chronic toxicity and carcinogenic evaluation of diisononyl phthalate in rats. *Fundamental Applied Toxicology*, 36, 79–89, 1997

MAFF (2000). BSE Enforcement Bulletin No. 43. Ministry of Agriculture, Fisheries and Food, London, February

NRC (1999). Hormonally active agents in the environment. US National Research Council, Washington, DC: National Academy Press, July 1999

Petridou, E (1997). Injuries from food products containing inedibles. University of Athens, April.

Poon, R., Lecavalier, P., Mueller, R. Valli,V.E., Procter, B.G. and Chu, I. (1997). Subchronic oral toxicity of di-n-octyl phthalate and di(2-ethylhexyl) phthalate in the rat. *Food and Chemical Toxicology*, **35**, 225–239.

Prost, A. (1998). Science and society: the dilemma facing the policy makers. *Eurohealth* **4**(4), 31, Autumn.

RIVM (1991). Update of the exploratory report on phthalates. Report No. 710401 008. Bilthoven, The Netherlands: National Institute of Public Health and Environmental Protection (RIVM).

RIVM (1992). Toxicological investigation of di(2-diethylhexyl)phthalate in rats. The determination of a no-effect level. Report No. 618902 007. Bilthoven, The Netherlands: National Institute of Public Health and Environmental Protection (RIVM).

RIVM (1998). Phthalate release from soft PVC baby toys – Report from the Dutch Consensus Group. Report No. 613320 002. Bilthoven, The Netherlands: National Institute of Public Health and Environmental Protection (RIVM).

Safe, S.H. (1995). Environmental and dietary oestrogens and human health: Is there a problem? *Environmental Health Perspectives*, **103**, 346–351.

Sessions, S.K., Franssen, R.A. and Horner, V.L. (1999). Morphological clues from multi-legged frogs: are retinoids to blame? *Science*, **284**, 29 April.

Shanker, R, Ramakrishna, C, and Seth, P.K. (1985). Degradation of some phthalic acid esters in soil. *Environmental Pollution*, **39**, 1–7.

Vikelsoe, J., Jensen, G.H., Johasen, E., Carlsen, I. and Rastogi, S.C. (1997). Migration of phthalates from teething rings., Roskilde: Danish National Environmental Research Institute, Environmental Chemistry Department, April.

Wilson, J.D. (1997). Thresholds for carcinogens: a review of the relevant science and its implications for regulatory policy. In *What Risk? Science, Politics and Public Health* (R. Bate, ed.). Oxford: Butterworth-Heinemann.

Zacharewski, T.R., Meek, M.D., Clemons, J.H., Wu, Z.F., Fielden, M.R. and Matthews, J.B. (1998). Examination of the 'in vitro' and 'in vivo' estrogenic activities of eight commercial phthalate esters. *Toxicological Sciences*, **46**, 282–93.

9 The precautionary principle as a force for global political centralization: a case-study of the Kyoto Protocol

Bruce Yandle

Introduction

In the aftermath of the December 1997 Kyoto Conference, participating nations are now grappling with the realities of a negotiated agreement to cut future carbon emissions below 1990 levels. Expressions of passionate concern about climate change and the prospects for doing something to relieve fears of global warming have given way to tough political bargaining over which countries, which industries, and which firms will actually bite the carbon emissions reduction bullet. Analyzing has given way to 'strategizing'. Kyoto policies defining US relations with the rest of the world are now being transformed to domestic industrial policy in nations worldwide.

The evolving policy we observe diverts efforts from meeting smaller but difficult challenges of managing the local commons to the ultimate challenge of managing the global commons. This shift of attention from local to global has been associated with perceived crises that seem always to be a prerequisite to formal governmental action.

The need to manage the commons, whether it be common hunting territories, fisheries, or a common air mantle that sustains life, defines a need for property rights and government enforcement of those rights (Anderson and Leal, 1991). The commons management imperative is a centralizing force in all human communities. Decentralized spheres of private action and exclusive private rights, what might be termed individual or local sovereignty, are reduced as government expands. Each step taken along the way involves collective decision making that unavoidably encounters special interest struggles to have wealth redistributed in favorable ways. And each step can generate social gains by denying a tragedy of the commons.

As the dimensions of the commons to be managed expand beyond community, state, region, and nation, rules that govern heterogeneous communities give way to ever more homogeneous regulations. Customs, traditions, and institutions like common law tend to be pushed to one side as statutes and treaties form a more extensive social order. Local sovereignty is compromised as collective decision making becomes delegated to state, national, and then international bodies. When nations collectively agree to pursue global environmental goals, state and national sovereignty is of necessity compromised.

An inevitable trade-off accompanies the transfer of sovereignty from smaller to larger communities (Yandle, 1997, p. 29–30; Ostrom and Schlager, 1996, p. 46). When remotely determined homogeneous rules are imposed on diverse communities, some efficiencies in resource use, where more readily measured costs are weighed against locally perceived benefits, are exchanged for the avoidance of more remote costs, not easily observed at local levels. As control becomes more remotely determined, the efficiency losses tend to increase. It is obviously important that the marginal benefits from avoiding global costs exceed the ever-increasing marginal costs of efficiency losses.

The Kyoto Protocol is a case in point. The December 1997 agreement to reduce greenhouse gases, endorsed by representatives from 174 nations, joins an estimated 180 other environmental treaties on deposit with the UN Secretary General (Committee to Preserve American Security and Sovereignty, 1998). Kyoto, if ratified, and the other treaties are fundamentally different from national decisions to legislate in the interest of cleaner air or water. Firstoff there is the remoteness issue. The Kyoto Protocol seeks to impose a homogeneous rule – greenhouse gas reductions based on 1990 emissions – on a diverse and heterogeneous set of communities. Just the task of getting 174 nations, let alone 174 people, to agree on substantive issues staggers the mind. Next, constitutional constraints and domestic rules of law and property that normally protect property rights and force competitive behavior in domestic economies can be compromised more readily at the post-Kyoto negotiators' table.

National legislative bodies accustomed to writing statutes and guiding the ship of state find themselves subject to political pressures from far-flung governing bodies as nations prepare to engage in trade with other nations. The items to be traded differ fundamentally from the array of goods and services that normally describe exports and imports. The Kyoto trade involves bartered off-setting actions to reduce greenhouse gases; the exchange of still undefined marketable emission permits, and bilateral agreements to engage in clean technology transfers and development assistance. Finally, actions that might otherwise be seen as attempts by industries to cartelize, restrict output, and raise competitors' costs are encouraged in the name of global environmental protection. National policies that affect the new tradeable goods that might otherwise be seen as violations of GATT are viewed benevolently. Kyoto provides extraordinary opportunities for all-encompassing cartelization that converts foreign policy to world industrial policy.

Those interest groups concerned about the environment may still find comfort in all this. Carbon emissions may be reduced and the prospect for global warming, if it exists, may be marginally diminished. Those who see Kyoto as an opportunity to gain a stronger toehold in markets will be comforted as well. Relative prices of major energy commodities will change. For example, the demand for natural gas will rise while the demand for coal plummets. Certain ozone-depleting chemicals will be banned; and comparative advantage enjoyed by nations worldwide will be altered. In short, there will be winners and losers in the post-Kyoto struggle. But as much as anything else, the Kyoto Protocol magnifies the pressure of well-organized interest groups to obtain transferred wealth and resources from the politically weak and unorganized masses. Kyoto, global warming, and greenhouse gas containment can be used as justification for accomplishing special interest goals. To the extent that the justification becomes accepted, Kyoto reduces the cost of political favour seeking.

This chapter examines the aftermath of Kyoto Protocol through the lens of Public Choice economics, the application of economic logic to political decision making. The chapter begins with a brief discussion of the predicted economic effects of Kyoto, a discussion that addresses the relative magnitude of change that may be forthcoming. The next section discusses briefly theories of political economy that offer useful insights for explaining the way in which the world of environmental regulation works. The section offers a series of episodes that illustrate the theories. It is here that the theory of Bootleggers and Baptists is offered as the best candidate for forecasting Kyoto outcomes.

Along with the more traditional political favour seeking, the Protocol establishes an enhanced stage for nations to pursue special interest benefits. The last major section of the chapter examines the political bargaining now underway in Europe, where emission allocations are being determined for member nations, and in the process, potential beneficiaries of managed trade in emission reductions are being identified. The results of some preliminary statistical modelling reported in the section shed some light on the potential winners and losers. The chapter ends with some final thoughts on Kyoto and sovereignty.

Kyoto's economic consequences: setting the stage for the struggle

The Kyoto Protocol is an evolved agreement rooted in the notion that developed countries, which are automatically large energy users and greenhouse gas producers, should bear the brunt of reducing emissions in the name of avoiding costly climatic changes. This idea was first discussed formally in Toronto in June, 1988. It was then addressed by Congress in 1989 in a proposed bill – the Global Warming Prevention Act – and later became fundamental to commitments reached in 1992 when representatives of 160 nations attended the Rio De Janeiro Conference on Environment and Development (Manne and Richels, 1991, p. 88).

Efforts to contain greenhouse emissions were bolstered further at a second Conference of Parties to the Rio De Janeiro Agreement held in Berlin in 1995, yielding the Berlin Mandate, which stressed the importance of gaining national commitments to greenhouse gas reductions. Then, an ad hoc group meeting in Geneva in 1995 and again in 1996 called for binding mandates for developed countries, 38 in number known as Annex I and including primarily the OECD and Eastern European states. Meaningful co-operation and emission reporting were expected of developing countries, but no quantifiable emission reduction commitments were called for.

Just what are the relative emission magnitudes involved here? In 1990 the Annex I countries, with the USA leading the pack, produced roughly 64 per cent of all greenhouse gases, which then totalled six billion tons annually. (The data here, from Antonelli and Schaefer, 1997, p. 18, were drawn from reports of the Intergovernmental Panel on Climate Change.) The developing countries, led by China, produced the remaining 36 per cent. Forecasts of emissions for the year 2015 predicted total emissions to be 8.45 billion tons, with the developing countries producing 52 per cent of the total. At that point, the developed countries would become minority players. By the year 2100, the forecast called for 19.8 billion tons of greenhouse emissions, with the developing world producing 66 per cent of the total.

Seen in this light, the Protocol is a very odd agreement, if reducing total greenhouse gases is its primary purpose. Under the Protocol, developed countries have agreed to reduce emissions by the period 2008–2012 so that their total will be five per cent less than 1990 levels. Meanwhile developing countries will be expanding emissions at roughly three per cent per year. With these opposing trends, it is impossible to see how 1990 targets can ever be achieved overall. Obviously, there is far more to Kyoto than reducing the threat of global warming. A review of research on the economic effects of greenhouse gas containment may provide some clues regarding other objectives.

The Academic Literature

Long before Kyoto, academic economists were busy turning out studies on the economic effects of controlling greenhouse gases (Manne and Richels, 1991; Nordhaus, 1991; Pearce and Barbier, 1991; Whaley and Wigle, 1991; Jorgenson and Wilcoxen, 1993; Kosobud, et al. 1994; Larsen and Shah, 1994; Sinclair, 1994; Holz-Eakin and Selden, 1995; Carrato, Galeotti, and Gallo, 1996; Chen, 1997). Some of the studies represent the economist's most sophisticated techniques for modelling national economies. Others focus solely on European issues. Still others compare various government instruments for reducing carbon emissions – taxes, regulation, and marketable permits.

The Jorgenson-Wilcoxen (1993) study uses a major macro model of the US economy that accounts for 35 industrial sectors, consumer behaviour, investment, and trade. The authors assume a policy goal of holding US carbon emissions constant at 1990 levels. As it turns out, they incorrectly assume that a 14.4 per cent reduction in year 2020 emissions will achieve 1990 levels. Recent data indicate reductions in the range of 36 per cent are necessary. Nonetheless, the Jorgenson-Wilcoxen model shows the level of taxes required on various fuels to achieve their stated goal. For example, one of their simulations calls for coal to be taxed at $US11.01 per ton; oil at $US2.31 per barrel, and natural gas at $US0.28 per thousand cubic feet. The resulting revenues will yield $26 billion annually to the federal government. The authors conclude that the tax policies considered will have effects on GDP (Gross Domestic Product) growth that range from fractions of a percentage point reduction to a one percentage point reduction from baseline growth. However, they show dramatic changes in the relative prices of energy, with coal sustaining a 40 per cent price increase and an associated 26 per cent reduction in production.

In a similar study that focuses on the United Kingdom, Pearce and Barbier (1991) estimate a 67 per cent increase in coal taxes, 40 per cent for gas, and 54 per cent for oil will be required to reduce UK carbon emissions by 20 per cent in the year 2005. They note that unilateral action can accomplish very little; domestic energy use and carbon emissions may fall, but importation of substitutes from elsewhere can lead to carbon emission replacement by exporting countries. These prospects for massive changes in relative prices and altered trade patterns provide clues for identifying players in Kyoto's special interest struggle.

Manne and Richels (1991) take a global approach in their study of emission reductions. They assume that countries worldwide seek to reduce carbon emissions 20 per cent by the year 2000. They accurately assume that the industrialized world will accept the 20 per cent reduction goal, but that the rest of the world will not. They calculate GDP losses associated with the carbon constraint and find that the USA would sustain rising GDP losses across the control period, hitting a net loss in growth of 3 per cent by the year 2030. Losses for the OECD countries are shown to be much lower, reaching 1–2 per cent in 2030. The estimate helps us to see how the EU countries could push so hard for US emission reductions. Mexico and oil producing countries would sustain even larger losses, and China the largest of all, losing 10 per cent of GDP in the last half of the twenty-first century. In the most stringent set of circumstances, the price of coal would increase fourfold, and the demand for oil would accordingly increase, not decrease. (Is it possible that some oil producers would favour Kyoto?)

Other studies reported in professional journals follow along the lines of these just summarized. The academics seem to agree that curtailment of carbon emissions to 1990 baseline levels places the brunt of the adjustment cost on the coal and coal-related sectors, that GDP growth rates in the industrial world will be affected by meaningful amounts. (For example, a loss of 1 per cent in US GDP is not small potatoes.) The studies also demonstrate the potential benefits of permit trading, as opposed to taxation and regulation. Of particular relevance to this paper, the research tells us:

1 that the potential cost of the Kyoto Protocol to the USA is far greater in total and in relative terms than that for other industrialized countries;
2 that a number of major European countries (UK and Germany) have already experienced adjustments that lighten their load;
3 that substitutes for coal have much to gain, and
4 that how control instruments and permit markets are defined will provide significant differential effects across countries.

Economic studies by consulting firms, government, and trade associations

As the time for the Kyoto conference drew near, a number of major economic studies were produced at the behest of trade associations, organized labour, and government. In most cases, these studies were performed by widely recognized and respected consulting firms whose reputations represent huge investments in brand-name capital. As might be expected, the studies focused on sectors or elements of the US economy that were of greatest interest to the sponsors. The findings help us to understand more about the stakes involved for special interest groups.

DRI/McGraw-Hill provided a major economic impact study for the United Mine Workers/Bituminous Coal Association, itself an interesting alliance (*The Impact of Carbon Mitigation Strategies*, 1997). The study, which was reviewed by the Economic Policy Institute, provides insights into estimates of the macroeconomic and sector effects of stabilizing greenhouse gas emissions at 1990 levels and reducing emissions by 10 per cent below 1990 levels by the year 2010. The study assumes government-issued marketable permits will constrain carbon emissions. These permits are predicted to fetch prices that range from $US180–280 per ton of emissions across the years 1995 through 2020 for the containment case. Permit prices will be higher in the 10 per cent reduction case.

The study shows a seven-fold price increase for coal, electricity prices increasing about 100 per cent, and retail gasoline prices rising 40 to 50 per cent. The change in fuel consumption generated by the controls is particularly interesting. Coal, which now provides 24 per cent of US energy, will provide 18 per cent. Petroleum's share increases, and natural gas maintains its current market share. The government's revenue from permit sales rises to $US776 billion in 2020, and yields a budget surplus of $US388 billion by 2020. Annual losses in employment reach 1.4 million for the years 2000–2020, and GDP growth is reduced by one percentage point as the economy adjusts to the constraints. Coal output is predicted to decline 45 per cent, rubber and plastics by 50 per cent, and electricity production by 18 per cent.

A major study by WEFA sponsored by the American Petroleum Institute assumes U.S. carbon emissions will stabilize at 1990 levels by the year 2010. The study realistically rejects the State Department's proposal for inter-country tradeable permits due to the lack of institutional infrastructure

(National Impacts, 1998). WEFA assumes a US permit market instead. The analysts assume uncontrolled emissions will be 27 per cent above 1990 levels by 2010, and 46 per cent above the target by 2020. To achieve the necessary reductions, carbon permit prices would rise across the control period from $US100 per ton/per year to $300 per ton.

The economic effects of the reductions would lead to a 30 to 55 per cent increase in consumer prices, with energy-intensive sectors sustaining shocks comparable to those associated with the Arab oil embargoes of the 1970s. Real GDP would fall 2.4 per cent below baseline 2010 estimates, with that loss alone amounting to $US227 billion 1992 dollars. Cumulative GDP losses across the years 2001 to 2020 would total 3.3 trillion dollars, which is roughly 48 per cent of 1996 GDP. Employment declines would exceed 22.8 million workers by the year 2010.

Addressing international competitiveness and trade, the WEFA study noted:

> One key reason for the lower level of real GDP is reduced global competitiveness. Because the imposition of the carbon target and permit system is not borne equally by all countries . . . US. exports are relatively more expensive on the world market, while the prices of many imported products will fall. As a consequence, exports are lowered dramatically, while imports are increased substantially.
>
> (National Impacts, 1998, 4–5)

The report notes that chemicals, paper, textiles and apparel, and computer and electronic parts production will be severely affected.

The US Department of Energy prepared an exhaustive study of Kyoto effects (Office of Policy and International Affairs, 1997). This report also assumes a control target of achieving 1990 emission levels by 2010 and considers both a US and international market for tradeable permits. If the market is strictly domestic, permit prices rise to $US150 per ton of carbon emissions. With a world market, the price falls to $US40. Assuming a domestic control scenario, US coal consumption will fall by 50 per cent by 2010, with the price tripling. Total GDP losses across the period will have a present value of $US418 billion. Revenues from permits will reach $US400 billion by 2010.

Ronald J. Sutherland, Senior Economist for the American Petroleum Institute, prepared an interesting analysis of Kyoto policy options. Using a simple econometric model for explaining carbon emissions, Sutherland (1998) shows that it is practically impossible for the US to achieve Kyoto's goals, especially if nuclear energy production is ultimately replaced by gas-fired turbines, which is now predicted. Three things happen. Clean nuclear is replaced with dirtier natural gas. Income growth leads to a predictable increase in the demand for energy, and therefore more carbon emissions. The price increases necessary for achieving Kyoto goals will not be accepted. For example, based on estimates of price elasticity of demand from 10 large-scale studies, gasoline prices would need to rise from $1.25 per gallon now to

$4.23 per gallon in 2010, just to achieve Kyoto levels. After that, prices would have to rise continuously to offset increases in demand generated by rising incomes. Sutherland's analysis demonstrates the hopelessness of relying on technical change, prices, and controls for reaching Kyoto's US goal for 2010. In a few words, the target date for achieving the goal comes too soon.

Faced with an array of studies forecasting a significant Kyoto burden, the US Congress held hearings on the matter in March, 1998, and heard from Dr Janet Yellen, Chairperson on the Council of Economic Advisors (Testimony of Dr Janet Yellen, 1998). Dr Yellen indicated that the cost imposed by Kyoto on the US economy would be quite small. Putting the burden in terms of the cost of reducing a ton of carbon emissions, she explained how the cost could fall from $US240 per metric ton to $US23 per ton. Her optimistic estimate assumed large gains in energy-production efficiencies, obtained through deregulation, expanded emission credit trading with developing and developed countries, and carbon reduction gains from natural sinks, such as the ocean and forests. She indicated that her estimates were not based on a single formal model of the economy, but were derived from assumptions applied to several major studies. It is worth noting that for Dr Yellen's forecast to obtain, all her assumptions would need to be met in a matter of 10 years, assuming the US Senate ratifies the Protocol this year.

There are other notable studies that might be mentioned, but the reports surveyed here serve the purpose of identifying strategic issues that motivate special interest groups either to rally around Kyoto or to take costly steps to stop the ratification process. Again, the relative effects on energy-intensive sectors are emphasized, with coal production carrying the brunt of the load. International competitiveness for identifiable sectors is at issue. And the scope of the permit market – whether domestic or international – is shown to have significant effects on the ultimate cost projected for the US economy.

Bootleggers and Baptists in the glow of Kyoto

In April, 1998, the European Union members officially ratified and signed the Kyoto treaty, accepting an 8 per cent reduction in carbon emissions below 1990 levels over the next 15 years (Leopold, 1998). The USA, which had accepted a 7 per cent reduction, had still not ratified the agreement, and the prospects for doing so were dim. In the same month, Japan, Australia, Brazil, Canada, Norway and Monaco signed. Argentina and Pacific island nations had signed earlier. As of January 2000, 84 nations have signed the Protocol, although only 22 have ratified. Perhaps the most notable non-ratifier is the United States (Status of Ratification, 2000). With 36 per cent of emissions among industrialized nations, and 23 per cent worldwide, the USA alone can prevent the agreeing nations from reaching the requisite 55 per cent reduction in emissions required for the agreement to be binding. Yet, even though the Protocol is not binding, its effects are real.

Some theoretical considerations

It is helpful to consider some theories of regulation when seeking to understand events related to the implementation of the Kyoto Protocol. The review of economic effects identified potential winners and losers and highlighted the exceptionally large value of wealth transfers that are at stake. Armed with the information, consider some theory.

There are three basic theories of regulation that may assist the analysis (see further Yandle, 1989). The first is called the **public interest** theory, which simply states that governments attempt to maximize the collective well being of citizens. Political actions, according to this theory, are efficiency driven, always weighing benefits and costs and attempting to maximize net benefits. If taxes are to be imposed to reduce quantifiable harms from global warming, the politicians will carefully calibrate and impose the taxes so that least-cost solutions emerge. When things turn out differently, the proponents of this theory respond that politicians, like everyone else, are fallible.

The second theory carries a note of political realism. The **capture** theory tells us to expect dedicated politicians attempting to serve the public interest to encounter persuasive special interest groups who have a substantial impact on political action. In effect, the political decision maker, though dedicated, is captured by the special interest group. Unfortunately, this theory does not help determine which of many special interest groups may succeed in winning the struggle.

The third theory, called the **economic** theory of regulation (Stigler, 1971; Posner, 1974; and Peltzman, 1976), asks us to consider the political arena as a market place where favours are bought and sold. Interest groups that have the most to gain or to lose will bid the highest prices for favours. Politicians dedicated to preserving their jobs, and needing large amounts of campaign funds to do so, auction off the favours. If carbon emissions are to be controlled, the politician, by this theory, will find the group with the largest economic stake in the outcome and favour that group. Other competing groups will attempt to outbid the winner. Special interest groups with large markets and revenues that can be enhanced by regulation can outbid other less organized groups that have less to offer. The smaller the group, holding the prize constant, the more each member can gain. The larger the group that bears the cost of the prize, the less likely it is that they will mount meaningful opposition.

My theory of **bootleggers and baptists**, a subset of the economic theory, calls attention to coalitions that seem to prevail when environmental and other social regulation is being formulated (Yandle, 1983). While powerful interest groups still matter, this theory tells us that there must be at least two interest groups working in the same the direction. Bootleggers like Sunday Closing laws that shut down legitimate sellers of alcoholic beverages; they get the market to themselves. Baptists support the same laws, but for entirely different reasons. When one group takes the moral high ground, it is easier for politicians to favour both groups, which is to say, the Baptists lower the costs of favour-seeking for the bootleggers. Kyoto promises to be rich with Bootlegger/Baptists coalitions. Each group is necessary for successful outcomes; if one defects, the other will lose benefits.

In the post-Kyoto period, we should expect to find environmentalists pushing for ratification, enforcement, and working to prevent backsliding. These are the 'Baptists' in the theory. They demand regulation of particular kinds. They do not favour voluntary action and co-operation. Traditional regulation theories tell us that we should search for other special interest groups who either are positioned to gain from regulatory enforcement and stringency or who must fend off losses that spring from proposed rules. Within industries, there may be firms that have specialized assets or output that are favoured by rules raising the cost of competing assets and products. With Kyoto, there are countries positioned to exploit carbon reductions already made; they are in a position to raise the cost of competing economies. There are other countries that can become lower cost suppliers of carbon reduction offsets. But unlike conventional regulatory episodes that involve one national government regulating domestic industries, Kyoto presents us with the unusual situation of countries behaving like firms strategically positioning themselves to benefit while gaining protection and credibility from international environmental groups that embrace Kyoto as a necessary part of their environmental cause.

Post-Kyoto episodes

In line with the Bootlegger–Baptist theory, the Kyoto Protocol provides environmentalists to run interference and reduce favour-seeking costs for interest groups already working to obtain political favours. For example, in January 1997, Enron Corporation, a major provider of low-carbon natural gas, announced the formation of Enron Renewable Energy Corporation indicating that it was 'preparing to take advantage of the growing interest in environmentally sound alternatives of power in the $US250 billion US electricity market' (Salisbury, 1998). The new division faces the difficult challenge of producing solar and other non-traditional energy products at costs that can compete with conventional energy sources. As a result, Tom White, Enron Renewable Energy CEO, understandably endorsed President Clinton's $US6.3 billion plan to fight global warming, which includes $US3.6 billion in tax credits to spur the production and purchase of renewable energy and related technologies (Salisbury, 1998). Kyoto-justified taxpayer subsidies will make life easier for firms like Enron.

Other US producers have long enjoyed federal subsidies they now hope can be global-warming justified. On 9April, 1998, the National Corn Growers Association launched a campaign hoping to stall congressional efforts to eliminate the 5.4 cents per gallon federal tax incentive provided to producers of corn-based ethanol (National Corn Growers Report, 1998). Originally enacted on the dubious basis of providing energy self-sufficiency, the large ethanol subsidies were on shaky ground. A few days later, the Renewable Fuels Association joined forces with ethanol producers to celebrate Earth Day, calling attention to ethanol's beneficial effects on global warming (Renewable Fuels Association, 1998b). On 20 April, Secretary of Agriculture Dan Glickman indicated his strong support for extending the ethanol subsidy, noting that 'renewable fuels provide an important opportunity ... to lower greenhouse gas emissions (Renewable Fuels Association, 1998a).

Just after Kyoto, Mary Nichols, US EPA Assistant Administrator for Air and Radiation, spoke at the National Ethanol Conference in Des Moines, Iowa, in January, telling the audience: 'One area where I think we do more together is the area of climate change and global warming' (Stark, 1998). Quite understandably, no one mentioned that ethanol production was so costly that it might be a net destroyer of energy, or that the federal government's $US600 million annual ethanol subsidy, half of which went to one ethanol producer, Archer-Daniel-Midland ($US7 billion in the last 16 years). Nor was a literal Bootlegger–Baptist connection described: The taxpayer subsidy assists the production of beverage as well as industrial alcohol (Bandow, 1997). On 6 May 1998, House Speaker Gingrich successfully salvaged the ethanol program, much to the dismay of Senator Bill Archer (Republican, Texas) who sought to level the playing field for oil producers in his state by ending the programme (Pianin, 1998). Global warming helped save the day for the corn producers.

Following in their American cousins' footsteps, the Canadian Commercial Alcohol Association trumpeted the products' carbon reducing virtues, suggesting that any CO_2 produced by burning ethanol would be recycled into corn plant tissue, thereby yielding a net reduction in atmospheric carbon dioxide levels (Canadian Commercial Alcohol Association, 1998). Not to be outdone, the National Biodiesel Board, representing farmers nationwide who produce soybean and other vegetable oil products, testified before Secretary of Energy Frederico Pena on 19 February 1998, pointing out the environmental benefits of blending farm-produced oil products with diesel fuel (National Biodiesel Board, 1998). Lobbying to persuade the Department of Energy (DOE) to give regulatory approval to biodiesel as an officially approved alternative fuel, insuring a market through DOE programmes, the trade association officials indicated 'biodiesel helps reduce the effects of global warming by directly displacing fossil hydrocarbons' (National Biodiesel Board, 1998).

Although corn producers with specialized assets for producing ethanol see a pot of gold in Kyoto, farmers who must fare in a globally competitive market generally oppose Kyoto. Dean Kleckner, president of the 4.8 million member American Farm Bureau Federation, opposed the signing of the protocol 'because of its potential harm to US farmers' (Farm-state senators sceptical, 1998). Reinforcing his concern, Mary Novak, senior vice president of WEFA, a major econometric consulting firm, predicted a Kyoto-induced 10 per cent increase in the cost of food, and substantially higher fertilizer taxes and fuel prices. There are winners and losers within the same economic sector.

While the ethanol and biodiesel 'bootleggers' were rapidly putting on the green, a coalition of major oil producers and thousands of other firms were having trouble keeping members on the anti-Kyoto reservation. Calling their trade group the Global Climate Coalition (GCC), major oil producers attempted to speak with one voice in debunking Kyoto's recognized shaky scientific underpinnings, calling attention to the economic effects of the protocol. In June 1998, Shell Oil announced it was leaving the GCC. Claiming credit for Shell's green conversion, Friends of the Earth spokesperson Anna Stanford indicated: 'We're delighted that our hard work has paid off, that Shell has bowed to public pressure and seen that the future lies in fighting climate change and investing in green energy. Now is the time to turn our attention to Exxon to make them follow Shell's lead' (Friends of the Earth, 1998). As to Shell's response, the firm indicated that 'there are enough indications that CO_2 emissions are having an effect on climate change' (Magada, 1998). Being more specific about the firm's strategy, Mark Moody-Stuart, Chairman of Shell Transport and Trading, indicated that Shell was 'promoting the development of the gas industry particularly in countries with large coal reserves such as India and China' (Magada, 1998). Obviously, tough support of Kyoto, at the margin, would imply growing demand for cleaner natural gas.

Shell's departure from GCC was made easier by an earlier defection by British Petroleum. John Browne, CEO of BP, stated that industry must play a 'positive and responsible part in identifying solutions' to the global warming problem (EDF, 1997). His comments came after having serious discussions with members of the Environmental Defense Fund and World Resources Institute, the 'Baptists' in the theory. BP, expecting to see increase in demand for oil as a cleaner substitute for coal, also announced a significant investment increase in solar and alternative energy technology development.

Support of Kyoto by environmentalists is certainly to be expected, even if global warming is purely a spurious event that will pass. Strict guardians of the environment are opposed to the any human action that might despoil the environment. Any discharge that can be counted in tons must therefore be opposed on principle. However, the Kyoto Protocol enjoys a 'Baptist' supporter that gets very close to the name itself. It is the United Methodist Church. On 17 December, just a few weeks after the Kyoto meetings, Jaydee R. Hanson, assistant general secretary of the United Methodist Board of Church and Society, announced his denomination's support for Kyoto ('Church executive calls for ratification', 1997). Hanson urged the US Senate to 'protect God's creation' by ratifying the agreement.

In spite of the potential benefits others find by teaming up with 'Baptists' to support the protocol, many major industries oppose Kyoto, or at least major firms in those industries do so. Coal producers and related unions are among the most vocal in their opposition. Indeed, coal interests in West Virginia were successful enough to obtain state legislation prohibiting the state's division of environmental protection from 'proposing or implementing rules regulating greenhouse gas emissions from industrial sites' ('Governor signs bill, 1998). On signing the bill, Governor Cecil Underwood indicated that while actions like the Kyoto Protocol must be opposed, we 'should continue to encourage the development and implementation of technologies that allow the clean burning of coal' (ibid.). Governor Underwood was joined by Kentucky's Governor Paul Patton in successfully gaining a Southern Governors Association resolution saying basically the same thing.

The Kyoto Protocol promotes an unusual trading environment, one that has governments, not individuals or firms, trading with other governments. Even before ratification, steps were already underway to capitalize on the protocol. Some found it possible to gain additional wealth for actions they were going to take anyway. In April 1998, Costa Rica announced a new version of its programme to save 1.25 million acres of rainforest by selling CO_2 allowances to industrial firms elsewhere (Allen, 1998). Announcing the programme, to be managed by the prestigious Swiss commercial inspection firm SGS, Costa Rican President Jose Maria Figueres described environmental bonds called Certified Tradeable Offsets, each one corresponding to one ton of carbon to be absorbed by trees. The planned offsets will accommodate one million metric tons of carbon annually. The zero cost programme generated an estimated $US20 million in revenues in 1998, or $US20 per ton of carbon emissions offset, and $US300 million over the life of the project, which is the life expectancy of the Kyoto Protocol.

In April 1998, Japan and Russia engaged in what is believed to be the world's first greenhouse gas emissions swap, which involved two countries, not two private parties (Takenaka, 1998). The alliance provides Japanese technicians to Russian power plants and factories who assist in cutting carbon emissions at some 20 facilities. As part of the agreement, Japan and Russia will share information on nuclear energy production. Both have something to offer. Japan is a leading producer of nuclear energy technology, and Russia a leader in the development of breeder reactors. Japan will also become a larger investor in the search for offshore gas and oil in Russian waters. This Kyoto-type arrangement is facilitated by the fact that Russia has no difficulty in meeting its zero carbon emission increase over the 1990 baseline. The Russian economy is in shambles. However, Japan, which promised to cut baseline emissions by 6 per cent, faces a real challenge.

Trimming the budding permit market

Marketable greenhouse gas emission permits, the centrepiece of the Kyoto Protocol, offer the prospect of significantly reducing the cost of achieving protocol goals and generated meaningful support for the protocol among major interest groups. Indeed, at times it appeared that having a permit market was justification enough for taking actions to address global warming, no matter what the economics or science might say. In any case, an unfettered permit market theoretically would provide countries such as the USA, which faces high incremental control costs, the opportunity to shop world markets for lower cost providers of emission reductions. Given Kyoto's constraints, incentives would be large for securing trades, wherever they might take place. Apparently, the prospect of having the USA provide reductions through the market, rather than internally, is more than some international politicians can bear.

Fear of trading

Deputy Prime Minister of the UK, John Prescott, for one, wants to make certain that the USA feels the pain of implementing the Kyoto accord, that higher cost solutions be imposed rather than lower cost ones. In an obvious move to raise rivals costs, Prescott expressed concern that Washington would 'buy tradeable greenhouse emission permits from Russia' ('EU urges US to implement Kyoto', 1998). As he put it, 'Europe has always been clear that while we accept the trading possibilities in this matter, they should not be used as a reason for avoiding taking action in your own country'.

It so happens that Russia's emissions have fallen 30 per cent below the country's target level of zero reduction. Russia can actually increase emissions to offset higher cost reductions that might be taken elsewhere, which is exactly what tradeable permits can accomplish. But Prescott is disturbed by the prospect of gains from trade for the USA. First off, he is simply opposed to an international market in carbon emission offsets. In addition, his idea of trade requires that one party always reduces emissions so that another party can increase them. In the present situation, where Russia is actually cleaner than necessary, both parties can increase emissions, and both will gain by doing so.

Support of trading unions

The European Commission's 3 June 1998 Communication setting out principles for the November Buenos Aires meeting of Kyoto Parties makes it clear that Europe's member states hope to minimize their emission reduction costs while limiting gains from trade for the USA (Climate Change, 1998). Noting the EU plan to use a bubble concept in achieving overall emission reductions for the member states, the Communication states:

> It is recognized that the flexible mechanisms can play an important role in meeting commitments at least cost, thereby safeguarding the competitiveness of EU industry. The existence of the EU bubble does not prevent the Community from fully participating in international emission trading

> (Climate Change, 1998, p. 2).

The EU expects to gain internally with its bubble and externally through emission trading. However, the Communication endorses Prescott's position regarding U.S. trading strategies:

At Buenos Aires, discussions on emission trading should focus on ensuring the establishment of strict rules and for setting minimum requirements that any Party or private entity needs to fulfil in order to participate in international trading ... It is also necessary to define the Protocol's use of the word 'supplemental' in respect to the contribution of the flexible mechanisms. In principle a ceiling should be set for trading to ensure that the main reduction in emissions are by domestic efforts.

(Climate Change, 1998, p. 2)

Europe's bubble was an item of contention during the Kyoto discussions. Playing the 'increase competitors' cost game,' the USA pushed for each European state to have specific reduction goals to be met internally. This strategy placed a heavy burden on southern European countries, such as Spain, Portugal, and Greece, lower income but high carbon emitters that are rapidly industrializing. Countries such as the UK, Germany, The Netherlands, and France were already relatively clean, having transformed their coal-based energy economies to cleaner fuels. If uniform reductions were imposed on each European member state, the EU would lose a cross-subsidization advantage of allowing some countries to actually increase emissions while others offset those emissions at relatively low cost. The Kyoto Protocol itself showed uniform reduction goals of eight per cent for each member country that were to be converted later to bubble-based reductions.

Analysing the EU's allocation scheme

In June 1998, EU leaders met to negotiate each member's reduction allocation (EU Greenhouse Deal, 1998). The draft proposal called for individual reductions shown in the accompanying table, which lists emission reductions in ascending order.

Modelling the proposal

In an attempt to explain these proposed targets, and recognizing the limitations of a small data set, I ran a regression using as a dependent variable the number of tons of CO_2 emissions to be released or reduced in the 1990–2010 time period for each EU country. This was calculated by using the percentages in the table (page 182) applied to each country's 1987 level of CO_2 emissions. (The data on emissions is taken from Larsen and Shah, 1994, p. 843; 1995 data for Luxemboug were not available in The World Bank Tables and were constructed by interpolation from Larsen and Shah, 1996.) Independent variables included in the linear model were 1995 per capita GDP in US dollars, the 1995 ratio of carbon emissions to GDP (kg/$US), 1998 country population, and the year when each country joined the European Union. (Data for the independent variables are for 1995, with the exception of population, which is for 1998, and are taken from *World Resources: 1998–99*, The World Bank, 1998.)

Table 9.1 EU member state emission reduction goals 1990–2010

Country	Per cent change from 1990 levels
Luxembourg	−28.0
Denmark	−21.0
Germany	−21.0
Austria	−13.0
UK	−12.5
Belgium	−7.5
Italy	−6.5
Netherlands	−6.0
France	−0.0
Finland	−0.0
Sweden	−4.0
Ireland	+13.0
Spain	+15.0
Greece	+25.0
Portugal	+27.0

Source: Friends of Earth Press Release (1998).

Examination of the carbon emissions per GDP unit and per capita GDP, shown in the accompanying chart, indicates that CO_2 emission intensity decreases with the level of per capita GDP. At first blush, the data and regression line suggest that the attainment of higher per capita GDP levels could reduce total worldwide carbon emissions. However, this conclusion is incorrect, at least on a historical basis. Higher income levels do lead to lower CO_2 intensity, but larger total carbon emissions.

Let us now turn to the underlying theory of the statistical model. The politics of redistribution suggest that richer countries will absorb more of the environmental load than poorer countries. All else equal, the coefficient on per capita GDP should be negative, fewer tons of emission allowances. However, the cost of emission reductions will be higher for those countries that have 'cleaner' GDP. Generally speaking, the lower the amount of CO_2 per dollar of output, the more costly it be to reduce a ton of emission. A positive coefficient on the carbon/GDP ratio will imply that countries with 'dirtier' GDP, which are the poorer countries, receive more allowances. A negative coefficient on the carbon/GDP ratio implies that richer countries deflect control costs to poorer countries. That is, those countries that face lower control costs (dirtier emissions) will be treated less favourably when emission allowances are distributed. The results of the modelling exercise will tell us just how generous the wealthier countries really are.

Population size tests for a redistribution argument that smaller groups value a one ton allowance more than larger groups, all else being equal. The argument is based on the Public Choice logic that a small concession to a

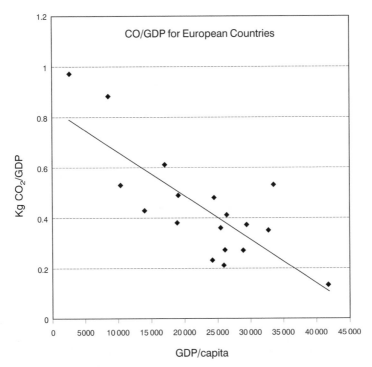

Figure 9.1 Relationship of carbon dioxide emissions to GDP per capita in European countries

smaller country is worth more per capita than the same concession to a larger country (Chen, 1997). This predicts the coefficient on population to be negative. The year of EU entry is included to test for side payments from older to newer members, all else being equal. The exit of new members is always a greater threat than for older ones. Side payments in the form of emission allowances help to keep newer members in the fold. By this argument, the coefficient on year should be positive. A competing argument suggests that new members are not well-seasoned in the bargaining process with older members, in which case the coefficient will be negative.

The estimate

The following ordinary least squares estimate, with intercept suppressed, was obtained:

$$\text{TONS} = -1.477\,\text{PERCAP} - 52046\,CO_2/\text{GDP} - 449.128\,\text{POP} + 31.173\,\text{YEAR}$$

$$(-2.934) \qquad\qquad (2.255) \qquad\qquad (-4.707) \qquad\qquad (2.980)$$

$$R^2\colon 0.63\ F_{(3,11)}\colon 9.04$$

T-ratios are shown below the coefficients, along with other relevant statistics. As indicated, the proposed reductions follow a rough pattern that yields lower tons of emission growth for higher income countries. All else equal, fewer tons are allowed for countries with high carbon to GDP concentrations, which means countries like Portugal and Spain will clean up more, at the margin. Fewer allowances are provided to higher population countries, and more allowances are allocated to newer members of the European Union. For example, Spain, a recent EU member, has lower income, and a 'dirtier' GDP than France does. Even though penalized for its 'dirtier' GDP, Spain is allowed to increase emissions over the 1990 baseline by 15 per cent. France is to achieve and then maintain the 1990 emission level.

At the mean of the estimate, which has large confidence intervals given the small sample, a $US1000 increase in per capita GDP yields a 1.47 ton reduction in carbon emissions. An increase of 1g per GDP dollar of carbon emissions (the sample mean is 420g) predicts 52 fewer tons in emission growth. An increase of one million in population is associated with a loss of 449 tons of emission allowances, and an increase of one year in the year of membership, say from 1974 to 1975, yields an increase of 31 tons in allowances.

Since it is always cheaper to reduce emissions when concentrations are higher, the EU proposal establishes future sellers and buyers of tradeable emission reduction permits. Populous nation states with lower emission allowances will buy permits from states with dirtier carbon streams and larger allowances for emission growth. The allocation scheme enables us to predict that wealth will flow generally from northern to southern European countries, at least for trades within the European bubble. The EU plan of encouraging bubble trading within the EU and managing external trades places the central government is the traditional protectionist position of controlling exports and imports. But in this case the items traded are permits (emission reductions), not commodities. Along these lines, an examination of the residuals for emission allowances, those larger than one standard deviation from the mean value, shows France gaining – being a potential seller – and Germany and Portugal losing disproportionately in the political process that determined emission allowances.

The results also confirm the Public Choice notion that a concession to a less populous group is worth more per member than the same concession to a larger group. Population size exercises a significant and independent effect in explaining the proposed EU allocation of future greenhouse emissions.

Protecting the tradeable rights

As post-Kyoto bargaining continues, there are at least two major institutional problems to be settled. The first relates to permit markets, how they will be defined and operated, and the extent to which this budding market will be unfettered by international rules and regulations. The second problem relates to enforcement of agreements within and among countries that ratify the Kyoto Protocol. While the first problem is set for discussion at the fall meeting in Buenos Aires, the second has already been discussed (Morrison, 1998). In efforts to clamp down on all forms of environmental cheating, ministers from the Group of Seven and Russia met recently to line up co-operation against environmental crime. Britain's Deputy Prime Minister John Prescott said that he 'wanted to see the equivalent of Interpol to allow police, customs and enforcement agencies to combat . . . global illegal trade' (Morrison, 1998, p. 1). While many issues were at stake in the discussion, the bootleg trade in chlorofluorocarbons, one of the greenhouse gases, was singled out for attention. Perhaps an international environmental police force is in the making.

Final thoughts

The Kyoto Protocol is perhaps one of the most far-reaching international accords to be settled in modern times. And for all we know, global climate change may be one of the most far-reaching threats faced in modern times. But while the theory and evidence of global warming is considered to be shaky or at least controversial (Lindzen, 1997), the theory and evidence that helps explain changing rules of sovereignty is rather well established. Sovereignty modification has to do with changing the locus and means of collective decision making. Human efforts to manage the commons have always involved sovereignty issues. Kyoto is no different.

While the principles are no different, the scope of Kyoto and the relative magnitude of affected wealth are different indeed. When countries become substituted for firms and conventional interest groups in struggles over politically determined favours, an entirely different set of forces is unleashed. There are no guiding rules of law, no overriding constitutional constraints, and no impartial judge to hear appeals and grievances. There is no international government, and if there were, by definition it would have extraordinary monopoly power. Since orthodox constraints are absent, Kyoto bargaining will involve the messy but beneficial activity of ministers of state and competing legislative bodies that must deal with costly proposals.

This chapter has examined Kyoto through the lens of Public Choice economics. Doing so enabled the identification of potential winners and losers in the political process that heads toward final ratification of a global greenhouse gas emission control system. There is ample evidence that Kyoto is already being used as a crutch for conventional special interest groups to secure political favours. There is some evidence that some nations and communities of nations are acting in strategic ways to enhance their positions relative to other nations. We should expect no less.

In the final analysis, we should hope that fears of global warming will subside and that efforts to control the world's energy economies will gradually dissipate. Yet while we might cling to these hopes, history teaches us that once a major concern becomes transformed into institutional rules, interest groups that invested in those rules will work to maintain them. The compromise of sovereignty delivered by Kyoto will tend to last. When efforts are made to manage a global commons, prior property rights and spheres of private action will of necessity be compromised.

References

Note: In all references containing web addresses, access date was in 1998 unless otherwise stated.

National Biodiesel Board (1998). Agricultural products are key to national energy security, 24 February .
http://biz.yahoo.com (2 March 1998).

Allen, V. (1998). Costa Rica to save forest with carbon credits. Reuters.
http//www.infoseek.com (4 May)

Anderson, T. and Leal, D.R. (1991). *Free Market Environmentalism*. San Francisco: Pacific Research Institute.

Antonelli, A. and Schaefer, B.D. (1997). The road to Kyoto. *Backgrounder*. Washington, DC: The Heritage Foundation (6 October).

Banbow, D. (1997). Ethanol keeps ADM drunk on tax dollars. Washington, DC: Cato Institute http://www.cato.org (4 May 1998).

Canadian Commercial Alcohol Association (5 May 1998). Fuel ethanol.
http://www.comalc.com (5 May 1998).

Carrato, C., Marzio G., and Massimo G. (1996). environmental taxation and unemployment: some evidence on the 'double dividend hypothesis in Europe'. *Journal of Public Economics*, **62**(1/2), 141–81.

Chen, Z. 1997). Negotiating an agreement on global warming. *Journal of Environmental Economics and Management*, **32**, 170–78.

Church executive calls for ratification (17 December 1997). Washington, DC: United Methodist News Service http://www.umc.org (17 December 1997).

Climate change (28 July 1998). European Union, DN: IP/98/498 http://europa.eu.int (28 July 1998).

Committee to Preserve American Security and Sovereignty (1998). *Treaties, National Sovereignty, and Executive Power: A Report on the Kyoto Protocol*. Alexandria, VA (18 May).

EDF (1997). British petroleum to take action on climate change. Letter, September.
http://www.edf.org (2 March 1998).

Friends of the Earth (1998). EU greenhouse gas deal too much hot air. Press Release, 11 July. http:// www.foe.co.uk (11 July 1998).

Farm-State senators skeptical of climate plan (1998). Reuters. http://www.yahoo.com (9 March 1998).

Governor signs bill critical of Kyoto Protocol (1998). http://www.state.wv.us. (11 July 1998).

Holtz-Eakin, D. and Selden, T.M. (1995). Stoking the fires? CO_2 emissions and economic growth. *Journal of Public Economics*, **57**: 85–101.

UMWA/BCOA (July 1997). The impact of carbon mitigation strategies on energy markets, the national economy, industry and regional economies. Prepared for UMWA/BCOA by DRI/McGraw-Hill.

Jorgenson, D.W. and Wilcoxen, P.J. (1993). Reducing US carbon dioxide emissions: an assessment of different instruments. *Journal of Policy Modeling*, **115** (5/6), 491–520.

Kosobud, R. F., Daly, T.A., South, D.W. and Quinn, K.G. (1994). Tradeable cumulative CO_2 permits and global warming control. *Energy Journal*, **15** (2), 213–32.

Kyoto Protocol to the United Nations framework on climate change (1997). http://www.cnn.com (27 July 1998).

Kyoto Protocol Status of Ratification (2000) http://www.unfccc.de (accessed 11 August 2000)

Larsen, B. and Shah, A. (1994). Global tradeable carbon permits, participation incentives, and transfers. *Oxford Economic Papers*, **46** (5), 841–56.

Leopold, E. (1998). European nations sign Kyoto global warming treaty. Reuters http://www.infoseek.com. (4 May 1998).

Lindzen, R.S. (1997). Can increasing atmospheric CO_2 affect global climate? *Proc. Natl. Acad. Sc.*, **94**, 8335–42.

Magada, D. ((21 April 1998). Focus: Shell revamps image. Reuters. http://wwwinfoseek.com. (4 May 1998).

Manne, A.S. and Richels, R.G. (1991): Global CO_2 emission reductions: the impacts of rising energy costs. *Energy Journal* **12**(1), 87–107.

Morrison, J. (1998). G8 countries to act against environmental crime. Reuters. http://www.infoseek.com. (4 May 1998).

National Biodiesel Board (21 February 21), 1998). Agricultural products are key to national energy security. http://biz.yahoo.com (2 March 1998).

National Corn Growers Association (1998). National Corn Growers Report http://www.ncga.com (5 May).

National impacts (1998). WEFA National Impacts Link. http://www.api.org (27 July).

Nordhaus, W.D. (1991).'The cost of slowing climate change: a survey. *Energy Journal*, **12** (1), 37–65.

Office of Policy and International Affairs (1997). Analysis of carbon stabilization cases. SR-OIAF/97–01. Washington, DC: U.S. Department of Energy (October).

Ostrom, E. and Schlager, E. (1996). The formation of property rights. In *Rights to Nature* (S.S. Hanna, C. Folke, and K.-G. Maler, eds.). Washington, DC: Island Press.

Pearce, D. and Barbier, E. (1991). The greenhouse effect: a view from Europe. *Energy Journal*, **12** (1), 147–161.

Pianin, E. (1998). Gingrich halts move to end ethanol subsidy. *The Greenville News*, 7 May, 6D.

Posner, R.A. (1974). Theories of economic regulation. *Bell Journal*, Autumn, 335–58.

Raven, G. (1998). EU urges US to implement Kyoto global warming deal. Reuters. http://www.infoseek.com (7 May 1998).

Renewable Fuels Association (1998a). RFA Ethanol Report Issue 72 (7 May) http://www/ethanolrfa.org/ erob0798 (7 May 1998).

Renewable Fuels Association (1998b). Ethanol's contributions to 'clean air celebrated on Earth day'. Press Release, (21 April). http://www.ethanolrfa.org/pr042198 (7 May 1998).

Salisbury, L. (1998) Enron exec wants clean energy tax break. Reuters (26 February) http://yahoo.com (2 March 1998).

Sinclair, P.J.N. (1994). On the optimum trend of fossil fuel taxation. *Oxford Economic Papers* **46** (5), 869–77.

Stark, C. (1998). Inventory of greenhouse gases. *Iowa Energy Bulletin*. http://www.state.ia.us/government (5 May).

Stigler, G.J. (1971) The economic theory of regulation. *Bell Journal*, Spring, 3–21.

Sutherland, R.J. (1998. Achieving the Kyoto Protocol: an analysis of policy options. Washington: American Petroleum Institute (March).

Takenaka, K. (1998). Japan, Russia conclude landmark greenhouse gas swap. Reuters. http://www.infoseek.com. (4 May).

Testimony of Dr Janet Yellen, Chair, Council of Economic Advisers Before the House Commerce Committee on the Economics of the Kyoto Protocol (1998). Washington, D.C.: Council of Economic Advisers (4 March 1998).

Whaley, J. and Wigle, R. (1991) Cutting CO_2 emissions: the effects of alternative policy approaches. *Energy Journal*, **12** (1), 109–24.

The World Bank (1998). *World Resources: 1998–99*. Washington: The World Bank.

Yandle, B. (1983).Bootleggers and Baptists: the education of a regulatory economist. *Regulation*, May/June, 12–16.

Yandle, B. (1989). *The Political Limits of Environmental Quality Regulation*. Westport, CT: Quorum Press.

Yandle, B. (1997): *Common Sense and Common Law for the Environment*. Lanham, MD: Rowman & Littlefield Publishers.

10 Applying the precautionary principle in a broader context

Indur M. Goklany

Introduction

A popular formulation of the precautionary principle is that contained in the Wingspread Declaration (Raffensperger and Tickner, 1999, p. 8): 'When an activity raises threats of harm to human health or the environment, precautionary measures should be taken even if some cause and effect relationships are not established scientifically'.

I will attempt in this chapter, as a *gedankenexperiment* (a thought experiment), to apply this formulation of the principle to devise precautionary policies for some of the most contentious environmental issues facing the globe, namely, the issues of DDT, global warming and bioengineered crops. In this *gedankenexperiment*, I will examine and apply the precautionary principle comprehensively to the entire set of public health and environmental consequences of inaction as well as actions designed to address each of these issues.

A framework for applying the precautionary principle under competing uncertainties

Few actions are either an unmitigated disaster or an unadulterated benefit and certainty in science is the exception rather than the rule. A fundamental question with regard to the precautionary principle, then, is: how do we formulate policies in situations where an action could simultaneously lead to uncertain benefits and uncertain harm to public health and the environment? Prior to applying the precautionary principle it is necessary to formulate hierarchical criteria on how to rank various threats based upon their characteristics and the degree of certainty attached to them.

First, I will postulate that, in general, threats to human health should take precedence over threats to the environment. In particular, the threat of death to a human being (even to the lowliest human being in, say, Rwanda) outweighs similar threats to members of other species (no matter how magnificent that species). I will call this unapologetically anthropocentric criterion, the 'human mortality criterion'.

Second, all else being equal, more immediate threats should be given priority over threats that could occur later. This is the 'immediacy criterion'.

Third, threats of harm that are more certain (or have higher probabilities of occurrence) should take precedence over those that are less certain (or have lower probabilities of occurrence) if otherwise their consequences would be equivalent. (I will, in this chapter, be silent on how equivalency should be determined for different kinds of threats.) This, I will label as the 'uncertainty criterion'.

Moreover, for threats that are equally certain, precedence should be given to those that have a higher expectation value. So, fourth is the 'expectation value criterion'.

Fifth, if technologies are available to cope with or adapt to the adverse consequences of an impact, then under the 'adaptation criterion', that impact can be discounted to the extent that threat can be nullified.

Finally, there is the 'irreversibility criterion' which gives greater priority to outcomes that are irreversible.

DDT

Applying the precautionary principle in developing countries

Each year over a million people die from malaria in developing countries (WHO 1999a). The global death rate due to malaria was 18 per 100 000 in 1998, down from 194 per 100 000 in 1900. This more than 10-fold reduction is due to better nutrition, new drugs, insecticide-impregnated mosquito nets and spraying of insecticides (particularly DDT) inside homes.

We know for certain that, despite build-up of any mosquito resistance to DDT, the death toll would be higher if DDT spraying inside homes in many areas where malaria is currently endemic were to be discontinued, and that mortality increases would follow relatively soon. We also know that alternatives to DDT, even if available, do not necessarily lead to equivalent reductions in malaria incidence if the alternatives are more expensive because cost is an important factor in developing countries. The additional cost inhibits their use and helps explain why, despite the theoretical availability of substitutes, malaria rebounded in areas where DDT usage was discontinued, and receded when it was recommenced (WHO 1999a; Roberts 1999; Roberts et al.; 1997; Sharma, 1996; Whelan, 1992; Guarda et al., 1999).

For instance, malaria incidences in Sri Lanka (Ceylon) dropped from over 2.5 million in the 1940s to less than 20 in 1963 (WHO 1999a; Whelan, 1992). DDT spraying was stopped in 1964, and by 1969 the number of cases had grown to 2.5 million. Similarly, malaria was nearly eradicated in India in the early 1960s, and its resurgence coincided with shortages in DDT

(Sharma, 1996). Roberts et al. (1997) showed that South American countries (for example, Guyana, Bolivia, Paraguay, Peru, Brazil, Colombia and Venezuela) which had discontinued or decreased spraying of DDT inside homes saw malaria rates increase, while Ecuador, which increased DDT use since 1993, reported a 61 per cent decline.

Guarda et al. (1999) note that, although in 1988 there were no cases of *P. falciparium* reported in Loreto, Peru, they increased to 140 in 1991, and over 54 000 cases and 85 deaths in 1997. Four pages later, they note that DDT use was discontinued in 1988, although, remarkably, they failed to note this coincidence. A cynic may attribute these oversights to the researchers not wanting to offend the environmental sensibilities of either the anonymous referees or their sponsors.

In developing areas, by contrast with the certain and the almost immediate loss of human lives due to discontinuation of DDT, the public health and environmental consequences of continuing DDT at the levels they need to be sprayed indoors are uncertain and, if they occur at all, delayed. Thus, applying the human mortality, uncertainty and immediacy criteria, one must conclude that the precautionary principle requires that DDT use should be continued – and even encouraged – in developing countries, at least until equally inexpensive and equally effective methods of controlling malaria are generally available. Accordingly, regulations specifying that DDT ought to be phased out by a certain date could well be counter-productive.

Once equally effective but cheaper options are available, become public knowledge, and are generally accepted as such by potential victims and public health officials, the market place will almost inevitably drive out DDT. Similarly, if malaria-carrying mosquitoes become sufficiently resistant to DDT, its use would no longer be cost-effective (compared to other options), and economics, again, would automatically phase out DDT use. Thus, it is superfluous to require that DDT be phased out once cost-effective alternatives become available. In fact, if the goal is to phase out DDT as soon as possible and without any counter-productive increases in human mortality, we should bolster programmes to: (a) research and develop equally safe and cost-effective alternatives to DDT; (b) constantly monitor and evaluate the effectiveness of DDT and potential substitutes; and (c) disseminate such cost-effectiveness information amongst users and public health authorities charged with controlling malaria.

It might be argued that for DDT, the immediacy criterion may be invalid and overruled by the irreversibility criterion because – over time – DDT accumulation in the environment may lead to irreversible environmental harm. There are two counters to this. First, the death of a human being is equally irreversible, and more heinous than the death of a bird, for instance. In fact, if DDT could reduce the global death rate due to malaria by 10 per cent for even 10 years, that would save over a million people from premature death.

Second, the experience of developed countries which have banned DDT indicates that its most critical adverse effects – the declines in avian species such as the bald eagle, the peregrine falcon, and the osprey – are reversible, albeit slowly. Thus, in the USA, a quarter-century after the ban on DDT, these avian species were no longer endangered, and levels of DDT and its metabolites (for example, DDE) in human adipose tissues, fish and gull eggs are now a fraction of what they used to be (CEQ, 1999; EDF, 1997; Goklany, 1994, 1998a).

Finally, it has been argued that DDT use should be discontinued because mosquitoes may develop resistance to it. If DDT is not used, though, what difference does it make whether they develop any resistance? It makes more sense to use DDT until its use ceases to be cost-effective, for whatever reason (whether due to the build-up of resistance or availability of more cost-effective alternatives). In fact, DDT's use buys time during which better alternatives can be developed and perfected while, in the meantime, reducing human mortality.

Applying the precautionary principle in developed countries

Although malaria once was prevalent in many of the richer countries, these countries have virtually no incidences of malaria today. DDT contributed significantly to the eradication of malaria in many of these countries including the USA (Zucker, 1996). However, today DDT plays virtually no role in reducing human mortality and improving public health in those countries. Even if it did, they could afford equally safe and effective substitutes, despite any extra cost. Therefore the major impact of DDT use in the richer countries would be its potential negative impacts on the environment and, more speculatively, on human health (NRC, 1999). Thus, a ban on DDT in the richer countries – which most of them have, in fact, instituted – can be justified under a precautionary principle.

Applying the precautionary principle worldwide

The above discussion indicates that the precautionary principle can lead to vastly different policies in different parts of the world, and that it does not support a one-size-fits-all approach to DDT, whether it is a worldwide prohibition or a worldwide sanction for its use.[1] In fact, the precautionary principle is a poor argument for imposing a uniform worldwide regime for controlling DDT use.

Global warming

The net impacts of global warming

The net global and regional impacts of human-induced climate change (or global warming) are inherently uncertain. This is because projections of future impacts are based on a series of model calculations with each succeeding model using as its inputs increasingly uncertain outputs of the previous model (IPCC, 1996a; Goklany, 1992b).

First, future emissions of greenhouse gases (GHG) have to be estimated using uncertain projections of future population, economic conditions, energy usage, land use and land cover. These emissions are themselves sensitive to climatic conditions and to atmospheric concentrations. Second, these emissions have to be converted into each GHG's atmospheric concentration. Third, these concentrations have to be used to determine future 'radiation forcing' which is then used (ideally) by coupled atmospheric-ocean models to project climatic changes (such as changes in seasonal temperatures and precipitation, seasonal highs and lows, and changes in diurnal variability).

These climatic changes should be estimated at relatively fine geographical scales. This is because geography, itself, is an important determinant of the climate. Moreover, the distribution and abundance of natural resources, which are the basis of most climate-sensitive natural and human systems, are spatially heterogeneous. However, regardless of how much confidence one may have in the ability of climate models to estimate globally-averaged climatic changes, the finer the geographic scale, the more uncertain the results.

Fifth, these uncertain location-specific climatic changes serve as inputs to simplified and often inadequate models which project location-specific biophysical changes (e.g. crop or timber yields). Then, depending on the human or natural system under consideration, the outputs of these biophysical models may have to be fed into additional models to calculate impacts on those systems, e.g. estimates of crop yields should serve as inputs for a model of the agricultural system in order to estimate overall impact on food security.

Ideally there ought to be dynamic feedback loops between several of the models in the entire chain of models going from emissions to impacts estimates. For instance, the climate affects photosynthesis and respiration on the earth's surface which, in turn, will affect global CO_2 emissions. Therefore, there ought to be dynamic feedbacks from the impacts and climate models to the emissions models. To ease calculations, though, these feedback loops are generally ignored or replaced by static inputs or 'boundary' conditions.

Thus, estimates of the impacts of global warming in any specific location at any particular time are probably even more uncertain than estimates of the globally-averaged temperature and/or precipitation. Moreover, net global impacts – because they are an aggregation of the various location-specific impacts – are also uncertain, although there may be some cancellation of errors. Nonetheless, the uncertainties are large enough that one cannot be confident either of the magnitude or, in many cases, even the direction of impacts, i.e., whether the net impacts are positive or negative. This is true not only for any specific geographic location , but also globally.

Moreover, for climate-sensitive systems or indicators that are affected by human actions (e.g., agriculture, forests, land use, land cover, habitat loss and biodiversity) impacts models should include socio-economic models which ought to – but often do not – fully incorporate (among other things) secular changes in technology and 'automatic' adaptations. Failure to account fully for such technological change and human adaptability results in a substantial upward bias in the negative consequences of climatic change because it underestimates the ability of human ingenuity not only to mitigate adverse effects but also to harness the positive consequences. Such failure is the major reason why much-heralded forecasts such as that of the Club of Rome's *Limits to Growth, Global 2000*, or Ehrlich's *The Population Explosion*, have proven to be spectacular duds (Frederick et. al., 1994; Goklany, 1992b, 1996, 1999a).

Regardless of the uncertainties regarding the impacts, unless fossil fuel emissions are curtailed drastically from both developed and developing countries:

- Atmosphere carbon dioxide concentrations will most likely continue to rise. All else being equal, higher carbon dioxide concentrations mean greater productivity for agriculture, if not vegetation in general (IPCC, 1996a). And greater agricultural productivity means more food, which leads to better nutrition, which, in turn, ought to result in better health, less disease and lower mortality (Goklany, 1999b). And, in fact, the remarkable increases in global agricultural productivity and global food supplies per capita since the end of the Second World War – despite a much larger population – have been accompanied by substantial worldwide improvements in health, reductions in mortality rates and increases in life expectancies (Goklany, 1999b). Most of the credit for these achievements is generally assigned to agricultural, medical and public health technologies and practices, economic development – which makes more productive and improved technologies more affordable) – and trade –which moves food surpluses to food deficit areas, and generally stimulates both economic growth and diffusion of technology (Goklany 1995, 1998a, 1998b, 1999c, 1999d). Nevertheless, some credit is due to the past increase in carbon dioxide concentrations and, perhaps, to any associated warming global warming (see below; Goklany 1998b, Wittwer 1995, Nicholls 1997).
- Globally averaged temperatures will be higher, but the degree of warming and its geographic distribution is uncertain. There ought to be greater warming in the higher latitudes, at night, and during the winter. In general this means, among other things, greater agricultural and forest productivity in the higher latitudes because of longer growing seasons, but it could increase heat stress and reduce productivity in the tropics (Goklany, 1992b 1999c; IPCC, 1996a). Although the contribution of warming *per se* to the historical increases in global agricultural productivity is not yet known, growing seasons and forest productivity have been increasing in the northern latitudes due, perhaps, to a combination of higher nighttime temperatures during the winter and higher carbon dioxide concentrations (Myneni, et al. 1997; Tans and White, 1998; Fan et al., 1998; Tian et al., 1998).
- Globally averaged precipitation may increase, although precipitation may decline in some areas. Also, the timing of rainfall may be altered.

Increased precipitation does not necessarily translate into greater avail-ability of moisture for growing crops and vegetation. In some areas, increased evaporation due to higher temperatures may, all else being equal, more than offset increased precipitation. On the other hand, the water-use efficiency of vegetation goes up with increasing carbon dioxide concentrations. Thus, the amount of water needed to grow specific crops and other vegetation may or may not decline at any given location (IPCC, 1996a).

- Although there has been no discernible increase in the rate of sea level rise over the past century due to global warming, it could conceivably accelerate in the future (IPCC, 1996b).
- Altered patterns of temperature and precipitation combined with increas-ing CO_2 concentrations will cause some animal and vegetation species to migrate. The ensemble of species or 'ecosystem' at any specific location today will, thus, be altered, as will the abundance of individual species at that location (Goklany 1992; IPCC, 1991, 1996a p. 451–54). But whether these changes constitute a net benefit or loss is unclear not only because the 'final' distribution is uncertain but also because there are no criteria for establishing whether the change has resulted in a net loss or benefit to either humanity or the rest of nature. Proponents of GHG controls implicitly assume that any change is inherently detrimental, more as an article of faith rather than as the product of a rational inquiry into aspects such as changes in net or gross productivity, or the mix and abundance of species.

Assessments of the future impacts of global warming suggest that in the absence of further GHG controls, over the next several decades the net impacts of global warming will be relatively small compared to the other environmental and natural resource problems facing the globe (see Table 10.1 on p. 203; Goklany 1998b, 1999c). Specifically, Table 10.1 shows that:

- With respect to agricultural production, in the absence of warming, global production would have to increase 83 per cent from 1990 to 2060 to meet additional food demand from a larger and richer global population, according to one study relied upon by the IPCC's 1995 assessment (IPCC, 1996a; Rosenzweig and Parry, 1994). Global warming may decrease production in developing, but increase it in developed, countries, resulting in a net change in global production of +1 or -2 per cent in 2060. Notably, Rosenzweig and Parry used a globally-averaged temperature change for 2060 which was higher than the IPCC's 'best estimate' for 2100 (Goklany, 1998b). Also, it considered only a few of the potential adaptations that could be available in 2060 (or, for that matter, 2100). It, for instance, did not consider the potential for productivity-enhancing techniques such as development of cultivars that can better tolerate drought, salt and acidic conditions, and which can better take advantage of higher atmospheric carbon dioxide concentrations – technologies which are merely gleams in our eyes today, but could be realities six decades from now (Goklany, 1998b, 1999c; see also the following section on bioengineered crops). On the other hand, the analysis did not consider any change in the proportion of crops lost to insects and other pests. However, crop protection is an ongoing challenge for farmers everywhere with or without climate change (Goklany, 1998a, 1999d).

● Regarding forest and habitat, greater agricultural and other human demands may reduce forest cover by 25 per cent (or more) by 2050 in the absence of any global warming, putting enormous pressure on the world's biodiversity (IPCC, 1996a, pp. 95–129, pp. 492–96). However, global warming alone (but ignoring the beneficial effects of carbon dioxide on photosynthesis and water-use efficiency) may actually increase forest cover by 1 to 9 per cent (IPCC, 1996a, pp. 492–96). The existing margins of current forest types, almost certainly, would shift poleward. *A priori*, there is no reason to believe that would lead to a diminution of global biological diversity in terms of the number of species or their abundance. It is worth noting that, often, wetter and warmer climatic conditions seem to harbor greater biodiversity, so long as sufficient water is available (Hawksworth et al., 1995, Huston, 1994).

● By 2060, incidences of malaria (which may be thought of as a metaphor for climate-sensitive infectious and parasitic diseases) may increase by about 5 to 8 per cent of the base rate in the absence of warming (IPCC, 1996a, pp. 561–84; Goklany, 1999c). The increase may be double that in 2100. These increases, although small compared to the baseline rate, are, nevertheless, likely to be overestimates because the analysis is based upon the notion that warming will expand the geographical ranges of the responsible vectors. However, this notion has been disputed by some authorities on tropical diseases (Reiter, 1996; Bryan et al., 1996; Taubes, 1997). More importantly, the current ranges of these diseases seem to be dictated less by climate than by human adaptability. Specifically, many infectious and parasitic diseases (e.g., malaria, yellow fever and cholera) have been virtually eradicated in richer countries although they were once prevalent there (e.g. the USA and Italy). This is because, in general, a wealthier society has better nutrition, better general health, and greater access to public health measures and technologies targeted at controlling these diseases. Also, given secular improvements in public health measures and technologies that ought to occur in the next several decades given the rapid expansion in our knowledge of diseases and development of the institutions devoted to health and medical research, the importance of climate in determining the ranges of these diseases is likely to further diminish.

● Sea level could rise about 10 inches by 2060 and 20 inches by 2100 due to global warming. The cost of protecting structures and populations against a 20-inch rise in sea level by 2100 has been estimated at about $US1 billion per year until 2100 or less than 0.005 per cent of global economic product (Goklany, 1999b; IPCC, 1996b, pp. 384–85, 1996c, p. 191).

Proponents of establishing GHG emission limits have also speculated that the frequency and intensity of extreme weather events may be increased by global warming, as would deaths and damages due to such events. But, so far, there seems to be little evidence of that. In fact, despite any increased global warming during the past century, US. data shows that in the past decades death rates due to hurricanes, floods, tornadoes and lightning have declined 60 to 99 per cent since their peaks (based on 9-year moving averages; see Figure 10.1; Goklany 1998b, 1999c). In addition, although property losses due to floods and hurricanes have increased somewhat in terms of 'real' dollars because a larger and richer population has more property at risk, losses have not increased in terms of per cent of wealth (Figures 10.2 and 10.3; Goklany 1998b, 1999c). Finally, there seems to be little scientific basis for concluding that in the future, extreme events will be more frequent or more intense due to global warming (Henderson-Sellers et al., 1998; Henderson-Sellers, 1998; IPCC,1996b, p. 7, 332–5).

Hence, stabilizing greenhouse gas concentrations immediately, even if feasible, would do little or nothing over the next several decades to solve those problems which are the major reasons for concern about warming, except, possibly, sea level rise (see Table 10.1). Specifically:

- Land and water conversion will continue virtually unabated, with little or no reduction in the threats to forests, biodiversity, and carbon stores and sinks.

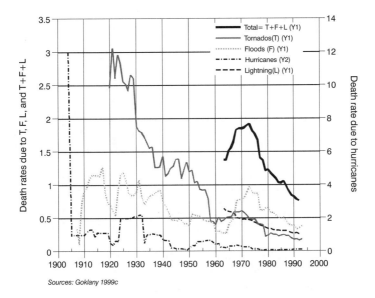

Sources: Goklany 1999c

Figure 10.1 Death rates due to tornados, floods, lightning and hurricanes (deaths per million population, 9-year moving averages, 1990–97)

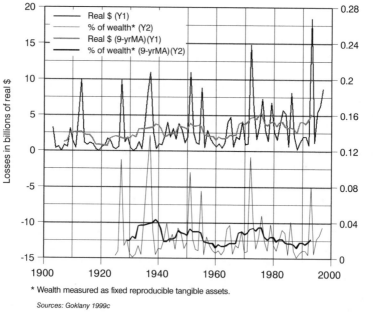

Figure 10.2 Property losses due to floods, 1903–97

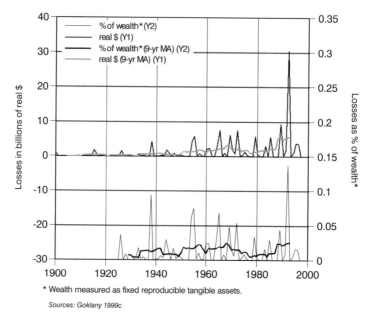

Figure 10.3 Hurricane property losses, 1900–97

- Chances of feeding, clothing and sheltering a larger world population will not have been substantially improved, if at all.
- Incidence rates of infectious and parasitic diseases will be virtually unchanged.
- Poorer nations, which by virtue of their poverty are deemed to be most vulnerable to the adverse impacts of climate change, will continue to be vulnerable to all kinds of adversity, natural or man-made.

Thus, while global warming may be a serious problem in the long run, other environmental and health problems are likely to be much more urgent for the next several decades (Goklany, 1998b, 1999c).

The net impacts of aggressively forcing the pace of GHG emission reductions

Attempts to reduce greenhouse gas emissions beyond what could occur with secular trends in technology and the withdrawal of some subsidies for energy will come at a cost to the world's economic development. We know that economic development, which creates wealth, helps increase food supplies per capita (Figure 10.4) which, then, reduces malnutrition, mortality rates (Figure 10.5) and increases life expectancies (Figure 10.6). Even if GHG control requirements were restricted to developed countries, economic growth would suffer in developing countries because trade between the two sets of countries

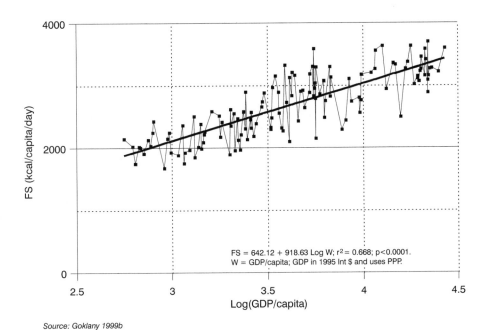

$FS = 642.12 + 918.63 \log W; r^2 = 0.668; p < 0.0001.$
$W = GDP/capita; GDP$ in 1995 Int \$ and uses PPP.

Source: Goklany 1999b

Figure 10.4 Daily food supplies per capita (FS), 1995

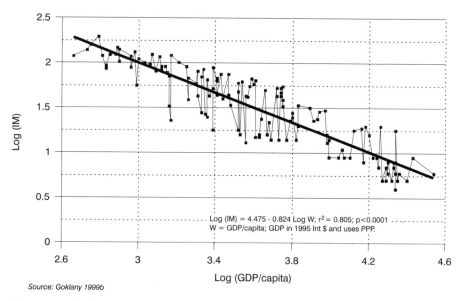

Source: Goklany 1999b

Figure 10.5 Infant mortality (IM), 1990–95

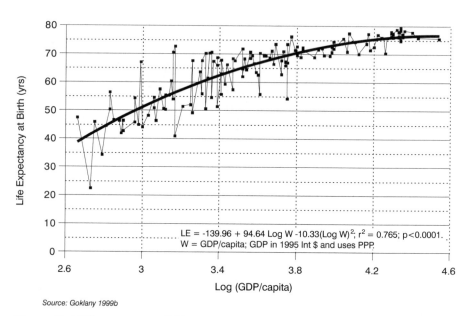

Source: Goklany 1999b

Figure 10.6 Life expectancy (LE), 1990–95

is an important factor in maintaining and enhancing the latter's economic output (Goklany, 1992b, 1995). Thus, aggressively forcing the pace of reductions will almost inevitably result in increased mortality rates and lowered life expectancies – to be balanced, if at all, by the more speculative benefits associated with a reduction in the impacts of reduced warming.

Reduced economic development has other down sides. First, lower levels of economic development are correlated with higher total fertility rates (Figure 10.7) which tends to push up population growth rates. Second, it diminishes a society's adaptability to adversity in general and to climate change in particular (Goklany, 1992, 1995, 1999b). This is because poorer societies have fewer resources available to research, develop, acquire, operate and maintain technologies that would help society better cope with whatever problems it may be plagued with, including unmet public health, environmental and social needs. As we have seen, future non-climate change related environmental and public health problems ought to substantially outweigh the adverse impacts of climate change for the next several decades. Third, a poorer society has lower crop yields (see Figure 10.8). For any specific level of crop production, to compensate for lower yields, more habitat and forest land have to be converted to cropland, which puts greater pressure on biodiversity, and reduces carbon stores and sinks. In fact, such conversion is the major threat to global biodiversity (Goklany 1992, 1995, 1999b). It is hardly surprising that between 1980 and 1995, forest cover in developing countries decreased by 190 million

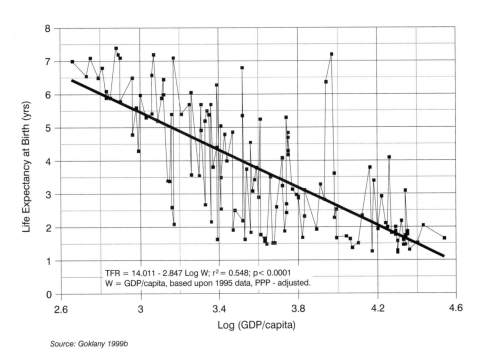

TFR = 14.011 - 2.847 Log W; r^2 = 0.548; p< 0.0001
W = GDP/capita, based upon 1995 data, PPP - adjusted.

Source: Goklany 1999b

Figure 10.7 Total fertility rate (TFR), 1990–95

hectares (Mha) while it increased 20 Mha in the developed countries (FAO, 1997). Finally, efforts to substantially reduce GHG emissions could, over the next several decades, divert scarce resources from addressing more urgent environmental and public health problems (see Table 1).

As an alternative to imposing additional GHG control requirements, energy prices could be increased through taxes or, in effect, through elimination of subsidies. Such price increases, however, could have unintended consequences. First, the productivity of the food and agricultural sector would be reduced because that sector is heavily dependent upon oil and gas for running its farm machinery, production of inputs such as fertilizers and pesticides, powering irrigation systems, and the movements of inputs and outputs from farms to markets. Thus, food production would decline and/or prices would go up. This is what happened following the oil shocks of the 1970s (Pinstrup-Andersen, 1999, Figure 24, p. 21). In either case, food would be less accessible to those who are less well off, and hunger and malnutrition would increase which, in turn, should increase rates of death and disease amongst those groups. Second, an estimated 2.8 million die annually because of indoor air pollution worldwide, mainly because of the burning of solid fuels (e.g. coal, wood and dung) for heating and cooking in the home in developing countries. Increasing fossil fuel prices would only make it harder for households using solid fuels to switch to cleaner, commercial fossil fuels. Third, increasing fuel prices would inhibit the operation of heaters in the winter and air conditioners in the summer, which could, in turn, lead to greater sickness, if not mortality, due to cold and heat waves.

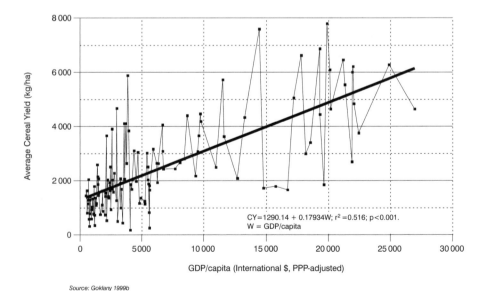

CY=1290.14 + 0.17934W; r^2=0.516; p<0.001.
W = GDP/capita

Source: Goklany 1999b

Figure 10.8 Cereal yields (CY), 1995

Table 10.1 Projected climate change impacts compared to other environmental problems

Climate-sensitive sector/indicator	Year	Impact/effect	
		Baseline, includes impacts of environmental problems other than climate	*Impacts of climate change, on top of the baseline*
Agricultural Production	2060 for baseline >2100 for climate change	must increase 83 per cent, relative to 1990	net global production would change −2.4 per cent to +1.1 per cent; but could substantially redistribute production from developing to developed countries
Global forest area	2050	decrease 25–30 (+) per cent, relative to 1990	*reduced loss of global forest area*
Malaria incidence	2060 2100	500 million 500 million	25 to 40 million additional cases 50 to 80 million additional cases
Sea level rise	2060 2100	varies varies	less than 25 cm (or 10 inches) less than 50 cm (or 20 inches)
Extreme weather events	2060 or 2100	NA	unknown whether magnitudes or frequencies of occurrence will increase or decrease

Sources: IPCC 1996a, 1996b; Goklany 1998b.

Applying the Precautionary Principle to Global Warming

The above analysis indicates that for the next several decades the impacts of climate change are probably relatively minor compared to other environmental hazards even without the imposition of additional control requirements (see Table 1). On the other hand, forcing the pace of GHG controls could result in numerous problems (namely, greater hunger; higher mortality; lower life expectancy; greater losses of habitat, biodiversity and carbon stores and sinks; and greater vulnerability to adversity in general, including those caused by climate change). Thus, in light of the human mortality criterion, the precautionary principle argues against *accelerating* GHG reductions for the next few decades beyond what would occur due to secular improvements in technology and normal measures to reduce air pollution and energy-related costs. This argument is strengthened by the immediacy criterion because the problems due to forcing the pace of GHG reductions are likely to occur sooner than the effects of deferring such reductions. The argument is further bolstered by the uncertainty criterion because the negative effects of greater poverty are also more certain than the positive effects of reducing climate change.

But there are counter-arguments against deferring requirements to reduce GHG emissions.

First, given that the impacts of climate change could be in addition to other environmental stresses on natural and human systems, climate change may be the straw that breaks the camel's back. Indeed, that may well be the case. Consider malaria, for instance, where, because of climate change, malaria incidences in 2100 may climb from 500 million to 550–580 million (Table 1).

However, there are at least two ways to address the problem of the last straw (Goklany, 1999c). The usual approach is to try to eliminate the last straw. This means trying to eliminate climate change completely in order to wipe out the 50–80 million additional cases in 2100. But we know that there will be some climate change even if atmospheric GHG concentrations could be stabilized immediately (a most unlikely occurrence). Alternatively, we could lighten the overall burden on the camel's back, by removing several other straws to make room for that proverbial last straw if, and when, it descends. That would also leave a margin for error. Accordingly, we could reduce, if not eliminate, the cumulative 550–580 million cases that may occur in 2100, rather than only the extra 50–80 million. In fact, if the baseline rate is reduced by 0.2 per cent per year from now to 2100, that would more than compensate for any increase in malaria due to climate change. This could provide more bang for the buck, and benefits to humanity will come sooner and more certainly, since the relationship between an increase in malaria incidence and global warming is tenuous, at best. In addition, if we eliminate malaria by 2100, we also eliminate a major reason for being concerned about warming. In effect, the first counter-argument against deferring requirements for GHG controls is nullified by the adaptation and uncertainty criteria.

A second counter-argument is that the assessment that impacts of climate change would be relatively small was based on net global impacts. It ignored the fact that there will be regional winners and regional losers because of non-uniform geographical impacts of warming. In particular, developing countries may be the biggest losers because being poor, they are the least able to adapt.

Consider food security. Developing nations already run food deficits. Their net imports of grain currently amount to more than 10 per cent of their production (FAO, 1999a). These deficits will get worse in the future because the increase in their food demand is expected to outstrip the increase in their productivity (Goklany, 1999c; Pinstrup-Andersen, 1999). Global warming is expected to further aggravate those food deficits. On the other hand, the food surpluses of developed countries are expected to increase further. However, it is not necessary to require GHG reductions in order to address this issue. The increase in food deficits due to climate change can be addressed in exactly the same way as we address current imbalances in production (and differences in comparative advantage) today, namely, through trade. Trade allows surpluses to flow voluntarily to deficit areas; but to expand such trade, developing countries will need to 'grow' the non-food sectors of their economies. Also, as noted previously, economic growth has other ancillary benefits for human well-being. Thus, the second counter-argument against aggressively forcing the pace of GHG controls is also invalidated by the adaptation criterion.

A third counter-argument is that, although climate change may not be the most urgent problem facing the globe over the next several decades, because of the inertia of the climate system, it may be too late to do anything about warming by the time its impacts become urgent. In other words, climate change may not be as urgent as other environmental problems today and tomorrow, but it could be crucial the day after tomorrow. Table 10.1, however, suggests that even if there is a 50-year lead time to implement climate change controls (Wigley, 1997, Wigley, et al., 1996, Ha Duong et al., 1997), we have a couple of decades leeway before commencing any costly control actions (Goklany, 1999c). Moreover, as noted previously, we may solve the problem of climate change but not most of the critical underlying problems that placed climate change on our agenda in the first place.

Consider forest and habitat losses. If climate change is completely halted, an unlikely proposition, we may lose 25 per cent of global forest area mainly because the increasing future human demand for food will increase pressures to convert additional habitat for agriculture (see Table 10.1). Discounting for the moment the notion that climate change could increase global forest cover, as suggested by Table 10.1 and IPCC (1996a, 1996b), eliminating climate change would do little or nothing to reduce the major, imminent threats to global forests, ecosystems, biodiversity and loss of carbon sinks and stores. Similarly, if climate change is halted, the challenge of adequately feeding the world's future population will be practically undiminished, as will be the underlying problems of malaria, or other infectious and parasitic diseases.

So how do we solve the urgent problems of today and tomorrow, without compromising our ability to address the climate change problem of the day after?

There are two complementary approaches to addressing these multiple problems. First, we can focus on fixing current environmental problems that might be aggravated by climate change. With respect to the problem of increasing forest and habitat loss, for instance, this means addressing its basic causes, namely, the increased demand for land and water to meet human needs for food, clothing, shelter, paper and other material goods. To reduce such demand, we should attempt to produce as much food, timber and other products per unit of land and water diverted to meet humanity's needs as is possible in an environmentally sound manner. This will also help solve the problem of food security because it will increase food production and help keep food prices in check. In addition, it would help maintain global carbon stocks and reservoirs, thereby mitigating carbon emissions. Also by containing land costs, it would reduce costs for carbon sequestration or energy farms, if they are ever needed (Goklany, 1998a, 1999d)

To increase the productivity and efficiency of land and water use, we ought to continue research and development (R&D), for instance, on precision farming, integrated pest management, and methods to reduce post-harvest and end-use crop and timber losses. Greater emphasis should also be placed upon R&D to increase agricultural and forest productivity under less-than-optimal conditions which might become more prevalent due to climate change, such as drought (due to higher temperatures and redistribution of precipitation), higher salinity (due to greater evaporation and saltwater intrusion in coastal agricultural areas), and higher carbon dioxide. As we shall see in greater detail later, biotechnology, unless *verboten*, can play a crucial role here.

The second approach to addressing the problems of today, as well as the long term, is to reduce the vulnerability of society in general by increasing its resilience to adversity, whatever its cause (Goklany, 1992b, 1995, 1999c). This can be accomplished by enhancing the mutually reinforcing forces of technological change, economic growth and trade. If we look around the world today, we find that virtually every indicator of human or environmental well-being improves with wealth. Poorer countries are hungrier and more malnourished, and their inhabitants suffer from higher mortality rates and live shorter lives (Figures 10.4–10.7; Goklany, 1999b). This is because they are less resilient and more vulnerable to any adversity owing to the fact that they have fewer resources (fiscal as well as human capital) to create, acquire and operate new *and* existing-but-underutilized technologies to cope with that adversity. Just as someone suffering from AIDS is less immune to an infectious disease, no matter what the infection, so is a poorer society less immune to adversity, no matter what its proximate cause. And just as AZT boosts the entire immune system of a person with AIDS helping that person combat any infection, so does economic growth boost the ability of society to combat any adversity, and not just the adverse impacts of climate change.

Thus, economic growth enhances technological change, making society more resilient. In turn, technological change reinforces economic growth. Trade is also an integral part of boosting society's resilience. Not only does it enable food and other natural resources to move from surplus to deficit areas voluntarily, in so doing, it discourages exploitation of marginal resources. It also helps disseminate new technologies and bolster economic growth.

To summarize, the precautionary principle argues for a cautious policy over the next few decades toward reducing GHG emissions; otherwise, that could retard increases in global wealth which, in turn, could lead to greater hunger, poorer health and higher mortality. Specifically, it argues against forcing the pace of controls, and, instead, for putting greater emphasis on research into the consequences of climate change, on solving current problems which may be worsened by climate change, and on enhancing society's adaptability and reducing its vulnerability to environmental problems in general by strengthening the institutions underpinning the mutually-reinforcing forces of technological change, economic growth, and trade. These institutions include free markets, secure property rights, and honest and predictable bureaucracies and governments. Moreover, enhancing adaptability and reducing vulnerability will raise the thresholds at which greenhouse gas concentrations become 'dangerous' which, in turn, would reduce the cost of controls. This is essentially a 'no-regrets' policy (Goklany, 1992b, 1995, 1999d).

Bioengineered crops

Environmental benefits

Agriculture and forestry, in that order, are the human activities that have the greatest effect on the world's biological diversity (Goklany, 1998a). Today, agriculture alone accounts for 37 per cent of global land area (FAO, 1999a), 70 per cent of water withdrawals and 87 per cent of consumptive use worldwide (UNCSD, 1997). It is also the major determinant of land clearance and habitat-loss worldwide. Between 1980 and 1995, developing countries lost 190 Mha of forest cover mainly because their increase in agricultural productivity was exceeded by growth in food demand, while developed countries increased their forest cover by 20 Mha because their productivity outpaced demand. Agriculture and, to a lesser extent, forestry also affects biodiversity through water pollution and atmospheric transport, for example, by release of excess nutrients, pesticides and silt into the environment (Wilcove, et al. 1998; Goklany 1998a).

The world's population will almost inevitably increase (from about 6 billion today to, perhaps, between 10 and 11 billion in 2100). It will also become richer. Accordingly, the predominant future environmental and natural resource challenge for the globe is likely to be the problem of meeting the human demand for food, nutrition, fibre, timber and other natural resource products while preserving land and water for the rest of nature and containing other impacts on the environment (Goklany 1998a, 1998b, 1999c).

In this subsection, I will address the role biotechnology can play in reconciling these often opposing goals. Although most of the following discussion focuses on agriculture with particular emphasis on developing countries, much of it is equally valid for developed countries, as well as for other human activities that use land and water, for example, forestry.

Decrease in land and water diverted to human uses

Figure 10.9 and Table 10.2 indicate, for a specific scenario, the amount of additional land that would have to be converted to cropland between 1993 and 2050 as a function of the future increase in productivity of the food and agricultural sector. This scenario assumes, for illustration, that global population will be 9.6 billion in 2050, that food supplies per capita will increase at the historical 1969–71 to 1989–91 rate, and that new cropland will, on average, be just as productive as cropland in 1993 (an optimistic assumption). Table 2 shows that if current productivity is maintained – hardly a foregone conclusion – the entire increase in production would have to come from an expansion in the amount of cropland, that is, cropland would have to increase by 121 per cent or 1753 Mha over the 1993 level of 1448 Mha. Much of that would necessarily have to come at the expense of forested areas. On the other hand, a productivity increase of 1.0 per cent per year, equivalent to a cumulative 76 per cent increase from 1993–2050, would reduce the amount of new cropland needed to 368 Mha (Goklany, 1998a, 1999a).

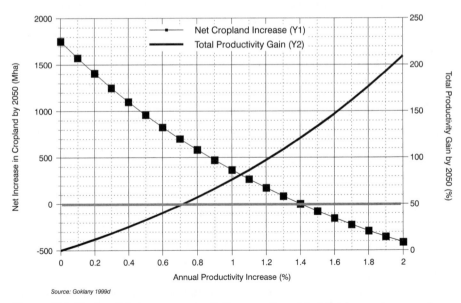

Source: Goklany 1999d

Figure 10.9 Trade-off between productivity growth and habitat loss net conversion of land to cropland from 1993 to 2050

Table 10.2 Global habitat conversion to cropland between 1993–2050

Increase in productivity, 1993–2050		
Annual increase (%)	*Total increase from 1993–2050 in %*	*Additional land cleared for cropland (Mha)*
0.0	0	1753
0.1	6	1576
0.2	12	1408
0.3	19	1251
0.4	26	1102
0.5	33	961
0.6	41	828
0.7	49	703
0.8	57	585
0.9	67	473
1.0	76	368
1.1	87	268
1.2	97	174
1.3	109	85
1.4	121	0
1.5	134	−78
1.6	147	−152
1.7	161	−223
1.8	176	−290
1.9	192	−353
2.0	209	−12

Note: In 1993, global cropland was 1,448 Mha. *Source*: Goklany 1999d.

Such an increase in productivity is theoretically possible without resorting to biotechnology, provided sufficient investments are made in human capital and research and development (in general, and in the food and agricultural sector), extension services, infrastructure expansion (to bring new lands, where needed, into production and integrate it with the rest of the world's agriculture system), inputs such as fertilizers and pesticides, and the acquisition and operation of technologies to limit or mitigate environmental impacts of agriculture (Goklany, 1998a, 1999a). A 1.0 per cent per year increase in the overall productivity of the food and agricultural sector is within the bounds of historical experience given that it increased 2.3 per cent per year between 1961–63 and 1995–97 (FAO, 1999a). What is more important, there are numerous existing-but-unused opportunities to enhance productivity in an environmentally sound manner – unused largely due to insufficient wealth (one reason why cereal yields are usually lower in poorer nations; see Figure 10.8). Merely increasing the 1992–94 average cereal yields in developing and transition nations to the level attained by the country with the highest average yield (i.e. the yield ceiling, YC) would have increased global production by 170 per cent (Goklany, 1999a). Best farming practices would increase yields even further. For instance, the 1992 US. champion maize grower's yield exceeded YC by a further 136 per cent (Waggoner, 1994). Also, there are large gaps between the average global cereal yield of 2.77 T/ha (in 1992–94; Goklany, 1999a), YC of 7.48 T/ha (in 1991–93) and the theoretical maximum yield of 13.4 T/ha (Linnemann, et al., 1979).

Specifically, conventional (i.e., non-biotechnological) methods could be used to increase agricultural productivity by: (a) further limiting pre-harvest crop losses to pests and diseases, which currently reduce global yields by an estimated 42 per cent (Oerke et al., 1994); (b) increasing fertilizer use; (c) liming acidic soils; and (d) adapting high yielding varieties to specific locations around the world, although many scientists believe that opportunities to further increase yields through conventional breeding techniques are almost tapped out (Mann, 1999b).

Net productivity of the entire food and agricultural sector (i.e., from farm to mouth) could also be increased by reducing post-harvest and end-use losses (Goklany and Sprague, 1991), which are estimated at about 47 per cent worldwide (Bender, 1994). In fact, combining pre- and post-harvest losses, I estimate that 69 per cent of the potential crop is lost one way or another. Reducing combined losses by a third would increase food availability by about 80 per cent. Post-harvest losses could be reduced through – among other things – greater irradiation, increased refrigeration and better packaging worldwide.

Conventionally-derived new technologies could also be employed to improve yields while limiting adverse environmental impacts, for example, through the development and deployment of location- and crop-specific integrated nutrient, water and pest management systems to help optimize the timing, quantities and mix of various inputs and chemicals used, i.e 'precision' farming (Goklany, 1998a, 1999a). Such optimization could, for instance, reduce, though not eliminate, the estimated 99 per cent (+) of pesticides that do not reach their targets (Pimentel, 1997), and excess nutrients in water systems.

Improvements based upon conventional technologies will depend, in large part, on the ability of developing nations to afford and operate (through economic development and growth of human capital) the necessary technologies. However, productivity improvements could come much more rapidly and more surely if biotechnology is used because that could more easily reduce current gaps between average yields and yield ceilings, and yield ceilings and the theoretical maximum yield, as well as push up the theoretical maximum yield. Whether biotechnology can also reduce net environmental impacts of agriculture will be discussed in greater detail later.

If, through biotechnology, the annual rate at which productivity can be increased sustainably goes up from 1.0 per cent to 1.5 per cent per year, then cropland could actually be reduced by 78 Mha rather than increased by

368 Mha (relative to 1993 levels), all the while meeting the increased food demand of a larger and richer population. (This corresponds to a net increase in productivity of 33 per cent in 2050 due to biotechnology alone.) In addition, if perchance productivity is increased to 2.0 per cent per year, then 412 Mha of current cropland could revert to the rest of nature, which corresponds to a net improvement of 76 per cent due to biotechnology (Table 10.2).

Several biotechnological crops, currently in various stages between research and commercialization, could increase yields and, more importantly, put more food on the table per unit of land and water diverted to agriculture. Such crops, which could be particularly useful in developing nations, include:

- Cereals which are tolerant of poor climatic and soil conditions; specifically, cereals which are tolerant to aluminum (so that they can grow in acidic soils), drought, high salinity levels, submergence, chilling and freezing. The ability to grow crops in such conditions could be critical for developing countries: 43 per cent of tropical soils are acidic (World Bank, 1994); more cropland is lost to high salinity than is gained through forest clearance; and salinity has rendered one-third of the world's irrigated land unsuitable for growing crops (Frommer, et al. 1999). Moreover, if the world warms, the ability to tolerate droughts, high salinity, submergence and acidity could be especially important for achieving global food security.
- Rice which combines the best traits of the African and Asian varieties, namely, the former's ability to shade out weeds when young (which, however, inhibits photosynthesis later in the 'pure' African variety) with the high yield capacity of the Asian variety. In addition, the bioengineered variety is highly resistant to drought, pests and diseases. This could be particularly useful for Africa because its increases in rice yields have so far lagged behind the rest of the world. This lag is one reason why malnourishment in sub-Saharan Africa has increased in the past several decades, in contrast to trends elsewhere.
- Rice with the property of being able to close stomata more readily. This ought to increase water use efficiency and net photosynthetic efficiency. Both aspects will be useful under dry conditions – conditions which may get more prevalent under global warming.
- Rice with the alternative C4 pathway for photosynthesis which could be especially useful if there is significant warming because the C4 pathway is more efficient at higher temperatures. In addition, efforts are underway to try to re-engineer RuBisCO, an enzyme that is critical to all photosynthesis, by using RuBisCO from red algae, which is a far more efficient catalyst for photosynthesis than that found in crops (Mann, 1999a).
- Maize, rice and sorghum with resistance to *Striga*, a parasitic weed which could decimate yields in sub-Saharan Africa.
- Rice with the ability to fix nitrogen.
- Rice and maize (which together account for 20 per cent of global cropland) with enhanced uptakes of phosphorus and nitrogen.

- Rice, maize, potato, sweet potato, and papaya with resistance to insects, nematodes, bacteria, viruses, and fungi. Papaya, which, for instance, had been ravaged in Hawaii by the papaya ringspot virus, has now made a come-back due to a bioengineered variety resistant to that virus.
- Cassava, a staple in much of Africa, with resistance to the cassava mosaic virus and including a gene with an enzyme (replicase) with the ability to disrupt the life cycles of a number of other viruses. This could, it is claimed, increase yields 10-fold. Also, because cassava naturally contains substances that can be converted to cyanide, it has to be adequately prepared before consumption. Work is proceeding on producing a genetically modified (GM) cassava which would be less toxic.
- Bananas in which ripening is delayed (similar to the commercially available Flavr Savr tomato). Bananas and plantains are an important source of food for many African nations. This would extend the shelf life of bananas and reduce post-harvest losses.
- High lysine maize and soybeans, maize with high oil and energy content, and forage crops with lower lignin content which ought to improve livestock feed and reduce the overall demand for land needed for livestock.

(Conway and Toennissien, 1999; MacIlwain, 1999; Jayaraman, 1999; Mann, 1999a, 1999b; Ferber, 1999; Moffat, 1999a; McCalla and Brown, 1999; Mazur et al., 1999; Prakash, 1998a, 1998b; see also Goklany, 2000)

If the methods and genes used to bioengineer the above crops can be successfully adapted and transferred to other vegetables, tubers, fruits and even trees, that would help reduce future land and water needs for feeding, clothing and sheltering humanity.

Reduction in the release of nutrients, pesticides and silt into the environment

Many of the above crops could also help reduce the release of nutrients and pesticides into the environment (Goklany, 2000). These include:

- Nitrogen-fixing rice, and rice and maize bioengineered with the ability to increase uptakes of phosphorus and nitrogen from the soil. In Europe and the USA, only 18 per cent of the nitrogen and 30 per cent of the phosphorus in fertilizers are incorporated into crops, between 10 and 80 per cent of the nitrogen and 15 per cent of the phosphorus end up in aquatic ecosystems, and much of the remainder accumulates in the soil, to be later eroded into aquatic systems (Carpenter, et al., 1998). Such crops would, therefore, reduce reliance on chemically fixed fertilizers and, thereby, reduce ground and surface water pollution, risks of chemical spills, and decrease atmospheric emissions of nitrous oxide (N_2O), a greenhouse gas which, pound for pound over a 100-year period, is 310 times more potent a greenhouse gas than is CO_2.

- Crops resistant to viruses, weeds, and other pests, e.g. *Striga*-resistant maize, rice and sorghum. Examples also include various *Bt* crops which contain genes from the *Bacillus thuringiensis* bacterium, which has been used as an insecticide (as a spray) for four decades. One evaluation of *Bt* cotton in the USA estimates its planting on 2.3 million acres in 1998 (as opposed to using the conventional variety) reduced chemical pesticide use by over a million pounds, increased yields by 85 million pounds and netted farmers $US92 million (Ferber, 1999). The usage of *Bt* maize which was planted on 14 million acres in the U.S. reduced pesticide spraying on 2 million of those acres. It would have been greater, but for the fact that many farmers do not normally spray for the European maize borer, the target of the *Bt* toxin (Ferber, 1999). Developing countries also can reduce pesticide usage by using pest resistant crops. Consider that in India, the world's third largest producer of cotton, although cotton occupies only 5 per cent of its land, cotton farmers alone buy about 50 per cent of all pesticide used in the country (Prakash, 1999). In 1998, the devastation caused by pests reportedly contributed to 500 suicides among Indian cotton farmers whose crops had failed. Field trials of Bt cotton at 30 locations in India show a 14 to 38 per cent yield increase despite suspension of any spraying (Hindu Business Line, 2000)
- Crops tolerant of various herbicides, so that those herbicides can be used to kill weeds, but not the crop itself. This would increase yields while also facilitating no-till cultivation, a highly effective method of stemming soil erosion. Such erosion not only jeopardizes future agricultural productivity but also leads to water pollution, and consequent damage to fish and other aquatic organisms. Herbicide tolerant crops are among the most common applications of biotechnology today. One commercially available example is 'Roundup Ready' soybean, which is engineered to be tolerant to glyphosate. However, so far results from the field are mixed. Planting of these crops seems to have reduced application of more hazardous and longer lasting herbicides (e.g., acetochlor), although overall herbicide use may have increased (Ferber, 1999).

Finally, any reduction in the amount of cultivated land due to increases in crop yields because of bioengineered crops would also reduce soil erosion, and its associated environmental effects on water bodies and aquatic species.

Other environmental benefits of bioengineered plants and trees

Crops can also be engineered to improve environmental conditions. For instance, GM plants can be used for bioremediation by developing crops that selectively absorb various metals and metal complexes such as aluminium, copper and cadmium from contaminated soils (Moffat, 1999b). Such plants could, for instance, detoxify methyl mercury in soils, thereby removing it from the food chain.

Researchers have also genetically modified aspen trees to produce 50 per cent less lignin and 15 per cent more cellulose. Lignin, a component of all wood, must be chemically separated from cellulose to make the pulp used in paper production. The GM tree has half the normal lignin:cellulose ratio of about 1:2. Overall, 15 per cent more pulp may be produced from the same amount of wood. Moreover, the GM trees are 25–30 per cent taller. Thus, the requirements of land, chemicals and energy used to make a given quantity of paper ought to be reduced substantially, and result in significantly lower environmental impacts at every stage, from tree farming to paper production (MTU. 1999).

Other potential applications of biotechnology which could reduce environmental impacts include production of biodegradable plastics using oilseed rape and coloured cotton (which could reduce reliance on synthetic dyes) (Lawrence, 1999).

Public health benefits

As noted previously, the increase in food supplies per capita is a major reason for the world-wide improvement in health status during this century. In turn, that helped lower mortality rates, increase life expectancies, and enable the average person to live a more fulfilling and productive life. The above discussion indicates that GM crops ought to increase the quantity of food produced per unit of land and water which ought to help sustain continued improvement in the average person's health status and general well-being, while reducing pressures on biodiversity.

Despite years of progress, during which food supplies per capita increased and malnourishment declined, about 825 million people worldwide still cannot meet their basic needs for energy and protein. Moreover, the nutritional quality of food is just as important as the quantity. The diets of over half the world's population are deficient in iron, vitamin A or other micronutrients. Such deficiencies can cause disease, if not death (WHO, 1999a; FAO, 1999b). About 2 billion people do not have enough iron in their diet, making them susceptible to anaemia. Another 260 million suffer from subclinical levels of vitamin A deficiency which causes clinical xerophthalmia which, if untreated may lead to blindness, especially in children. Vitamin A is also crucial for effective functioning of the immune system (WHO, 1999b).

Through the cumulative effect of these deficiencies, in 1995, malnutrition was responsible for 6.6 million or 54 per cent of the deaths worldwide in children under five years of age, stunting in 200 million children, and clinical xerophthalmia in about 2.7 million people (WHO, 1999c).

Bioengineering can not only increase food production which could go a long way toward reducing protein and energy deficits, but it could also help ward off many of the above micronutrient deficiencies. Scientists at Zurich's Swiss Federal Institute of Technology have developed 'golden rice' which is rich in beta-carotene, a precursor to vitamin A, and crossed it with another bioengineered strain rich in iron and cysteine (which allows iron to be absorbed in the digestive tract). Two-thirds of a pound of rice, an average daily ration in the tropics, will provide the average daily vitamin A requirement while reducing iron deficiency. An important bonus from golden rice is that would reduce the need for red meat – one of the primary sources for dietary iron – which, in turn, could somewhat reduce overall demand for livestock feed, and the land, water and other inputs necessary to produce that feed (Gura, 1999; Guerinot, 2000; Ye et al., 2000; Goklany, 2000).

Scientists are also working on using bananas and other fruits as vehicles to deliver vaccines against the Norwalk virus, *E. coli*, hepatitis B and cholera (Moffat, 1999a, Smaglik, 1998). This could eventually lead to low cost, efficient immunization of whole populations against common diseases with broader coverage than likely with conventional needle delivery.

Bioengineered crops can also help battle the 'diseases of affluence', namely, heart disease, hypertension and cancer. Genetically enhanced soybeans that are lower in saturated fats are already in the market. The International Food Information Council (1999) also notes that biotechnology could also make soybean, canola and other oils and their products such as margarine and shortenings more healthful; peanuts with improved protein balance; tomatoes with increased antioxidant content; potatoes with higher starch than conventional potatoes, which ought to reduce the amount of oil absorbed during processing of foods like French fries or potato chips; fruits and vegetables fortified with or containing higher levels of vitamins such as C and E; and higher-protein rice, using genes transferred from pea plants.

Finally, to the extent pest resistant GM plants reduce the amount, toxicity and/or persistence of pesticides used in agriculture (by themselves or as parts of integrated pest management systems), that would reduce accidental poisonings and other untoward health effects on farm workers.

Adverse environmental consequences

The major environmental concerns regarding GM crops are those related to crops which are designed to be resistant to pests and tolerant of herbicides. One potential risk is that target pests will become resistant to toxins produced by pest resistant GM crops, such as *Bt* corn or *Bt* cotton. Although this is a possibility even if *Bt* is delivered via conventional sprays on non-GM plants, it is of greater concern with *Bt* plants. This is because under conventional spraying target pests are exposed to *Bt* toxins only for brief periods, whereas currently available *Bt* crops produce toxins throughout the growing season, which could increase the chances of developing *Bt*-resistant pests (Gould, 1998; see also Walliman, 2000). Moreover, some laboratory studies suggest that target pests may evolve resistance more rapidly than had previously been thought possible (Liu, et al. 1999, Agbiotechnet, 1999).

Strategies used to address pest resistance due to conventional pesticide spraying can – and should – be adapted for GM crops. Such strategies include ensuring plants deliver high doses of *Bt*, while simultaneously maintaining refuges for non-*Bt* crops to ensure pest populations remain susceptible to *Bt*. The Environmental Protection Agency (EPA) has established the requirement that *Bt* corn farmers plant 20 per cent of their land in non-*Bt* corn, as refuges. For *Bt* corn grown in cotton areas, farmers must plant at least 50 per cent non-*Bt* corn. In addition, EPA requires expanded monitoring to detect any potential resistance (EPA, 2000). Other strategies to delay development of pesticide resistance include crop rotation (Gould, 1998), developing crops with more than one toxin gene acting on separate molecular targets (Conway, 2000) and inserting the bioengineered gene into the chloroplast since that ought to express *Bt* toxin at higher levels (Daniell, 1999; Kota et al., 1999). Notably, farmers have an economic stake in implementing such adaptive strategies so that their crop losses to pests are kept in check in the long, as well as short, term.

Another source of risk is that *Bt* from pest resistant plants could harm, if not kill, non-target species. This could happen if, for instance, *Bt*-laden pollen were to drift away from the field or if the toxin were to leak through the roots and was consumed by non-target organisms (Losey et al., 1999; Walliman, 2000; Saxena et al.; 1999). Losey et al. (1999) showed in a laboratory study that the mortality rate of Monarch butterfly larvae fed for four days with milkweed dusted with *Bt* maize pollen was 44 per cent, compared to zero for the control case (which used milkweed dusted with ordinary pollen). However, whether – and the extent to which – the Monarch butterfly population would be affected in the real world is a matter of debate (Ferber, 1999). One study suggests that under a worst-case scenario as much as 7 per cent of the North American population (estimated at 100 million) may die, although the real-world effect would probably be smaller (Ferber, 1999; see also Milius, 1999). The inadvertent effects of *Bt* crops due to pollen dispersal or root leakage could be virtually eliminated by bioengineering genes into the chloroplast rather than into nuclear DNA (Kota et al., 1999; Scott and Wilkinson, 1999, Chamberlain and Stewart, 1999).

Bt could also enter the food chain through root leakage or if predators prey on target pests. For instance, studies have shown that the green lacewing larvae, a beneficial insect, which ate maize borers fed with *Bt* maize were more likely to die (Hilbeck et al., 1998), but the real world significance of this has also been disputed based on the long history of *Bt* spraying on crops and other studies which showed beneficial insects essentially unharmed by such spraying (Gray, 1998).

There is also a concern that bioengineered genes from herbicide or pest tolerant crops might escape into wild relatives leading to 'genetic pollution' and creating 'superweeds'. This would have an adverse economic impact on farmers. It would reduce crop yields and detract from the very justification for using such GM crops (Gray and Raybould, 1998). Clearly, the farmer has a substantial incentive for preventing weeds from acquiring herbicide tolerance and, if that fails, to keep such weeds in check.

Gene escape is possible if sexually compatible wild relatives are found near fields planted with GM crops, as is the case in the USA for sorghum, oats, rice, canola, sugar beets, carrots, alfalfa, sunflowers and radish (Mann, 1999c; Regal, 1994; Lemaux 1999). However, the most common GM crops, namely, soybeans or corn, have no wild US relatives (Cook, 1999; Mann, 1999c) Moreover, centuries of conventional breeding have rendered a number of important crops, e.g. maize and wheat, 'ecologically incompetent' in many areas (Royal Society, 1998), although that is no guarantee of safety (Regal, 1994). Moreover, despite the use of conventionally-bred herbicide tolerant plants, there has been no upsurge in problems due to herbicide tolerant weeds (Royal Society, 1998). However, if any weeds develop such tolerance, available crop management techniques (such as another herbicide) can be used to control them.

Gene escape from GM crops to wild relatives is also an environmental concern. It has been argued that herbicide tolerant 'superweeds' could invade natural ecosystems. It is unclear why such a weed would have a competitive advantage in a natural system unless that system is treated with the herbicide in question. But if it is so treated, does it still qualify as a natural system? Moreover, if it is to be treated, another herbicide to which the so-called superweed is not resistant could be used. On the other hand, if the area is not treated with the herbicide in question, what difference does it make to the ecosystem whether the weed is tolerant? Moreover, regarding ecosystem function and biodiversity, the significance of genetic pollution, per se, is unclear. Would gene escape affect ecosystem function negatively?[3] To bring this issue into focus, consider the case of human beings: if an Indian from Calcutta comes to Washington, DC, and has an offspring with a native-born American would that not, as the term has been used, be considered genetic pollution? (Not very long ago, xenophobes labelled that, miscegenation.) Does that diminish, or expand, biological diversity? Is such genetic pollution acceptable for human beings, but not for other species? But if the answer varies with the species, it raises questions about the validity of the notion that gene escape can be equated to pollution – genetic, or otherwise (see also Sagoff 1999; for a different viewpoint, see Johnson 1999). A similar argument can be made regarding the hypothetical offspring of a union of two human beings, with one having been treated to reduce the likelihood of passing on a genetically determined disease. Would it diminish or expand biodiversity (Sagoff, 1999; Rayl 2000)?

In addition, genes may escape from GM crops to non-GM crops of the same species. If this were to occur, it would be unpopular with organic farmers, who are afraid it might 'adulterate' their produce, as well as producers and farmers of GM seeds, who are not eager to have someone else profit from their investments. The chances of such gene escape can be reduced by maintaining a buffer between the two crops. The Royal Society (1998) also notes that because more crops (including corn, sorghum, sugar beet and sunflower) are now grown from hybrid seeds, that provides a measure of built-in security against such gene transfers.

Of course, gene escape could be limited if the GM plant was engineered to be sterile or prevented from germinating using, for instance, 'terminator technology'. An alternative approach would be to insert the gene into the chloroplast which would preclude their spread through pollen or fruit, as well as prevent root leakage (Daniell, 1999; Royal Society, 1998).

Finally, there is a concern that in the quest to expand yields, GM plants will work too well in eliminating pests and weeds, leading to a further simplification of agricultural ecosystems and further decreasing biodiversity. This concern, in conjunction with the other noted environmental concerns, needs to be weighed against the cumulative biodiversity benefits of reduced conversion of habitat to cropland, and decreased use of chemical inputs.

Adverse public health consequences

A major health concern is that the new genes inserted into GM plants could be incorporated into a consumer's genetic makeup. This, however, seems unlikely. First, not all the products made from a GM crop contain the gene inserted into it. For instance, refined soy oil made from Roundup Ready soy does not contain any of the glyphosate resistant genes, although the unrefined oil may have detectable amounts (May 1999, Royal Society 1998). However, there is no evidence that any genes have ever been transferred to human beings through food or drink despite the fact that plant and animal DNA has always been a part of the daily human diet (Royal Society, 1998). In fact, an estimated 4 per cent of human diet is composed of DNA (Chassy and Sheppard, 1999), and an average adult Briton consumes 150 000 km of DNA in an average meal (Lewis and Palevitz, 1999).

Another concern is that genes transferred from foods to which many people are allergic could trigger allergies in unsuspecting consumers of such GM crops. Between 1–3 per cent of the adults and 5–8 per cent of the children in the USA suffer from food allergies, and each year, food allergies cause 135 fatalities and 2500 emergency room visits (Buchanan, 1999). This concern regarding allergic reactions to GM foods can be traced to pre-commercialization tests conducted by Pioneer Hi-Bred which showed that a soybean which had been bioengineered to boost its nutritional quality using a gene from the brazil nut was, in fact, allergenic. Although this example shows that GM foods can be tested prior to commercialization for their allergic potential, opponents of GM foods have used this as an argument against bioengineered crops. Notably, several databases of known allergens could be used to help identify problematic GM products before they are developed (Royal Society, 1998; Gendel, 1999). In fact, because bioengineering allows more precise manipulation of genes than does conventional plant breeding, it could be used to render allergenic crops non-allergenic (Buchanan, 1999; Scalise, 1997).

Yet another potential negative effect on public health is that antibiotic resistant 'marker' genes which are used to identify whether a gene has been successfully incorporated into a plant could, through consumption of the antibiotic gene by humans, accelerate the trend toward antibiotic-resistant diseases. However, by comparison with the threat posed by the use of antibiotics in feed for livestock and their overuse as human medicines, the increased risk due to such markers is slight (Royal Society 1998; see also May, 1999).

Applying the precautionary principle

The above discussion indicates there are risks associated with either the use – or the non-use – of GM crops. With respect to public health, limiting GM crops will almost certainly increase hunger and malnutrition because that would reduce the quantity and quality of food which would otherwise be produced. In turn, that will increase death and disease, particularly among children in the developing world. The loss of these benefits far outweigh the speculative adverse consequences of eating GM foods. Thus, employing the human mortality, expectation value and uncertainty criteria, the precautionary principle *requires* that we continue to develop and commercialize, with appropriate safeguards (of course), those GM crops which would increase food production, and improve nutrition and health generally for the developing world.

Some have argued that many developed countries are 'awash in surplus food' (see, for example, Williams, 1998). Thus, goes this argument, developed countries have no need to boost food production. However, this argument ignores the fact that reducing those surpluses would be almost as harmful to public health in developing countries as curtailing the latter's food production. At present, net cereal imports of the developing countries exceed 10 per cent of their production. Without trade (and aid) based on the surpluses of the developed countries, food supplies available to the populations of developing countries would be higher and their food prices would be steeper; in turn, this would increase undernourishment and any associated health problems. In addition, as already noted, food deficits of developing countries are only expected to increase in the future because of high population growth rates and, possibly, global warming. Therefore, food surpluses of developed countries will at least be as critical for future global food security as it is today.

The above argument against GM crops also assumes that such crops will produce little or no benefits for the inhabitants of developed countries. However, as noted, GM crops are also being engineered to improve nutrition in order to combat diseases of affluence afflicting populations in developed, as well as developing, nations. Similarly, the health benefits of 'golden rice', for instance, are available to all.

Hence, the human mortality and uncertainty criteria also require developed countries to develop, support and commercialize yield-increasing and health- and nutrition-enhancing GM crops in order to improve public health worldwide.

A second argument against using GM foods to increase food production is that there is no shortage of food in the world today, that the problem of hunger and malnutrition is rooted in poor distribution and unequal access to food because of poverty; therefore, it is unnecessary to increase food production; ergo, there is no compelling need for biotechnology (MacIlwain, 1999). However, even if everyone had equal access (an unlikely proposition, at best), finite levels of food, fibre and timber would still have to be produced to meet the demand. A figure similar to Figure 9 could be developed for any level of food demand whether it is, say, half that of today (perhaps because of a perfect, cost-free distribution system and a magical equalization of income) or whether it is four times that (possibly due to runaway population growth). Thus, regardless of the level of demand, limiting GM crops would lower crop and forest yields per unit of land and water used. And to compensate for the lower yields, more land and water would have to be pressed into mankind's service, leaving that much less for the rest of nature. Moreover, if bioengineering succeeds in improving the protein and micronutrient content of vegetables, fruits and grains, it might persuade many to adopt and persevere with vegetarian diets and, thereby, reduce the additional demand meat-eating places on land and water. In addition, giving up GM crops will, more likely than not, increase pressures on biodiversity due to excess nutrients, pesticides and soil erosion. Finally, reduced conversion of habitat and forest to crop and timber land would help limit losses of carbon reservoirs and sinks.

Against these reductions in threats to biodiversity and carbon stores and sinks, on the other sides of the scales we have the environmental benefits of limiting pest resistant and herbicide tolerant GM crops (minus the environmental costs of conventional farming practices). These include a potential increase in the diversity of the flora and fauna associated with or in the immediate vicinity of GM crops if they are more effective in reducing non-target pests and weeds than conventional farming practices, and the possible consequences of gene escape to weeds and non-GM crops.

Hence, even if one were to ignore the likely benefits to humanity from GM foods due to reduced mortality and improved public health, based on the uncertainty and expectation value criteria, one must still conclude that the precautionary principle also requires the cultivation of GM crops in order to conserve the planet's biodiversity, provided due caution is exercised, particularly with respect to herbicide tolerant and pest resistant GM crops.

It is worth noting that the precautionary principle supports using terminator-type technology which would, one way or another, disable a GM plant's ability to reproduce because that would minimize the possibility of gene transfer to weeds and non-GM plants. Notably, some of the same groups that profess environmental concerns about genetic pollution subjected terminator technology to sustained criticism (Greenpeace, 1998; Friends of the Earth, 1999). Does that mean that they believe that concerns about genetic pollution may, in the larger scheme of things, be overblown?

Conclusion

The precautionary principle has been invoked to justify policies for a world-wide ban on DDT, aggressive GHG emission controls, and a prohibition on GM crops. However, these justifications are based upon a selective application of the precautionary principle on a limited set of consequences of the policies themselves. Specifically, these justifications overlook the likely outcome of a global DDT ban on human health and mortality in developing countries. Regarding global warming, these justifications ignore the probable, though indirect, impacts of an effective regime to significantly slow down the increase in GHG atmospheric concentrations in the short- to medium-term. By slowing economic growth and/or increasing energy prices, such regimes could, in the final analysis, decrease overall access to food which could lower health status and increase death and disease in the poorer segments of society, especially in the developing world. In addition, justifications for banning GM crops omit consideration of their probable world-wide benefits to public health and in reducing threats to biological diversity, forests, habitats, and carbon stores and sinks. Thus, contrary to claims that the above policies are based on caution, they would, in fact, increase overall risks to public health and the environment. In other words, the above policy cures may be worse than the underlying diseases.

The precautionary principle properly applied, with full consideration of all the public health and environmental consequences of action and inaction, argues for substantially different policies. Specifically, the precautionary principle argues that:

- DDT use should not be banned worldwide because it will surely lead to increased human mortality in human beings. In fact, indoor spraying of DDT ought to be encouraged in countries where malaria is an ongoing threat until it is automatically phased out because of market forces, once equally safe and cost-effective substitutes are available and have been accepted by the beneficiaries of indoor spraying in the developing world.
- GHG emission reduction requirements that go beyond secular improvements in technology and elimination of unjustified energy subsidies ought to be eschewed for the next few decades because they are likely to retard economic development which, in turn, would lead to greater hunger, poorer health and higher mortality in human beings. Moreover, oil and gas prices ought not to be raised because that would reduce food availability, as well as retard the abandonment of solid fuels for heating and cooking in the developing world, which would then delay reductions in mortality from indoor air pollution. The precautionary principle argues, instead, for placing a much higher priority on solving current problems which may be aggravated by climate change, and on increasing society's adaptability and decreasing its vulnerability to environmental problems, in general, and climate change, in particular. These could be achieved by bolstering the

institutions that are the foundations of the mutually-reinforcing forces of technological change, economic growth, and trade. These institutions include free markets, secure property rights, and honest and predictable bureaucracies and governments. Moreover, consistent with the precautionary principle, enhancing adaptability and reducing vulnerability will raise the thresholds at which greenhouse gas concentrations become 'dangerous'.

• Research and development into, and commercialization of, GM crops ought to be encouraged, provided due caution is exercised. By comparison with conventional crops, such crops would increase the quantity and nutritional quality of food supplies and, thereby, improve public health and reduce mortality rates worldwide. In addition, cultivation of GM, rather than conventional, crops would be more protective of biological diversity, since it would, by increasing productivity, reduce the amount of land and water that would otherwise be diverted to mankind's needs. It could also reduce the environmental damage from the use of fertilizers and pesticides, and from soil erosion, while also conserving carbon reservoirs and sinks.

Notes

1 In fact, the precautionary principle is a poor argument for imposing a uniform worldwide regime for controlling DDT use.

2 To bring this issue into focus, consider the case of human beings: if an Indian from Calcutta comes to Washington, DC, and has an offspring with a native-born American would that not, as the term has been used, be considered genetic pollution? (Not very long ago, xenophobes labelled that, miscegenation.) Does that diminish, or expand, biological diversity? Is such genetic pollution acceptable for human beings, but not for other species? But if the answer varies with the species, it raises questions about the validity of the notion that gene escape can be equated to pollution, genetic, or otherwise (see also Sagoff, 1999; for a different viewpoint, see Johnson, 1999). A similar argument can be made regarding the hypothetical offspring of a union of two human beings, with one having been treated to reduce the likelihood of passing on a genetically determined disease.

3 This, however, seems unlikely. First, not all the products made from a GM crop contain the gene inserted into it. For instance, refined soy oil made from Roundup Ready soy does not contain any of the glyphosate resistant genes, although the unrefined oil may have detectable amounts (May, 1999; Royal Society, 1998).

References

Agbiotechnet (1999). Hot topic: Bt plants: resistance and other issues. July 1999 www.agbiotechnet.com/topics/hot.asp (4 February, 2000).

Bender, W.H. (1994). An end use analysis of global food requirements. *Food Policy* **19**, 381–95.

Bryan, J.H., D.H. Foley and R.W. Sutherst (1996). Malaria transmission and climate change in Australia. *Medical Journal of Australia*, **164**, 345–347.

Buchanan, R.. (6 October 1999). Statement to the Senate Committee on Agriculture, Nutrition, and Forestry.
www.senate.gov/~agriculture/buc99106.htm (11 January, 2000).

Carpenter, S.. Caraco, N. F., Correll, D.L., Howarth, R.W., Sharpley, A.N. and Smith, V.H.. (1998). Nonpoint pollution of surface waters with phosphorus and nitrogen. *Issues in Ecology*, Number 3, Summer 1998

esa.sdsc.edu/carpenter.htm (10 February, 2000).

Council on Environmental Quality (CEQ) (1999). *Environmental Quality*. CEQ: Washington, DC.

Chamberlain, D., and Stewart, C.N. (1999). Transgene escape and transplastomics. *Nature Biotechnology*, **17**, 330–31.

Chassy, B., and Sheppard, L.. (1999). GMO food safety risk is negligible. *ACES News*. University of Illinois.

www.ag.uiuc.edu/news/articles/943382465.html (10 December, 1999).

Conway, G. (2000). Food for all in the twenty-first century. *Environment*, **42**, 9–18.

Conway, G. and Toenniesen, G. (1999). Feeding the world in the twenty-first century. *Nature*, **402** (supplement), C55–C58.

Cook, R.J. (1999). Toward science-based risk assessment for the approval and use of plants in agriculture and other environments. CGIAR/NAS Biotechnology Conference, October 21–22, 1999.

www.cgiar.org/biotechc/mccalla.htm (11 November, 1999).

Daniell, H.. (1999). the next generation of genetically engineered crops for herbicide and insect resistance: containment of gene pollution and resistant insects. *AgBiotechNet* 1999, **1**, August, ABN 024.

www.agbiotechnet.com/reviews/aug99/html/Daniell.htm (12 February 2000).

Environmental Defense Fund (EDF) (1997). 25 years after DDT ban, bald eagles, osprey numbers soar. Press release 13 June.

www.edf.org/pubs/NewsReleases/1997/Jun/e_ddt.html (21 December, 1999).

Environmental Protection Agency (EPA) (2000). *Bt*. corn insect resistance management announced for 2000 growing season. EPA Headquarters Press Release. January 14.

Fan, S. et al. 1998. A large terrestrial carbon sink in North America Implied by atmospheric and oceanic carbon dioxide data and models. *Science*, **282**, 442–446;

Food and Agricultural Organization (FAO) (1997). *The State of the World's Forests 1997*. Rome: FAO:

FAO (1999a) *FAO Database*
apps.fao.org (12 January 2000).

FAO (1999b). *The State of Food Insecurity in the World*. Rome: FAO.

www.fao.org/FOCUS/E/SOFI/home-e.htm (12 January 2000).

Ferber, D. (1999). Risks and benefits: GM crops in the cross hairs. *Science*, **286**, 1662–1666.

Friends of the Earth (FOE). (1999). FoE Remains Sceptical about Monsanto's terminator pledge. Press Release. 5 October.

http://www.foeeurope.org/press/foe_remains_sceptical.htm (21 February 2000).

Frederick, K.M., Goklany, I.M. and Rosenberg, N.J. (1994). Conclusions, remaining issues, and next steps. *Climatic Change*, **28**, 209–219.

Frommer, W.B., Ludewig, U. and Rentsch, D. (1999). Taking transgenic plants with a pinch of salt. *Science*, **285**, 1222–1223.

Gendel, S. (1999). *The Biotechnology Information for Food Safety Database*
www.iit.edu/~sgendel/fa.htm (11 January 2000).

Goklany, Indur M. et al. (1992a). *America's Biodiversity Strategy: Actions to Conserve Species and Habitat.* US Department of Agriculture and Department of the Interior, Washington, DC.

Goklany, I.M. (1992b). Adaptation and climate change. Paper presented at the Annual Meeting of the American Association for the Advancement of Science, Chicago, February 6–11, 1992.

Goklany, I.M. (1994). *Air and Inland Surface Water Quality: Long Term Trends and Relationship to Affluence.* Office of Program Analysis, US Department of the Interior, Washington, DC.

Goklany, I.M. (1995). Strategies to enhance adaptability: technological change, economic growth and free trade. *Climatic Change,* **30**, 427–449.

Goklany, I.M. (1996). Factors affecting environmental impacts: the effects of technology on long-term trends in cropland, air pollution and water-related diseases. *Ambio,* **25**, 497–503.

Goklany, I.M. (1998a) saving habitat and conserving biodiversity on a crowded planet. *BioScience,* **48**, 941–953

Goklany, I.M. (1998b). The importance of climate change compared to other global changes. In Proceedings of the Second International Specialty Conference: Global Climate Change – Science, Policy, and Mitigation/Adaptation Strategies. Crystal City, Virginia, 13–October 1998. Sewickley, PA: Air and Waste Management Association, pp. 1024–1041.

Goklany, I.M. (1999a). *Clearing the Air: The Real Story of the War on Air Pollution.* Washington, DC: Cato Institute.

Goklany, I.M. (1999b). *The Future of the Industrial System.* International Conference on Industrial Ecology and Sustainability, University of Technology of Troyes, Troyes, France, 22–25 September, 1999.

Goklany, I.M. (1999c). Richer is more resilient: dealing with climate change and more urgent environmental problems. In *Earth Report 2000: Revisiting the True State of the Planet* (R. Bailey, ed.). New York: McGraw-Hill, pp. 155–187.

Goklany, I.M. (1999d). Meeting global food needs: the environmental trade-offs between increasing land conversion and land productivity. In *Fearing Food: Risk, Health and Environment.* (J. Morris and R. Bate, eds). Oxford: Butterworth-Heinemann, pp. 256–289.

Goklany, Indur M. et al. 1992. *America's Biodiversity Strategy: Actions to Conserve Species and Habitat.* U. S. Department of Agriculture and Department of the Interior, Washington, DC.

Goklany, I.M. (2000). Biotechnology and biodiversity: the risks and rewards of genetically modified crops. In review.

Goklany, I.M., and Sprague, M.W. (1991). *An Alternative Approach to Sustainable Development: Conserving Forests, Habitat and Biological Diversity by Increasing the Efficiency and Productivity of Land Utilization.* Washington, DC: Office of Program Analysis, Department of the Interior.

Gould, F. (1998). Sustaining the efficacy of Bt toxins. In *Agricultural Biotechnology and Environmental Quality: Gene Escape and Pest Resistance* (R.W.F. Hardy and J.B. Segelken, eds). National Agricultural Biotechnology Council (NABC) Report 10. Ithaca (NY): NABC, pp. 77–86

Gray, A. (15 October 1998). Nature debates: be careful what you wish. . .. http://www.biotech-info.net/monarch_Q&A.html (February 12, 2000).

Gray, A.J., and. Raybould, A.F. (1998). Reducing transgene escape routes. *Nature* **392**, 653–654.

Greenpeace. 1998. Stop Monsanto's terminator technology.
www.greenpeace.org/~geneng/highlights/pat/98_09_20.htm (12 January 2000).

Guarda, J.A., Asayag, C.R. and Witzig, R. (1999). Malaria re-emergence in the Peruvian Amazon Region. *Emerging Infectious Diseases*, **5**, 209–215.

Guerinot, M. (2000). The Green Revolution strikes gold. *Science*, **287**, 241–243.

Gura, T. (1999). New genes boost rice nutrients. *Science* **285**, 994–995.

Ha-Duong, M., Grubb, M.J. and Hourcade, J.-C. (1997). Influence of socio-economic inertia and uncertainty on optimal (sic) CO_2-emission abatement. *Nature*, **390**, 270–273.

Hawksworth, D.L., et al. (1995). Magnitude and distribution of biodiversity. In *Global Biodiversity Assessment*. (V.H. Heywood et al., eds). Cambridge University Press, Cambridge (UK), pp. 107–192.

Henderson-Sellers, Ann, et al. 1998., Tropical Cyclones and Global Climate Change: A Post-IPCC Assessment. *Bulletin of the American Meteorological Society* 79: 19–38.

Henderson-Sellers, Ann. 1998. Climate Whispers: Media Communication About Climate Change. *Climatic Change* 40: 421–456.

Hilbeck, A.M., Baumgartner, P., Fried, P.M. and Bigler, F. (1998). Effects of transgenic *Bacillus Thuringiensis* corn-fed prey on mortality and development time of immature *Chysoperla Carnea (Neuroptera: Chrysopidae)*. *Environmental Entomology* 27(2): 480–487.

Hindu Business Line. 2000. *Bt* Cotton Trials Show Yield Rise.
www.indiaserver.com/bline/2000/01/19/stories/071903a1.htm (19 January 2000).

Huston, Michael A. 1994. *Biological Diversity*. Cambridge (UK): Cambridge University Press, pp. 30–35.

International Food Information Council (IFIC) (1999). *Backgrounder – Food Biotechnology*. Updated April 1999.
ificinfo.health.org/backgrnd/BKGR14.htm (12 January 2000).

Intergovernmental Panel on Climate Change (IPCC) (1991). resource use and management. In *Response Strategies: The Intergovernmental Panel on Climate Change*. Washington, DC: Island Press.

IPCC (1996a). (R. Watson et al., eds) *Climate Change 1995: Impacts, Adaptations and Mitigation of Climate Change*. Cambridge, UK: Cambridge University Press,.

IPCC (1996b). (J.T. Houghton et al., eds). *Climate Change 1995: The Science of Climate Change*. Cambridge, UK: Cambridge University Press,.

Jayaraman, K.S. (1999). India intends to reap the full commercial benefits. *Nature* **402**: 342–343.

Johnson, B. (1999). Conserving our natural environment. *Nature Biotechnology*. **17**, BV29–BV30.

Kota, M.,. Daniell, H., Varma, S. Garczynski, F. Gould, F and Moar, W.J. (1999). Overexpression of the *Bacillus Thuringiensis* (*Bt*) CRY2A2 protein in chloroplasts confers resistance to plants against susceptible and Bt-resistant insects. *Proceedings of the National Academy of Sciences*. **96**, 1840–1845.

Lawrence, E. 1999. Biotechnology: plastic plants. *Nature Science Update*, 28 September.
helix.nature.com/nsu/990930–5.html (11 January 2000).

Lemaux, P.G. (1999). Plant growth regulators and biotechnology. Paper presented at the Western Plant Growth Regulator Society; 13 January 1999; Anaheim, CA.
plantbio.berkeley.edu/~outreach/REGULATO.HTM (19 January 2000.

Lewis, R., and Palevitz, B.A. (1999). Science vs. PR: GM crops face heat of debate. *The Scientist*. **13**,. 11 October
www.the-scientist.library.upenn.edu/yr1999/oct/lewis_p1_991011.html (19 January, 2000.

Linnemann, H., De Hoogh, J.,. Keyzer, M.A,. Van Heemst, H.D.J.,. Brolsma, R.J.,. Bruinsma, J.N., Buringh, P. Staring, G.J. and. De Wit, C.T. (1979). *MOIRA: Model of International Relations in Agriculture*. Amsterdam: North Holland.

Liu Y-B, Tabashnik, B.E., Dennehy, T.J., Patin, A.J. and Bartlett, A.C. (1999). Development time and resistance to Bt crops. *Nature,* **400**, 519.

Losey, J.E., Rayor, L.S. and Carter, M.E. (1999). transgenic pollen harms Monarch larvae. *Nature,* **399**, 214.

MacIlwain, C. (1999). Access issues may determine whether agri-biotech will help the world's poor. *Nature,* **402**, 341–345.

Mann, C.C. (1999a). Genetic engineers aim to soup up crop photosynthesis. *Science* **283**, 314–316.

Mann, C.C. (1999b). Crop scientists seek a new revolution. *Science,* **283**, 310–314.

Mann, C.C. (1999c). Biotech goes wild. *Technology Review.* July/August.

May, R. (1999). *Genetically Modified Foods: Facts, Worries, Policies and Public Confidence.* Briefing from the Chief Science Officer, February.
www.gn.apc.org/pmhp/dc/genetics/cso-gmos.htm (21 February 2000).

Mazur, B., Krebbers, E. and Tingey, S.. 1999. Gene discovery and product development for grain quality traits. *Science* **285**, 372–375.

McCalla, A.F., and. Brown, L.R. (1999). *Feeding the Developing World in the Next Millennium: A Question of Science?* CGIAR/NAS Biotechnology Conference, October 21–22, 1999. www.cgiar.org/biotechc/mccalla.htm (11 November 1999).

Milius, S. (1999)New studies clarify Monarch worries. *Science News,* **156**, 391.

Moffat, A.S. (1999a). Crop engineering goes south. *Science* **285**: 370–371.

Moffat, A.S .(1999b). Engineering plants to cope with metals. *Science,* **285**: 369–370.

Michigan Technological University (MTU) 1999. New Aspen could revolutionize pulp and paper industry. 11 October.
www.admin.mtu.edu/urel/breaking/1999/aspen.htm (10 January 2000).

Myneni, R.B. et al. (1997). Increased plant growth in the northern high latitudes. *Nature,* **386**, 698–702.

National Research Council (NRC). (1999). *Hormonally Active Agents in the Environment.* Washington, DC: NRC.

Nicholls, N. (1997). Increased Australian wheat yield due to recent climate trends. *Nature,* **387**, 484–485.

Pinstrup-Andersen, P., Pandya-Lorch, R. and Rosegrant, M.W. (1999). *World Food Prospects: Critical Issues for the Twenty-First Century.* Washington, DC: International Food Policy Research Institute.

Oerke, E.-C, Weber, A., Dehne, H.-W. and Schonbeck, F. (1994). Conclusion and Perspectives. In *Crop Production and Crop Protection: Estimated Losses in Food and Cash Crops* (E.-C. Oerke, A. Weber, H.-W. Dehne, and F. Schonbeck, eds.) Amsterdam: Elsevier, pp. 742–770.

Pimentel, D. (ed.) (1997). *Techniques for Reducing Pesticide Use: Economic and Environmental Benefits.* Chichester: John Wiley.

Prakash, C.S. (1999). *Relevance of Biotechnology to Indian Agriculture.*
www.teriin.org/discuss/biotech/abstracts.htm (15 January 2000).

Prakash, C.S. (1998a). Engineering cold tolerance takes a major step forward. *ISB News,* May 1998.
http://www.isb.vt.edu/news/1998/news98.may.html may9802 (15 January 2000).

Prakash, C.S. (1998b). A first step towards engineering improved phosphorus uptake. *ISB News,* May 1998.
http://www.isb.vt.edu/news/1998/news98.may.html may9802 (15 January 2000).

Raffensperger, C. and Tickner, J. (eds) (1999). *Protecting Public Health & the Environment: Implementing the Precautionary Principle*. Washington, DC: Island Press.

Rayl, A.J.S. (2000). Are all alien invasions bad? *The Scientist*, **14** (20 March 2000). http://www.the-scientist.com/yr2000/mar/rayl_p15_000320.html (21 March 2000).

Regal, P.J. (1994). Scientific principles for ecologically based risk assessment of transgenic organisms. *Molecular Ecology*, **3**, 5–13. www.psrast.org/pjrisk.htm (11 January 2000).

Reiter, P. (1996). Global warming and mosquito-borne disease in USA. *Lancet*, **348**, 622.

Roberts, D.R. (1999). Foreword: DDT is still needed for malaria control. In, *The Economic Costs of Malaria in South Africa: Malaria Control and the DDT Issue*. (R. Tren, ed.) www.iea.org.uk/env/malaria.htm (12 December 1999).

Roberts, D.R. et al. (1997). DDT, global strategies, and a malaria control crisis in South America. *Emerging Infectious Diseases*, **3**, 295–301.

Rosenzweig, C., and Parry, M.L. (1994). Potential impacts of climate change on world food supply. *Nature*, **367**, 133–138.

Royal Society (1998). Genetically modified plants for food use. www.royalsoc.ac.uk/st_pol40.htm (11 January 2000).

Sagoff, M. (1999). What's wrong with exotic species? *Report from the Institute for Philosophy and Public Policy*, **19** (Fall), 16–23.

Saxena, D., Flores, S. and Stotzky, G. (1999). Transgenic plants: insecticidal toxin in root exudates from *Bt* Corn, *Nature*, **402**, 480.

Scalise, K. (1997). New Solution for Food Allergies Effective with Milk, Wheat Products, Maybe Other Foods, UC Researchers Discover. University of California, Berkeley News Release. 19 October 1997. www.urel.berkeley.edu/urel_1/CampusNews/PressReleases/releases/10_19_97a.html5 January 2000).

Scott, S.E., and Wilkinson, M.J. (1999). Low probability of chloroplast movement from oilseed rape (*Brassica Napus*) into wild *Brassica Rapa*. *Nature Biotechnology*, **17**: 390–392.

Sharma, V.P. (1996). Re-emergence of Malaria in India. *Indian Journal of Medical Research*, **103**, 26–45.

Smaglik, P. (1998). Success of edible vaccine may depend on picking right fruit. *The Scientist* **12** (August 17). <www.the-scientist.library.upenn.edu/yr1998/August/pg4_story2_980817.html> January 7, 2000.

Tans, P.P., and White, J.W.C. (1998). The global carbon cycle: in balance, with a little help from the plants. *Science* **281**, 183–184.

Taubes, G. (1997). Global warming: apocalypse not. *Science*, **278**: 1004–1006.

Tian, H. et al. (1998). effect of interannual climate variability on carbon storage in Amazonian ecosystems. *Nature*, **396** 664–667.

UN Commission on Sustainable Development (UNCSD) (1997). Fifth Session. Document E/CN.17/1997/9. gopher://gopher.un.org:70/00/esc/cn17/1997/off/97–9.EN (23 July 1999).

Waggoner, P.E. (1994). *How Much Land Can Ten Billion People Spare for Nature?* Ames (IA): Council for Agricultural Science and Technology.

Walliman, T. (2000). *Bt* toxin: assessing GM strategies. *Science*, **287**, 41.

Whelan, E.M. (1992). *Toxic Terror: The Truth Behind the Cancer Scares*. Buffalo, NY: Prometheus Books.

WHO (1998). The Kyoto Protocol: CO_2, CH_4 and climate implications. *Geophysical Research Letters*, **25**, 2285–2288.

WHO (1999a). *The World Health Report 1999*. Geneva: WHO.

WHO (1999b). *About WHO: Nutrition*. 21 September.
www.who.int/aboutwho/en/promoting/nutrtion.htm (5 January, 2000).

WHO (1999c). *Malnutrition Worldwide*. 22 November.
www.who.int/nut/malnutrition_worldwide.htm (5 January 2000).

Wigley, T.M.L. (1997). Implications of recent CO_2 emission-limitation proposals for stabilization of atmospheric concentrations. *Nature*, **390**, 267–270.

Wigley, T.M.L. et al. (1996). Economic and environmental choices in the stabilization of atmospheric CO_2 concentrations. *Nature*, **379**, 240–243.

Wilcove, D.S., et al. (1998). Quantifying threats to imperilled species in the United States. *BioScience*, **48**: 607–615.

Williams, J. (1998). Organic farming in the uplands of mid Wales. Statement at Earth Options, Second 'Look Out Wales' Environmental Forum, May 1998.
www.wyeside.co.uk/expotec/earth_options.htm (19 March 2000).

Wittwer, S.H. (1995). *Food, Climate and Carbon Dioxide: The Global Environment and World Food Production*. Boca Raton, LA: Lewis Publishers, pp. 56–57.

World Bank (1994). *New & Noteworthy in Nutrition*. Issue 24.
www.worldbank.org/html/extdr/hnp/nutrition/nnn/nnn24.htm   (5   January 2000).

Ye, Xudong et al. (2000). Engineering the provitamin A (ß-Carotene) biosynthetic pathway into (Carotenoid-Free) rice endosperm. *Science*, **287**, 303–305.

Zucker, J.R. 1996. Changing patterns of autochthonous malaria transmission in the united states: a review of recent outbreaks. *Emerging Infectious Diseases*, **2**, 37–43.

11 A Richter scale for risk?

John Adams

The scientific management of uncertainty versus the management of scientific uncertainty

Risk management involves balancing risks and rewards. Figure 11.1 is a simplified model of this process. The model postulates that: everyone has a propensity to take risks; this propensity varies from one individual to another; this propensity is influenced by the potential rewards of risk taking; perception's of risk are influenced by experience of accident losses – one's own and others'; individual risk taking decisions represent a balancing act in which perceptions of risk are weighed against propensity to take risk; accident losses are, by definition, a consequence of taking risks; the more risks an individual takes, the greater, on average, will be both the rewards and losses he or she incurs.

There has been a long-running and sometimes acrimonious debate between 'hard' scientists – who treat risk as capable of objective measurement – and social scientists – who argue that risk is culturally constructed. In earlier papers discussing how these perspectives might be reconciled (Adams, 1997a, b),

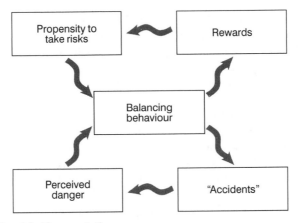

Figure 11.1 The risk 'thermostat'

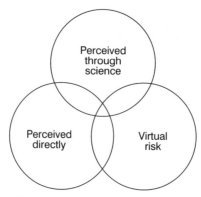

Figure 11.2 Three types of risk

I suggested that it would be helpful, when considering how the balancing act is performed, to distinguish three categories of risk:

- *directly perceptible risks*: e.g. climbing a tree, riding a bicycle, driving a car;
- *risks perceptible with the help of science*: e.g. cholera and other infectious diseases;
- *virtual risks* – scientists do not know or cannot agree: e.g. BSE/CJD and suspected carcinogens.

In Figure 11.2, these categories are represented by three overlapping circles to indicate that the boundaries between them are indistinct, and also to indicate the potential complementarity of approaches to risk management that have previously been seen as adversaries.

Directly perceptible risks

The management of *directly perceptible risks* – by toxicologists, doctors, the police, safety officials and numerous other 'authorities' – is made difficult and frustrating by individuals insisting on being their own risk managers, and overriding the judgements of risk experts and the interventions of safety regulators – a phenomenon routinely attested to by millions of smokers, sunbathers, consumers of cream buns, and drinking and speeding motorists. Why do so many people insist on taking more risks than safety authorities think they should? It is unlikely that they are unaware of the dangers; there can be few smokers who have not received the health warning. It is more likely that the safety authorities are less appreciative of the *rewards* of risk taking. (Variable perceptions of risk will be discussed further in the section on *virtual risk* below.)

Directly perceptible risks are 'managed' instinctively; our ability to cope with them has been built into us by evolution; contemplation of animal behaviour suggests that it has evolved in non-human species as well. Our method of coping is intuitive; everyone ducks if they see something that might hit them, without first doing a formal probabilistic risk assessment. There is now abundant evidence, particularly with respect to directly perceived risks on the road, that *risk compensation*, sometimes referred to as offsetting behaviour, accompanies the introduction of safety measures (Wilde, 1994; Wildavsky, 1988). Statistics for death by accident and violence, perhaps the best available aggregate indicator of the way in which societies cope with directly perceived risk, display a stubborn resistance, over many decades, to the efforts of safety regulators to reduce them (see Adams, 1995; see also Peterson and Hoffer, 1996, for recent evidence concerning airbags).

Risk perceived through science – some limitations

The risk and safety literature does not cover all three categories equally. It is overwhelmingly dominated by the second category – *risks perceived through science*, which is expanded in Figure 11.3. Does science deserve its current dominance in risk debates?

Central to this literature is the *rational actor paradigm* (Renn et al., 1998), the advice of the risk experts about how to manage risks is based upon their judgement about how a rational optimiser would, *and should*, act if in possession of all relevant scientific information. In this literature economists and scientists strive together to serve the interests of someone we might call *homo economicus-scientificus* – the offspring of the ideal economist and the ideal scientist.

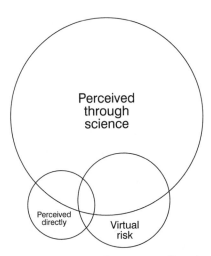

Figure 11.3 The dominance of the rational actor paradigm in the risk and safety literature

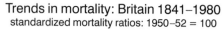

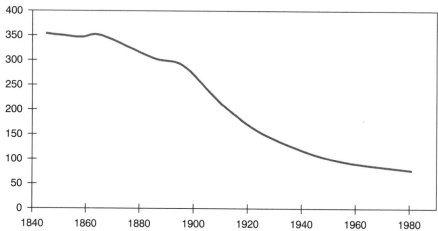

Figure 11.4 Trends in mortality. Source: *Living with risk*, British Medical Association, 1987

Infectious diseases such as cholera are not directly perceptible. One requires a microscope to see them, and a scientific training to understand what one is looking at. Science has an impressive record in making invisible, or poorly understood dangers perceptible, and in providing guidance about how to avoid them. Large decreases in premature mortality over the past 150 years, such as those shown for Britain in Figure 11.4, have been experienced throughout the developed world. Such trends suggest that ignorance is an important cause of death, and that science, in reducing ignorance has saved many lives. When the connection between the balancing-behaviour box and the accident box in Figure 11.1 is not perceptible, there is no way that it can inform behaviour.

A Richter scale for risk?

Where this connection is poorly understood it is usually expressed in probabilistic terms, or sometimes in chains of probabilities in the form of fault trees or event trees. *Homo economicus-scientificus* is an expert gambler, sensitive to small variations in the odds associated with the risks he runs. The adherents to the rational actor paradigm, the authors of most of the 'scientific' risk literature, frequently express their dismay at the inability of *ordinary* people to make sensible use of such information, and seek ways to make their risk taking decisions better informed and more rational.

In Britain, in 1996 the Department of Trade and Industry has proposed the development of a 'Richter scale for risk' which would 'involve taking a series of common situations of varying risk to which people can relate'

(Taylor, 1996); the Royal Statistical Society similarly called for 'a simple measure of risk that [people] can use as a basis for decision making' (RSS News, 1996); and the Chief Medical Officer of Health has called for the development of an agreed standard scale for communicating information about risk to the general public (see the source of Table 11.1 below). The collection of risks presented in Table 11.1 is a typical example of what they have in mind.

The risk of dying in a road accident (1:8000) is commonly found about halfway down such tables. It is included because road accidents are the most common cause of accidental death – and hence assumed to be a familiar 'benchmark' risk to which people can relate for purposes of seeing other risks in their proper perspective. However, there are a number of problems with this number which place in doubt the utility of the table as a guide to individual risk taking decisions.

Table 11.1 Risk of an individual dying (D) in any one year or developing an adverse response (A)

Term used	Risk estimate	Example	
High	Greater than 1:100	A. Transmission to susceptible household contacts of measles and chickenpox	1:1 –1:2
		A. Transmission of HIV from Mother to child (Europe)	1:6
		A. Gastro-intestinal effects of antibiotics	1:10- 1:20
Moderate	Between 1:100–1:1000	D. Smoking 10 cigarettes per day	1:200
		D. All natural causes, age 40 years	1:850
Low	Between 1:1000–1:10000	D. All kinds of violence and poisoning	1:3300
		D. Influenza	1:5000
		D. Accident on road	1:8000
Very low	Between 1:10000–1:100000	D. Leukaemia	1:12000
		D. Playing soccer	1:25000
		D. Accident at home	1:26000
		D. Accident at work	1:43000
		D. Homicide	1:100000
Minimal	Between 1:100000–1:1000000	D. Accident on railway	1:500000
		A. Vaccination-associated polio	1:1000000
Negligible	Less than 1:10000000	D. Hit by lightning	1:10000000
		D. Release of radiation by nuclear power station	1:10000000

Source: Department of Health (1996), p. 13.

First, the number is out of date even when proposed. 1:8000 was calculated by dividing the number of people dying in a road accident in Britain by the population of Britain. The most recent number then available for *Road Accident Statistics Great Britain 1995* is about half the number in Table 11.1 (1:15686), moving road accidents from the 'low' to the 'very low' category. But this error is trivial compared to the complications that would arise should an individual seek to base a risk-taking decision upon it.

A trawl through the road safety literature reveals that a young man is 100 times more likely to die in a road accident than a middle-aged woman; someone driving at 3 a.m. on Sunday is 134 times more likely than someone driving at 10 a.m. on Sunday; someone with a personality disorder 10 times, and someone two and half times over the alcohol limit 20 times (examples from Evans, 1991). If these factors were all independent of each other, one could predict that a disturbed, drunken young man driving at 3 a.m. on Sunday would be about 2.7 million times more likely to die than a normal, sober, middle-aged woman driving to church seven hours later (Evans, op. cit., whose statistics are from the USA).

These four factors, of course, are not independent; there are almost certainly proportionately more drunken and disturbed young men on the road in the early hours of the morning than at other times of day. But I have listed only four complicating factors from a very long list. Does the car have worn brakes, bald tyres a loose suspension, a valid tax disc . . .? Is the road well-lit, dry, foggy, straight, narrow, clear, congested . . .? Does the driver have good hearing and eyesight, a reliable heart, a clean licence . . .? Is the driver sleepy, angry, aggressive, on drugs . . .? All these factors, plus many more, can influence a motorist's chances of arriving safely. Whether the number used for road accidents in the Richter scale is 1:8000 or 1:16000, it is difficult to see how it could serve as a guide to an individual risk-taking decision.

Consider another 'familiar' comparator for risk frequently found in risk tables: the risk of death in an air crash. It is commonly asserted that the fear of flying is irrational, because 'objectively' flying is safer than driving. John Durant (1997), in a paper for the Royal Society's conference on *Science, Policy and Risk*, sets out what might be called the orthodox-expert view of the safety of flying and the problem created by popular 'subjective biases':

> the fact that many people behave as if they believe that driving a car is safer than flying in an aeroplane (when on objective criteria the opposite is the case) has been attributed to a combination of the greater dread associated with plane crashes and the greater personal control associated with driving. Faced with a mismatch between scientific and lay assessments of the relative risks of driving and flying, few of us [presumably Durant is referring here to his scientific audience at the Royal Society, and not the lay public] are inclined to credit the lay assessment with any particular validity. On the contrary we are more likely to use the insight to help overcome our own subjective biases in the interests of a more 'objective' view'.

(Durant, 1997).

Evans (1991; which contains a summary of Evans et al., 1990) succinctly deconstructs this view. He begins with the most commonly quoted death rates for flying (0.6/billion miles) and road travel (24/billion miles) and comes to a much less commonly-quoted conclusion. He notes:

1 that the airline figure includes only passengers, while the road figure includes pedestrians and cyclists;
2 that the relevant comparison to make with air travel is the death rate on the rural interstate system which is much lower than the rate for the *average* road;
3 that the average road accident death rates that lead to the conclusion that it is safer to fly are strongly influenced by the high rates of drunken young men, while people dying in air crashes are, on average, much older and, when on the road, safer-than-average drivers; and
4 that, because most crashes occur on take-off or landing, the death rate for air travel increases as trip length decreases.

Taking all these factors into account he concludes that a 40-year-old, belted, alcohol-free driver in a large car is slightly *less* likely to be killed in 600 miles of interstate driving – the upper limit of the range over which driving is likely to be a realistic alternative to flying – than in trip of the same distance on a scheduled airline. For a trip of 300 miles, he calculates that the air travel fatality risk is about double the risk of driving. This comparison, of course, is not the complete story. The risks associated with flying also need to be disaggregated by factors such as aircraft type and age, maintenance, airline, the pilot's age, health and experience, weather, air traffic control systems etc.

The cost of insurance as a measure of risk?

The insurance industry uses, generally successfully, past accident rates to estimate the probabilities associated with future claim rates. This success is sometimes offered as an argument for using the cost of insuring against a risk as a measure of risk that would be a useful guide to *individual* risk takers. Weinberg (1996) has argued that 'the assessment is presumably accurate, since in general it is carried out by people whose livelihood depends on getting their sums right'.

However, the fact that the livelihoods of those in the insurance business depend on 'getting their sums right' does not ensure that the cost of insuring against a risk provides a good measure of risk *for individuals*. The sum that the insurance business must get right is the *average* risk. For most of the average risks listed in Table 11.1 the variation about the average will range, depending on particular circumstances, over several orders of magnitude. Insurers depend on ignorance of this enormous variability because they need the good risks to subsidize the bad. If the good and bad risks could be accurately identified the good ones would not consider it worthwhile to buy insurance and the bad ones would not be able to afford it. This is precisely the threat to the insurance business posed by discoveries about genetic predispositions to fatal illness. The greater the precision with which individual risks can be specified, the less scope remains for a profitable insurance industry. The current debate about whether insurance companies should be allowed to demand disclosure of the results of genetic tests focuses attention on the threat to the industry of knowledge that assists the disaggregation of these averages. If disclosure is not required, people who are poor risks will be able to exploit the insurance companies, and if it is required the insurance companies will be able to discriminate more effectively against the bad risks – making them, in many cases, uninsurable.

Accident statistics do not measure danger

If a road has many accidents it might fairly be called dangerous; but using past accident rates to estimate future risks can be positively misleading. There are many dangerous roads that have good accident records *because* they are seen to be dangerous – children are forbidden to cross them, old people are afraid to cross them, and fit adults cross them quickly and carefully. The good accident record is purchased at the cost of community severance – with the result that people on one side of a busy road tend no longer to know their neighbours on the other. But the good accident record gets used as a basis for risk management. Officially – 'objectively' – roads with good accident records are deemed safe, and in need of no measures to calm the traffic.

The meaning of **probability**

Britain's Chief Medical Officer of Health (Sir Kenneth Calman) says that 'it is possible for new research and knowledge to change the level of risk, reducing it or increasing it.' (Department of Health, 1996) This view sits uncomfortably alongside the Royal Society's view of risk as something 'actual' and capable of 'objective measurement' (Royal Society, 1992). The probabilities that scientists attach to accidents and illnesses, and to the outcomes of proposed treatments, are quantitative, authoritative, confident-sounding expressions of uncertainty. They are not the same as the probabilities that can be attached to a throw of a pair of dice. The 'odds' cannot be known in the same way, because the outcome is not independent of previous throws. When risks become perceptible, when the odds are publicly quoted, this information is acted upon in ways that alter the odds. One form that this action might take is new research to produce new information.

Einstein famously argued with the quantum physicists about whether God played dice. The argument remains in the realm of theology. The current majority view among scientists is that He does. But to the extent that scientists, insurance company actuaries, and other risk specialists are successful in identifying and publicizing risks that have previously been shrouded in ignorance, they shift them into the directly perceptible category – and people then act upon this new information. Risk is a continuously reflexive phenomenon; we all, routinely, monitor our environments for signs of safety or danger and modify our behaviour in response to our observations – thereby modifying our environment and provoking a further round of responses *ad infinitum*. For example, the more highway engineers signpost dangers such as potholes and bends in the road, the more motorists are likely to take care in the vicinity of the now perceptible dangers, but also the more likely they are to drive with the expectation that *all* significant dangers will be signposted.

What Calman perhaps meant when he said that new research might change the level of risk is that the probabilities intended to convey the magnitude of the scientist's uncertainty are themselves uncertain in ways that cannot be expressed in probabilities. He should perhaps have said that a scientific risk estimate is the scientist's 'best guess at the time, but subject to change in ways that cannot be predicted.' This brings us to uncertainty and *virtual risk*.

Virtual risk

We do not respond blankly to uncertainty; we impose meaning(s) upon it. These meanings are virtual risks. Whenever scientists disagree or confess their ignorance the lay public is confronted by uncertainty. Virtual risks may or may not be imaginary, but they have real consequences – people act upon the meanings that they impose upon uncertainty.

The 1995 contraceptive pill scare in Britain is an example of a 'scientific' risk assessment spilling over into the virtual category. On the basis of preliminary, unpublished, non-peer-reviewed evidence suggesting that the new third generation pill was twice as likely to cause blood clots as the second generation pill, Britain's Committee on the Safety of Medicines issued a public warning to this effect. The result was a panic in which large numbers of women stopped taking the new pill, with the further result that there were an estimated 8000 extra abortions plus an unknown number of unplanned pregnancies. The highly-publicized two-fold increase in risk amounted to a doubling of a very small number, which might have caused, according to the original estimates, an extra two fatalities a year (BBC, 1997); even when doubled the mortality risk was far below that for abortions and pregnancies. Such minuscule risks are statistical speculations and cannot be measured directly. Subsequent research cast doubt on the plausibility of *any* additional risk associated with the new pill. The lesson that the Chief Medical Officer of Health drew from this panic (i.e. behavioural response to new information) in his annual report (Department of Health, 1996) was that 'there is an important distinction to be made between relative risk and absolute risk'.

Perhaps a more important lesson is that scientists, by combining uncertainty with potential dire consequences can frighten large numbers of people.

Dressing up their uncertainties in very low absolute probabilities does not seem to help, especially when they are presented via a hastily called press conference which begins with the advice 'Don't panic'. Calman observed that 'although the increased risk was small, women did need to be informed that there was a difference in risk between the oral contraceptives available to them' and that 'the message, to continue to take the oral contraceptive pill, seemed to be ignored in the pressure for action.' From where, he might have asked himself, did this pressure for action come? Why, women might sensibly ask themselves, are they giving us this new information with such a sense of urgency if they expect us to take no action?

Cultural filters

The women who stopped taking the pill were imposing meaning upon the uncertainties of the British medical establishment. This uncertainty was projected through, and amplified by the media. The fact of the hastily convened press conference, the secretive procedures by which the Committee on the Safety of Medicines and other government agencies arrive at their conclusions, and histories of government cover-ups of dangers such as radiation and mad cow disease have resulted in a very low level of public trust in government to tell the truth about environmental threats. A recent survey which asked people if they would trust institution X to tell them the truth about risks found that only 7 per cent would trust the Government, compared to 80 per cent who said they would trust environmental organizations (Marris et al., 1996). This mistrust feeds a paranoid tendency which can hugely exaggerate trivial dangers.

We all, scientists included, perceive virtual risks through different *cultural filters* (Figure 11.5; see Adams, 1995, Chapter 3). The cultural filters of scientists are usually referred to as paradigms. The discovery of the Antarctic ozone hole was delayed by such a filter. US satellites failed to pick it up because their computers had been programmed to reject as errors the data that their instruments were collecting; their values lay beyond the range that the programmers had considered credible.

The influence of filters can also be detected in the debate about the effects of low-level radiation. Despite the accumulation of many decades of evidence, there is still no agreement about whether or not there is a safe dose, or perhaps even a therapeutic dose. The July 1997 issue of *Chemistry in Britain* continued a long-running debate on the effects of radon. The April issue contained an article (Eric Hamilton, p. 49) noting that 'large epidemiological studies for radon levels in parts of the US, Sweden, Finland and China show that the incidence of lung cancer actually decreases with increasing radon exposures, even for levels of up to 300 Bq m^{-3}' and that 'even in Cornwall and Devon, where soils and houses contain the highest levels of uranium and radon in the UK ... the number of lung cancers is lower than in most other regions of the UK – despite the fact that the south-west includes a high proportion of cigarette smokers'. This provoked a strong reply in the July 1997 issue from G.M. Kendall and C.R Muirhead of Britain's National Radiological Protection Board who insisted that radon caused about 2000 deaths a year in Britain and suggested that the effect in Devon and Cornwall was probably obscured by smoking. Neither side of the argument presented any statistics on smoking in Devon and Cornwall.

John Graham (1996), vice-president in charge of environment, safety and health for British Nuclear Fuels Inc., takes the argument one step further, advancing the hypothesis that low-level radiation can have beneficial effects. He argues that background radiation routinely causes cell damage, for which effective repair mechanisms exists, and that there are optimum exposure levels at which the stimulation of the repair mechanisms outweighs the damage. This lay spectator judges the debate to be still unresolved.

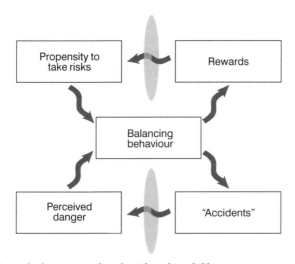

Figure 11.5 The risk thermostat fitted with cultural filters

Figure 11.6 helps to explain why the debate is likely to remain unresolved for some time yet. It is taken from *Risk Assessment in the Federal Government: Managing the Process* – a report for the US Government by the National Research Council on the assessment of the risk of cancer and other adverse health effects associated with exposure to toxins. It shows the very different dose-response relationships for low levels of exposure that it is possible to derive from the same experimental data. At high dose levels there is a predictable response. At low dose levels one is in the realm of assumption and speculation. Data simply do not exist to settle the argument about whether or not there is a 'safe dose' or threshold below which one can assume no harmful effect.

But what about possible *beneficial* effects? It is not possible to display such effects on the typical dose-response graph. It is possible only to show harmful effects approaching zero. This method of presenting the data might be considered as both the product of a cultural filter that precludes the possibility of beneficial effects, and as a cultural filter in its own right.

Why, one wonders, when virtually all of the therapies produced by the pharmaceutical industry, including aspirin, are toxic above certain doses and beneficial below certain doses, should the conventional dose-response curve preclude the possibility of a benign effect? The answer, perhaps lies in the division of labour that one discovers in the risk-management literature. 'Risk management' usually means 'risk reduction'. The remit of most risk managers is to focus on the bottom loop of Figures 11.1 and 11.5, to try to minimize the number and magnitude of adverse outcomes. Thus the first question that the US Food and Drug Administration or the British Committee on the Safety of Medicines will ask of a new food or drug is: Does it have *harmful* effects? The emphasis of the manufacturers, the food and drug companies, is likely to be on the top loop, the rewards to the customer and the profits to themselves. For medical risks there is a dearth of risk management institutions that seek to strike a balance between potential adverse and beneficial consequences.

Anthropologist Michael Thompson has developed a typology of cultural filters that helps to account for the different meanings imposed on

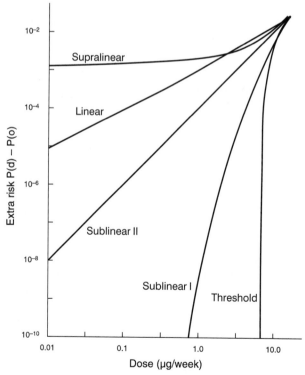

Figure 11.6 A family of dose-response curves

uncertainty (Thompson et al., 1990). Some people, he calls them *egalitarians*, view environmental threats as punishment for technocratic hubris, and failure to respect a fragile nature and obey its commands. They, the egalitarians, urge a retreat to practices that they label sustainable. Others, *individualists*, consider nature to be robust and capable of looking after itself, and argue that the best protection in an uncertain world is power over nature; they advocate more science and technology to buttress our defences against any nasty surprises that nature might have in store. The Government, the *hierarchists*, assure everyone that everything is under control, their control, and commission more research that they hope will prove it. And the *fatalists*, who harbour no illusions about their power to guide events, continue to read *The Sun*, watch videos, drink lager and buy lottery tickets; *que sera sera*.

Long-running controversies about large-scale risks are long-running because they are scientifically unresolved, and unresolvable within the time-scale imposed by necessary decisions. The clamorous debates that take place in the presence of uncertainty are characterized not by irrationality, Thompson argues, but by *plural rationalities.* The contending parties argue logically, but from different premises.

Figure 11.7 illustrates this typology with reference to the diverse postures adopted in the controversy about whether or not new variant CJD is caused by eating BSE infected meat. This is yet another question that remains to be resolved by science. A 1997 survey of the epidemiological evidence published in the *British Medical Journal* summed up the then current state of knowledge: 'we do not know how or indeed if bovine spongiform encephalopathy is transmitted to humans' (Cousens *et al.*, 1997). One of the report's 'key messages' is that 'the observation of a group of comparatively young patients with Creutzfeldt-Jakob disease characterized by unusual neuropathological features during 1994–6 remains unexplained'. Yet a leading researcher in the field, Professor John Collinge, proclaims in an interview with *The Times'* medical correspondent (7 August 1997) that 'CJD could become an epidemic of biblical proportions' (this dramatic quotation served as the headline for the article). Professor Collinge went on to say 'I am now coming round to the view that doctors working in this field have to say what they think, even though this may give rise to anxieties which later turn out to be groundless. . . . we have to face the possibility of a disaster with tens of thousands of cases . . . we just don't know if this will happen, but what is certain is that we cannot afford to wait and see.' This *egalitarian* call for precautionary action in the face of uncertainty met, two days later in the *Sunday Telegraph*, a robust *individualist* response which also raised the question of what the nation could afford: 'the efforts of the scientists behind last year's BSE scare to defend their alleged link with "new variant Creutzfeldt Jacob disease" become ever more comical as the epidemic they promised fails to materialize . . . how much longer should we continue to look for objective guidance on this matter to experts who have invested so much of their own personal reputations in the theory that a link between BSE and new variant CJD exists . . . faced with a bill now rising above £5 billion . . . how much longer can we afford it?'

Fatalist

- "They should shoot the scientists, not cull the calves. Nobody seems to know what is going on." Dairy Farmer quoted in *The Times* (2.8.96)

- **"Charles won't pay for Diana's briefs"** Main headline in *The Sun* on 21.3.96, the day every other paper led with the BSE story.

Hierarchist

- "We require public policy to be in the hands of elected politicians. Passing responsibility to scientists can only undermine confidence in politics and science." John Durant, *The Times Higher* 5.4.1996

- "As much as possible, scientific advice to consumers should be delivered by scientists, not politicians." *The Economist*, 21 March 1996

- "I believe that British beef is safe. I think it is good for you." (Agriculture Minister Douglas Hogg 6.12.95) "I believe that lamb throughout Europe is wholly safe." (Douglas Hogg, 23.7.96)

- "I felt the need to reassure parents." Derbyshire Education chief quoted in *The Sun*, 21,3.96

- "I have not got a scientific opinion worth listening to. My job is simply to make certain that the evidence is drawn to the attention of the public and the Government does what we are told is necessary." Health Secretary Stephen Dorrel, *Daily Telegraph*, 22.3.96

- "We felt it was a no-goer. MAFF already thought our proposals were pretty radical." Richard Southwood explaining why he had not recommended a ban on cattle offal in human food in 1988, quoted by B Wynne, *Times Higher* 12.4.96

Individualist

- "The precautionary principle is favoured by environmental extremists and health fanatics. They feed off the lack of scientific evidence and use it to promote fear of the unknown." T. Corcoran, *The Toronto Globe and Mail*

- "I want to know, from those more knowledgeable than I, where a steak stands alongside an oyster, a North Sea mackerel, a boiled egg and running for the bus. Is it a chance in a million of catching CJD or a chance in ten million? I am grown up. I can take it on the chin." Simon Jenkins, *The Times*, quoted by J. Durant in *Times Higher*, 5.4.96

- "'Possible' should not be changed to 'probable' as has happened in the past." S.H.U. Bowies, FRS, *The Times* 12.8.96

- "It is clear to all of us who believe in the invisible hand of the market place that interference by the calamity-promoting pushers of the precautionary principle is not only hurtful but unnecessary. Cost-conscious non-governmental institutions are to be trusted with the protection of the public interest." P. Sandor, *Toronto Globe* and *Mail* 27.3.1996

- "I shall continue to eat beef. Yum, yum." Boris Johnson, *Weekly Telegraph*, no 245.

Egalitarian

- Feeding dead sheep to cattle, or dead cattle to sheep, is "unnatural" and "perverted". "The present methods of the agricultural industry are fundamentally unsustainable." "Risk is not actually about probabilities at all. It's all about the trustworthiness of the institutions which are telling us what the risk is." (Michael Jacobs, *The Guardian*, 24.7.96)

- "The Government... choose to take advice from a small group of hand-picked experts, particularly from those who think there is no problem." Lucy Hodges, *Times Higher* (5.4.96)

- "It is the full story of the beginnings of an apocalyptic phenomenon: a deadly disease that has already devastated the national cattle herd... could in time prove to be the most insidious and lethal contagion since the Black Death." "The British Government has at all stages concealed facts and corrupted evidence on mad cow disease."

- "Great epidemics are warning signs, symptoms of disease in society itself." G. Cannon in the foreword to *Mad Cow Disease* by Richard Lacey

- "My view is that if, and I stress if, it turns out that BSE can be transmitted to man and cause a CJD-like illness, then it would be far better to have been wise and taken precautions than to have not." Richard Lacey, ibid.

Figure 11.7 BSE/CJD: a typology of bias. Source: Adams (1997c)

The contending rationalities not only perceive risk and reward differently, they also differ about how the balancing act ought to be performed. *Hierarchists* are committed to the idea that the management of risk is the job of 'authority' – appropriately advised by experts. They cloak their deliberations in secrecy because the ignorant lay public cannot be relied upon to interpret the evidence correctly or use it responsibly. The *individualist* scorns authority as 'the Nanny State' and argues that that decisions about whether to wear seat belts or eat beef should be left to individuals. *Egalitarians* focus on the importance of *trust*; risk management, they argue, should be a consensual activity requiring openness and transparency in considering the evidence.

These different styles of balancing act respond differently to uncertainty. Ignorance is a challenge to the very idea of authority and expertise. The response of *hierarchists* is to conceal their doubts and present a confident public face. Confession of ignorance or uncertainty does not come easily to authority; in the face of uncertainty about an issue such as BSE, they seek to reassure. *Individualists* are assiduous collectors of information – even paying for it – but are also much more comfortable with uncertainty. Their optimism makes them gamblers – they expect to win more than they lose. Markets, in their view, are institutions with a record of coping with uncertainty successfully. If the experts cannot agree about BSE, there is no basis upon which central authority can act; the risk should be spread by letting individual shoppers decide for themselves. The *egalitarian* instinct in the face of uncertainty is to assume that authority is covering up something dreadful, and that untrammelled markets will create something dreadful. They favour democratizing the balancing act by opening up the expert committees to lay participation and holding public inquiries to get at the truth – which, when known, will justify the intervention in the markets that they favour.

Conclusions

Science has been very effective in reducing uncertainty, but much less effective in managing it. The scientific risk literature has little to say about virtual risks – and where the scientist has insufficient information even to quote odds, the optimizing models of the economist are of little use. A scientist's 'don't know' is the verbal equivalent of a Rorschach Inkblot: some will hear a cheerful reassuring message; others will listen to the same words and hear the threat of catastrophe.

Science has a very useful role in making visible dangers that were previously invisible, and thereby shifting their management into the directly perceptible category. Where science has been successful it has reduced uncertainty, and thereby shrunk the domain of risk perceived through science; now that its causes are well understood, cholera, for example, is rarely discussed in terms of risk. But where the evidence is simply inconclusive and scientists cannot agree about its significance we all, scientists included, are in the realm of virtual risk – scientists usually dignify the virtual risks in which they take an interest with the label hypothesis. Figure 11.8 indicates the relative significance that I suggest hypotheses should be accorded in risk debates.

The role of science in debates about risk is firmly established; clearly we need more information and understanding, of the sort that only science can provide, about the probable consequences of 'balancing behaviours' for both 'rewards' and 'accidents'. But equally clearly, we must devise ways of proceeding in the absence of scientific certainty about such consequences – science will never have *all* the answers – and in so doing we must acknowledge the scientific elusiveness of risk. The clouds do not respond to what the weather forecasts say about them. People do respond to information about risks, and thereby change them.

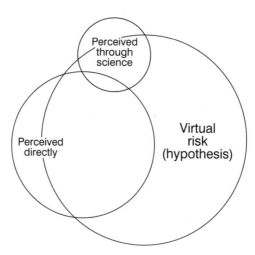

Figure 11.8 Reality?

In the presence of virtual risk even the precautionary principle becomes an unreliable guide to action. Consider the ultimate virtual risk, discussed from time to time on television and in our newspapers. Edward Teller and NASA invoke the precautionary principle to argue for the commitment of vast resources to the development of more powerful H-bombs and delivery systems to enable the world to fend off asteroids – *even if the odds of them ever being needed are only one in a million*. But we are also told by Russia's then Defence Minister that 'Russia might soon reach the threshold beyond which its rockets and nuclear systems cannot be controlled' (quoted in *The Times*, 8 February 1997). Which poses the greater danger to life on earth – asteroids or H-bombs and delivery systems out of control?

Debates about BSE, radiation and asteroid defences are debates about the future, which does not exist except in our imaginations. They are debates to which scientists have much to contribute, but not ones that can be left to scientists alone. An understanding of the different ways in which people tend to respond to uncertainty cannot settle arguments. It does offer the prospect of more coherent and civilized debate amongst all those with a stake in such issues.

Acknowledgement

I would like to thank Ragnar Lofsedt for his editorial help.

References

Adams, J. (1995). *Risk*. London: UCL Press.

Adams, J. (1997a).Virtual risk and the management of uncertainty. Paper presented to the Royal Society Conference on Science, Policy and Risk 18 March 1997; short version published in the *Times Higher*, 14 March.

Adams, J. (1997b). What do mad cows, Brent Spar, the NHS and contaminated land have in common?,' in Bate (1997) op.cit.

Adams, J. (1997c). Cars, cholera and cows: virtual risk and the management of uncertainty. *Science Progress*, **80** (2).

Bate, R. (1997): *What Risk?: Science, Politics and Public Health*. Oxford: Butterworth-Heinemann.

BBC (1997). *Anxiety Attack*. London: BBC2, broadcast 11 June.

British Medical Association (1987). *Living with Risk*. London: BMA.

Cousens, S.N., Zeidler, M., Esmonde, T.F., De Silva, R., Wilesmith, J.W., Smith, P.G., Will, R.G. (1997). Sporadic Creutzfeldt-Jakob disease in the United Kingdom: analysis of epidemiological surveillance data for 1970–96. *BMJ*, 16 August.

Department of Health (1996). *On the State of the Public Health: the Annual Report of the Chief Medical Officer of the Department of Health for the Year 1995*. London: HMSO.

Durant, J. (1997). Overcoming the fear of flying with Joe-Public as co-pilot. *The Times Higher Education Supplement*, 14 March.

Evans, L., Frick, M.C., and Schwing, R.C. (1990). Is it safer to fly or drive? A problem in risk communication. *Risk Analysis*, **10**, 259–268.

Evans, L. (1991). *Traffic Safety and the Driver*. New York: Van Nostrand Reinhold.

Graham, J. (1996): 'The benefits of low level radiation,' *Uranium and Nuclear Energy 1996*. Proc. of Annual Symposium of the Uranium Institute, London, September.

Marris, C, Langford, I. and O'Riordan, T. (1996). *Integrating sociological and psychological approaches to public perceptions of environmental risks: detailed results from a questionnaire survey*. CSERGE Working Paper GEC 96–07, University of East Anglia.

Peterson, S. and Hoffer, G.E. (1996). Auto insurers and the airbag: comment. *The Journal of Risk and Insurance*. **63**, (3), 515–523.

Renn, O., Jaeger, C., Rosa, E., and Webler, T. (1998). The rational action paradigm in risk theories: analysis and critique. In *Risk in the Modern Age: Science, Trust, and Society* (M.J. Cohen, ed.). London: Macmillan Press.

Royal Society (1992). *Risk: Analysis, perception and management*. London: Royal Society.

RSS News (1996). Editorial in *RSS News*, **24** (4), December.

Taylor, I. (1996). Minister Ian Taylor in DTI Press Notice P96/686, 11 September.
Thompson, M., Ellis, R. and Wildavsky, A. (1990). *Cultural Theory*, Boulder, CO: Westview Press.
Weinberg (1996). Letter to *The Times*, 28 December.
Wildavsky, A. (1988). *Searching for Safety*. New Brunswick, NJ: Transaction Press.
Wilde, G.J.S. (1994). *Target Risk*. Toronto: PDE Publications,

12 Facts versus factions: the use and abuse of subjectivity in scientific research

Robert A. J. Matthews

Summary

This chapter explores the use and abuse of subjectivity in science, and the ways in which the scientific community has attempted to explain away its curiously persistent presence in the research process. This disingenuousness is shown to be not only unconvincing but also unnecessary, as the axioms of probability reveal subjectivity to be a mathematically ineluctable feature of the quest for knowledge. As such, concealing or explaining away its presence in research makes no more sense than concealing or explaining away uncertainty in quantum theory. The need to acknowledge the ineluctability of subjectivity transcends issues of intellectual honesty, however. It has profound implications for the assessment of new scientific claims, requiring that their inherent plausibility be taken explicitly into account. Yet as I show, the statistical methods currently used throughout the scientific community lack this crucial feature. As such, they grossly exaggerate both the size of implausible effects and their statistical significance, and lend misleading support to entirely spurious 'discoveries'. These fundamental flaws in conventional statistical methods have long been recognized within the statistics community, but repeated warnings about their implications have had little impact on the practices of working scientists. The result has been an ever-growing number of spurious claims in fields ranging from the paranormal to cancer epidemiology, and continuing disappointment as supposed breakthroughs fail to live up to expectations. The failure of the scientific community to take decisive action over the flaws in standard statistical methods, and the resulting waste of resources spent on futile attempts to replicate claims based on them, constitutes a major scientific scandal.

Introduction

There can be no doubt that science advances. Even the most casual review of the scientific literature shows that our knowledge of the universe, its contents and our place within it is greater and more reliable now than at any other time. This more or less steady progress from ignorance to insight is widely ascribed to the insistence of scientists on the dispassionate and rational assessment of quantitative facts. In other academic disciplines such convincing evidence of progress is more elusive, as fashionable ideas come and go. In science, however, objectivity paves the Golden Road to knowledge.

The need to base science on objective fact rather than mere opinion, prejudice or authority is regarded as axiomatic by the scientific community. Galileo's dispute with the Vatican ultimately centred on a battle between objectivity and religious dogma. Objectivity has allowed phenomena quite beyond the bounds of human experience and common sense, from antimatter to curved space-time, to be discovered, studied and exploited. It has cut through bitter arguments in fields as diverse as human evolution to the cause and cure of disease. Such successes have led to objectivity being regarded as a hallmark that distinguishes genuine science from pseudoscience, quackery and fraud. As the philosopher of science Imre Lakatos puts it:

> The objective, scientific value of a theory is independent of the human mind which creates it or understands it. Its scientific value depends only on what objective support these conjectures have in facts.

> (Lakatos, 1978, p. 1).

Einstein admitted that he found the objectivity of science to be one of its most powerful personal attractions:

> A finely tempered nature longs to escape from the personal life into the world of objective perception and thought

> (quoted in Hoffman, 1975, p. 221).

Hardly surprisingly, therefore, any attempt to argue that subjectivity may still be a potent force in science tends to provoke a vociferous response from the scientific community. Those who make such claims – especially if they are themselves non-scientists – are often accused of being supporters of the so-called 'anti-science' movement, in which all scientific knowledge is seen as merely a social construct, a product of the prevailing intellectual milieu (see, e.g. Theocharis & Psimopolous 1987). Sociologists and historians of science who back their claims by specific examples of the use of subjectivity in science find themselves confronted with a variety of reactions, ranging from special pleading – 'Great scientists have great judgement' (cf. Wolpert, 1992 p. 95), through complacency – 'We know better now' (cf. Feynman, 1985 p. 342) – to *ad hominem* attack: 'These people are out of their depth' (cf. Dunstan, 1998 p. 15).

Such responses hint at a more complex relationship between scientific research and subjectivity, one with which many scientists feel somewhat ill at ease. As I now show, one reason is the recognition by working scientists that they routinely rely on subjective criteria to help them in their working lives.

The use of everyday subjectivity in research

Despite their public image as dispassionate seekers after truth, it is common knowledge within the scientific community that subjective methods have a vital role to play in everyday research. All working scientists are constantly bombarded with new research findings and theoretical claims, put forward in seminars, conferences, pre-prints, journals and books. Many of these new claims appear at odds with current belief. If all scientists were truly objective, however, they would have no alternative but to refuse to hold any view on the correctness or otherwise of these new claims until they had first carried out their own extensive studies.

In practice, of course, they do no such thing, for it is simply impracticable. If every more or less ludicrous claim were objectively researched, scientific progress would slow to a crawl. Even so, scientists do need a way of judging which claims to take seriously and pursue, and in the absence of any hard evidence, they resort to a range of criteria which are shot through with subjectivity. These range from personal experience and knowledge about the plausibility of the claim and its consequences to more *ad hoc* criteria such as the reputation of the researchers making the claims, their academic affiliation, and the quality of the journal in which their claims appear. As even Lewis Wolpert, one of the staunchest defenders of the public image of science, has admitted: 'One of the reasons for going to meetings is to meet the scientists in one's own field so that one can form an opinion of them and judge their work' (quoted in Collins, 1998, p. 20).

To criticize researchers for relying on subjectivity at this level of the scientific process is clearly absurd. There is simply not enough time, resources or money to appraise objectively each new scientific claim that emerges. The fact remains, however, that while its use may be justified on the grounds of expediency, the exercise of personal judgement, no matter how professional, is patently subjective, and has inherent dangers. Of these, the one that seems uppermost in the minds of researchers is that admitting to the presence of subjectivity in science is to play straight into the hands of their perceived enemies among post-modern philosophers and sociologists, who maintain that science is no more objective than literary criticism (Aronson, 1984, p. 12). This fear contains a deep irony, however, and one with which I shall deal in greater detail later.

A more pragmatic concern centres on the belief that unbridled subjectivity can seriously undermine the scientific process, leading to major discoveries being overlooked, dismissed or ignored. As I now show, this concern is well-placed.

Abuses of everyday subjectivity

Robert Millikan is widely regarded as one of the founders of modern American science, his determination of the charge on the electron winning him the 1923 Nobel Prize for physics. In a now-famous study, the physicist and historian Gerald Holton examined the log-books for Millikan's experiments with the electron, and revealed that he repeatedly rejected data that he deemed 'unacceptable' (Holton, 1978). The criteria he used were blatantly subjective, as revealed by the comments in the log-books, such as 'Very low – something wrong' and 'This is almost exactly *right*'. Throughout, Millikan appears to have been driven partly by a desire to get results that were self-consistent, broadly in agreement with other methods, and consistent with his personal view that the electron is the fundamental and indivisible unit of electric charge.

While these criteria may seem reasonable enough, they carry inherent dangers. Even today a fundamental explanation of the precise numerical value of the charge on the electron remains lacking, so Millikan was hardly in a position to decide objectively which values were high and which ones low. Previous results may have been fundamentally flawed, while the demand for self-consistent results may mask the existence of subtle but genuine properties of the electron. Millikan could also have been proved wrong in his belief that the electron was fundamental.

However, it is also clear that Millikan had another powerful motivation for using all means to obtain a convincing determination of the electronic charge: he was in a race against another researcher, Felix Ehrenhaft at the University of Vienna. Ehrenhaft had obtained similar results to those of Millikan, but they were interspersed with much lower values that suggested that the electron was not, in fact, the fundamental unit of charge. Millikan had no such doubts, published his results, and went on to win the Nobel Prize.

To many, this will seem like an egregious example of subjectivity in experimental science. Yet within the scientific community, it has been excused on the grounds that Millikan was, in the final analysis, correct: the electron is the fundamental unit of electric charge. For example, while conceding that 'Millikan may have taken his judgement beyond reasonable boundaries', Wolpert argues that the episode provides an object lesson in what distinguishes great scientists from the common herd: 'It is that remarkable ability not only to have the right ideas but to judge which information to accept or reject' (Wolpert, 1992, p. 95). This overlooks the fact that Millikan was *not* correct: fractional units of electronic charge do exist in Nature, in the form of quarks. The discovery in the 1970s of the concept of asymptotic freedom in quantum chromodynamics is now believed to prevent individual quarks from being observed; working 60 years previously, however, Millikan had no such basis for his beliefs. We can only be thankful that Millikan's 'remarkable ability' to spot the truth was not available during the early days of the quark hypothesis.

Apologists for Millikan's hand-picking of data also point out that the numerical result he obtained, -1.592×10^{-19} coulombs, is just 0.6 per cent below the modern value of $-1.6021892 \times 10^{-19}$ C (Weinberg, 1993, p. 99). At first sight, this does indeed seem impressive. However, Millikan's stated result was based on a faulty value for the viscosity of air, which when corrected changes Millikan's result to -1.616×10^{-19} C, increasing the discrepancy with the modern value by over 40 per cent. More importantly, however, it puts the latter well outside the error-bounds of Millikan's central estimate. Indeed, the discrepancy is so large that the probability of generating it by chance alone is less than one in a thousand. Millikan's 'remarkable ability' to scent out the correct answer was clearly not as great as his apologists would have us believe. Rather more remarkable is Millikan's ability, almost half a century after his death, to evade recognition as an insouciant scientific fraudster who won the Nobel Prize by deception. (Millikan's cavalier attitude towards scientific research is further evidenced by his dealings with his young assistant Harvey Fletcher over authorship of the key papers on the properties of the electron: Fletcher, 1982; and his role in early cosmic ray studies: Crease and Mann 1996, pp. 150–155.)

The dangers of the injudicious use of subjective criteria is further highlighted by the aftermath of Millikan's experiments. In the decades following his work and Nobel Prize, other investigators made determinations of the electronic charge. The values they obtained show a curious trend, creeping further and further away from Millikan's 'canonical' value, until finally settling down at the modern figure with which, as we have seen, it is wholly incompatible. Why was this figure not reached sooner? The Nobel Prize-winning physicist Richard Feynman has given the answer in his own inimitable style (Feynman, 1988, p. 382):

It's apparent that people did things like this: when they got a number that was too high above Millikan's, they thought something was wrong – and they would look for and find a reason why something might be wrong. When they got a number closer to Millikan's value they didn't look so hard. They thus eliminated the numbers that were too far off.

Feynman described this example of subjective influence of personality in science as 'A thing that scientists are ashamed of'. Yet even Feynman, one of the most individualistic of scientists, fell back into line with the rest of the scientific community when assessing the ultimate relevance of the Millikan case for contemporary science: 'We've learned those tricks nowadays', he insists, 'And now we don't have that kind of disease'. Such complacency is hard to reconcile with the many examples of scientific fraud by influential individuals that have come to light since the Millikan case (see e.g. Grayson, 1995, 1997 and references therein).

Experimental science is not alone in being vulnerable to abuses of subjective criteria; theoretical advances can and have been gravely affected as well. Some of the most egregious examples centre on the influence of the brilliant but notoriously arrogant theorist Wolfgang Pauli, whose dismissive opinions of the work of a number of theoreticians led to their being denied credit for major scientific discoveries in elementary particle physics. For example, the discovery of the key quantum-theoretic concept of spin is widely ascribed to Uhlenbeck and Goudsmit. However, it was first put forward by the young American theorist Ralph Kronig, who was persuaded not to publish after being ridiculed by Pauli and informed that while 'very clever', the concept of spin 'Of course has nothing to do with reality' (quoted in Pais, 1991 p. 244). Caustic *ad hominem* remarks by Pauli similarly led to the Swiss theorist Ernst Stueckelberg failing to publish his exchange model of the strong nuclear force; Yukawa subsequently published essentially identical ideas, and won the 1949 Nobel Prize for Physics. (Stueckelberg's work on renormalization of quantum electrodynamics met a similar fate, being later duplicated by three other theorists who went on to win the 1965 Nobel Prize for physics (Crease and Mann 1996, p. 142–3)). During the 1950s, Pauli together with the charismatic and influential theorist Robert Oppenheimer succeeded in stifling discussion of the de Broglie–Bohm interpretation of quantum theory by a combination of spurious arguments and subjective criticism. After being told that supposedly knock-out arguments against the de Broglie-Bohm interpretation were invalid, Oppenheimer is alleged to have remarked that 'Well. . .we'll just have to ignore it' (quoted in Matthews, 1992, p. 146); ironically, Oppenheimer went on to write a book whose central thesis was the need for an open mind in science (Oppenheimer, 1955).

Of all concepts in particle physics, however, none so vividly displays the presence of subjectivity within the 'hard' sciences as the nature of the fundamental constituents of matter. The concept of the atom – the ultimate, indivisible particle of matter – was first raised by the Greek philosopher Leukippos in the fourth century BC, yet even as late as 1900 the physical reality of atoms was still rejected by influential scientists, most notably the Austrian physicist Ernst Mach, and the German chemist Wilhelm Ostwald. Their refusal to countenance the existence of atoms was based largely on a Positivist agenda, in which the lack of direct evidence for atoms – and supposed impossibility of obtaining any – *ipso facto* implied their non-reality. This view led them to mount a sustained and vociferous campaign against the views of the Austrian physicist Ludwig Boltzmann, who had shown that the presumption of the physical reality of atoms led to natural explanations for the bulk properties of matter. Boltzmann and his work was successfully marginalized for many years, and by the time of his suicide in 1906, he was regarded as a scientific 'dinosaur' (Greenstein, 1998, p. 50). Ironically, barely a year before his death, a paper appeared which ultimately established the reality of atoms. It was an analysis of the phenomenon of so-called Brownian motion, the random movement of particles in a suspension which was shown to be explicable by the existence of atoms; the author of the paper was a young patents clerk named Albert Einstein. Within two years of Boltzmann's death, experimental studies of Brownian motion had compelled even Ostwald to accept the reality of atoms.

The Boltzmann case shows how the subjective (in this case, philosophical) prejudices of a few influential individuals can prevent the acceptance and application of fundamental advances for decades. What makes the case especially interesting, however, is the way in which its principal features emerged again 60 years later, with the controversy over the concept of quarks. The claim that the neutron and proton, supposedly fundamental components of atoms, are not indivisible was first put forward in 1964 in an eight-paragraph note in *Physics Letters* by the American physicist Murray Gell-Mann (Gell-Mann, 1964). Like Boltzmann, Gell-Mann based his claim on a mathematical demonstration of the explanatory power of the new concept; in this case, the ability of quarks to explain the properties of hadrons. This in turn led Gell-Mann to predict that quarks had fractional electric charges. The absence of evidence for such charges he ascribed to the permanent confinement of the quarks within their host particles.

Like Boltzmann, Gell-Mann found considerable resistance to his proposal within the physics community, stemming from two subjective prejudices. The first was a throw-back to the days of Millikan, and the insistence that electronic charge was indivisible. The second was an echo of the Positivist arguments against Boltzmann. Gell-Mann put forward the concept of confinement – and thus the impossibility of the direct observation of individual quarks – to avoid the philosophical wrangling that had dogged Boltzmann (Gell-Mann, 1994, p. 182). Ironically, his rather opaque statement that quarks 'exist but are not *real*' had precisely the opposite result: according to Gell-Mann, quarks 'went over like a lead balloon', with colleagues refusing point-blank to take them seriously, ridiculing the concept in the professional literature (Crease and Mann, 1996, p. 283–5). This was, however, a relatively mild reaction compared to those encountered by George Zweig, a young American theorist who proposed essentially the same explanation (based around 'Aces' rather than quarks) in 1964, but emphasized their physical reality. His papers were summarily rejected, and his appointment to a position at a major university blocked by the head of department on the grounds that he was a 'charlatan' (Crease and Mann, 1996, p. 285). Even so, in yet another parallel with the Boltzmann case, within five years experiments at the Stanford Linear Accelerator had demonstrated the reality of quarks within hadrons. They are now at the heart of quantum chromodynamics, the most successful theory for the strong nuclear force.

It is not difficult to find examples of where subjective prejudice has seriously delayed progress in many other fields:

- Semmelweiss's long and unsuccessful struggle during the 1840s to introduce antiseptic practices into hospitals (Asimov, 1975, p. 348). Despite the existence of a dramatic fall in the numbers of cases of childbed fever produced by the use of antiseptics, the practice was rejected because of resentment by the doctors that they could be causing so many deaths, nationalistic prejudice against a Hungarian working in a Viennese hospital, and annoyance at the way the antiseptics eliminated the 'professional odour' on their hands after returning to the wards from working in the mortuary.

- The refusal of the astronomical community to accept reports of 'stones falling from the sky', as had been long reported by many ordinary people, until investigations by Biot in the early nineteenth century (Milton, 1994, pp. 3–4). This refusal seems to have had stemmed from a combination of disdain for the claims of non-scientific outsiders, and a prejudice against the notion that the Earth could be subject to potentially serious bombardment.

- The rejection and ridiculing of Francis Peyton Rous's evidence for the existence of viruses capable of transmitting cancer (Williams 1994, p.422). First put forward in 1911, Rous's evidence came at a time when the existence of viruses was still controversial – they were beyond the reach of contemporary microscopy – and when cancer was thought to be caused by 'tissue irritation'. Rous's claim was finally vindicated 25 years later. In 1966 he was awarded the Nobel Prize – at the age of 87.

- The vociferous response of geologists to the proposal by Alfred Wegener, a German astronomer and meteorologist, that the continents moved across the face of the Earth. Having found considerable evidence for the phenomenon, but unable to propose a physical mechanism for it, Wegener's proposal was dismissed as a 'fairy tale', the product of 'auto-intoxication in which the subjective idea comes to be considered as an objective fact' (Hellman, 1998, p. 150). His claims were subsequently vindicated in the 1960s, 50 years after he first proposed them, and 30 years after his death.

- In the early 1980s, the Australian physician Barry Marshall encountered derision and hostility for his claim that a previously unknown bacterium, *Helicobacter pylori*, was responsible for stomach ulcers. Marshall's evidence went against the prevailing view that bacteria were incapable of thriving within the acidic conditions of the stomach. *H. pylori* is now accepted as the principal cause of stomach ulcers, and has also been implicated in gastric cancer.

Together with the battles faced by advocates of the atomic and quark concepts, these examples hardly support the complacent view that the scientific community has 'learned its lesson', and now 'knows better' how to recognize when professional judgement slips into subjective prejudice. Indeed, it is clear from these examples that subjectivity has played, and continues to play, a considerable role in the development of science. My principal aim in choosing these specific examples is not, however, to suggest that subjectivity is a uniquely evil force in science. Rather, it has been to show that the official responses to such examples – that they have only short-term effects, or are confined to less quantitative sciences, or are 'all behind us now' – are not sustainable.

A rather more cogent response is that which many working scientists give, at least when out of earshot of the guardians of the public image of science: that while regrettable, the cases cited above represent a 'price worth paying' for retaining subjective criteria to separate the scientific wheat from the chaff.

I shall now show that this pragmatic view is not only supported in practice, but also has a firm theoretical basis in the mathematics of scientific inference. In short, the presence and use of subjectivity in science *need not* be glossed over, explained away or concealed. Indeed, I shall demonstrate that subjectivity *must* not be treated in this way. For as we shall see, the continuing and misguided attempts to portray scientific research as a wholly objective pursuit has led to practices which threaten its reputation as a source of reliable knowledge.

Subjectivity in the testing of theories

The value of any scientific theory, no matter how theoretically elegant or plausible, is ultimately tested by experiment. Conventionally, this crucial element of the scientific process involves extracting a clear and unequivocal prediction from the theory, investigating this prediction experimentally, and assessing the outcome objectively. Exactly how this comparison is performed, and what conclusions are drawn, has long been a subject of debate among scientists and philosophers. Many scientists consider themselves to be followers of Karl Popper and the concept of falsifiability (Popper, 1963): that to be considered scientific, a theory must be capable of being proved wrong. On this view, the experiment and the analysis of data should be performed to discover if the theory is falsified, and if it is, it must be abandoned. As such, theories are never proved correct: they merely survive until the next experimental attempt at falsification.

There are a great many fundamental problems with Popper's widely-held – and admittedly appealing – view of the scientific process (see especially Howson and Urbach, 1993). Put simply, these problems boil down to the fact that the concept of falsification is supported neither in principle nor in practice. Over 90 years ago the French physicist and philosopher Pierre Duhem pointed out that the testable consequences of scientific theories are not a pure reflection of the theory itself, but are based on many extra assumptions. As a result, if an experiment appears to falsify a theory, this does not automatically imply that the theory must be false: it is always possible to blame one of the auxiliary assumptions.

It should be stressed that this is not merely a philosophical objection to the concept of falsifiability: there are many cases of now well-attested theories being falsified, from the Standard Model of elementary particle physics (Crease and Mann, 1996, pp. 383–390) through to the concept of cancer viruses (Wolpert and Richards, 1989, Chapter 12). Even Einstein's special theory of relativity was falsified barely a year after its publication. In what appears to be the very first published response citing Einstein's famous paper, Walter Kaufmann at the University of Gottingen reported that two rival theories gave a better fit to data from studies of beta particles than relativity. Einstein conceded that Kaufmann's work was carefully executed, based on solid theory, and that the results showed a better fit with rival theories. Even so, he bluntly refused to concede defeat, arguing on the entirely subjective grounds that the rival theories seemed to him inherently less plausible. It took another decade for Einstein's view to be vindicated (Pais, 1982, p. 159).

Once again we see a major disparity between the way science is said to operate and how it actually does. We again see scientists applying subjective criteria for essentially pragmatic reasons: it simply makes no sense to take seriously every apparent falsification of a plausible theory, any more than it makes sense to take seriously every new scientific idea. Judgements based on considerations ranging from the reputation of the experimentalists to a hunch about the correctness of a theory may not be utterly reliable, but they appear to work pretty well most of the time.

Yet, once again, there is a reluctance by the scientific community to admit to what every working scientist knows: that, for all its faults, subjectivity plays a key role in setting objective experimental findings in their proper context. The need to accept this fact transcends the demands of intellectual honesty, however. For as I shall now show, past attempts to sweep subjectivity 'under the carpet' have led to the adoption of apparently objective methods for analysing experimental data that are neither objective nor reliable.

The standard theory of statistical inference

The Popperian image of an experiment is one of clear-cut falsification. Yet, as ever, working scientists readily admit that such black and white, pass/fail outcomes are rarely possible (e.g. Medawar, 1979, Chapter 9). This raises another major objection to the Popperian scheme: for if falsification cannot be clear-cut, what criteria should be used to decide whether a theory has been at least partly falsified ? This problem is most acute where data are *statistical* in nature – the common outcome of experimental investigations in fields from particle physics to psychiatry. Faced with a set of results from, say, a group of depressives where 79 per cent of those given cognitive therapy improved, compared to 68 per cent of those given tricyclics, how is one to decide when the difference between the two groups is significant ?

Clearly, there is considerable scope for subjective criteria to be applied here: psychopharmacologists sceptical of 'talk therapy' may well demand more impressive findings than their cognitive therapist colleagues. However, the standard techniques for gauging the statistical significance of an experimental result seem to eliminate such vexations. These textbook methods of apparently wholly objective statistical inference were developed largely by Ronald Fisher, Jerzy Neyman and Karl Pearson during the 1920s and 1930s. Their aim was to provide objective mathematical tests capable of falsifying theories, and to this end they developed the methods still widely used by the scientific community.

One key feature of these statistical tests is that they appear to require no skill or training in statistics, and seem to lead to a single, objective and easily-understood result. They typically appear in the form of a kind of cook-book recipe, as follows:

1. Specify the hypothesis under test. This is usually the 'null hypothesis' of no real difference; for example, that the difference in the proportions of patients benefiting in both the treatment and the control groups is no greater than that due to mere chance. The 'alternative' hypothesis would then be that there is an improvement in the treated group that cannot be ascribed to fluke alone.
2. Execution of the experiment (for example, as a double-blind randomized case-control clinical trial), and conversion of results into a so-called test-statistic that captures both the size and variation of the effect under study.
3. Determination of the so-called P-value of the test statistic, that is, the probability of obtaining a test-statistic at least as large as that actually observed, on the assumption that the null hypothesis is actually true.
4. If the P-value is less than a certain cut-off figure (the 'level of significance', usually denoted by α), the null hypothesis is held to be 'rejected', and the experimental result is deemed 'significant at the α level'.

While such a recipe is certainly easy to carry out, it undoubtedly contains many perplexing features. Most obvious among them is the strangely convoluted definition of the key determinant of falsifiability, the P-value. This is said to give the probability of obtaining results *at least* as impressive as those actually observed *on the assumption* that the null hypothesis is true. Put another – hardly more illuminating – way, *assuming* the null hypothesis is true, if the same experiment were repeated many times, the frequency with which we would obtain data at least as impressive as those obtained is equal to the P-value (this latter definition leads to these conventional text-book methods being called 'frequentist').

Those who bother to analyse either of these convoluted definitions are apt to ask themselves why they should care about a probability involving results never actually obtained, and calculated assuming the very hypothesis under test. Why is the measure of the significance of the results not simply the probability of the hypothesis under test being true ?

A little more reflection suggests that these cook-book recipes are not, in fact, truly objective. For example, what objective principle underpins the choice of α, the cut-off level for significance, or the preference of one frequentist method over another?

Many of those coming to significance testing for the first time find these issues confusing, and somewhat disturbing (see, e.g. Sivia, 1996 ,p *vi*; Lee, 1997, p *ix*). Yet the widespread use of frequentist methods suggests that most statistical neophytes decide that their qualms must stem from some minor philosophical or mathematical misapprehension of little consequence.

It is one of the most disturbing yet poorly recognized facts of contemporary science that such qualms are far from misplaced. There are indeed fundamental problems with the standard methods of statistical inference, and warnings about their impact on scientific research have been repeatedly pointed out for over 30 years in mathematical research papers (e.g. Edwards *et al.*, 1963; Berger & Sellke, 1987), textbooks (e.g. Jeffreys, 1961; Lindley, 1970; Howson and Urbach, 1993; O'Hagan 1994; Lee, 1997) and even general science publications (e.g. Berger and Berry, 1988; Matthews, 1997). All these authors have pointed to the conceptual flaws in the standard methods of statistical inference, and the logical and practical dangers they present to the scientific enterprise. So far, however, these warnings have had virtually no effect beyond the community of mathematical statisticians. The bulk of the scientific community still uses the standard techniques, at best only vaguely aware of some apparently esoteric concern over their reliability. As we shall see, this concern could hardly be more serious.

Flaws and failings of standard statistical inference

The failure to provide objectivity

The most obvious failing in the standard textbook methods of statistical inference is that they are not objective. This is most clearly apparent in their requirement for a value of α, the cut-off level for significant P-values. Textbooks on classical inference typically introduce a value for $\alpha = 0.05$, stating blandly that it is 'conventionally used', 'widely used', or 'accepted' as the value below which a P-value is deemed significant. Similarly, values of $\alpha = 0.01$ are quoted as being the standard cut-off for highly significant P-values, and $\alpha = 0.001$ for very highly significant results. Yet these same textbooks typically give no clue to the objective underpinnings of these choices. The disturbing truth is that these ubiquitous standards of significance, by which research findings are held to stand or fall, have their origins in nothing more objective or statistically defensible than a coincidence. Through a mathematical quirk of the Normal distribution, 95 per cent of the area under this distribution is enclosed within almost exactly two standard deviations of the mean value. It was this juxtaposition of an integer value for the ordinate and a seemingly convenient 95 per cent probability led Fisher to set $\alpha = 0.05$ as the cut-off for judging significance (Fisher quoted in Jeffreys, 1961, pp. 388–9). As we shall see, it was both an indefensible and unhappy choice.

Altogether more subtle are the logical fallacies lurking in the definitions of frequentist measures of significance. The strangely convoluted definition of the P-value, for example, stems from the fact that it is calculated from an integral, that is, the area under a probability curve such as the familiar bell-shaped normal distribution. This curve is calculated on the *assumption* of the null hypothesis; the fact that the required probability is given by the area under this curve forces the inclusion of entirely hypothetical data points that were, in fact, never observed.

All this is reflected in the more formal mathematical definition of the P-value of Prob(data | null hypothesis). In other words, the P-value is the probability of getting at least as impressive data from an experiment *given* the null hypothesis. While this explains the far-from-intuitive nature of the P-value, it is still far from clear why anyone should be interested in the final result. Working scientists typically want something far more straightforward: the probability that the null hypothesis *really is* correct, *given* the data they observed, that is, Prob(null hypothesis | data).

The difference between this and a P-value seems to be nothing more that switching the order of null hypothesis and outcome. Indeed, the two are often taken to be equivalent even by the authors of some standard statistics texts (see, e.g. Bourke *et al.*, 1985, p. 71, Heyes *et al.*, 1993, p. 116). This is, however, a fundamental and potentially disastrous fallacy known as 'transposition of conditioning': the fallacy of taking Prob(A | B) to be always identical to Prob(B | A).

Risk of false interpretation

To see the dangers inherent in this fallacy, suppose a patient walks into a doctor's surgery covered with spots. The doctor knows that the probability of getting spots *given* a measles infection is very close to certainty, i.e. Prob(spots | measles) $\simeq$ 1. However, it clearly does not follow that the probability that the patient really *has* got measles is also close to 1, i.e. that Prob(measles | spots) $\simeq$ 1: there is a vast number of other diseases apart from measles that produce spots. Deciding which the patient has will involve taking into account other sources of information, such as whether there is chicken pox in the family, and whether the patient has recently travelled abroad.

Clearly, mistaking Prob(spots | measles) for Prob(measles | spots) could lead to a doctor being struck off. Yet the standard methods of statistical inference can and do prompt working scientists to fall into precisely the same trap: P-values are all too easily taken to be identical to Prob(null hypothesis | data), so that a low P-value is taken to imply that the probability that chance alone explains the data is similarly low. There is no simple relationship between P-values and the probability working scientists actually want, and as I shall show shortly, confusing the two can and does lead to meaningless fluke results being regarded as significant.

There is a further serious logical fallacy lurking in the interpretation of a P-value: simply because a result has a low probability on the basis of the null hypothesis, this does not imply that a specific alternative hypothesis is confirmed to a corresponding degree. For example, suppose that a case-control trial shows that a higher proportion of patients on the drug benefited relative to the control group, with a P-value of 0.02. In conventional parlance, as the P-value is below 0.05, this is a significant result. As we have seen, however, this does *not* imply that the probability P of the results being a fluke is 1 in 50. Still less does it imply that the probability of the drug being efficacious are 49/50: Prob(efficacy | outcome) does not equal 1-P, and in any case the efficacy of the drug is just one out of a host of possible explanations for a positive result.

It must be said that the existence of these problems has been acknowledged by some advocates of standard inference, who have put forward a number of rejoinders. For example, some concede that P-values may not be particularly relevant, but insist that they are still a simple and convenient way of summarizing a research finding. This is hardly convincing. Any summary of data worthy of the name must not mislead those without access to the full results – and as we have seen, P-values are all too likely to mislead. Arguing that they are a 'convenient summary' is equivalent to claiming that 'A patient with glandular fever has a high probability of swollen glands' is a convenient summary of a diagnosis of the Black Death.

In an attempt to rid frequentist methods of some of their subjectivity, some authors recommend that the P-value alone should be stated, without comparison to the entirely subjective standard cut-off levels for significance (see e.g. Freedman *et al.* 1998 pp. 547–8). It is usually conceded, however, that this does nothing to prevent others – especially editors and referees of journals – from making the comparison themselves, and acting accordingly.

Yet others eschew use of P-values altogether, arguing instead for so-called estimation methods and the use of 'confidence intervals' (CIs). Rather than using just a single figure, confidence intervals summarize a finding as a central figure, plus a range of values for a parameter of interest, e.g. the relative risk of contracting cancer from some carcinogen. If this range excludes the value corresponding to no additional risk, then the results are deemed to be 'significant'.

Conscious of the criticisms of P-values, many medical journals now ask for results to be quoted in terms of CIs. Despite appearances, however, CIs still fail to resolve the key issue of the interpretation of the outcome of conventional statistical tests. At first sight, a 95 per cent CI *seems* to imply that there is a 95 per cent probability that the true value of the parameter of interest will lie within the stated bounds. Its correct interpretation, however, is just as convoluted as that of the P-value: the 95 per cent actually refers to the frequency with which the statistical test used will generate bounds capturing the true figure. That is, the '95 per cent confidence' refers to the reliability of the *test*, not to the *parameter*. Indeed, so subtle is this distinction that 95 per cent CIs are arguably even more confusing than P-values. Defenders of their use typically respond that – unlike P-values – the distinction between the perceived and correct meanings of 95 per cent CIs can often be ignored. However, as we shall see, this is true only when there is no prior reason for suspecting that the true value of a parameter lies within a well-defined range of values. It is rare that a claim of such complete ignorance can be justified. In any case, the choice of the value of 95 per cent for the CI is entirely arbitrary and subjective, so that in the end a 95 per cent CI is no more 'objective' a measure of significance than a P-value.

Nothing so clearly illustrates the many flaws of frequentist inference than the way in which the scientific community feels able – indeed, sometimes obliged – to decide on entirely subjective grounds which 'objectively significant' results they are going to take seriously, and which they will reject.

Subjective interpretations of study outcomes

If scientists and their statistical methods were truly objective, then the research enterprise would be relatively simple. When a carefully designed study finds a sizeable effect with a P-value of less than 0.05 (or, equivalently, a 95 per cent CI that excludes no effect), then everyone would agree that a significant effect potentially worthy of further investigation had been found. If, on the other hand, a large study failed to reveal a significant outcome despite having the statistical power to do so, then researchers would know to start to looking elsewhere.

This is, of course, not at all how scientists respond to research findings. Large and 'objectively significant' effects found in some fields of research are repeatedly ignored by the scientific community, while small and non-significant effects found in other fields are deemed to be impressive.

For example, researchers at a number of respected academic institutions have investigated the concept of telepathy, the transmission of information from one person to another by extrasensory means. The most highly regarded studies centre on the so-called autoganzfeld technique (see, for example, Radin, 1997, Chapter 5), in which subjects have to identify one of four images which a 'sender' attempts to transmit to them by telepathic means. The null hypothesis of no telepathy suggests a random hit rate of 0.25; a recent meta-analysis of over 2,500 sessions (Radin, 1997 p. 87) showed an average hit-rate of 0.332, with an extraordinarily significant P-value of less than 10^{-15}. By the usual criteria of objective statistical inference, such a finding should convince even the most sceptical of the existence of telepathy. Yet many if not most scientists continue to reject the existence of telepathy out of hand, often citing past examples of fraud and incompetence in parapsychology to support their stance (Radin, 1997, Chapter 13). Similarly, recent trials of a number of homeopathic treatments have been found to produce large and highly significant effects for some ailments, such as migraine and allergy (for a review, see Vallance, 1998). Even so, homeopathy is still regarded with suspicion by much of the medical profession (see for example Vanden-broucke, 1997).

Both these examples are clear cases of the use of double standards. Many scientists feel entirely comfortable about their stance, however, citing the lack of any mechanism to explain telepathy or homeopathy, and past evidence of fraud and incompetence by researchers in these areas.

Given the lack of clear mechanisms for the action of many drugs, and the cases of fraud and incompetence in entirely conventional fields of research, this defence of the use of double standards is hardly convincing. It seems particularly disingenuous when one considers the response of the scientific community to findings in other, more conventional areas of research. Now results that are both minor and statistically non-significant are said to constitute substantial support for the prevailing wisdom. For example, the World Health Organization (WHO) and International Agency for Research on Cancer (IARC) recently conducted the largest case-control study of the effects of passive smoking ever performed in Europe (Bofetta *et al.*, 1997). The aim was to establish, as unequivocally as possible, the extra risk of lung cancer faced by non-smokers who live with smokers. This extra risk is typically quantified by the so-called Odds Ratio (OR), in which an OR greater than 1 constitutes an additional risk.

The WHO/IARC study found only a small and non-significant Odds Ratio (OR) for lung cancer for spouses exposed to environmental tobacco smoke (ETS) of 1.16 with a 95 per cent CI of (0.93 1.44). As well as being statistically non-significant, so small an effect size lies within the range at which the IARC itself concedes that unequivocal results may be forever unachievable (Breslow and Day, 1980). Yet following the publication of a negative interpretation of their results in the media (Macdonald 1998), the WHO/IARC team publicly insisted that their findings 'add substantially' to previous evidence for the link between ETS and lung cancer. The WHO went on to issue a press release clearly implying that the results proved a link between passive smoking and lung cancer.

No competent statistician would agree that the WHO/IARC results add substantially to the case against ETS, much less that they prove the existence of a link with lung cancer. Moreover, the WHO's interpretation of such weak evidence is in striking contrast to the official interpretation of very similar findings in studies of other supposed health risks, in which the 'politically correct' line is one of considerable scepticism. For example, a recent major study of the supposed link between electric power lines and childhood leukaemias (Linet, *et al.* 1997) produced an OR of 1.24, with a 95 per cent CI of (0.86 1.79). This result is very similar to that obtained by the WHO/IARC passive smoking study; this time, however, the researchers concluded that so small and non-significant effect provided 'little evidence' of a link between power lines and leukaemia. The team's funding organization, the US National Cancer Institute, went further, declaring that the study showed magnetic fields 'do not raise children's leukaemia risk'.

Similarly, a recent study of women with breast implants (Nyren *et al.*,1998) found an OR for hospitalization for connective tissue disorders of 1.3, with a non-significant 95 per cent CI of (0.7, 2.2). This is again similar to the WHO/IARC study findings, but again the lack of significance was held to add weight to the conclusion that silicone breast implants 'are *not* associated with a meaningful excess risk of connective tissue disorder' (Cooper and Dennison, 1998, emphasis added).

There are many other examples of where the results of supposedly objective statistical methods are interpreted according to the prevailing subjective opinion of the scientific community. Together, they provide further evidence of the gulf between how scientists are supposed to conduct even quantitative research, and how they actually go about it. The insouciance with which subjectivity is used in the assessment of scientific claims suggests that many working scientists accept – consciously or otherwise – that a key feature is missing from conventional statistical methods: specifically, an explicit means of taking into account the *plausibility* of the claim under study. Indeed, as one leading advocate of frequentist inference has noted, it is 'curious that personal views intrude always' (Kempthorne, 1971, p. 480).

This curious fact, combined with the many problems and pitfalls associated with frequentist measures of significance, raises an obvious question: is there a better way? As I now show, the answer is *yes*.

Bayesian inference

The classical frequentist techniques of inference are not, in fact, classical at all, but relative newcomers in the long history of statistical inference. Before the 1920s, another approach to statistical inference was in general use, based on a result that flows directly from the axioms of probability. As such, this approach has solid theoretical foundations, produces intuitive, readily-understood measures of significance, and remains as valid today as it did before it was eclipsed by the flawed attempts of Fisher *et al.* to create an objective theory of statistical inference. It is known as Bayesian inference, after the eighteenth century English cleric Thomas Bayes who first published the key theorem behind it: Bayes's theorem.

The power and importance of this theorem is immediately apparent in its solution to one of the central problems of standard statistical inference. As we have seen, frequentist methods do not tell us Prob(theory | data); that is, they do not tell us what our belief in a theory should be, given the data we actually saw. To answer that question, we must turn to the axioms of probability theory, from which we find that (see, e.g. Feller, 1968, Chapter 5):

$$\text{Prob}(A \mid B) = \text{Prob}(B \mid A).\text{Prob}(A)/\text{Prob}(B) \tag{1}$$

This is Bayes's theorem, which becomes the basis of Bayesian inference when A is the event of a specific hypothesis being true, and B as the event of observing specific data. Bayesian inference was the standard means of performing statistical inference prior to Fisher's work in the 1920s, and it allows us to calculate a clear and unambiguous measure of support for a theory, Prob(theory | data) directly from experimental results via the relationship:

$$\text{Prob}(\text{theory} \mid \text{data}) = \text{Prob}(\text{data} \mid \text{theory}).\ \text{Prob}(\text{theory})/\text{Prob}(\text{data}) \tag{2}$$

This formulation of Bayes's theorem shows clearly that while we can calculate the quantity we are interested in, namely Prob(theory | data), this is not equivalent to Prob(data | theory), much less to a P-value. However, the formula also highlights the key stumbling-block to the application of Bayesian inference. To work out the value of Prob(theory | data), we must first establish Prob(theory); that is, we must be able to put some prior probability on the theory we are testing. As I shall show later, setting this prior probability is often far less problematic than some critics claim: it is rare that there are absolutely no previous findings or plausibility arguments available to constrain our estimate. It remains true, nevertheless, that in those cases where there is a complete absence of any previous results or insight, the prior probability of the correctness of the hypothesis will be based largely on opinion. In short, it will be *subjective*.

It is this unequivocal use of subjectivity that has made Bayesian inference so controversial, and has led to such determined attempts to find alternatives. As we have seen, working scientists may routinely use subjectivity when it suits them, but the idea of explicitly incorporating it into the very heart of data analysis remains anathema. But this attitude overlooks a striking fact about the scientific process: that all attempts to rid it of subjectivity have failed. By the usual standards of scientific research, the repeated failure of these attempts would be taken to imply that the basic thesis was flawed. And from (2) we now see that this would, indeed, be the correct conclusion to draw. For the axioms of probability, via Bayes's theorem, show that subjectivity cannot be wrung out of the scientific process for the simple reason that it is mathematically *ineluctable*. Much as we might want to, it is *impossible* to obtain the value of Prob(theory | data) without having some value for the prior probability Prob(theory).

The plain fact is that subjectivity in statistical inference is as unavoidable as uncertainty in quantum mechanics. Yet while we have all grown accustomed to the latter – not least because of the welter of theoretical and empirical support for its existence – there remains a deep-seated reluctance to embrace the presence of subjectivity in scientific research.

We have seen that this reluctance stems in part from concern about playing into the hands of the enemies of science, and also from past abuses in the application of subjectivity. Further barriers exist to the adoption of Bayesian methods in data analysis, however. Some of these are entirely pragmatic: it is undoubtedly harder to boil down Bayesian inference to the same 'cook-book' approach used in standard frequentist methods. Except in simple cases, Bayesian inference is also more mathematically and computationally demanding than frequentist methods. The dearth of textbooks and software suitable for the non-specialist wanting to carry out real-life data analysis does nothing to help (see, however, O'Hagan 1997).

None of this would matter, however, were the working scientist convinced that the effort involved in getting to grips with Bayesian methods was worthwhile. This leads one to suspect that there are other, more fundamental reasons for the failure of Bayesian inference to regain its primacy over frequentist methods.

First, advocates of Bayesian inference have failed to tackle the widely held belief that Bayesian prior probabilities are never more than wholly subjective guesses, 'plucked out of the air' to suit some or other prejudice or preconception. It cannot be stressed too highly that only rarely will there be *absolutely nothing* on which to base a reasonable prior. In many cases, there will be sources of evidence on which to base a sensible prior probability: for example, results from previous studies of similar drugs and plausibility arguments concerning, say, cancer risks from radiation based on insights from physics. Even if there really is little solid evidence on which to base a prior probability, Bayesian inference can still provide insight by allowing one to study the effect of different levels of prior belief (see, for example, Spiegelhalter et al. 1994). It is also possible to invert Bayes's theorem, and estimate what prior belief is needed for data to reach a given level of plausibility; I give examples of such 'inverse Bayesian inference' below.

The second key feature of Bayesian inference that is not sufficiently appreciated is that initial prior beliefs in a specific hypothesis become progressively less important as data accumulate. It can be shown mathematically (see, for example, O'Hagan, 1994 p. 74 et seq.) that whatever prior probability is used at the outset, Bayes's theorem ensures that everyone is driven towards the same conclusion as the data accumulate. Unless one's prior is precisely zero (which is not a rational stance), the only long-term effect of the prior belief is that a sceptic starting from a low prior probability will require more data to reach the same level of belief as an enthusiast for the theory – which is hardly an egregious feature of a theory of inference. Indeed, it is striking that this mathematical feature of Bayesian inference mirrors so well how science actually operates. Starting from a wide variety of opinions about, say, the link between some chemical and cases of cancer, the accumulation of experimental and epidemiological evidence drives the scientific community toward the same conclusion about the reality or otherwise of the link, with sceptics merely taking longer to be convinced.

In short, Bayesian inference provides a coherent, comprehensive and strikingly intuitive alternative to the flawed frequentist methods of statistical inference. It leads to results that are more easily interpreted, more useful, and which more accurately reflect the way science actually proceeds. It is, moreover, unique in its ability to deal explicitly and reliably with the provably ineluctable presence of subjectivity in science.

These features alone should motivate many working scientists to find out more about applying Bayesian inference in their own research. For those who still need to be convinced, however, I now demonstrate perhaps the most impressive reason for using Bayesian inference: its ability to provide a far greater level of protection than frequentist methods against seeing significance in entirely spurious research findings. For as we shall see, while frequentist methods are still widely used within the scientific community, they routinely exaggerate the real significance of implausible data, with results that can and do bring the scientific process into disrepute.

How P-values exaggerate significance

As we have seen, frequentist methods of inference provide measures of significance that are neither objective nor intuitive. More importantly, however, they give a fundamentally misleading view of the significance of data. To see this, take the simple case in which a hypothesis is to be tested via measurements of a specific parameter, θ; for example, the hypothesis may be that a toxin is linked to some disorder in children, so that θ is the level of this toxin in children suffering from the disorder. Such an investigation would then consist of measuring values of θ in a group of affected children, θ_i, computing the data mean and variance, and comparing it with θ_0, the value of θ found among normal children. We would then test the null hypothesis that any difference we find is merely the result of chance by setting up a test-statistic, z, which takes into account the sample size, its mean and variance, and compares it to θ_0, the value expected if the null hypothesis is correct. Following the frequentist approach, one would typically convert this z-score to a P-value, the probability of obtaining at least as large a value of z, *assuming* the null hypothesis that chance alone is the cause. According to convention, if the P-value is less than 0.05, then the data are taken to be significant.

However, as we have seen, a much more meaningful measure of significance is Prob(Null hypothesis | data), the probability that the difference in θ *really is* the product of chance alone. Just how big is the disparity between this measure of significance and the frequentist P-value? To find out, we can use Bayes's theorem (2), which with a little algebra becomes

$$\text{Prob(Null hypothesis | data)} = \left(1 + \frac{1 - \text{Prob(Null)}}{\text{Prob(Null).BF}}\right)^{-1} \tag{3}$$

where Prob(Null) is the prior probability for the null hypothesis that there is no real difference in the toxin level in the children, and BF is the so-called Bayes Factor, which measures how much we should alter our prior belief about the null hypothesis in the light of the new data, as captured by z. For the value of the Bayes Factor, one can show (see, for example, Lee, p. 131) that under very general conditions BF has a *lower* limit of

$$\text{BF} \geq \exp(-z^2/2) \tag{4}$$

As an example, suppose that past evidence concerning the toxin leads us to an agnostic view of the possibility that there are higher levels of the toxin in the children with the disorder; this is equivalent to setting Prob(Null) = 0.5. Inserting this and (4) into (3) we find that, for a given value of z, our initial agnosticism leads us to a probability that the null hypothesis of no real difference is indeed correct of *at least*

$$\text{Prob}(\text{Null} \mid \text{data}) \geq [1 + \exp(z^2/2)]^{-1} \qquad (5)$$

Suppose, for example, that the measurements of the toxin levels in the two groups revealed a difference with a z-value of 2.0. On the frequentist viewpoint, standard statistical tables shows that this implies a P-value of 0.044; as this is less than 0.05, the difference is deemed significant at the P = 0.05 level. As we have stressed, however, this does *not* mean that the probability that the difference *really is* a fluke is also 0.044; we can only calculate this latter probability via Bayes's theorem. Plugging in z = 2 into (5), we find that our data actually imply that Prob(null | data), the probability the difference is just a fluke, is *at least* 0.12. In other words, while the frequentist methods led us to conclude that the difference was significant, the Bayesian calculation pointed to a much higher probability of the finding being a mere fluke.

This conclusion, moreover, was based on an agnostic prior of Prob(Null) = 0.5. If there are no strong grounds for believing that the effect is genuine, then – in contrast to frequentist methods – Bayesian inference allows us to factor in this lack of plausibility explicitly into our analysis. This can have particularly dramatic effects in the assessment of 'anomalous' phenomena (Matthews, 1999), as the following example shows (Nelson, 1997).

For over 250 years, Princeton students have attended Commencement on a Tuesday in late May or early June, an outdoor event for which good weather is vital. According to local folklore, good weather does usually prevail, prompting claims that those attending may 'wish' good weather into existence. By analysing local weather records spanning many decades, Nelson found that Princeton's weather was generally no different from that of its surroundings. However, he did find some evidence that the town was less likely to be rained on during the outdoor events. The phenomenon gave z-scores as high as 1.996, which on a frequentist basis gives a significant P-value of 0.046. Properly mindful of the implausibility of the phenomenon, however, Nelson was reluctant to take this objective finding at face value, and instead reached a more subjective conclusion: 'These intriguing results certainly aren't strong enough to compel belief, but the case presents a very challenging possibility'.

A Bayesian analysis allows a far more concrete assessment of plausibility to be made. Clearly, with such a bizarre claim, there is little one can say about the precise value of a sensible prior probability for the null hypothesis of no real effect, other than to say that the probability is likely to be pretty high. In such cases, Bayesian inference still gives valuable insight, as it allows one to estimate the level of prior probability necessary to sustain a belief that the effect is illusory, even in the light of Nelson's data. Using (4) and (3) and z = 1.996, this inverse Bayesian inference shows that Prob(Null | data) > 0.5 for all Pr(Null) > 0.88 In other words, for anyone whose prior scepticism about the effectiveness of wishful thinking exceeds 90 per cent, the balance of probabilities is that the effect is illusory, despite Nelson's data.

As this example shows, frequentist methods greatly exaggerate the significance of intrinsically implausible data. However, as we shall now see, frequentist methods can also seriously exaggerate both the size and significance of effects in much more important mainstream areas of research, such as clinical trials.

Misleading significance of clinical trial results

Misleading P-values

The classic method for investigating the efficacy of a new drug or therapy, or the impact of exposure to some risk factor, is the so-called randomized case-control clinical trial. In such trials, a group of people given the new treatment or exposed to the risk-factor are compared with an unexposed control group. One common frequentist method of analysing the outcome is to reduce the results to a test-statistic (such as χ^2), which is then turned into a P-value; as before, if this is less than 0.05, then the difference between the two groups is deemed to be significant. Again, however, a Bayesian analysis reveals that the real significance of such a finding is typically much less impressive than the P-values imply.

As before, I shall demonstrate this by taking a real-life case. During the early 1990s, research emerged to suggest that the risk of coronary heart disease (CHD) is associated with childhood poverty (Elford, et al. 1991). Following the discovery that infection with the bacterium *H. pylori* is also linked to poverty, some researchers suspected that the bacterium might form the missing link between the two. Precisely how a bacterium in the stomach might cause heart disease is less than clear – raising the key issue of plausibility, to which we shall return shortly. Nevertheless, a number of studies were undertaken to investigate the link between CHD and *H. pylori*. In one of the first such studies (Mendall, et al. 1994), 60 per cent of patients who suffered CHD were found to be infected with *H. pylori*, compared with 39 per cent of normal controls. When the effects of age, CHD risk factors and current social class had been controlled for, the results led to a χ^2 value of 4.73. Using frequentist methods, this leads to a P-value of 0.03, implying that the rate of CHD among those infected with *H. pylori* is significantly higher than those without.

On the face of it, this finding raises the intriguing prospect of being able to tackle one of the major killers of the western world using nothing more than antibiotics. Yet while the evidence that both CHD and *H. pylori* infection are more common among the poor is suggestive of a link between the two, it is hardly unequivocal. Such scepticism is underscored by the lack of any convincing mechanism by which a gastric bacterium could trigger heart disease. The frequentist P-value, however, cannot reflect any of these justifiable qualms; sceptics of the link have no option but to say that on this occasion they are just going to ignore the supposed significance of Mendall *et al.*'s finding.

In contrast, Bayesian inference requires no such arbitrary 'moving of the goalposts': it allows explicit account to be taken of the plausibility of the findings. In the case of the supposed link between CHD to *H. pylori*, the lack of any convincing mechanism balanced against the socio-economic evidence of a link suggests that an agnostic prior probability of Prob(Null) = 0.5 would be a reasonable starting-point for assessing results like those found by Mendall *et al.* Inserting this into (3) implies that the probability of the results being due to chance, given the observed data, is

$$\text{Prob(Null | data)} = BF/(1 + BF) \tag{6}$$

where BF is the Bayes Factor for the null hypothesis of chance effect. One can show that for in a wide range of practical situations, including this type of case-control study, the *lower* bound on BF is given by (see, for example, Berger and Sellke, 1987)

$$BF \geq \sqrt{(\chi^2)}.\exp[(1 - \chi^2)/2] \tag{7}$$

Inserting the value of $\chi^2 = 4.73$ found by Mendall *et al.* into (6) shows that the BF is *at least* 0.337. Putting this in (6) we find that Prob(Null | data), the probability that Mendall *et al.*'s results are due to nothing more than chance is *at least* 0.25. In other words, even using an agnostic prior, the frequentist P-value has over-estimated the real significance of the findings by almost an order of magnitude.

Those taking a more sceptical view of a link between a gastric bacterium and CHD would, of course, set Prob(Null) somewhat higher. Applying the concept of inverse Bayesian inference used earlier, it emerges that even a relatively modest sceptical prior of just Prob(Null) = 0.75 is enough to lead to a balance of probabilities that Mendall *et al.*'s findings are entirely illusory.

Misleading confidence intervals

Some defenders of frequentist methods regard criticism of P-values as an attack on a straw man, pointing out that P-values are increasingly being supplanted by 95 per cent confidence intervals (CIs), which convey more information about effect size than a single-figure P-value. Yet as we have seen, frequentist CIs share many of the same problems of interpretation as P-values. Most importantly, they also share an inability to take into account the plausibility of the hypothesis under test. As such, 95 per cent confidence intervals are also prone to exaggerate both the size and the significance of intrinsically implausible effects.

In contrast – and as one might expect by now – the Bayesian counterpart of CIs (known as Credible Intervals or Highest Density Regions), are more comprehensible, more meaningful and more reliable indicators of real significance. With frequentist CIs, the 95 per cent refers to the reliability of the statistical test; the Bayesian CI, in contrast, means precisely what it seems to mean: that there is a 95 per cent probability that the true value of the parameter lies within the stated range.

As already noted, Bayesian CIs are numerically identical to their frequentist counterpart if there is only very vague prior knowledge about plausible values of the parameter of interest (see, for example, Berger and Delampady, 1987 p. 328, and Appendix to this chapter). However, such complete ignorance about the likely size of the effect under study is rarely defensible, and in general frequentist and Bayesian CIs will not coincide. In such cases, a Bayesian CI is always a more reliable guide to the true significance of a finding than its frequentist counterpart.

Again, let us illustrate this through a real-life example. In the early 1990s, the Grampian region early anistreplase trial study (GREAT Group, 1992) generated considerable interest in the medical community, as it seemed to show that heart-attack victims given this clot-busting drug at home had a 50 per cent higher chance of survival than those given the drug once they arrived in hospital. While there were good reasons for expecting that early intervention with the drug would produce some improvement, the size of the claimed benefit surprised many. Nevertheless, frequentist measures of significance appeared to give objective support to the finding: the team found a relative risk (RR) of death for those given the drug early of 0.52 – i.e. a 48 per cent risk reduction – with a 95 per cent CI of (0.23 0.97). As this excludes an RR of 1, this surprising result is also significant in frequentist terms, the equivalent P-value being 0.04.

However, as was pointed out shortly after the publication of the GREAT results (Pocock and Spiegelhalter, 1992), a considerable amount of prior information existed with which to assess the plausibility of the GREAT finding; for example, a much larger European study involving the same drug pointed to a much smaller benefit. Drawing on this existing knowledge, Pocock and Spiegelhalter carried out a Bayesian re-assessment of the GREAT results; an outline of how such an analysis can be performed is given in the Appendix to this paper. The prior information was captured through a probability distribution which peaked at an RR of 0.83 while giving low probabilities to RRs greater than 1.0 (no benefit) or less than 0.6 (dramatic improvement). When combined with the GREAT data, the resulting ('posterior') probability distribution peaked at an RR of around 0.75, with a 95 per cent Bayesian CI of (0.57 1.0). While still pointing to a more impressive effect than that suggested by previous studies, the GREAT results emerge from the analysis as markedly less impressive than suggested by the frequentist methods.

At this point, it is natural to ask whether this Bayesian analysis really did give a more accurate picture of reality than the frequentist methods. The simple answer is yes. Six years after the publication of the GREAT findings, the overall picture emerging from international studies is that early use of clot-busters like anistreplase does indeed confer extra benefit, with RRs of around 0.75 to 0.8 (Fox, quoted in Matthews 1997). This is only half the improvement suggested by the frequentist analysis of the GREAT data, but in impressive agreement with Pocock and Spiegelhalter's Bayesian analysis.

In a similar vein, the current consensus concerning the supposed *H. pylori*-CHD link is that a plausible mechanism relating the two is lacking, and that a causal link remains dubious (Danesh, *et al.*, 1997). This suggests that the basis of the above Bayesian analysis of the supposed link remains valid – a conclusion supported by a recent large-scale study that failed to find any convincing evidence for an association (Wald *et al.*, 1997).

These cases are hardly the only examples of the tendency of frequentist methods to exaggerate both effect size and significance of clinical findings. Undoubtedly the most disturbing evidence comes from the continuing failure of many impressive drug trial results to produce similarly impressive results once approved for general release. It is widely recognized that most new therapies for cancer and heart disease have proved far less effective than initially believed (e.g. Fayers, 1994, Yusuf *et al.*, 1984). Very recently, a UK study uncovered evidence that the use of 'clinically proved' drugs for myocardial infarction since the early 1980s has had no effect on mortality, with death-rates on the wards at least double those found in trials (Brown *et al.*, 1997).

Such a finding would come as no surprise to those familiar with the inherent ability of frequentist methods to exaggerate both effect sizes and significance. It is of course perfectly possible that at least part of the explanation for such disappointing findings lies elsewhere: the greater care taken of all patients in clinical trials, for example, and the fact that trials tend to be conducted in centres of excellence. Brown *et al.* suggest that their disappointing findings may be due to a failure to optimize the use of the available treatments for myocardial infarction. This highlights another factor in the continuing failure of Bayesian methods to supplant frequentist methods: the existence of many other apparently plausible explanations capable of masking the failings of frequentist methods.

'Explaining away' frequentist failures

The most common explanation for studies whose spuriously significant findings fail to be confirmed is that the sample size was too small. This seems plausible enough: after all, everyone knows that the smaller a sample, the less reliable its conclusions. Yet the argument overlooks two key facts. First, the calculation of a P-value takes full account of sample size. On the frequentist viewpoint, we must regard a P-value of 0.03 as significant whether it is based on a sample of 10 or 10 000 people; larger samples are just more likely to detect significance in smaller effects. This is related to the second flaw in the sample size defence of frequentist failures. Small samples are indeed more susceptible to statistical noise than large ones, but only in the sense that their lack of statistical power makes them more prone to missing real effects. For a given P-value, both small and large studies of the same quality are equally likely to see significance in results that are really due to chance. As such, blaming the failure of large studies to replicate significant positive findings from smaller studies purely on sample size is simply fallacious.

A more sophisticated, and plausible, defence of frequentist failures is that the original studies were undermined by biasing and confounding factors. Bias undermines the separation of subjects into cases and controls, due to, say, misdiagnosis of the disease whose cause is under investigation. Confounding undermines attempts to link a cause to its effects; for example, failure to take into account dietary differences can undermine attempts to link carcinogens to observed cases of cancer.

Both bias and confounding are exceptionally difficult to deal with, and undoubtedly explain many failures to replicate results. For example, when Mendall *et al.* applied further controls for the confounding effect of overcrowding and hot water supplies in childhood risk-factors for infection by *H. pylori*, the link between the bacterium and CHD remained, but its P-value was no longer significant.

The undoubted power of bias and confounding to undermine clinical research findings has provided defenders of frequentist methods with a further reason for shunning Bayesian inference. The argument is that while Bayesian methods may indeed deal more effectively with the risk of seeing significance in fluke results, it is no better at dealing with bias and confounding than the standard frequentist methods, and these are typically far more important.

This is also incorrect. Even relatively simple Bayesian analysis does allow concern about bias and confounding to be taken into account, via the form of the prior probability distribution, in the assessment of the posterior probability. Similar remarks apply to the supposed inability of Bayesian methods to take into account the many other potential influences on trial outcome, from poor randomisation to the better care received by patients in clinical trials. All these can be captured by a prior reflecting past real-life experience of just how successful drugs usually turn out to be.

Ultimately, however, all these supposed objections to the use of Bayesian methods serve only to conceal the key advantage of Bayesian inference: that it offers far greater protection against seeing significance in implausible results. The importance of this can best be seen through another real-life example, and one of great contemporary interest: the assessment of the risk of lung cancer faced by passive smoking of environmental tobacco smoke (ETS). The strongest evidence for this risk is generally held to be a recent meta-analysis of 37 published studies (Hackshaw *et al.*, 1997). This found a relative risk (RR) for lung cancer among life-long non-smokers living with smokers of 1.24 with a 95 per cent CI of (1.13, 1.36). A detailed assessment of both bias and confounding was carried out, but the central estimate for the RR remained essentially unchanged at 1.26 with a 95 per cent CI of (1.07, 1.47). On the basis of standard inference methods, this implies a highly significant link between passive smoking and lung cancer (P < 0.006). To underline the credibility of their results, Hackshaw *et al.* performed an informal plausibility assessment of their findings, using indirect measures of the likely intake of ETS by passive smokers. These suggest that passive smokers have about 1 per cent the exposure to cigarettes of their smoking partners. Assuming smokers typically consume 25 cigarettes a day, face an RR of 20 and that there is a linear dose-risk relation, Hackshaw *et al.* reached an estimate of RR ~ 1.19 for passive smokers.

While broadly similar to the RR found by the meta-analysis, this plausibility argument has itself been criticized as implausible (Lee 1998; Nilsson 1998, p. 20). However, both Hackshaw *et al.* and their critics underestimate the crucial importance of a much more rigorous assessment of the plausibility of such weak results. Hackshaw *et al.* devoted about 10 times more of their paper to the assessment of bias and confounding than to plausibility; as I now show, however, a Bayesian analysis reveals that plausibility has a far more dramatic effect on the significance of the results.

Of the many criticisms that can be levelled at Hackshaw *et al.*'s plausibility argument, the most serious is their reliance on markers of ETS exposure which are both indirect and not linked to carcinogenicity. The use of such markers is especially hard to justify in the face of evidence from *direct* studies of ETS exposure that consistently point to much lower levels of exposure. An ongoing series of such studies (see e.g. Phillips *et al.*, 1994; Phillips *et al.*, 1998 and references therein) has found median exposures figures of ~ 0.02 cigarettes a day for the most exposed passive smokers. Even adopting the same linear dose-risk relation as Hackshaw *et al.* (which again is questionable, Nilsson, 1998, pp, 21–22) this suggests a plausible RR for passive smoking of around 1.02, an excess risk 10 times lower than that estimated by Hackshaw *et al.* Only the top 10 per cent of the most exposed passive smokers in the studies by Phillips *et al.* were found to face anything like the risk predicted by Hackshaw *et al.*

Incorporating these results into a plausibility argument via a Bayesian prior distribution leads to an altogether different view of the risks of passive smoking. Specifically, it suggest that the excess lung-cancer risk is both 11 times smaller, with a 95 per cent CI of (1.00. 1.04) than that given by Hackshaw *et al.*, and statistically non-significant. Bayesian inference thus strongly suggests that the growing consensus that ETS is a proven and major health risk is misplaced. Whether or not the outcome of this Bayesian analysis will be borne out is as yet unclear. What is clear is that there is a very real danger of the frequentist evidence for a 'significant extra' risk from ETS becoming canonical. This, in turn, raises the possibility that Hackshaw *et al.*'s risk figure will be used routinely to subtract out the confounding effect of passive smoking in future studies of the causes of cancer. If this risk figure has been substantially over-estimated – as the above Bayesian analysis strongly suggests it has – attempts to assess the true risk posed by many other health hazards will be seriously undermined (Nilsson, 1997, p. 140).

This example of passive smoking and lung cancer provides the final strand in the case for the widespread and routine use of Bayesian inference in the analysis of data. This can be summed up as follows:

1 It allows both previous knowledge and the inherent plausibility of a hypothesis to be explicitly taken into account.
2 It gives measures of significance that are more meaningful than those generated by frequentist methods.
3 These measures have more intuitive and straightforward definitions than their frequentist counterparts, and are thus much less prone to misinterpretation.
4 Bayesian inference is less likely to see significance in entirely spurious findings, especially in poorly motivated research of low inherent plausibility. As such, it provides more protection against seriously – even dangerously – misleading findings whose attempted replication or extension will ultimately prove futile.

Conclusions

In this chapter, I have shown that the scientific community has a deeply ambiguous attitude towards the presence of subjectivity in research. While both desiring and proclaiming objectivity, working scientists routinely use subjective criteria in their everyday research. The justification is pragmatic, and entirely reasonable: it is impossible for working scientists to deal with the plethora of new results and theories that constantly present themselves in any other way. However, mindful of past abuses in the history of science, the scientific community remains committed to keeping the presence of subjectivity in the research enterprise to a minimum.

This commitment has led to the widespread adoption of techniques for statistical inference that appear to be objective. Known as frequentist methods, they have become central to the research enterprise, with their outcomes – P-values and 95 per cent confidence intervals – becoming a *sine qua non* for acceptance by leading science journals. As I have shown, however, these textbook methods are neither objective nor reliable indicators of either effect size or statistical significance of research findings. By failing to take into account the intrinsic plausibility of the hypothesis under test, frequentist methods are capable of greatly exaggerating both the size and the significance of effects which are in reality the product of mere chance.

The implicit recognition of these failings by the scientific community is evidenced by the way in which essentially identical results from the supposedly objective frequentist methods are interpreted in entirely different ways, according to the subjective belief of researchers. Thus, a large and highly statistically significant result in parapsychology will be ignored, while a small and statistically non-significant link between passive smoking and cancer will be deemed to add considerably to the case against environmental tobacco smoke.

The persistent failure of scientists to rid the research process of subjectivity, and the failings of frequentist techniques, can both be traced to the same fundamental source: the axioms of probability. These show that in the assessment of hypotheses, subjectivity is mathematically *ineluctable*. All attempts to banish subjectivity from the research process are thus ultimately futile, and are at best no more than exercises in sweeping subjectivity 'under the carpet'.

The vexed problem of subjectivity in science has its solution in those same axioms, however. Bayes's theorem provides the underpinning for an entire theory of statistical inference which takes explicit account of plausibility, and supplies measures of statistical significance that are more relevant, more comprehensible and more reliable than those of frequentist methods. As such, the wider adoption of Bayesian inference will undoubtedly save substantial amounts of time, resources and public money currently spent on futile attempts to replicate significant support for intrinsically implausible hypotheses.

Some idea of the extent of this waste can be obtained by noting that each month journals covering disciplines from sociology and psychology to geology and genetics carry many papers claiming to have results significant at the 0.05 level with P-values in the range $0.01 < P \leq 0.05$. Even assuming that these claims are all sufficiently well-motivated to merit an agnostic prior, it can be shown that (6) and (7) point to *at least* a quarter of such claims are meaningless flukes (Matthews, 1999). For research meriting even a very moderate level of scepticism, this proportion rapidly rises to over 50 per cent. This is a finding that should worry anyone concerned with the reliability and funding of scientific research.

The fact that just two independent clinical trials with results significant at the 0.05 level are sufficient for new therapies to win approval from national regulatory bodies is hardly less worrying. As so often with frequentist concepts, this P-value standard can and is misinterpreted as implying that the probability of the therapy being ineffective is less than 1 in 400 (see, for example, Buyse, 1994). The true proportion will be far higher, especially among therapies whose claims of efficacy are poorly motivated – a fact reflected in the many cases of where initial euphoria over some new breakthrough turns into disappointment (Yusuf et al., 1984; Pocock and Spiegelhalter, 1992; Fayers, 1994; Brown et al. 1997). Bayesian assessment of trial results give regulatory bodies a formal means of incorporating this crucial 'reality check' into their deliberations. In contrast, the frequentist methods currently used by regulatory bodies have no means of incorporating such key knowledge: given the same raw data, they cannot distinguish between streptokinase or snake-oil. A number of regulatory bodies will accept Bayesian assessments of drug trials; in the light of the above, the use of such methods should not be optional but mandatory.

Lack of theoretical underpinning has an especially large impact on areas of research such as parapsychology and alternative medicine. Bayesian inference applied here would certainly cast grave doubt on claims that appear impressive from a frequentist viewpoint. It is important to stress, however, that this does not imply that all research into alternative or anomalous fields should be abandoned. Bayesian inference merely implies that the standard frequentist criteria for judging statistical significance in these areas are especially inadequate. It can be shown that in such fields of research, there are few grounds for viewing as significant any result whose two-tailed P-value exceeds 0.003 (Matthews 1998). This value assumes an agnostic prior of Pr(Null) = 0.5, which is undoubtedly generous for most claims for the existence of anomalous phenomena; even so, the resulting P-value is 17 times more demanding than the conventional 0.05 criterion used for gauging significance, and it is clear that many current claims for anomalous phenomena fail to meet it.

Reputable researchers would no doubt feel more confident defending evidence for an anomalous phenomenon by applying at least a mild level of scepticism in their assessment of significance. In this case, a P-value of no more than around 2×10^{-4} is appropriate, a value 250 times more demanding than the conventional 0.05 criterion. These technical results can be stated much more succinctly, however: extraordinary claims require extraordinary evidence. This is a well-attested and widely-accepted principle, yet it is noticeable by its absence in the mathematics of frequentist inference.

It must also be emphasized that many of the concerns about frequentist inference expressed here have been recognized by leading statisticians for decades (see for example Jeffreys, 1961; Edwards et al., 1963; Lindley, 1970). This inevitably raises the question of why Bayesian inference is still failing to (re)gain its central role in the scientific enterprise. This is, I believe, due largely to the failure of its advocates to convey three key facts to working scientists:

- That while subjectivity may be an unwelcome feature of the scientific process, the axioms of probability show that it is unavoidable, and that Bayes's theorem is the correct way to deal with it;
- That while Bayesian inference does allow subjective prior knowledge to be incorporated into the assessment of data, such knowledge is not 'plucked out of thin air'. Rather, it allows an entirely reasonable yet crucial assessment of plausibility to be factored into the analysis.
- That, in any case, the effect of the choice of prior becomes increasingly irrelevant as data accumulates, with the only persistent effect of priors being the entirely natural one that sceptics of a specific claim require stronger evidence to reach the same level of belief than its advocates.

There is a dangerous irony in the continuing reluctance of the scientific community to adopt Bayesian inference. For this reluctance stems largely from a deep-rooted fear that adopting methods that embrace subjectivity is tantamount to conceding that the scientific enterprise really is a social construct, as claimed by the post-modern advocates of the 'anti-science' movement. The central lesson of Bayes's theorem is, however, quite the opposite. It shows, with full mathematical rigour, that while evidence for a specific theory may indeed start out vague and subjective, the accumulation of data progressively drives the evidence towards a single, objective reality about which all can agree.

It is ironic indeed that by failing to recognize this, the scientific community continues to use techniques of inference whose unreliability undermines confidence in the scientific process, and which thus threatens to deliver science into the hands of its enemies.

Appendix: Bayesian inference using confidence intervals

A growing proportion of research findings are reported via confidence intervals, in which a central parameter value, M, is accompanied by a range of values of the form (L , U), which form the so-called 95 per cent confidence interval (CI) for the results. As discussed in the main article, the frequentist interpretation of a CI is not as straightforward as it may appear: the 95 per cent figure refers to the reliability of the statistical test applied, and not to the probability that the true parameter value lies in the stated range. In contrast, a Bayesian 95 per cent CI (often also called a Credible Interval) means precisely what it seems to mean: there is a 95 per cent probability that the true value lies within the stated range.

We now outline the procedure for calculating Bayesian CIs for a given set of data. For both frequentist and Bayesian CIs, the range (L, U) is calculated from the mean parameter value, M and its standard deviation SD, via the formulas

$$L = M - 1.96.SD \tag{A1}$$

$$U = M + 1.96.SD \tag{A2}$$

In the textbook frequentist approach, M and SD are calculated directly from the raw data. In the Bayesian approach, however, the M and SD are the so-called 'posterior' mean and standard deviation, formed by combining the raw values extracted from the data with prior values based on extant knowledge and insight about the effect under study. The resulting posterior mean and standard deviation thus sets the new findings into their proper context, taking explicit account of their intrinsic plausibility.

The first step in a Bayesian analysis is thus to capture this prior knowledge and insight. In many real-life cases, this can be achieved by specifying a Normal distribution which peaks at the most plausible value for the parameter of interest, M_o, and whose 95 per cent 'tails' (L_o, U_o) reflect the plausible range of that parameter. The standard deviation of this prior distribution, SD_o can then be calculated from (A1), (A2):

$$SD_o = (U_o - L_o) /3.92 \tag{A3}$$

The next step is to combine this prior distribution with the experimental data, whose mean is M_d and standard deviation is SD_d; the resulting posterior distribution will have a mean M_p and standard deviation SD_p. It can be shown that Bayes's theorem leads to a posterior distribution with parameters given by (see, for example, Lee, 1997 Chapter 2):

$$SD_p = 1/\sqrt{[1/SD_o^2 + 1/SD_d^2]} \qquad \text{A4}$$

$$M_p = (SD_p)^2 \cdot [(M_o/SD_o^2) + (M_d/SD_d^2)] \qquad \text{A5}$$

The Bayesian 95 per cent CI then follows putting A4 and A5 into A1 and A2; the result is a range of values for the parameter of value in which the true value will lie with 95 per cent probability. Two key implications of equations A4 and A5 should be noted. First, they show that the frequentist and Bayesian definitions of the CI are equivalent only when SD_o is infinite, corresponding to a stance of complete ignorance about the plausible range of values for the parameter of interest. This is rarely justifiable, and in general the frequentist and Bayesian CIs will not coincide. Equations A4 and A5 also show that the inclusion of prior information has the effect of moving the posterior probability distribution in the direction of the prior. Thus if results from, say, a clinical trial are strikingly more impressive than seems plausible, failure to account for this lack of plausibility via a prior distribution will exaggerate both the size of the effect, and its statistical significance. As we have seen, frequentist methods cannot explicitly incorporate such plausibility arguments, and are thus especially prone to lend unjustified credibility to remarkable data.

The growing tendency to state results in terms of frequentist 95 per cent CIs does at least summarize results in a form that can easily be combined with prior knowledge using the techniques given above, as I now show.

Example: In their analysis of the GREAT study, Pocock and Spiegelhalter captured the implications of previous studies via a prior relative risk (RR) of death of 0.825, with a 95 per cent CI of (0.6, 1.0). To apply the above formulas, a logarithmic transformation has to be applied to the central estimate and range (strictly speaking, RRs should also first be transformed into a so-called Odds Ratio, but in many cases – including this one, and epidemiological studies of rare diseases such as lung cancer – the difference is immaterial). Thus we take the prior distribution to be Normal, with a peak at $\ln(RR_o)$, with its standard deviation SD_o being calculated from A3 using the natural logarithms of the upper and lower ranges of the CI, $\ln(U_o)$ and $\ln(L_o)$. This leads to a prior distribution that peaks at $M_o = -0.19$, with a standard deviation of 0.13.

To calculate M_d and SD_d, we note that the GREAT study found a mean RR of 0.515, with a (frequentist) 95 per cent CI of (0.23, 0.97). We can convert this into the mean and standard deviation required by A4 and A5 by taking natural logarithms and using A2: this gives $M_d = -0.664$, and $SD_d = 0.367$. Using A4 and A5 we can now work out the posterior probability distribution; we find $M_p = -0.245$ and $SD_p = 0.123$.

Using A1 and A2 and then transforming back out of natural logarithms, we finally arrive at a posterior RR figure of 0.78 with a Bayesian 95 per cent CI of (0.6, 1.0). This central risk figure is substantially less impressive than the value that emerges from the raw data; this reflects the impact of the inclusion of a prior reflecting the implausibility of gaining so large a risk reduction. Furthermore, the Bayesian 95 per cent CI encompasses an RR of 1.0, which implies that the possibility that there is no benefit is not entirely ruled out by this (small) study. As discussed in the main article, the results of Pocock and Spiegelhalter's Bayesian analysis ultimately proved more realistic than those suggested by the raw GREAT data alone.

Acknowledgements

In arriving at the arguments presented in this chapter, I have benefited enormously from the assistance, advice and comments of many researchers. I should particularly like to thank David Balding of Reading University, James Berger of Purdue University, Colin Howson of the London School of Economics, Robert Nilsson of Stockholm University, and Stuart Pocock and Ian White of the London School of Hygiene and Tropical Medicine. I am also most grateful to Roger Bate of ESEF for originally inviting me to collect together my thoughts presented in this chapter. I would also like to thank the three anonymous referees who provided useful criticisms of the chapter. My biggest debt, however, is to Dennis Lindley, from whom – like so many others working in this field – I have learned so much.

References

Aronson, J.L. (1984). *A realist philosophy of science.* London: Macmillan.

Asimov, I. (1975). *Asimov's Biographical Encyclopaedia of Science and Technology.* London: Pan Books

Barber, B. (1961). Resistance by scientists to scientific discovery. *Science, 134,* 596

Berger, J. and Berry, D. (1988) Statistical analysis and the illusion of objectivity *American Scientist, 76,* 159.

Berger, J. and Delampady, M. (1987) Testing precise hypotheses. *Stat. Sci.* **2** 317.

Berger, J. & Sellke, T. (1987).Testing a point null hypothesis: the irreconcilability of P-values and evidence. *J. Amer. Statist. Ass., 82,* 112.

Bofetta, P., Brennan, P., Lea, S. Ferro, G. (1997) Lung cancer and exposure to environmental tobacco smoke. *Biennial Report 1996/7.*Lyon: IARC/WHO.

Bourke, G.J., Daly, L.E. and McGilvray, J. (1985) *Interpretation and Uses of Medical Statistics* (3rd edn). St Louis: Mosby.

Breslow, N., Day, N.E. (1980). Statistical methods in cancer research. Vol. 1: The analysis of case-control studies. *IARC Scientific Publication No. 32* Lyon : IARC.

Brown, N., Young, T., Gray, D., Skene, A., Hampton, J.R. (1997). Inpatient deaths from acute myocardial infarction, 1982–92: analysis of data in the Nottingham heart attack register. *Brit Med J., 315,* 159.

Buyse, M.E. (1994). Remarks in response to Spiegelhalter et al. 1994 (op.cit), p. 399.

Collins, H. (1998) What's wrong with relativism? *Physics World*, **11** (4), 19.

Cooper, C. Dennison, E. (1998). Do silicone breast implants cause connective tissue disorder? *Brit Med J.*, **316**, 403

Crease, R.P., Mann, C.C. (1996). *The Second Creation*. London: Quartet.

Danesh, J., Collins, R. and Peto, R. (1997). Chronic infections and coronary heart disease: is there a link? *Lancet* **350**, 430.

Dunstan, D. 1998 Letter *Physics World* **11** (6), 15.

Edwards, W. Lindman, H. and Savage, L. J. (1963). Bayesian statistical inference for psychological research. *Psychol. Rev.*,**70**,193.

Elford, J., Whincup, P. and Shaper, A.G. (1991). Early life experience and adult cardiovascular disease. *Intl J Epid.*, **20**, 833.

Fayers, P. (1994). Remarks in response to Spiegelhalter et al. (op.cit), p. 402.

Feller, W. (1968). *An Introduction to Probability Theory and its Applications* (3rd edn). New York: Wiley.

Feynman, R.P. (1985). *Surely you're joking Mr Feynman*. London: Unwin.

Fletcher, H. (1982). *Physics Today*, **43**

Freedman, D. Pisani, R. and Purves, R. (1998). *Statistics* (3rd edn). New York: Norton.

Gell-Mann, M. (1964). A schematic model of baryons and mesons. *Physics Letters*, **3**, 214.

Gell-Mann, M. (1994). *The Quark and the Jaguar* London: Little, Brown.

Grayson, L. (1995). *Scientific Deception*. London: The British Library.

Grayson, L. (1997). *Scientific Deception – An Update*. London: The British Library).

GREAT Group (1992) Feasibility, safety and efficacy of domiciliary thrombolysis by general practitioners: Grampian region early anistreplase trial. *Brit. Med. J.*, **305**, 548.

Greenstein, G. (1998). *Portraits of Discovery*. New York: Wiley.

Hackshaw, A.K. Law, M.R., and Wald, N.J. (1997). The accumulated evidence on lung cancer and environmental tobacco smoke. *Brit. Med. J.*, **315**, 980.

Hoffmann, B. (1975). *Albert Einstein*. London: Paladin.

Holton, G. (1978). Sub-electrons, presuppositions and the Millikan-Ehrenhaft dispute. *Historical Studies in the Physical Sciences* **9**, 161

Hellman, H. (1998). *Great Feuds in Science*. New York: Wiley.

Heyes, S., Hardy, M., Humphreys, P., Rookes, P. (1993). *Starting Statistics in Psychology and Education* (2nd edn). London : Weidenfeld & Nicolson.

Howson, C. Urbach, P. (1993). *Scientific Reasoning* (2nd edn). Chicago: Open Court.

Jeffreys, H. (1961) *Theory of Probability* (3rd edn). Oxford : Oxford University Press.

Kempthorne, O. (1971). Probability, statistics and the knowledge business. In *Foundations of Statistical Inference* (Godambe V.P. and Sprott, D.A., eds) Toronto: Holt, Rinehart & Winston.

Lakatos, I. (1978). *The Methodology of Scientific Research Programmes* (Philosophical Papers Volume 1) (Worrall, J. and Currie, G. eds). Cambridge: Cambridge University Press.

Lee, P.N. (1997). *Bayesian Statistics: An Introduction* (2nd edn). London : Arnold.

Lee, P.N. (1998). Difficulties in assessing the relationship between passive smoking and lung cancer. *Stat Meth Med Res*, **7**, 137.

Lindley, D. V. (1970). *Introduction to Probability & Statistics Part 2: Inference*. Cambridge: Cambridge University Press.

Linet, M. et al. (1997). Residential exposure to magnetic fields and acute lymphoblastic leukaemia in children. *New Eng. J Med*, **337**, 1.

Macdonald, V. (1998). Official: passive smoking does not cause cancer. *The Sunday Telegraph* 8 March, p. 1.

Matthews, R.A.J. (1992). *Unravelling the Mind of God*. London: Virgin.

Matthews, R.A.J. (1997). Faith, hope and statistics. *New Scientist*, **156**, 36

Matthews, R.A.J. (1999). The statistical assessment of anomalous phenomena. *J Sci Expl*. **13**(1), 1–7.

Medawar, P. (1978). *Advice to a Young Scientist*. New York: Harper and Row.

Mendall, M.A. et al. (1994). Relation between *Helicobacter pylori* infection and coronary heart disease. *B Heart J*. **71**, 437.

Milton, R. (1994). *Forbidden Science*. London: Fourth Estate.

Nelson, R. (1997). Wishing for good weather: a natural experiment in group consciousness. *J. Sci. Expl*. **11**, 47.

Nilsson, R. (1997). Is environmental tobacco smoke a risk factor for lung cancer? In *What Risk: science, politics and public health* (Bate, R. ed.) Oxford: Butterworth-Heinemann.

Nilsson, R. (1998). *Environmental Tobacco Smoke Revisited: The reliability of the evidence for risk of lung cancer and cardiovascular disease* (Cambridge: The European Science and Environment Forum).

Nyren, O. et al. (1998). Risk of connective tissue disease and related disorders among women with breast implants: a nationwide retrospective cohort study in Sweden *Brit Med J*, **316**, 417.

O'Hagan, A. (1994). *Kendall's Advanced Theory of Statistics Vol. 2B: Bayesian Inference*, London: Arnold).

O'Hagan, A. *FirstBayes -freeware Bayesian inference software*. Available from http://www.nott.ac.uk/maths/aoh/.

Oppenheimer, J.R. (1955). *The Open Mind*. New York : Simon & Schuster.

Pais, A. (1982). *Subtle is the Lord*. Oxford: University Press.

Pais, A. (1991). *Niels Bohr's Times*. Oxford: Clarendon Press.

Phillips, K. Howard, D.A., Browne, D. and Lewsley, J.M. (1994). Assessment of personal exposures to environmental tobacco smoke in British non-smokers *Environment International*, **20**, 693.

Phillips, K. Howard, D.A., Bentley, M. C. and Alvan, G. (1998) Measured exposures by personal monitoring for respirable suspended particles and environmental tobacco smoke of housewives and office workers resident in Bremen, Germany. *In.t Arch. Occup. Environ. Health*, **71** 201.

Pocock, S.J. and Spiegelhalter D. J. (1992) Letter. *Brit Med J* , **305**, 1015

Popper, K. (1963). *Conjectures and Refutations*. London: Routledge.

Radin, D. (1997). *The Conscious Universe: the scientific truth of psychic phenomena* San Francisco: Harper.

Sivia, D.S. (1996). *Data Analysis: A Bayesian Tutorial* Oxford: Oxford: University Press.

Spiegelhalter, D.J., Freedman, L.S., and Parmar, M.K.B. (1994). Bayesian approaches to randomised trials (with discussion). *J Roy Stat Soc A*. **157**, 357.

Theocharis, T. and Psimopolous, M. (1987). Where science has gone wrong. *Nature*. **329** 595

Vallance, A.K. (1998). Can biological activity be maintained at ultra-high dilution? an overview of homeopathy, evidence, and Bayesian philosophy. *J Alt Comp Med* **4**, 49.

Vandenbroucke, J.P. (1997). Homeopathy trials: going nowhere. *The Lancet*, **350**, 824.

Wald, N., Law, M.R., Morris, J.K., and Bagnall, A.M. (1997). *Helicobacter pylori* infection and mortality from ischaemic heart disease: negative result from a large prospective study. *Brit. Med J* **315**, 1199.

Weinberg, S. (1993). *The Discovery of Sub-atomic Particles*. London: Penguin.

Williams, T. (1994). *Biographical Dictionary of Scientists*. London: Collins.

Wolpert, L. (1992). *The Unnatural Nature of Science,* London: Faber.

Wolpert, L., Richards, A. (1989). *A Passion for Science*. Oxford: Oxford University Press.

Yusuf, S., Collins, R. and Peto, R. (1984). Why do we need some large, simple randomized trials? *Statistics in Medicine,* **3**, 409.

Index